Current Topics in Human Intelligence

Volume 3

Individual Differences and Cognition

Current Topics in Human Intelligence

Volume 3

Individual Differences and Cognition

Editor

Douglas K. Detterman

Case Western Reserve University

 Ablex Publishing Corporation
Norwood, New Jersey

ISBN: 0-89391-860-1

ISSN: 8755-0040

Ablex Publishing Corporation
355 Chestnut Street
Norwood, New Jersey 07648

Contents

Section IV: Information-Processing Approaches

List of Contributors

Numbers in parentheses indicate the pages on which the authors' contributions begin.

A.A. Baumeister, John F. Kennedy Center, George Peabody College for Teachers, Vanderbilt University, Nashville, Tennessee 37203 (283)

Carmilla Persson Benbow, Department of Psychology, Iowa State University, Ames, Iowa 50001 (85)

Monte S. Buchsbaum, Department of Psychiatry and Human Behavior, College of Medicine, University of California, Irvine, California 92717 (157)

M.T. Carlin, Department of Psychology and Human Development, George Peabody College for Teachers, Vanderbilt University, Nashville, Tennessee 37203 (283)

Frank M. Crinella, Director, California State Developmental Research Institutes, Costa Mesa, and Clinical Professor of Psychiatry and Human Behavior, University of California, Irvine, California 92717 (157)

Veronica J. Dark, Department of Psychology, Iowa State University, Ames, Iowa 50001 (85)

William P. Dunlap, Department of Psychology, Tulane University, 2007 Percival Stern Boulevard, New Orleans, Louisiana 70118 (259)

Lynne V. Feagans, Department of Human Development and Family Studies, College of Health and Human Development, 110 Henderson Building South, The Pennsylvania State University, University Park, Pennsylvania 16802 (121)

Lee Friedman, Laboratory of Biological Psychiatry, Department of Psychiatry, Case Western Reserve University School of Medicine, Cleveland, Ohio 44106 (189)

Richard J. Haier, Department of Psychiatry and Human Behavior, College of Medicine, University of California, Irvine, California 92717 (157)

Daniel J. Hannon, Department of Psychology, 430 Huntington Hall, Syracuse University, Syracuse, New York 13244-2340 (55)

William J. Hoyer, Department of Psychology, 430 Huntington Hall, Syracuse University, Syracuse, New York 13244-2340 (55)

Robert S. Kennedy, Essex Corporation, 1040 Woodcock Road, Orlando, Florida 32803 (259)

John T. Kenny, Department of Psychiatry, Hanna Pavilion, University Hospitals of Cleveland, Cleveland, Ohio 44106 (189)

Robert B. McCall, Office of Child Development, University of Pittsburgh, 411 LRDC Building, 3939 O'Hara Street, Pittsburgh, Pennsylvania 15260 (3)

Ann Merriwether, Department of Human Development and Family Studies, College of Health and Human Development, 110 Henderson Building South, The Pennsylvania State University, University Park, Pennsylvania 16802 (121)

Ethel L. Parker, Department of Psychology, Florida State University, Tallahassee, Florida 32306-1051 (241)

Susan A. Rose, Departments of Pediatrics and Psychiatry, Rose F. Kennedy Center for Research in Mental Retardation and Mental Development, Albert Einstein College of Medicine, 1300 Morris Park Avenue, New York, New York 10461 (31)

Dennis P. Saccuzzo, Joint Doctoral Program in Clinical Pychology, San Diego State University, 6363 Alvarado Court, Suite 104, San Diego, California 92120-4913 (219)

Benjamin V. Siegel, Jr., Department of Psychiatry and Human Behavior, College of Medicine, University of California, Irvine, California 92717 (157)

S.A. Soraci, Department of Psychology and Human Development, Box 154, George Peabody College for Teachers, Vanderbilt University, Nashville, Tennesse 37203 (283)

Janet J. Turnage, Department of Psychology, University of Central Florida, Orlando, Florida 32826 (259)

Philip A. Vernon, Department of Psychology, University of Western Ontario, London, Ontario, Canada N6A 5C2 (171)

Richard K. Wagner, Department of Psychology, Florida State University, Tallahassee, Florida 32306-1051 (241)

Robert L. Wilkes, Department of Psychology, Casper College, 125 Casper Drive, Casper, Wyoming 82601 (259)

Current Topics in Human Intelligence
Foreword to the Series

Douglas K. Detterman, Editor

The purpose of this series is to focus on single issues of importance to the study of human intelligence. Unlike many edited volumes, this one is designated to be thematic. Each volume will present a detailed examination of some question relevant to human intelligence and, more generally, individual differences.

The reason for beginning this series is that a forum is needed for extensive discussions of pertinent questions. No such forum currently exists. A journal does not allow an author sufficient space or latitude to present fully elaborated ideas. Currently existing edited series are not thematic but, instead, offer researchers an opportunity to present an integrative summary of their own work. Both journals and edited, nonthematic monographs are essential to the advancement of the study of human intelligence. But they do not allow collective intelligence to be brought to bear on a single issue of importance.

Why is it important to examine specific issues in detail? The answer to this question depends on an appreciation of the historical development fo the study of human intelligence. For at least 40 years, and perhaps longer, the study of human intelligence has been less than highly regarded as an academic pursuit. The reasons for this attitude are many and have been discussed elsewhere. Despite the reasons, the lack of academic sanction for the study of individual differences in human intelligence has produced a discipline without a unifying paradigm. When researchers study human intelligence, it is almost always from the perspective of training in a related, but different, discipline. Disciplines which have "sacrificed" researchers to human intelligence include: cognitive, developmental, and educational psychology, behavior genetics, psychometrics, mental retardation, neuropsychology, and even experimental psychology. Each of these researchers has brought a different set of assumptions and methods to the study of human intelligence.

That so many different points of view have been applied to a single subject area has, in my opinion, brought vitality to the endeavor, a vitality currently lacking in so many areas of the social sciences. But this vitality does not arise from the isolation and fractionation which can be the result of different points of view. On the contrary, it results from the juxtaposition of these different points of view, a juxtapositioning which has occurred with increasing frequency over the last 10 years.

Therefore, it is the purpose of this series to bring different points of view together on issues of importance to understanding human intelligence. The hope is that, at the very least, researchers will find more reason to give their primary allegiance to the study of human intelligence and, at the most, the series will contribute to the emergence of a unifying paradigm.

Foreword to Volume 3:
Individual Differences
and Cognition

As editor of this volume, I have been impressed by the amount of individual differences research that is being done. The research does not always involve human intelligence directly. But it frequently focuses on cognitive behavior that is a part of intelligence. So even though the researchers don't measure intelligence directly, what they are doing is important for understanding intelligence and cognition. Some areas that are making important contributions to the understanding of individual differences include aging, infancy, development, exceptionality, schizophrenia, and mental retardation, to name just a few.

Another thing that has impressed me as editor of this volume is how little communication there is between the various areas in which people study individual differences. As an example, many who study intelligence are completely unaware of the work being done in infancy and aging. It is not a conscious neglect that leads to the lack of communication among these areas. It is probably more likely due to the fact that people who study intelligence and aging move in different circles, perhaps because of the differences in origins of their disciplines. The study of intelligence is closely associated with psychometrics, while individual differences work in aging had its origins in experimental psychology.

Because work in individual differences is fragmented across various areas of study, and because these areas do not communicate with each other, it is easy to get the mistaken impression that there is very little research being done on individual differences. The truth is that there is a lot of good individual differences research. In fact, there may be more work on individual differences being done than there is straight experimental work. It's just spread out instead of piled up.

This volume provides a sampler of the research on individual differences in different content areas of study. All of the work is relevant to intelligence, though much of it does not directly measure intelligence. But the book is only a sampler. It does not represent all of the areas that are doing good individual differences research. The omissions are glaring. For example, there are no chapters about human factors, brain damage, selective ablation, psychometrics, factor analysis, early intervention, psychopharmacology, or behavior analysis. The list could go on and on. What has been omitted from this volume makes as good a case for the quantity and quality of individual differences research, as does what has been included. Unfortunately, the book had to be limited in length.

What has been included in this book is a sampling of the work of people who are doing outstanding individual differences research in their chosen area of study. These people are stars in their respective areas but may not even know each other. However, as you read the chapters in this volume, you cannot help but be impressed by the similarity in outlook, in the consonant world view each author presents. All of the authors in this volume are soul mates, even if they don't know each other. Perhaps the common features in their work suggest that they should know each other.

The book is divided into four sections. The first section presents authors whose concern is with development at some stage. The second section presents chapters on exceptionality. There is a chapter on learning disability and another on gifted children. The third section includes chapters that take a biological approach to understanding individual differences in cognition. Finally, the fourth section includes chapters that take an information-processing approach. As you read these chapters, you will see that this division was arbitrary. Chapters in each section have commonalities with chapters in several other sections. These commonalities suggest other organizations and also show that the chapters have a great deal in common even though they are written by people who seldom, if ever, talk to each other.

As you may have guessed by now, it is my hope that this book will stimulate a union of individual differences researchers. There are a lot of us working on similar problems. We would probably be better working together than apart. Think about it as you read the chapters in this book.

Developmental Life Spans

Chapter *1*

Developmental Functions for General Mental Performance

Robert B. McCall

University of Pittsburgh

The modern developmental study of general mental performance (i.e., typically, but not exclusively, the study of IQ over age) began with the milestone longitudinal studies (e.g., Berkeley, Fels, etc.) in the late 1920s and early 1930s. It consisted primarily of the search for stability or lack of stability of individual differences on standardized assessments of general mental performance across various age spans, and the correlates of those differences with other variables at different ages.

In the 1960s, Piaget began to have a substantial influence on American developmental psychology, which stimulated an independent thrust to study the age at which children acquire Piagetian skills and the factors that influence such skill acquisition. Piaget and most of his followers were not concerned with individual differences, their stabilities over age, or their correlates; instead, they focused on describing the sequence of fundamental skills acquired by essentially all children during the course of early development.

These two themes—individual differences and species-general ability or skill acquisition—progressed rather independently. Research in one domain was conducted by different scholars and sometimes published in different journals from research in the other domain. Rarely, for example, were individual differences considered in studies of Piagetian skill acquisition, and rarely was the changing qualitative nature of the particular abilities required on standardized assessments of general mental performance considered by those who studied the stability of individual differences.

Eventually, Wohlwill (1973) and his followers (e.g., McCall, 1977a) labeled these two general domains of inquiry to be studies of *individual differences* and of the *developmental function* of general mental performance. They pointed out that findings in the two domains could be independent, and that both strategies should be adopted in pursuing an issue, preferably within the same sample. The admonition, however, generally did not catch hold. For one thing, the infrequent studies of individual differences within the Piagetian tradition failed to reveal strong or consistent cross-age stabilities or contemporary correlates (e.g., Corman & Escalona, 1969; Uzgiris, 1973, 1989), thereby squelching interest in a joint pursuit of both domains. Further, the structure and scoring of standardized infant developmental tests, and especially of the IQ test, were not conducive to describing quantitative or qualitative changes in mental performance over age. IQ, for example, is a unitless index of relative position deliberately designed to have constant psychometric parameters and to be comparable across age so that its qualitative nature might be ignored. As a result, the "two disciplines of psychology" (Cronbach, 1957) remained distinct with respect to the study of general mental performance and perhaps other areas of developmental psychology in general (McCall, 1977a).

The purpose of this chapter is to bridge this schism, at least partially. Specifically, the neglected concept of a developmental function for general mental development will be considered, as well as individual differences in such developmental functions.

Terminology and Distinctions

It will be helpful to clarify the use of certain terms and maintain certain distinctions.

The stability of rank ordering. Typically, students of individual differences rely statistically on the correlation coefficient and its derivatives to describe the consistency in relative rank ordering of individuals within a group on a variable at two different ages. Following others (Emmerich, 1964; McCall, 1977a, 1981b; McCall, Appelbaum, & Hogarty, 1973; Wohlwill, 1973), this phenomenon will be referred to as *stability of relative rank ordering of individual differences.* Specifically, if individuals on a given assessment retain their relative rank ordering on a second assessment of the same variable, then *stability* exists in relative rank ordering of individual differences. If not, then individual differences are *not stable*. *Stability* differs from test–retest reliability with respect to the length of time between the two assessments (typically less than a month for "reliability" but more than a month for "stability," although no standard is widely accepted). It should be noted that individual differences may exist with respect to attributes other than relative rank ordering, some of which will be discussed below.

Developmental functions. A *developmental function* is the plot of the average quantity of a characteristic across age. A plot of the heights of a group of children between 3 and 18 years of age would constitute a developmental function. Developmental functions may be plotted for species, groups (e.g., males versus females, preterm versus full-term infants), and individuals.

Developmental functions have several characteristics. For one thing, they may be *continuous* or *discontinuous*. A continuous developmental function is one in which the same qualitative characteristic is assessed at every age, while a discontinuous developmental function is one in which the qualitative nature of the variable changes from one age to another. A plot of height for a group of subjects across age may be considered continuous, whereas a plot of Piagetian skills across age would be discontinuous because different skills emerge at different ages. Notice that continuity may refer to a conceptual rather than to a measured variable. The Piagetian concept of intelligence may be discontinuous, but the measurement of that concept using the Uzgiris and Hunt (1975) scale might produce total scores that could be plotted in a continuous manner. The same may be said for IQ.

Developmental functions also have *general levels*. The general level is the central tendency across all the ages in the developmental function. It is typically measured by the average of all points in the function. In contrast, the *developmental profile* refers to the shape of the quantitative changes in the function over age regardless of what segment of the measurement scale the function occupies (i.e., its general level). It is typically represented by the plot of the deviation scores across age (each score minus their mean).

Developmental profiles may be characterized in several ways. First, they have varying amounts of *variability*. Variability refers to the general extent to which the values in the developmental profile vary one from another, and it is often assessed by the standard deviation of the developmental profile, or less precisely, by the range of values in the profile (i.e., the highest minus the lowest score). Profile variability may apply to species, groups, or individuals, depending on the sample on which the developmental profile is based. In the later case, it may be measured by the *intra-individual standard deviation*.

Developmental profiles also have *form*, which is the particular shape or pattern in the profile. A developmental profile may be *unpatterned*, containing points that are the same value within sampling error across the entire age span (i.e., essentially a horizontal line paralleling the *X* axis). In contrast, they may be *patterned*, in which case significant changes occur from age to age. A patterned developmental profile is also assumed to have a statistically significant trend that reflects some pattern other than random fluctuation around a constant value.

Notice that general level and developmental profile are potentially independent of one another. That is, one might have a patterned or unpatterned form at nearly any general level (ignoring issues of floors and ceiling to scales), although empirically certain patterns may be more characteristic of high scoring subjects than low scoring subjects. Similarly, in the middle ranges, the amount of profile variability is potentially independent of the particular profile form, although empirically they may not be independent, especially in the extreme (i.e., very low variability will be unpatterned or a horizontal line).

Notice also that individual differences may be studied with respect to any of the characteristics of developmental functions. That is, in principle, one could study differences between species, groups, or individual subjects in their general levels, amounts of variability, and specific patterns. However, in practice, it is difficult to study differences between species, because it may be difficult or unreasonable to measure the same variable on a decent sample of different species. For example, it may be practical and reasonable to study race or ethnic differences in the variability or pattern of developmental profiles for general mental performance, but it may be difficult the study mammalian species differences. This is an important consideration for behavioral genetics, because current methods of estimating heritabilities require individual differences, which means that heritability estimates will typically apply to individual differences within a species rather than describing the genetic contribution that makes humans different from the ants (which involves nearly all of one's genes).

Importance of these distinctions. These distinctions are important, because most of the several attributes described above are potentially independent of one another. This means that one may not glibly generalize from one characteristic to the next. For example, as indicated above, behavioral genetic estimates of heritability are typically based upon individual differences within a group assessed at a single age. Such heritabilities do not necessarily apply to the species at that age or to the developmental profile for individuals. For example, human intelligence is not 50% heritable; individual differences in intelligence are 50% heritable. Also, Bloom's (1964) classic conclusion that half of adult intelligence is formed by age 4, an assertion based on a correlation of .71 of IQ at age 4 and IQ in adulthood ($.71^2 = .50$), completely ignores the fact that the developmental function for children might increase $4^{1}/_{2}$ times (if the variable is mental age) between ages 4 and 18. Further, because of their potential independence, factors that influence one characteristic may be different than the factors that influence another characteristic. As will be described below, genes may be associated more strongly with individual differences in general level than developmental profile.

It should be emphasized that, while these several characteristics are potentially independent, it is an empirical question whether they actually are independent. For example, McCall, Eichorn, and Hogarty (1977) studied the pattern of correlations in relative rank ordering across age for the first principal components of standardized infant tests and found dips in such correlations at 8, 13, and 21 months of age. They also observed changes in the qualitative character of the components, presumably reflecting discontinuities in the qualitative character of the developmental function at the same ages. In this case, the discontinuities in the developmental function occurred at the same ages as the nodes of relative instability, a conclusion supported in part by other data (e.g., McCall, 1979; Uzgiris, 1989). Similarly, the prediction from early assessments of habituation and recognition memory during infancy to childhood IQ (Bornstein & Sigman, 1986) represents stability of relative rank ordering across a substantial discontinuity in the quality of the developmental function.

Focus of This Chapter

This chapter focuses on developmental functions for general mental performance, typically assessed by standardized tests of infant development and childhood intelligence tests. Characteristics of functions for the human species, certain groups, and individuals will be considered. This emphasis has been selected for the purpose of attempting to summarize what little research has been conducted on these issues and to encourage greater attention to this domain.

IQ is not the most popular variable of the day, and in some respects it is ill suited to the study of developmental functions. Specifically, it is artificially constructed to be a unitless index with a flat developmental profile for the population. It reflects only relative standing for individuals within a group. Therefore, it has no species-general developmental profile of interest, and individual differences are regarded as being among the most stable across substantial age spans of any behavioral characteristic. Why would one study developmental functions or individual differences in developmental profiles for such a variable?

For one thing, IQ is essentially the only measure of mental performance that has been studied systematically in this way, and it is among the most researched measures of any kind in the developmental literature. Further, for all the current debate over its usefulness and appropriateness, IQ is still probably the best single predictor of educational and occupational achievement. This is true for all major groups in American society (McCall, 1977b), and such predictions to adult status approach asymptote at approximately age 7 (McCall, 1977). Finally, if one can determine meaningful results for developmental profile in a variable known to display minimum change in either average value or stability, then how much more fruitful might this type of inquiry be for variables that display greater developmental change?

DESCRIBING SPECIES-GENERAL DEVELOPMENTAL FUNCTIONS FOR GENERAL MENTAL PERFORMANCE

Studies are reviewed in this section that attempt to describe or theorize about the species-general developmental function.

The nature of any developmental function, of course, will depend upon how it is measured. Presumably, the species-general developmental profile for IQ is flat, reflecting the intent of the test constructors to have a population average of 100 at every age. Similarly, the species-general developmental function for Mental Age should be linear with a slope of 45°, reflecting the intent of test constructors to have samples average identical mental and chronological ages at each age. Of course, one might not find these protypical forms for the developmental profile of any particular subsample.

In contrast, the developmental function for Piaget's stages might look quite different. Depending upon the nature of the measurement, one might expect discontinuities or major inflection points at or shortly after the ages at which Piaget hypothesized a new stage. A developmental function would be discontinuous if each stage were measured by an independent and qualitatively distinct instrument, or it might be highly inflected but continuous if performances were measured on a single scale.

Piaget's Theory of Mental Development

Piaget (1952; Flavell, 1963; Hunt, 1963) proposed a theory of mental development that emphasized a relatively discontinuous sequence of stages, each building upon the previous but each characterized by the emergence of a qualitatively unique skill, ability, or attribute. Piaget's intent was to describe the species-general developmental function for mental development; he was not particularly interested in individual differences of any kind. Since Piaget's theory (e.g., Flavell, 1963; Hunt, 1963; Piaget, 1952) and Neo-Piagetian theories (e.g., Fischer, 1980) have been described frequently, they will not be reviewed here. Instead, some thoughts about research strategy in defining Piaget's developmental function are presented.

Although Piaget's theory and efforts by some neo-Piagetian theorists represent perhaps the only major, well-articulated theories of mental development from birth to adulthood, American researchers did not set out to conduct longitudinal studies that would validate the qualitative characteristics of Piaget's development function for mental development. An exception was Uzgiris (1973, 1989), who followed a small group of infants from birth to 31 months of age. Therefore, a broad-based literature empirically describing the Piagetian development function is largely missing. Instead, Piaget was adopted in pieces, especially insofar as his theoretical formulations fit the experimental dispositions of American researchers at the time. The American focus was on the age at which infants and children displayed the theorized behavior characterizing a stage and the influence of particular characteristics of the assessment context and procedure and of the child on the demonstration of stage acquisition. At the risk of overgeneralizing, the conclusion from this literature indicates that Piaget's stages do emerge approximately in the sequence described and at approximately at the ages he proposed, although a variety of assessment parameters influence the acquisition of stages. This history illustrates that even when a major theory describes a developmental function, American researchers do not invest heavily in empirically describing that function.

Why? One reason is certainly practicality. It is expensive and time consuming to conduct the longitudinal studies, especially over substantial age spans, that would be necessary to empirically describe the species-general developmental function for mental development. Concentrating on one or two stage transitions is more manageable, and it fits with the scholarly reward system that values numerous publications of empirically tidy, preferably experimental, research.

A second reason is that the nature of Piaget's theory—discontinuous stages coupled with a disregard for individual differences—does not fit with the tradition and methods of American developmental psychology. Longitudinal studies were conducted primarily by people interested in individual differences and their stability, and a theory that proposed qualitative discontinuities from stage to stage obviated a common measurement instrument across age (or at least made it obvious that measurement instruments of all kinds were not comparable across large age spans). Further, when attempts were made to study the stability or predictability of Piaget-type behaviors across age, the results were no better and often worse (as might have been expected) than for traditional standardized psychometric instruments (Birns & Golden, 1972; King & Secgmiller, 1973; Kopp, Sigman, & Parmelee, 1974; Lewis & McGurk, 1972; Uzgiris, 1973, 1989; Uzgiris & Hunt, 1975; Wachs, 1976). The tendency has always been strong to search for stabilities in mental performance, and when none are found, researchers do not conclude that instability or discontinuity exists but that they should search elsewhere (McCall, 1981a).

A case can be made then for two conclusions. First, more scholarly energy needs to be devoted to describing the nature of developmental functions (Wohlwill, 1973). To continue to ignore this pursuit is, for the discipline of developmental psychology, to avoid its essential purpose. Second, new methods must be developed to cope with developmental functions that are continuous and for which individual differences may not be stable. In the absence of such statistical tools, the tendency will persist to believe that a behavior that is discontinuous and unstable is necessarily chaotic, error, and beyond the grasp of science. But early mental development and perhaps many social and temperamental characteristics may be developmentally discontinuous and lack stable individual differences as traditionally assessed. To persist exploring such phenomena with methods designed to reveal other characteristics represents the folly of scientists attempting to impose truth on nature rather than to describe nature's truth. Fortunately, some new methods are available (e.g., see Appelbaum, Burchinal, & Terry, 1989), although they are not often used.

Epstein's Phrenoblysis Hypothesis of Brain
and Mental Periodization

Piaget is not the only theorist to postulate discontinous or periodic growth spurts in mental performance. Epstein (1974a,b, 1976, 1978; Epstein & Toepfer, 1978) proposed that the brain does not grow smoothly during the first 18 years of life but develops unevenly, with peaks in the growth rate occurring between 3 and 10 months and between 2 and 4, 6 and 8, 10 and 12 (or 13), and 14 and 16 (or 17) years of age. Further, Epstein proposed that such spurts in brain growth produce similar spurts in mental performance growth rates at essentially the same age. He called the hypothesis *brain growth periodization* or "phrenoblysis (derived from the Greek meaning of welling-up or spurting of mind and/or skull) to signify these correlated brain and mind growth spurts" (Epstein, 1978, p. 356).

With respect to mental growth Epstein (1978) claimed that Piagetian theory, and data from numerous longitudinal studies, showed increments in mental performance growth rates during the hypothesized intervals. He asserted that brain and mental growth periodization, and their direct relationship, were scientific facts (Epstein, 1978, p. 345). He then offered as working hypotheses the propositions that children learn most during the growth-spurt periods, and that major educational efforts to introduce new material should be timed to match these receptive ages (1978, p. 362). Conversely, new material introduced during brain-growth lulls should be relatively ineffective. As a result, little progress should be expected in learning new material during the junior high school years (Epstein, 1974b, p. 223), and Head Start programs "should fall short of their cognitive goals for *biological* reasons" (1978, p. 360). Further, practicing educators were urged to change their curricula, or at least interpret certain episodes of slow learning in view of the phrenoblysis theory, and a few extremists have suggested that the theory may rival in importance the discovery of DNA (Toepfer, 1979) and that its application could virtually eliminate school failure (Hart, 1981).

The evidence. Presumably, Epstein's theory explains possible inflections in the developmental function for mental growth. Epstein cites a variety of longitudinal studies that he claims demonstrate growth spurts during the hypothesized periods for head circumference and other measures of brain growth (Epstein, 1974a) and for mental growth rates for standardized tests of intelligence, tests of memory or vocabulary, "grade age," and "schooling quotient" (Epstein, 1974b).

While ages at which major Piagetian stages are hypothesized to commence roughly coincide with Epstein's hypothesized growth spurts, the evidence for mental age or IQ (and head circumference) is less persuasive. McCall (1988) evaluated and reanalyzed all of the longitudinal studies Epstein claimed to be concordant with his theory. Strategically, McCall (1988) observed that Epstein's (1974b) summaries were difficult to evaluate because he gave few procedural details, it was not always clear which data in the original reports were used in his summaries, "peaks" and "troughs" in growth rates were not defined, statistical analyses demonstrating conformity with the theory were not presented, and the chance rate concordance with the theory is substantial because approximately 60% or more of the ages between birth and 18 years fall within developmental periods hypothesized to contain spurts. More importantly, no data cited by Epstein were collected or analyzed deliberately for the purpose of testing the theory, and no data were presented to suggest that brain growth changes are directly associated with mental growth changes in the same subjects, either with respect to group profiles or individual differences.

McCall (1988) then reanalyzed all of the longitudinal data that Epstein found compellingly consistent with his theory, and McCall concluded that the reanalyses were considerably less concordant with the theory than were Epstein's results. "At best, mental age may show a growth-rate peak at approximately nine years age, and some fluctuation may occur during preschool. But the size of these variations is relatively small. The maximum total fluctuation in IQ . . . across the entire age span is about 5 points, and the maximum year-to-year change represents about 1 IQ point" (McCall, 1988, p. 229).

The most decisive data come from a direct test of the theory conducted by McCall, Meyers, Hartman, and Roche (1983), who analyzed the head circumference growth rates and mental age growth rates between 2.5 and 17 years of age for a single sample subjects from the Fels Longitudinal Study. The group results for head circumference growth rate (top) and mental age growth rate (bottom) are presented in Figure 1, in which the shaded areas represent age periods hypothesized by Epstein to show growth-rate spurts.

With respect to head circumference, the only statistically significant peaks are at 3 years for females and at 15 years for males. While these spurts do fall within periods hypothesized by Epstein to contain peaks, only one out of four hypothesized peaks was supported statistically for each sex, those significant peaks were not the same for the two sexes, and the chance rate of a peak occurring during a hypothesized age period for these data was .75.

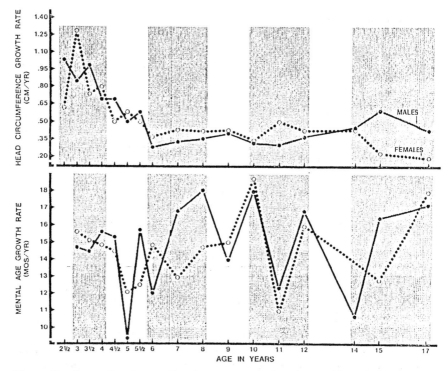

Figure 1.   Annualized growth rates over age of males and females for head circumference (top) and mental age (bottom). Shaded areas correspond to periods hypothesized by Epstein to contain growth spurts in both variables. (Reprinted with permission from McCall et al., 1983.)

With respect to mental age growth rate, the data support peaks at ages 8 and 15–17 for males and at 10 and 17 years for females, all of which did fall within the hypothesized peak ages. Again, however, results were not replicated across sex, and nothing in the theory predicts or explains sex differences. In addition, more hypothesized peaks failed to receive empirical support than did receive it, and the chance rate of having a significant peak fall within the hypothesized age period was so high (.75) that it was difficult to evaluate the significance of the timing of the statistically reliable peaks.

Perhaps of greater importance were the data relating individual differences in head circumference and mental age growth rates. Numerous analyses failed to reveal any relationship of any form between head circumference growth rate pattern and mental age growth rate pattern within individuals (McCall et al., 1983). Presumably, if brain growth-rate changes are driving mental performance growth-rate changes, a relation must exist between the developmental profile of head circumference growth rate and mental performance growth rate in individuals, which was not found in this singular test of this crucial proposition.

Conclusion. McCall (1988, 1990) concluded that insufficient evidence exists for the variables of head circumference and mental age growth rates (and several other mental performance variables suggested by Epstein) to validate the theory and certainly to encourage its application in school systems even as a "working hypothesis" (Epstein, 1990). On the other hand, it was exceedingly unlikely that head circumference or mental age based upon standardized intelligence tests would yield any meaningful relations in this regard. Head circumference, for example, is not generally related to mental performance except in the extremes (A.F. Roche, 1990, personal communication), and standardized intelligence tests are designed to minimize age-to-age changes in the performance of large samples.

It is possible, of course, that such growth periodicity will be found in other variables, and three independent studies of quantitative electroencephalograms (QEEG) have shown spurts at Epstein's hypothesized age periods (Hudspeth & Pribram, 1990). While this is very encouraging, McCall (1990) pointed out that data in each of the three cases are based on cross-sectional samples at each age, which Wohlwill (1973) argues and forcefully illustrates is an inadequate method of measuring growth rates, which occur within individuals, not between independent samples. Further, more research is needed to relate QEEG periodicity (not simply scores on a single assessment) to mental and educational performances of practical educational consequence in normal samples. Finally, while the QEEG and Piagetian growth curves are remarkably similar, no data yet exist to demonstrate any relationship between the two in the same sample, either with respect to group performance (which is likely, however) or with respect to individual differences.

While a neuroscience of education that can be put into practice does not yet exist (McCall, 1990), these data do provoke the scholarly possibility that developmental functions for mental performance might be related to developmental functions in another domain, specifically, brain growth. While the empirical and methodological requirements to demonstrate a causal relationship are substantial, development psychology must examine such relationships if it is ever going to explain changes in the form of the developmental profile or in individual differences in developmental profile for mental performance or any other characteristic.

INDIVIDUAL DIFFERENCES IN THE DEVELOPMENTAL FUNCTION FOR GENERAL MENTAL PERFORMANCE

Although Binet never claimed cross-age consistency for scores on his tests, it has long been thought that IQ is perhaps the most developmentally stable, continuous, and constant behavioral characteristic for individuals across large age spans. Indeed, year-to-year correlations average approximately .85, especially after 5–7 years of age. On the other hand, early reports from longitudinal studies indicated that at least some individuals did change substantially and systematically (e.g., Bayley, 1949, 1956; Hilden, 1949; Honzik, Macfarlane, & Allen, 1948; Sontag, Baker, & Nelson, 1958). These reports documented the existence of change in what was thought to be the most developmentally consistent behavioral measure, presented developmental profiles for individual subjects, categorized subjects into those having ascending versus descending patterns, and investigated the correlates of these groupings.

Three Studies of Developmental Profiles

More recently, however, three studies have attempted to describe individual differences in developmental functions for IQ over substantial age spans.

Fels. McCall et al. (1973) used a factoring and clustering procedure to describe the predominant developmental functions for 80 subjects from the Fels Longitudinal Study who had been given a maximum of 17 Stanford-Binet IQ tests between 2½ and 17 years of age. Statistical procedures grouped subjects into clusters that were homogeneous within but heterogeneous between clusters for developmental profile exclusive of general level (although the resulting profiles did differ with respect to general level as an empirical consequence). The average developmental functions for the main clusters are presented in Figure 2.

Several conclusions can be drawn. First, 45% of the subjects displayed essentially a flat or slightly rising profile (i.e., Cluster 1). Therefore, nearly half of the subjects show essentially no change or random changes about a constant value—that is, a flat developmental profile.

Second, 55% of the subjects showed rather substantial changes in IQ. McCall et al. (1973) found that the average range of IQ (highest minus lowest score) between 2½ and 17 years of age for individuals was 28.5 IQ points (the standard deviation of the test is approximately 16). More than one of every three children displayed a range of more than 30 points, and more than one in seven had a range of more than 40 points. One child increased 74 IQ points, or 4.63 standard deviation units. Moore (1967) reported a child who changed 73 IQ points, and these two cases are the largest known individual shifts in IQ performance.

Third, these changes were progressive, systematic, and relatively simple profiles, not random ups and downs about an apparently constant value. Indeed, another analysis of 136 subjects (including the 80 reported above) who had a maximum of 11 scores between 3 and 12 years of age revealed that 65% displayed a significant (.05 level) linear, quadratic, or cubic trend, whereas random fluctuation might have produced a much more even distribution of cases at each polynomial from the first to the tenth degree (McCall, 1970). This result seems to demonstrate that such patterns are not simply random error about a constant value.

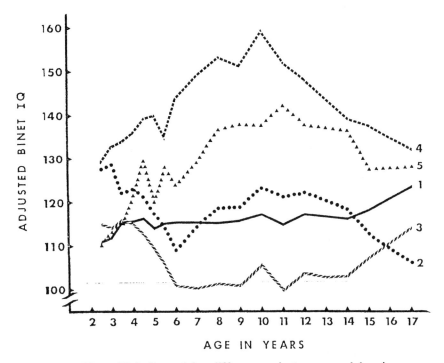

Figure 2. Mean IQ (adjusted for differences between revisions) over age for five IQ profile groups for the Fels data. (Reprinted with permission from McCall et al., 1973.)

Fourth, even though clusters were determined on the basis of profile alone, clusters that showed ascending patterns during the preschool years had higher average IQ's than groups showing decreasing patterns during this period.

Finally, major inflection points occurred at approximately age 6, 10–11, and 14. The inflection point at 6 (see also Hilden, 1949) is reminiscent of the shift to a more cognitive style that occurs between 5 and 7 years of age (White, 1965).

London. Hindley and Owen (1979) conducted a similar study but with several methodological differences. Subjects came from the London Longitudinal Study and were assessed at 6 and 18 months with the Griffith's Scale of Infant Development; at 3, 5, 8, and 11 years with the Stanford-Binet; and at 14 and 17 years with the AH4, a group test with verbal and nonverbal subscales (Heim, 1970). Notice that the inflection point at age 6 found by McCall et al. (1973) was not assessed in this study, and that assessments were made only every 3 years surrounding the inflections found by McCall et al. at ages 11 and 14. This means that it would be difficult for Hindley and Owen to replicate the ages of inflections found by McCall et al. (1973). Eighty-four subjects had scores on eight

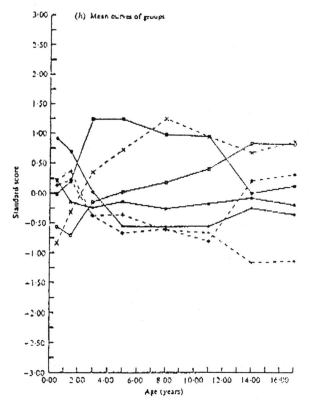

Figure 3.   IQ profiles over age for the London study. (Reprinted with permission from Hindley & Owen, 1979.)

assessments between 6 months and 17 years, and 109 subjects had seven assessments between 6 months and 14 years. As in the Fels Study, subjects were above average in IQ (122 at 11 years).

Clusters representing individual differences in developmental profile were determined visually by two independent investigators using seven a priori descriptive prototypes: (a) up, (b) up with hump, (c) hump, (d) down, (e) down with U, (f) U, and (g) horizontal or no definite trend. These classifications were made according to developmental profile excluding general level. The mean curves for these groups, including general level, are presented in Figure 3.

The results were in large part similar to those of McCall et al. (1973). First, approximately half the subjects (less over the shorter time spans) had nonsignificant trends, while the remaining subjects showed significant and simple patterns—linear, quadratic, or cubic for the 6-month to 17th-year sample, linear and quadratic for the 3–17-year sample, and linear only for the 3–11-year sample. Second, the amount of change was substantial, although somewhat less than in the Fels Study. The average estimated range was approximately 16 IQ points, and 11% of the subjects had a range of 33 IQ points. Third, approximately half the patterns were progressive, simple, and substantial in form, not random fluctuations about a constant value. Indeed, the systematic variance associated with the simple fitted curves accounted for 58% of the within-subjects variance between 3 and 11 years of age and 75% between 6 months and 14 years. Fourth, again there was a relation between increasing profiles and higher general levels. Fifth, inflection points occurred at 18 months, 36 months, 11 years, and 14 years. The 11- and 14-year points replicate McCall et al. (1973), but as indicated above, it was difficult to replicate McCall et al.'s 6-year inflection, because no assessment was made at this age.

North Carolina. The third study, by Ramey, Lee, and Burchinal (1989), followed the methodology of McCall et al. (1973) but was conducted on 129 low-income children, 61 of whom had been enrolled in the Frank Porter Graham Child Development Center's Enrichment Program. A maximum of eight assessments were made between 6 and 54 months. The Bayley was administered at 6, 12, and 18 months; the Stanford-Binet was given at 24, 36, and 48 months; and the McCarthy was administered at 42 and 54 months. Note that, in the Hindley and Owen and in this study, developmental profile is confounded with particular type of test. While standardizing scores within ages makes them statistically comparable across age, it does not make them psychologically comparable.

Four clusters were determined, and their average profiles are given in Figure 4. Some of the results were similar and some were different from those reported above. First, substantial numbers of children showed minimum change over the age span investigated. As can be seen in Figure 4, 59 of 129 (46%) subjects showed essentially no change, and 38 additional subjects showed only a gradual and minimally increasing pattern. The amount of intraindividual variation was less than for samples of higher SES children spanning much larger age ranges. While the amount of change was not reported for individuals, the range of values for the average curves (which would be less than for individuals) for the two groups showing the most change was 13.8 (above-average increase), which is somewhat less than for the other studies.

Second, patterns were quite simple, either essentially linear or quadratic, but they were not random fluctuations about an essentially constant value. Third, inflection points were not prominent but did appear in two groups at 18 months, which is similar to Hindley and Owen's results, but the previously observed inflection at 36 months was not clearly evident in these data. Finally, increasing patterns tended to have higher average scores than decreasing patterns.

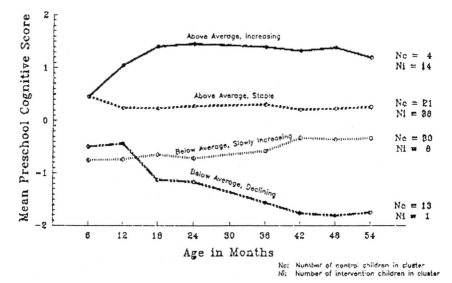

Figure 4. Mean standardized cognitive scores over the preschool ages for the North Carolina study. (Reprinted with permission from Ramey et al., 1989).

Conclusions. These three studies converge on a common set of conclusions:

1. When substantial age spans are considered (e.g., 2½ to 17 years), approximately half the subjects display essentially flat developmental profiles while the remaining subjects show substantial amounts of change that are described by simple, progressive linear, quadratic, and sometimes cubic trends. They are definitely not random fluctuations about a constant value. Since Hindley and Owen's patterns showed marked fluctuations during the preschool years but Ramey et al.'s low-income subjects did not, presumably lower scoring children show lower magnitudes of change than do higher scoring children.

2. Individual children display inflections at 18 months, possibly at 36 months, 5–7 years, 10–11 years, and 14 years (although confounding changes in test instruments were common at 14 years, even though scores were standardized within tests within ages). Inflections seem larger at the younger ages up to and including the 5–7-year period than at later ages, and the total amount of change tends to be larger for longer age spans, especially when it includes the younger ages.

3. Empirically, the form of the developmental profile is not independent of general level, even though profile form was determined independently of general level. As might be expected (but is not necessarily the case),

increasing patterns have higher general levels than do decreasing patterns. In part, this may be associated with the scoring system of some of the childhood tests which assign more months of mental age to higher level items, thereby increasing variability at higher levels of performance.

Potential Causes of Changes in Developmental Profile

Except for intervention studies, including Ramey et al., which found that a disproportionate number of children in their intervention group showed increasing developmental profiles, no experimental work has been done to determine possible causes of these shifts in IQ. However, several factors are, or are not, associated with changes in IQ that point in interesting directions.

Changing structure of the tests. As noted above, a different test was used at age 14 relative to the preceding years in both the McCall et al. and Hindley and Owen studies, both of which displayed a minor inflection point at age 14. Although standardized scores were used in both studies, it is possible that some subjects responded differently to the new test than did others, producing an inflection point in their developmental profiles at that age. Therefore, the presumed inflection at age 14 may be associated with a change in test instrument rather than any real change in general mental performance profile.

Of course, it is also possible that a test changes in the abilities reflected in the score from age to age, even though the name of the test remains the same. McCall et al. (1973), whose sample took the Stanford Binet tests exclusively between $2\frac{1}{2}$ and 17 years of age, investigated changes in the Meeker (1969) categorization of items on the Binet according to Guilford's (1967) Structure of the Intellect model. Thus, for example, any item might contribute to a particular Content, Operation, or Product in Guilford's terms. McCall et al. found that the distribution of items across the Guilford-Meeker categories varied substantially from age to age through the 4-year level, but not thereafter. Recall that major inflection points in IQ patterns occurred after 4 years. Further, when Guilford-Meeker variables were plotted across age for individuals, the individual's total IQ pattern was essentially replicated by each of the Guilford-Meeker variables after age 4. Therefore, at least in this case, major inflections in developmental profile do not appear to be obviously associated with a changing character of the abilities reflected on the assessment instrument, although changes during the first 4 years may be associated with such factors.

Major societal events. It is possible that major events occur in the life of a family that have the same influence on all children within the family but that will be displayed at different ages corresponding to the ages of the children at the time of that event. McCall et al. attempted two crude inquiries in this regard. First, they observed that the average year of birth for their five clusters differed by only 3.4 years—an amount sufficiently small to eliminate secular trends as a major factor in contributing to different IQ patterns because change trajectories often exceeded 3–4 years. However, the end of World War II (i.e., 1945) occurred between $10^1/_2$ and $13^1/_2$ years of age for this sample, years that marked the start of a long sustained rise in IQ performance for Clusters 1 and 3 and a long sustained decline in IQ for clusters 2, 4, and 5. Of course, because these secular differences between groups were not very great, it is difficult to tell whether inflections in IQ patterns are really associated with the termination of World War II or whether such inflections commonly occur between $10^1/_2$ and 13 years of age.

A second analysis was done more informally. In a sample of siblings from the Fels study, sibling pairs were aligned according to calendar year rather than chronological age to observe whether developmental profiles were more similar among siblings when this was done than matched unrelated children. While formal statistics were not conducted, visual inspection of the curves indicated that they were not. Therefore, it did not appear that major environmental events affected children the same way at the same calendar years.

Hereditary contributions. Traditionally, heritability calculations are made on single assessments based upon pairs of related individuals. But single assessments include variation associated with development profile, general level, and error. Evaluating the heritability of developmental functions has the potential of separating these sources of variance and assessing the heritability of general level more or less separately from the heritability of developmental profile. Attempts to conduct such analyses have been done in two laboratories.

McCall (1970, 1972a, b; McCall et al., 1973) has compared the general levels and developmental profiles of mental test performance of siblings versus matched unrelated control pairs at 6 and 12 months, 18 and 24 months, and with various numbers of assessments between 6 and 24 months, 42 and 66 months, 74 and 132 months, and 42 and 132 months. In each case, siblings were more similar to one another in general level than were matched unrelated children, but in no case were siblings more similar with respect to developmental profile than were matched unrelated children. Also, a small set of twins revealed a similar pattern of results across the childhood years (McCall et al., 1973).

In contrast, McCall (1979) calculated heritabilities for developmental profiles for Wilson's Louisville Twin Study reports (Wilson, 1974; Wilson & Harpring, 1972) for varying numbers of assessments between 9 and 12 months, 9 and 24 months, 12 and 36 months, 18 and 24 months, 36 and 60 months, and 60 and 72 months. These heritabilities ranged from .10 to 82 and averaged .45, with no obvious systematic increase or other pattern over age.

How shall these apparently contradictory results—no heritability for developmental profile for siblings, but heritability for twins—be resolved? First, Wilson's methodological approach has been debated (McCall, 1972b; McCall et al., 1973; see Wilson's 1973, rebuttal). A major point in these debates is that it appears uncertain that Wilson's procedures actually separate out the heritability for general level from the heritability of developmental profile. As a result, a substantial amount of the obtained heritability for twins may be associated with general level and not with developmental profile as defined here, which would make the sibling and twin results consistent in showing heritability for general level but not for developmental profile.

Second, Wilson assessed the heritability of development profiles over much shorter age spans, often involving only two or three assessments. This may favor within-pair similarity because profiles must necessarily be simple in form, especially if no-change patterns are regarded as similar.

Third, the heritability estimates in Wilson's data for single assessments do not show the typical increasing pattern. This presumably indicates differential shared environments between MZ an DZ twins, which may also produce artifactually high heritabilities for developmental pattern as well as for single-age assessments.

As a working hypothesis, then, it seems reasonable to conclude that, noting Wilson's exception, genetics makes increasing contributions to mental test performance, especially between 2 and 5–7 years of age, and that these contributions are more substantially associated with general level than with developmental profile. This has prompted some investigators to assert that genetics "sets" the general level or range of potential IQ while environment determines where within that genetic range one actually functions. While this conclusion appears to be a simple description of the data, it implies more structure and function than is warranted. If the "genetically set range" were fairly narrow and few individuals ever exceeded it, this interpretation might have some credence. But the studies of IQ change reviewed above showed that one in seven individuals changed 40 points or more, and that two changed as much as 73–74 IQ points, which essentially covers the entire range of IQ distribution. Therefore, the "genetically set range" seems so broad as to be meaningless. Further, developmental profile and general level are not independent in nature. Therefore, it is not really possible to totally ascribe one attribute to genetics and the other to environment. Instead, general level and developmental profile are convenient, if not totally precise and independent, descriptors or partitions of developmental variability that may help us think about these issues but which should not be interpreted so rigidly.

Environmental contributions. Two of the three studies of individual differences in developmental function report environmental correlates of the different developmental functions described in those studies. Recall, however, that general level and developmental profile were correlated in these studies, so the environmental correlates observed cannot be attributed separately to general level versus developmental profile.

More specifically, McCall et al. (1973) found that developmental patterns showing increases during the preschool years and having higher general levels were associated with parents who were rated as providing more attempts to accelerate the intellectual development of their children and to provide firm discipline with moderate levels of punishment, reminiscent of Baumrind's (1967) "authoritative" approach to discipline. Parents of these children themselves had higher education levels than the parents of children displaying predominantely decreasing developmental functions.

Ramey et al. (1989) also found that development functions that were above average in general level and increasing in developmental profile were associated with higher maternal IQ, higher scores on the HOME environmental assessment, and more likely to belong to subjects in the intervention than in the control group. Clearly, acceleratory attempts and higher parental IQs are associated with increasing developmental profiles.

Within-family, nonshared environmental factors. But environmental contributions may be more complicated than this. For example, Rowe and Plomin (1981) estimated that half the variation in IQ for a given group of subjects at a single age is nongenetic, presumably environmental plus error. Moreover, half of this environmental variation occurs within families and is not shared by siblings. Subsequently, McCall (1983) showed that essentially the same amount of variance was associated with development profile, and his other studies reviewed above indicate that developmental profile variation does not tend to be highly heritable nor is it's form shared by siblings.

The two analyses converge on the proposition that roughly half the variation in IQ is environmental and half the environmental variation is associated with development profile, that is, age-to-age changes in IQ that are systematic as opposed to random error. Further, since such changes are not shared by siblings, they are not likely to be associated with gross indices of the general intellectual climate of the home (e.g., general intellectual atmosphere, parental stimulation, etc.) that are frequently cited as major contributors to IQ (they may contribute to general level but not to developmental profile).

The conclusion is that one needs to examine a forgotten realm—that is, environmental factors that occur within families as opposed to between families, which are not shared by siblings, or that do not influence siblings in the same way. There are three types of these nonshared, within-family changes:

1. The general environment changes over the course of a child's life. Such changes may produce one consequence for mental development in the case of one sibling and another consequence in the case of another sibling, depending upon their ages and individual skills and interests at the time of major events. While no direct evidence exists on this point, it is known that the environment is not as consistent across age as one might suppose. For example, in the first 2 years of life, there is only moderate stability in the subscales of the HOME environmental assessment, with correlations between 6, 12, and 24 months ranging from .40 to .70 (Bradley, 189). It is likely that at least some of these changes will influence the mental development of one sibling differently from another sibling within these families.

2. Different environments for different siblings. Students of mental development frequently focus on the general home environment as the major contributor to mental development, and they often overlook teachers and peers, who are usually different individuals who likely provide different experiences for one sibling versus another within a family. Further children are likely to "niche pick" (Scarr & McCartney, 1983), and those niches are likely to be different for siblings. For example, siblings are more likely to develop different interests, skills, and experiences if they live together than if they live apart (McCartney, Harris, & Bernieri, 1990). Unfortunately, systematic studies of different environmental experiences and their contribution to the mental performance per se of siblings within families are lacking.

3. The same environmental event may produce different effects on different siblings. It is possible that a single environmental event has differential effects on different children within the family, partly because of their age differences at the time of the event, different perspectives by different children of the same environment event, and interactions with different interests, skills, and motivations. For example, a family with a 15-year-old and a 9-year-old might visit the space center in Florida. The older youth may be unaffected by it, preoccupied instead with sports and members of the opposite sex. The 9-year-old, however, might be fascinated and return home to study a science unit on aviation and space flight taught by a teacher who is a private pilot. Suddenly, a latent interest in science and math is kindled by these experiences, and the child's mental performance increases.

Empirically, divorce seems to affect children differently depending on their ages (Wallerstein & Kelly, 1980), and one might suppose that most other major environmental events would have differential effects on children of different ages within a family. Another example is the birth of a sibling, which obviously influences existing children differently than it does the child who is born.

Effects of the birth of a sibling. In fact, the birth of a sibling has been theorized by Zajonc (1976; Zajonc & Markus, 1975; Zajonc, Markus, & Markus, 1979) to contribute to the dilution of the intellectual atmosphere of the home and thereby produce a decline in intellectual growth for existing children during the years following the birth. The Confluence Model, which rests on this crucial dynamic, is highly controversial, largely because early tests of the model were based mostly on single cross-sectional assessments of one child per family (Berbaum & Moreland, 1985; McCall, 1985). But McCall (1984) found some support for the fundamental proposition that the birth of a sibling should be associated with a longitudinal and temporary decline in IQ for existing children in the family.

Specifically, three groups of subjects were selected and matched for sex, family size (when appropriate), age at IQ assessment, and IQ before the birth of the sibling. The focal groups consisted of children from two- and three-child families who experienced the birth of one younger sibling during their lives.

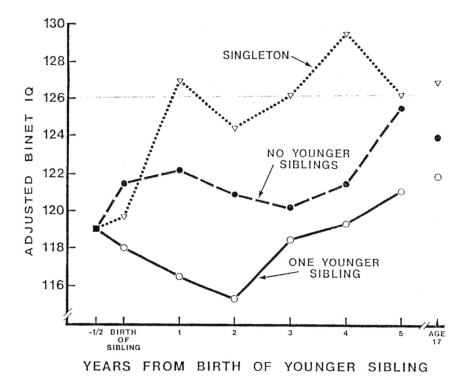

Figure 5. Adjusted Binet IQ over age for the singleton, no-younger, and one-younger sibling groups after equating the groups for IQ 6 months prior to the birth of a sibling and controlling for sex, age at testing, and family size where appropriate. (Reprinted with permission from McCall, 1984.)

They were compared with children from two- and three-child families who had no younger siblings born to them (i.e., they were the youngest child) plus a group of singletons who had no siblings at all. According to the Confluence Model, singletons should show the highest IQ and a development profile that is relatively smooth through the relevant age period. In contrast, those children experiencing the birth of a sibling should show a drop relative to singletons and to the most precise comparison group, namely, those children from similarly sized families who do not experience the birth of a younger sibling. The data are presented in Figure 5.

The three groups were adjusted to be equivalent in IQ on the assessment that occurred one-half year prior to the birth of a sibling. Thereafter, the groups diverged, with the birth of a sibling being associated with a 10-point disadvantage relative to singletons and a 5.8-point disadvantage relative to last-born children from families of comparable size. That the curves already begin to diverge on the IQ assessment closest in time to the birth of a sibling reflects the fact that such an assessment sometimes occurred before and sometimes after the birth.

These data clearly show that a nonshared (or differentially shared) environmental event within a family can have nontrivial effects on the developmental profile for general mental performance for different siblings within the family. It illustrates a class of variables that is often neglected in the study of mental performance that becomes crucial when considering developmental profile. Further, studies suggest that such factors collectively may account for half of the environmental variance and approximately 25% of the total variance in IQ at a given age (McCall, 1983; Rowe & Plomin, 1981).

CONCLUSION

If developmental psychologists indeed are interested in development, which means change within individuals over time (Wohlwill, 1973), then they must spend more of their energies describing developmental changes in behaviors of interest (McCall, 1977a, 1981b). This means they must conduct more longitudinal studies, and analyses must be directed at describing developmental functions and individual differences in developmental functions as vigorously as they describe cross-age stabilities in relative rank orderings.

The study of developmental functions has just begun, and it consists of describing functions for the species, for major groups within the species, and for individuals. Developmental functions can be broken down somewhat artificially into having general levels and developmental profiles, the latter being the patterns of ups and downs over age that may occur potentially independently of the average score (i.e., general level). Existing data suggest that some factors (e.g., genetics) may be more strongly associated with one of these domains (e.g., general level) than the other. Further, individual differences in developmental profiles are substantial, even for a variable with the known consistency of IQ. Moreover, the environmental factors that contribute to such changes are rarely studied. Such factors include changing environments, environmental events that impinge on one but not another sibling, and environmental events that are perceived or interpreted differently for different siblings. This will be painstaking work, difficult to fund, and increasingly complex, but it is also the essence of our discipline, whether it focuses on the development of general mental performance or any other variable.

REFERENCES

Appelbaum, M.I., Burchinal, M.L., & Terry, R.A. (1989). Quantification methods and the search for continuity. In M.H. Bornstein & N.A. Krasnegor (Eds.), *Stability and continuity in mental development: Behavioral and biological perspectives* (pp. 251–272). Hillsdale, NJ: Erlbaum.

Baumrind, D. (1967). Child care practices anteceding three patterns of preschool behavior. *Genetic Psychology Monographs, 75*, 43–88.

Bayley, N. (1949). Consistency and variability in the growth of intelligence from birth to eighteen years. *Journal of Genetic Psychology, 75*, 165–196.

Bayley, N. (1956). Individual patterns of development. *Child Development, 27*, 45–75.

Berbaum, M.L., & Moreland, R.L. (1985). Intellectual development within transracial adoptive families: Retesting the confluence model. *Child Development, 56*, 207–216.

Birns, B., & Golden, M. (1972). Prediction of intellectual performance at 3 years from infant tests and personality measures. *Merrill-Palmer Quarterly, 18*, 53–58.

Bloom, B.S. (1964). *Stability and change in human characteristics.* New York: Wiley.

Bornstein, M.H., & Sigman, M.D. (1986). Continuity in mental development from infancy. *Child Development, 57*, 251–274.

Bradley, R.H. (1989). The use of the HOME inventory in longitudinal studies of child development. In M.H. Bornstein & N.A. Krasnegor (Eds.), *Stability and continuity in mental development: Behavioral and biological perspectives.* Hillsdale, NJ: Erlbaum.

Corman, H.H., & Escalona, S.K. (1969). Stages of sensorimotor development: A replication study. *Merrill-Palmer Quarterly, 15*, 351–361.

Cronbach, L.J. (1957). The two disciplines of scientific psychology. *American Psychologist, 12*, 671–684.

Emmerich, W. (1964). Continuity and stability in early social development. *Child Development, 35*, 311–332.

Epstein, H.T. (1974a). Phrenoblysis: Special brain and mind growth periods. II. Human mental development. *Developmental Psychobiology, 7*, 217–224.

Epstein, H.T. (1974b). Phrenoblysis: Special brain and mind growth periods. I. Human brain and skull development. *Development Psychobiology, 7*, 207–216.

Epstein, H.T. (1976). A biologically-based framework for intervention projects. *Mental Retardation, 14*, 26–27.

Epstein, H.T. (1978). Growth spurts during brain development: Implications for educational policy and practice. In J.S. Chall & A.F. Mikky (Eds.), *Education and the brain: The seventy-seventh yearbook of the National Society for the Study of Education, part II.* Chicago: University of Chicago Press.

Epstein, H.T. (1990). Stages in human mental growth. *Journal of Educational Psychology, 82*, 876–880.

Epstein, H.T., & Toepfer, C.F., Jr. (1978). A neuroscience basis for reorganizing middle grades education. *Educational Leadership, 35*, 656–660.

Fischer, K.W. (1980). A theory of cognitive development: The control and construction of hierarchies of skills. *Psychological Review, 87*, 477–531.

Flavell, J.H. (1963). *The developmental psychology of Jean Piaget.* New York: Van Nostrand.

Guilford, J.P. (1967). *The nature of human intelligence.* New York: McGraw-Hill.

Hart, L.A. (1981). Brain language and new concepts of learning. *Educational Leadership, 38*, 443–445.

Heim, A.W. (1970). *Manual for the AH4 Group Test of General Intelligence.* Slough: NFER.

Hilden, A.H. (1949). A longitudinal study of intellectual development. *Journal of Psychology, 28*, 187–214.

Hindley, C.B., & Owen, C.F. (1979). An analysis of individual patterns of DQ and IQ curves from 6 months to 17 years. *British Journal of Psychology, 70*, 273–293.

Honzik, M.P., Macfarlane, J.W., & Allen, L. (1948). The stability of mental test performance between two and eighteen years. *Journal of Experimental Education, 18*, 309–324.

Hudspeth, W.J., & Pribram, K.H. (1990). Stages of brain and cognitive maturation. *Journal of Educational Psychology, 82*, 881–884.

Hunt, J. McV. (1963). *Intelligence and experience.* New York: Ronald Press.

King, W., & Seegmiller, B. (1973). Performance of 14–22-month-old black, firstborn male infants on two tests of cognitive development: The Bayley Scales and The Infant Psychological Development Scale. *Developmental Psychology, 8*, 317–326.

Kopp, C.B., Sigman, M., & Parmelee, A.H. (1974). Longitudinal study of sensorimotor development. *Developmental Psychology, 10*, 687–695.

Lewis, M., & McGurk, H. (1972). Evaluation of infant intelligence. *Science, 178*, 1174–1177.

McCall, R.B. (1970). IQ pattern over age: Comparisons among siblings and parent-child pairs. *Science, 170*, 644–648.

McCall, R.B. (1972a). Similarity in developmental profile among related pairs of human infants. *Science, 178*, 1004–1005.

McCall, R.B. (1972b). Similarity in IQ profile among related pairs: Infancy and childhood. *Proceedings of the American Psychological Association* (pp. 79–80). Washington, DC: American Psychological Association.

McCall, R.B. (1977a). Challenges to a science of developmental psychology. *Child Development, 48*, 333–334.

McCall, R.B. (1977b). Childhood IQ's as predictors of adult educational and occupational status. *Science, 197*, 482–483.

McCall, R.B. (1979). The development of intellectual functioning in infancy and the prediction of later IQ. In J.D. Osofsky (Ed.), *Handbook of infant development* (pp. 707–741). New York: Wiley.

McCall, R.B. (1981a). Early predictors of later IQ: The search continues. *Intelligence, 5*, 141–147.

McCall, R.B. (1981b). Nature-nuture and the two realms of development: A proposed integration with respect to mental development. *Child Development, 52*, 1–12.

McCall, R.B. (1983). Environmental effects on intelligence: The forgotten realm of discontinuous non-shared within-family factors. *Child Development, 54*, 408–415.

McCall, R.B. (1984). Developmental changes in mental performance: The effect of the birth of a sibling. *Child Development, 55*, 1317–1321.

McCall, R.B. (1985). The confluence model and theory. *Child Development, 56*, 217–218.

McCall, R.B. (1988). Growth periodization in mental test performance. *Journal of Educational Psychology, 80*, 217–233.

McCall, R.B. (1990). The neuroscience of education: More research is needed before application. *Journal of Educational Psychology, 82*, 885–888.

McCall, R.B., Appelbaum, M.I., & Hogarty, P.S. (1973). Developmental changes in mental performance. *Monographs of the Society for Research in Child Development, 32* (Serial No. 150).

McCall, R.B., Eichorn, D.H., & Hogarty, P.S. (1977). Transitions in early mental development. *Monographs of the Society for Research in Child Development, 42* (Serial No. 171).

McCall, R.B., Meyers, E.D. Jr., Hartman, J., & Roche, A.F. (1983). Developmental changes in head circumference and mental-performance growth rates: A test of Epstein's phrenoblysis hypothesis. *Developmental Psychobiology, 16*, 457–468.

McCartney, K., Harris, M.J., & Bernieri, F. (1990). Growing up and growing apart: A developmental meta-analysis of twin studies. *Psychological Bulletin, 107*, 226–237.

Meeker, M.N. (1969). *The structure of intellect: Its interpretation and uses.* Columbus: Charles E. Merrill.

Moore, T. (1967). Language and intelligence. A longitudinal study of the first eight years. Part I. Patterns of development in boys and girls. *Human Development, 10*, 88–106.

Piaget, J. (1952). *The origins of intelligence in children* (M. Cook, Trans.). New York: International Universities Press.

Ramey, C.T., Lee, M.W., & Burchinal, M.R. (1989). Developmental plasticity and predictability: Consequences of ecological change. In M.H. Bornstein & N.A. Krasnegor (Eds.), *Stability and continuity in mental development: Behavioral and biological perspectives* (pp. 217–234). Hillsdale, NJ: Erlbaum.

Rowe, D.C., & Plomin, R. (1981). The importance of non-share (E₁) environmental influences in behavioral development. *Developmental Psychology, 17*, 517–531.

Scarr, S., & McCartney, K. (1983). How people make their own environments: A theory of genotype—environment effects. *Child Development, 54*, 424–435.

Sontag, L.W., Baker, C.T., & Nelson, V.L. (1958). Mental growth and personality development: A longitudinal study. *Monographs of the Society for Research in Child Development, 23* (Serial No. 68).

Toepfer, C.F. (1979). Brain growth periodization—A new dogma for education. *Middle School Journal, 10*(3), 20.

Uzgiris, I.C. (1973). Patterns of cognitive development in infancy. *Merrill-Palmer Quarterly, 19*, 181–204.

Uzgiris, I.C. (1989). Transformations and continuities: Intellectual functioning in infancy and beyond. In M.H. Bornstein & N.A. Krasnegor (Eds.), *Stability and continuity in mental development: Behavioral and biological perspectives* (pp. 123–143). Hillsdale, NJ: Erlbaum.

Uzgiris, I.C., & Hunt, J. McV. (1975). *Assessment in infancy: Ordinal scales of psychological development.* Urbana: University of Illinois Press.

Wachs, T.D. (1976). Utilization of a Piagetian approach in the investigation of early experience effects: A research strategy and some illustrative data. *Merrill-Palmer Quarterly, 22*, 11–30.

Wallerstein, J.S., & Kelly, J.B. (1980). *Surviving the breakup: How children actually cope with divorce.* New York: Basic Books.

White, S.H. (1965). Evidence for a hierarchical arrangement of learning processes. In L.P. Lipsitt & C.C. Spiker (Eds.), *Advances in child development and behavior* (Vol. 2, pp. 187–220). New York: Academic Press.

Wilson, R.S. (1973). Testing infant intelligence. *Science, 182*, 734–737

Wilson, R.S. (1974). Twins. Mental development in the preschool years. *Developmental Psychology, 10*, 580–588.

Wilson, R.S., & Harpring, E.B. (1972). Mental and motor development in infant twins. *Developmental Psychology, 7, 277–287.*

Wohlwill, J.F. (1973). *The study of behavioral development.* New York: Academic Press.

Zajonc, R.B. (1976). Family configuration and intelligence. *Science, 192*, 227–236.

Zajonc, R.B. & Markus, G.B. (1975). Birth order and intellectual development. *Psychological Review, 82*, 74–88.

Zajonc, R.B., Markus H., & Markus, G.B. (1979). The birth order puzzle. *Journal of Personality and Social Psychology, 37*, 1325–1341.

Chapter *2*

Infant Information Processing and Later Intelligence*

Susan A. Rose

Departments of Pediatrics & Psychiatry
Rose F. Kennedy Center for Research in
Mental Retardation & Human Development
Albert Einstein College of Medicine

INTRODUCTION

At the turn of the century, Alfred Binet developed the first intelligence test (Binet & Simon, 1905). Binet's primary goal was to identify children who did not have the mental capacity to profit from regular instruction. Although his test included three or four items applicable to very young children, it was primarily

_____

* This chapter was written while the author was the Flora Stone Mather Visiting Professor at Case Western Reserve University. Preparation of this chapter, and of the author's research that is reported in it, was assisted by Research Grant HD-13810 from the National Institute of Child Health and Human Development. The author is indebted to Judith F. Feldman, Ina F. Wallace, and Cecelia McCarton for their collaboration in this research, and to Frances Goldenberg for her assistance in all phases of the work.

oriented towards those of school-age. This new tool rapidly gained wide acceptance and stimulated considerable research. One striking and consistent finding was the relative stability school children showed on repeated administrations of Binet's test. These stabilities were widely accepted as evidence that intelligence was constant, and intelligence soon came to be viewed as a capacity that each person was born with and that increased in a systematic fashion as the child matured (Bayley, 1958).

Tests of infant development were an outgrowth of the flurry of research spawned by Binet's effort to develop practical instruments of intellectual functioning. It was thought that infant tests would be not only of practical value, but of theoretical value as well. Because of the less complex behavior of infants, it was expected they would throw light on the fundamental processes involved in intelligence. The development of such tests signalled a recognition of the significance of infant behavior and ushered in an era that was to be marked by the beginning of serious scientific study of the infant.

By the 1930s several groups of researchers were attempting to develop measures of infant intelligence that would be reliable and predictive. These efforts resulted in a number of widely used tests, such as the Cattell Infant Scale (Cattell, 1940); the Gesell Developmental Schedule (Gesell & Amatruder, 1954); an early version of the Bayley, called the California First Year Mental Scale (Bayley, 1933); and, most recently, the Bayley Scales of Infant Development (Bayley, 1969). The Bayley Scales are currently the best standardized of the infant scales. All the infant tests developed in a tradition where researchers in the field were convinced of the constancy of intelligence (Bayley, 1958).

Unhappily, as predictors of later intelligence the infant tests have proved largely disappointing. Although they are useful as descriptive instruments, providing normative data on various aspects of current functioning and development, and allowing for the identification of certain sensorimotor deficits, scores on these tests have proven largely unrelated to scores on intelligence tests in later childhood. Numerous studies have shown that, when administered in the first 2 years of life (especially in the 1st year), existing psychometric tests have little prognostic value for normal children and even for those considered seriously compromised or clinically at risk (for reviews, see Kopp & McCall, 1982; McCall, 1979). For normal children, prediction of IQ scores in school years increases steadily after the 1st year, begins to stabilize around 24 months, and then increases rapidly until approximately 5 years. Kopp and McCall (1982) reported that, in unselected groups of normal infants, the median correlation between developmental tests administered in the first 6 months of life and IQ scores at 2–4 years is only .21; the correlation drops to near zero when IQ scores at 5–7 years are considered as the outcome variable. Prediction to later IQ is better from 2 years on, although at 2 years it is still relatively poor; for example, the correlation between 2 and 5 year scores is only .32 (Hoznik, Macfarlane, & Allan, 1948). By contrast, correlations obtained over a similar 3-year age span in later childhood are relatively high (e.g., IQ's assessed at 9 and 12 years correlate with one another in the neighborhood of .85). Kopp and McCall concluded that "cross-age correlations for performance on standardized tests are very low during the first 2 or 3 years of life, and individual differences assessed during this period do not predict IQ in childhood or adulthood at clinically useful or theoretically interesting level of accuracy" (1982, p. 35).

As it became clear that the infant tests failed to predict later IQ, ideas about the nature of intelligence came under closer scrutiny. For the most part, the view of continuity in intelligence gave way to one of discontinuity, in which intelligence was considered as either inherently unstable or as consisting of a series of qualitatively distinct stages. In particular, it has been suggested that the achievements in abstract, verbal, and symbolic reasoning that are possible after the onset of language reflect aspects of intelligence that are qualitatively and fundamentally different in nature from preverbal competencies (see McCall, 1979; McCall, Hogarty, & Hurlburt, 1972; Piaget, 1954). According to this view, it is hardly surprising that infant (preverbal) competencies fail to predict mature cognition, since such competencies are thought to undergo a fundamental change.

An obvious alternative to the above line of reasoning, and one being adopted with increasing frequency, is that the standard tests of early intelligence fail to predict because they aren't tapping the same domains of behavior as the tests used in later childhood. Whereas tests of more mature cognition are heavily weighted with assessments of information processing, many items in the standard infant scales assess imitation, sensorimotor maturity, and emotional expressiveness. For example, between 6 and 12 months the infant is evaluated on a variety of behaviors such as retrieving toys, placing cubes in a cup, exploring a formboard, cooperating in games, attending to and imitating scribbling, picking up a pellet, attempting to secure a third cube while holding two others, etc. Most of the childhood intelligence tests, on the other hand, consist of tasks tapping different functions, such as digit span, short-term memory, verbal comprehension, vocabulary, the perception and manipulation of geometric patterns, deductive reasoning, and general information. The infant skills clearly bear no obvious connection to those assessed at older ages.

It seems obvious that measures assessing specific aspects of information processing in infancy might prove more appropriate for evaluating the presence of cognitive continuities. And indeed, that seems to be the case. In the sections below, I shall (a) discuss some of the data that have accumulated over the past 20 years illustrating infant's capacity for, and skill at, information processing; (b) indicate how groups expected to differ in intelligence later in life differ during infancy on such measures; (c) summarize studies showing that individual differences in such abilities are proving to be more predictive of later cognitive ability than are traditional measures; and (d) present results from an ongoing study of these issues from our own laboratory.

INFANT INFORMATION PROCESSING:
A THUMBNAIL SKETCH

The studies of early information processing have, for the most part, used measures of habituation or recognition memory—generally visual habituation or visual recognition memory. The processes involved in both can be conceptualized as basic to the acquisition of new information and to the ability to deal with novelty, abilities similar to those singled out by Berg and Sternberg (1985) as integral components of individual differences throughout the entire life span. *Habituation* is commonly assessed by the decrement in response that occurs to an unchanging stimulus. Following habituation, the infant is tested for *dishabituation,* or attention to stimulus change. *Recognition memory,* on the other hand, is assessed by the differential preference for novel and familiar stimuli that occurs following a period of familiarization. (In this paradigm, the initial familiarization period is preset in duration so, unlike habituation, no waning of attention to the stimulus need occur.) Measures of habituation are taken as presumptive evidence of how fast and completely the infant encodes the stimulus and constructs an engram or trace of it. Measures of dishabituation, and of recognition memory, are taken as presumptive evidence of both the accuracy or completeness of the engram formed and the ability to distinguish the memory trace of the old from the new.

The picture that emerges from work using the habituation and paired-comparison paradigms is one in which infants show strong age-related increases in the speed of information processing, robust memory, and a clear capacity to recognize relatively abstract representations of what they initially saw. The evidence for each of these abilities is compelling and helps to validate the cognitive nature of the infant measures. Although considerable data can be brought to bear on each point, I'll make no attempt to be comprehensive here but instead offer a brief sketch of the nature of this support.

Speed of Processing

In an early study, Fagan (1974) compared the amount of familiarization time 5–6 month-olds needed to recognize three types of stimuli: simple, abstract patterns; more subtle patterns consisting of different rearrangements of identical elements; and photographs of faces. These tasks were chosen on the basis of previous studies that had shown variations in the age at which novelty preferences are first shown for each type of stimuli: The simple abstract patterns were first recognized at 2½ months, the more subtle patterns at 4 months, and faces not until 5–6 months. Of particular interest was the finding that stimuli recognized by younger infants were recognized increasingly faster (after less familiarization) at older ages: The 5–6-month-olds needed 3.4 sec to recognize simple patterns, but they needed close to 17 sec to recognize the more subtle patterns and at least 22 sec to recognize photos of faces. In effect, the amount of familiarization needed for recognition was inversely related to the age at which memory for each type of stimulus was first shown. Similar findings were reported by Rose (1983), who, using parametric variations in familiarization time, found that 1-year-olds needed only half the time 6-month-olds did to recognize simple three-dimensional shapes (10 vs 20 sec).

Demonstrations of age-related increases in the speed of visual habituation also exist. Fantz (1964) presented 10 pairs of stimuli to 28 1- to 6-month-olds. One member of the pair remained constant throughout the 10 1-minute trials; the other changed from trial to trial. The youngest group, 1–2 month-olds, showed no decrement over trials in their looking to either stimulus, whereas infants older than 2 months reliably decreased their attention to the previously exposed target. More recently, extensive data on the developmental course of habituation were reported by Colombo and Mitchell (1990). In a cross-sectional study, 186 infants from four age groups were studied at 3, 4, 7, and 9 months, and another group of 69 infants was studied longitudinally at these same ages. All infants were habituated to color photos of faces. There were developmental changes in a number of parameters of the habituation curve, including an age-related decrease in the total fixation time needed to reach a constant habituation criterion. Bornstein, Pecheux, and Lecuyer (1988) showed a similar effect in infants between 2 and 7 months of age.

Memory

Although there are a number of reports showing the robustness of infant memory, the best known is a trio of studies that appeared in 1977 (Cohen, DeLoache, & Pearl, 1977; Fagan, 1977; McCall, Kennedy, & Dodds, 1977). Using different methodologies, all three studies showed that memory in the 3- to 6-month-old is quite resistant to interference from intervening stimuli. There was little evidence in any of these studies of forgetting, with delays of a few minutes to a few hours. In an earlier study, Fagan (1973) had found that 5-month-olds recognized a photograph of a face as much as 2 weeks later. In related work, Rovee-Collier and her colleagues (Rovee-Collier, Sullivan, Enright, Lucas, & Fagan, 1980), using a conjugate reinforcement technique, have shown that 3-month-olds can readily learn a contingency between footkicking and the movement of a crib mobile and remember it for as long as 1 week; moreover with a brief reminder, memory can be reactivated after periods as long as 2 or 4 weeks. It should be noted, however, that, although infant memory is surprisingly robust, it is not invulnerable. Rose (1981) compared 6- and 8-month-olds' memory for briefly presented stimuli. Whereas immediate memory was present at both ages, delayed recognition was impeded in the younger infants.

Abstraction

Considerable research has been concerned with understanding the nature of the cognitive representations present in infants. It now appears that such representations can be quite abstract—that they are often encodings or interpretations that go well beyond exact "snap-shot" perceptions.

Rose (1977) reported that infants as young as 6 months were able to recognize pictures of an object they had seen only briefly. In this study, infants were familiarized with an object for 30 sec and then, on test, were shown a picture of the familiar object paired with the picture of a new object. In most studies of visual recognition, infants show a novelty response—when they recognize an object, they look longer at that which is new. That is what they did here—they looked significantly longer at the picture of the new object than at the picture of the old one. A control study indicated that infants were not confusing the object with its representation. Quite the contrary, they recognized the difference between the two while at the same time appreciating their similarities. These general findings were replicated in a related study with 1-year-olds, in which it was shown that infants recognized not only pictures, but line drawings of the objects as well (Rose, Gottfried, & Bridger, 1983).

Recently, Rose (1988) reported that, at least by 1 year, infants not only recognized degraded static representations, but could integrate visual information across space and time into the perception of a complete shape. After watching the contour of a shape being traced out by a moving point source of light, 1-year-olds recognized the similarity between the object and its tracing, 6-month-olds did not. Thus, by 1 year, infants can store successive bits of information and integrate them into some sort of perceptual schema or figural whole.

In work on categorization, infants are generally habituated to exemplars from one category and then tested for recognition of category membership by contrasting behavior to new exemplars from the familiar category with exemplars from a new category. If the infant appreciates category membership, it is anticipated that habituation will generalize to new exemplars from the old category and dishabituation will occur only to exemplars from the new category. Strauss (1979) and Sherman (1985) have presented evidence of face categorization in infancy. Their studies indicate that 10-month-olds have available strategies for abstracting category-level information from their perceptual experience with discriminable exemplars. Similarly, Fagan (1977) reported that 7-month-olds familiarized with a face in one pose recognized it in a totally new pose; Ruff (1978) found that 9-month-olds recognized the shape of objects independent of changes in size, color, and orientation, and Ross (1980) showed that 1-year-olds recognized toys representing real-world catagories such as animals, vehicles, and furniture.

Another conceptual process that indicates abstraction is that of *cross-modal transfer,* or the transfer of information from one sensory modality to another (Gottfried, Rose & Bridger, 1977; Rose, Gottfried, & Bridger, 1978, 1979, 1981a, 1981b, 1983). The study of cross-modal transfer would seem to have special significance for the issue of abstraction and mental representation, since recognition depends on comparing stimulus information presented to one modality with a stored mental representation of the stimulus acquired in a different modality. The procedure used by Rose and her colleagues to assess cross-modal transfer is based on an adaptation of the paradigm used to test for visual memory. In the original paradigm, a stimulus is displayed for a period of visual inspection, and then the now-familiar stimulus is presented again, paired with a novel stimulus. In adapting this paradigm to study cross-modal transfer, the stimuli are presented either tactually or orally during familiarization and visually during the test phase. When the stimuli are presented in different modalities during familiarization and test, the occurrence of recognition memory demonstrates cross-modal transfer.

Using this technique, Rose and her colleagues have found that 1-year-olds can visually recognize shapes that they have previously explored only tactually (with their hands) or orally (with their mouths). Younger infants also achieve some measure of tactual–visual transfer, but the phenomenon is not as robust at 6 months and requires double the familiarization at this early age (60 vs 30 sec). The slower rate of information processing seen in younger infants mirrors findings from studies of visual processing (Rose, 1983) and multimodal processing (Rose, Gottfried, & Bridger, 1979) and seems to be a basic characteristic of development. Once cross-modal recognition is achieved, the infant can also recognize degraded or impoverished versions of the object previously touched or mouthed (Rose, Gottfried, & Bridger, 1983).

In tasks of cross-modal transfer, the infant is called upon to integrate temporally distribute inputs into a unitary spatial percept in order to visually recognize the stimuli after tactual exploration. A similarity must be recognized between phenomena that, at least on one level, are ostensibly unrelated. Since the infant is able to transfer information from one sense system to another, the similarities abstracted must transcend modality-specific perception.

Although little is yet known about the mechanisms that underlie infant visual memory, habituation, and cross-modal transfer, the data clearly suggest that conceptual processes tapped by these paradigms reflect the infant's representation of experience and, as such, encapsulate important facets of infant information processing.

INFORMATION PROCESSING IN RISK INFANTS

There are a growing number of studies showing that children expected to differ in intelligence later in life differ during infancy on the information-processing skills discussed in the previous section. These include infants suffering from Down Syndrome, failure-to-thrive, malnutrition, nonoptimal perinatal events, exposure to chemical teratogens, and prematurity.

Down Syndrome infants have been found to be delayed in both visual recognition memory and visual habituation. Miranda and Fantz (1974) compared the performance of 16 Down Syndrome and 16 normal infants at each of three ages—3, 5, and 8 months—on three types of stimuli: simple abstract patterns, more subtle patterns consisting of rearrangements of component elements, and photographs of faces. For each type of stimulus the normal infants showed a preference for the novel stimulus several weeks earlier than the Down Syndrome infants, indicative of a clear superiority for the normal infants. Similar results were obtained by Cohen (1981) on a task of visual habituation. He compared eight Down Syndrome and eight normal infants at each of three ages—4, 5, and 6 months. Although normal infants habituated to the familiar stimulus (a 24″ × 24″ black-and-white checkerboard) and dishabituated to the novel stimulus at all three ages, the Down Syndrome babies did not habituate until 5 months and did not dishabituate to the new stimulus until 6 months. Thus, not until 6 months did those suffering from Down Syndrome appear to be as capable as their 4-month-old normal counterparts on these tasks.

The effect of nutritional insult has been examined in two studies. Singer, Drotar, Fagan, Devost, and Lake (1983) compared the performance of 13 organic failure-to-thrive infants with that of 13 non-organic failure-to-thrive and 13 normal controls on several problems of visual recognition memory. These problems used simple designs and photographs of faces as stimuli. Infants suffering organic failure-to-thrive demonstrated only chance performance, whereas the other two groups demonstrated recognition memory. Rose (1993) found that nutritional factors were associated with performance among infants growing up in India. The performance of 109 5–12-month-olds suffering mild-to-moderate malnutrition was compared with that of 74 adequately nourished infants on tasks of visual recognition memory and cross-modal transfer. Each task used a variety of familiarization times to capture age-related changes in performance. At all ages the malnourished infants performed poorly on both tasks, even controlling for birthweight. The poor performance of the malnourished infants still persisted even after controlling for family income and parental education. The deficits or delays associated with malnourishment were evident in both tasks.

In the only study to examine the effects of chemical teratogens on infant information processing (Jacobson, Fein, Jacobson, Schwartz, & Dowler, 1985), 123 infants followed from birth were administered Fagan's test of visual recognition memory at 7 months. Prenatal exposure to PCB was assessed by evaluating cord serum PCB level and by maternal report of contaminated fish consumption. Both measures were negatively associated with visual recognition memory and, in fact, preference for novelty actually decreased in a dose-dependent fashion with increasing levels of PCB exposure.

By far the greatest number of studies looking at the effects of risk have used preterm infants. Preterms have been compared with full-terms on visual recognition memory, visual and auditory habituation, the learning of and memory for an instrumental response, exploratory behavior, multimodal learning, and cross-modal transfer. In all the studies considered below, preterms were tested at "corrected age" (i.e., age from the expected date of birth).

Sigman and Parmelee (1974) compared 20 term and 20 preterm 4-month-olds on several types of problems, including four problems of visual recognition memory, each consisting of pairings of a previously exposed 24 × 24 checkerboard with a different novel stimulus. Full-terms exhibited recognition memory, as indicated by a significant overall preference for novelty, whereas preterms gave no evidence of recognition memory at all. Caron and Caron (1981), using the habituation design, compared about 20 preterms and 20 full-terms at each of four ages—3, 4, 5, and 6 months—in their ability to abstract categorical and relational information from a series of stimuli. Infants were habituated to multiple instances of one class of stimuli (e.g., schematic faces) and, in the test phase, shown stimuli that were all made up of new elements, on some trials arranged in a familiar configuration and on others in a totally new configuration. At each age, full-terms showed significantly greater recovery to the change in configuration-plus-elements than to the change in elements alone; preterms did not. The preterms focused primarily on the change in individual elements, ignoring the configural whole created by the relations between elements. Caron, Caron, and Glass (1983) found similar deficits among full-terms who had experienced a variety of nonoptimal perinatal events. Gekoski, Fagen, and Pearlman (1984) compared 10 preterms and 10 full-terms at 3 months of age in the acquisition and retention of a contingency in which they had learned to move a crib mobile by their footkicks. (A ribbon tied at one end to their ankle and at the other end to the mobile insured that footkicks would move the mobile.) The full-terms learned the contingency more quickly than the preterms, and showed superior 1-week retention. Indeed, the preterms showed no retention at all over this interval.

With respect to infant exploration, Sigman (1976) examined the behavior of 32 preterm and 32 full-term 8-month-olds. Infants were given a 6-minute period to explore a small bell and, immediately following, the familiar bell was paired with 10 novel objects, each presented for 1 min. The groups differed in the first 2 minutes following familiarization, with preterms exploring the familiar object for a longer duration and showing less preference for the novel object. In a detailed analysis of exploratory strategies used by infants around this age, Ruff, McCarton, Kurtzberg, and Vaughan (1984) found that immature strategies were favored by the group of 9 high-risk preterms they studied. These infants engaged in less fingering, rotating, and hand-to-hand transfer of new objects than did the group of either 9 low-risk preterms or 20 normal full-term infants. If high-risk preterms normally make poor use of such mature exploratory strategies, they may be handicapped in acquiring the information needed for discrimination and recognition.

In a series of investigations in our laboratory, we have found that preterms did poorly on a variety of information-processing tasks. In one of these studies (Rose, 1980), 18 preterm and 18 full-term 6-month-olds were tested on three problems of visual recognition memory. The preterms failed to differentiate between novel and familiar test stimuli on any of three problems, whereas the full-terms showed significant novelty preferences on two of them. The poor performance of preterms was replicated with another group of 18 infants. Of particular interest was the fact that the performance of preterms improved dramatically for a group (N = 18) given substantially increased familiarization times. This success suggests that, in general, the preterms were unable to encode the information as quickly as the full-terms.

We replicated and extended these findings in a study that introduced parametric variations in familiarization time, using 10, 15, 20, and 30 s of familiarization (Rose, 1983). This study was carried out with 20 preterm and 20 full-term infants at each of two ages, 6- and 12-month-olds. Although the older infants required less familiarization time than the younger ones, preterms of both age groups required considerably longer familiarization than full-terms. At 6 months, full-terms achieved significant scores with only 15 s of familiarization, whereas preterms needed 30 s; at 12 months, full-terms achieved significant scores with as little as 10 s of familiarization (the briefest interval used), whereas preterms required 20 s. These results suggest that there are persistent differences between preterms and full-terms throughout at least the first year of life in this very fundamental aspect of cognition.

These findings were further buttressed by results from a study of cross-modal transfer in 12-month-olds. In this study (Rose, Gottfried, & Bridger, 1978), we investigated infants' ability to recognize an object visually when the initial inspection or familiarization had been either tactual or oral—the infant must visually recognize a stimulus never seen, but only felt or mouthed. A group of 39 middle-class full-terms, 28 preterms, and 27 lower class full-terms were tested. Although the middle-class full-terms achieved successful transfer, the other two groups did not. Those not achieving transfer either failed to gain knowledge about the shape of an object by feeling it and mouthing it or were unable to make this information available to the visual system.

Preterms also seem to have more difficulty than do full-terms in another aspect of intersensory functioning, namely, extracting visual information from objects that are explored in a multimodal fashion—by visual regard, touch, mouthing, and manipulation (Rose, Gottfried, & Bridger, 1979). Contrary to our expectations, a brief period of such multimodal exploration turned out to impede rather than facilitate subsequent visual recognition. Whereas this was true at more than one age, and for full-terms as well as preterms, the negative effect was decidedly more pronounced for preterms.

PREDICTIVE VALIDITY OF
INFORMATION-PROCESSING MEASURES

Unlike the early Bayley scales, information-processing measures are proving to have a significant relation to later outcome. Although the longitudinal studies are still few in number, and many are based on small sample sizes, the weight of evidence is beginning to suggest that measures of infant recognition memory, selective attention, habituation, and cross-modal transfer have some predictive validity. Infants who habituate quickly, recognize new stimuli readily, and transfer information across modalities tend to perform well on traditional assessments of cognitive competence in later childhood.

The first report of the predictive value of infants' response to novelty was published by Yarrow, Klein, Lomonaco, and Morgan (1975), who, as part of a larger study, presented $5^1/_2$-month-olds (N = 39) with a series of 10 trials in which a familiar object was repeatedly paired with a novel one. The amount of time infants spent handling and mouthing the new objects correlated .35 with Stanford-Binet IQ at 3 years. In 1981, these findings were supported by two studies which appeared back to back in the journal *Intelligence*. In one, Lewis and Brooks-Gunn (1981) presented two samples of 3-month-olds (N = 22, N = 57) with six repeated presentations of a 30-s stimulus followed by a single dishabituation (recovery) trial with a new stimulus. They found correlations of .52 and .40 between recovery of attention to a change in color or form and 24-month Bayley scores. In the other study, Fagan and McGrath (1981) presented follow-up data for four samples of infants who had participated some years earlier in experimental studies where they had received two or three problems of visual recognition memory (sample sizes ranged from N = 19 to N = 35). The infant scores obtained at 4–7 months correlated .33 to .66 with scores obtained at 4–7 years on the Peabody Picture Vocabulary Test and/or other vocabulary scales.

Confirmatory findings have been reported by Fagan in several subsequent studies. In one (Fagan, 1984) 36 children originally tested for novelty preferences at 7 months and for performance on the Peabody Picture Vocabulary Test at 3 years were retested on the Peabody at 5 years. Predictive correlations of .42 were found at both ages. Fagan has been developing a screening test based on visual recognition memory. In an early version of the test (Fagan, Singer, Montie, & Shepherd, 1986), 62 infants suspected of being at risk for later cognitive development were administered 12 problems of visual recognition over a 5-month period, when they were between the ages of 3 and 7 months. Scores obtained on this battery showed a 75% sensitivity to retardation at 3 years (IQ ≤70) and a 91% specificity to normality. Similar results were obtained for a cross-validation sample of another 62 infants (Fagan & Montie, 1986). In a later version of the test, designed for 6.5- to 12-month-olds, infants were presented a series of 10 problems at each of four ages: 6, 7, 9, and 12 months (Fagan, Shepherd, & Montie, 1987). Although predictive validity has not yet been presented for this version of the test, significant differences in novelty preference were reported between 119 normal and 22 at-risk infants. In the largest study yet published in this area, DiLalla et al. (1990) examined the predictive validity of seven different measures of infant cognitive development, including the Fagan, in a sample of 208 twin pairs. Infants were followed longitudinally at 1, 2, and 3 years. The Fagan test, when administered at 7 (but not 9) months correlated significantly (.29) with 3-year Stanford-Binet scores.

Findings linking dishabituation to later outcome have been reported by Caron et al. (1983), who found that the extent to which 5–6-month-olds showed recovery to a novel facial expression in the habituation paradigm correlated .32 with Stanford-Binet IQ at 3 years (N = 31). The results of O'Connor, Cohen, and Parmelee (1984) indicate that such findings are not modality specific: Recovery to a new auditory stimulus at 4 months correlated .60 with 5-year Stanford-Binet scores (N = 28).

Similar predictive relations have been reported for measures of habituation and attention. The first such relation was reported by Miller and her colleagues (Miller et al., 1979), who found that the extent to which the attention of 2–4-month-olds waned during habituation correlated .39 with language comprehension at 2–4 years (N = 29). The rapidity with which attention wanes over a series of habituation trials is thought to be a measure of the infant's speed of information processing. Similar findings were reported by Lewis and Brooks-Gunn (1981) but for only one of the two samples of 3-month-olds in their study (N = 22). Sigman, Cohen, Beckwith, and Parmelee (1986), in a longitudinal follow-up of a large sample of preterms, found a relationship between attention and IQ at two different ages. At term age, greater habituation to a stimulus over the first minute of its presentation correlated .29 with 5-year IQ (N = 100) and .27 with 8-year IQ (N = 91). At 4 months, greater habituation to a stimulus over a series of trials (i.e., greater percentages of decrement) correlated .44 with 5-year IQ (N = 58) and .28 with 8-year IQ (N = 56). Rose, Slater, and Perry (1986) found similar results using an infant-control version of the habituation design. Here, the number of trials is not predetermined but instead continues until a criterion is reached. They found a negative correlation of − .69 between measures indexing the duration of looking during habituation at 1.5–6.5 months and 5-year IQ (N = 16). Finally, in a short-term longitudinal study, Tamis-LeMonda and Bornstein (1989) found that more mature habituation at 5 months predicted greater language comprehension and a higher percentage of pretend play at 13 months. The 5-month habituation measures also predicted a 13-month latent variable of representational competence (made up of language and play), even after the influence of maternal stimulation was removed, suggesting that there are direct links between early habituation and later cognition that are not attributable to child-rearing styles.

The literature that appeared through 1986 has been summarized in two studies. Fagan and Singer (1983) reported a median correlation of .40 (mean = .44) between novelty scores (representing infants' differential fixation to novel visual stimuli) and later outcome. This predictive validity coefficient, based on 12 samples, included a number of published and unpublished studies from their own laboratory, along with the samples tested by Lewis and Brooks-Gunn (1981) and Yarrow et al. (1975). Bornstein and Sigman (1986), in a subsequent review, reported a median predictive correlation of .46 between infant measures of habituation, dishabituation, and response to novelty and measures of later cognitive functioning obtained between 2 and 7.5 years. This correlation was based on 23 samples of children taken from 14 studies.

LONGITUDINAL STUDIES FROM OUR LABORATORY

Preliminary Studies

In two preliminary studies from our laboratory, we found results consistent with those cited in the preceding section. Both studies dealt largely with the follow-up of preterms who, as infants, had participated in experimental studies in our laboratory. As part of a longitudinal project being conducted by another group of investigators at our Kennedy Center, many of these same infants had received a series of developmental assessments, including the Bayley scales at 12 and 24 months, Stanford-Binet at 34 and 40 months, and the WISC-R at 6 years. In the first of our preliminary longitudinal studies (Rose & Wallace, 1985a), we found correlations of .53 to .66 between measures of visual recognition memory obtained at 6 months and developmental outcomes from 2–6 years (N = 14 to N = 35, depending on age at follow-up). In the second study (Rose & Wallace, 1985b), 1-year measures of cross-modal transfer and visual recognition memory both showed significant correlations with developmental outcomes at these same ages: Correlations of the 1-year measures with 2–6-year developmental assessments ranged from .38 to .64 (N = 19 to N = 26). Full-terms, tested in follow-up at 2 years, showed similar predictive correlations across this 1-year span.

Like many of the early studies in this area, our samples were small and the longitudinal follow-up was boot-strapped on studies initially designed as experimental investigations. However, the findings were particularly encouraging for several reasons. First, they indicated the predictive validity of a measure not previously examined in infancy work, namely, cross-modal transfer. Second, unlike many early studies, outcomes were assessed not at a single age, but repeatedly, and over a fairly lengthy time span. Having done this, we could see that the pattern of predictive relations was a consistent one, evident across the entire preschool period. Moreover, the results were similar even though somewhat different subgroups received follow-up exams at each age, making it unlikely that the predictive validity of the early measures was spurious or caused by idiosyncracies in any one subgroup. Third, early Bayley scores, whether obtained at 6 months or 1 year, failed to predict these same outcomes. Fourth, these information processing measures predicted variance in later outcome that was not accounted for by parental education, a background measure which, beginning about 2 years, is consistently associated with childhood IQ.

Current Study

Encouraged by these early findings, we begin a relatively large scale study to investigate more extensively the relation between information processing in infancy, biological risk, and later cognition. The sample includes 109 infants. Although there is a large literature indicating that perinatal factors can adversely affect outcome (e.g., Drillien, Thompson, & Burgoyne, 1980; Kitchen et al., 1980), medical risk has often been confounded with social risk. Unfortunately, the latter also has adverse sequalae (Escalona, 1982; Kopp & Kaler, 1989). To assess the impact of biological risk apart from social risk, we included two groups, one comprised of 63 high-risk preterms (born weighing <1500 g), the other of 46 healthy full-terms. Since both groups are drawn from the same predominately disadvantaged backgrounds, both can be considered at social risk, while the preterms can be considered additionally at biological risk.

In the initial report on this cohort, we replicated earlier findings of poor performance among preterms (Rose, Feldman, McCarton, & Wolfson, 1988). The problems used in this study included nine of visual recognition memory (Abstract Patterns, Faces, and Geometric Forms) and two of cross-modal transfer. Novelty scores, which reflect the relative amount of time infants look at a new stimulus compared with a familiar one, were computed for each problem and aggregated over problems. At 7 months of age, preterms not only had lower novelty scores than full-terms (particularly on Abstract Patterns and Face problems) but also required longer exposure times to accrue the preset amounts of looking at the familiarization stimulus. These longer exposure times were due primarily to longer pauses between fixations, although the two groups also differed during familiarization in the duration of fixation and the frequency in shifts of gaze. For the preterms, performance on both measures was depressed by several risk factors, particularly by respiratory distress syndrome. In general then, high-risk preterms exhibited deficits in visual recognition memory, and in the ability to recruit, maintain, and sustain attention. It should be noted that the measures of recognition memory and attention were uncorrelated, suggesting that each taps a different developmental process.

Stability and Reliability. In two reports we showed that various aggregates of these measures of early infant information processing had moderate stability from 6 to 8 months (Rose & Feldman, 1987; Rose, Feldman, & Wallace, 1988). Cross-age correlations for novelty scores (measuring visual recognition memory) ranged from .30 to .50 over the 1- to 2-month period, and those for exposure-time (measuring visual attention) ranged from .32 to .38.

Although the infant measures showed moderate stability over 1- and 2-month intervals, their internal consistency, as indexed by Chronbach's alpha, was surprisingly low. Whether computed at 6, 7, or 8 months, alphaes did not exceed .24, even for composites containing up to 11 problems. Alphas were slightly higher when scores on similar problems were averaged and these averages were used as components of the larger composite; however, even here the median alpha for nine scores (three at each of three ages) only equalled .18. Colombo, Mitchell, and Horowitz (1988) also reported moderate stability coefficients along with similarly low estimates of internal consistency reliability (see also Colombo, Mitchell, O'Brien, & Horowitz, 1987).

We initially interpreted these low reliablities as indicating that the variance contributed by each problem is unique. However, because the test periods in problems of visual recognition memory are so brief (10–20 s), it is equally possible that individual scores are unduly influenced by what Cattell (1982) termed *fluctuation variance.* Momentary fluctuations in state, arousal level, and fussiness could disrupt the infant's attention, thus making each score but a poor indicator of the underlying cognitive process or processes. Under these circumstances, one would not expect high alphas, even when processes assessed by each problem were identical.

Since measures that are unreliable cannot correlate with anything else (and these measures do) the stability figures would lead one to conclude that, unless interitem correlations can be substantially improved, reliability for measures of visual recognition memory will be better estimated by test–retest methods.

Prediction of Later Intelligence. In the first of two studies using this cohort (Rose, Feldman, & Wallace, 1988), scores for aggregates of 6–11 problems were created at each age (6, 7, and 8 months) and then correlated with 3-year IQ. Aggregate scores from all three ages significantly predicted 3-year Binet IQ with correlations ranging from .37 to .63; predictive correlations clustered between .50 and .60. The magnitude of the predictive relations was similar for aggregates based on scores obtained at each age (i.e., 6, 7, and 8 months) and similar for preterms and full-terms. Combining data across age increased predictability and led to multiple correlations as high as $R = .72$. In addition, cut-offs predicting children at risk for mental retardation (IQ <70) or cognitive delay (IQ <85) show reasonable sensitivity and specificity.

These results were extended in a second study, where a single aggregate created from all nine 7-month visual problems was found to relate to later intelligence (Rose, Feldman, Wallace, & McCarton, 1989). Novelty scores were significantly and consistently related to outcome beginning at 2 years—2-year Bayley Mental Development Index (MDI), 3- and 4-year Stanford-Binet IQ, 5-year Wechsler Preschool and Primary Scale (WPPSI) IQ. Correlations ranged from .37 to .65 and again were similar for both groups. An alternative index of visual recognition memory, created by considering performance on each problem as indicating the presence or absence of recognition, was related to outcome too, but not as strongly as the original novelty score. This finding indicates that variations in the actual magnitude of the novelty score capture significant individual differences. The infant's ability to sustain attention at 7 months was also predictive of later outcomes, although again, not as strongly as the novelty score. By contrast, correlations between concurrent (7-month) Bayley scores and outcome were generally lower: None were significant for full-term and, with one exception, none were significant beyond 1.5 years for preterms. Novelty scores were related to later intelligence independently of socioeconomic status, maternal education, 7-month Bayley, and medical risk. When taken together in multiple regressions, novelty scores consistently made a larger independent contribution to prediction than did any of these more traditional predictors. Together, novelty scores, maternal education, and 7-month Bayley scores accounted for anywhere between 18% and 44% of the variance (14% to 39% adjusted variance) in outcomes from 2 to 5 years.

Prediction of Later Language. Since many of the intelligence tests are dependent on linguistic skills, and since early infant measures have been found to predict later language proficiency as well as IQ, a question arises of whether the relation between infant recognition memory and later IQ is due entirely, or in part, to variance that the early measures share with language (e.g., Bornstein & Sigman, 1986). Unlike earlier studies, we had included assessments of language as well as intelligence at some ages, so we were in a position to examine this issue directly (Rose, Feldman, Wallace, & Cohen, 1991). The 7-month novelty scores turned out to be nearly as strongly related to 3- and 4-month measures of comprehension and expression (assessed by the Reynell Development Language Scales—Reynell, 1969) as they were to IQ. Although the novelty–IQ correlations were considerably reduced when language was controlled, they did not disappear; on the contrary, they remained significant and moderate in magnitude, .20 to .51. In other words, a substantial relation between novelty and IQ exists that is independent of language. These results obtained whether language was assessed contemporaneously with IQ or anywhere from 1 to 2.5 years earlier than IQ. Regression analyses and path diagrams indicated that novelty had an indirect impact on 3-year IQ that went through language. There was also a direct relation between early novelty and 3-year IQ that appears to have nothing to do with language. Beyond 3 years, all further developmental effects linking novelty to later IQ (at 4 and 5 years) were entirely indirect; the indirect path through language went by way of comprehension, not expression. Overall, the results indicate that the novelty score captures multiple processes, some shared with language (especially comprehension) and IQ, and some that are relatively language free and shared only with IQ.

CONCLUSIONS

Theoretically, the research on infant cognition and the demonstrations of predictive validity from infancy into later childhood raises issues of enormous significance for developmental psychology. This work provides a much firmer foundation for notions of cognitive continuity than has ever existed. There is now clear evidence that cognitive abilities can be assessed in infancy and that individual differences in these abilities are importantly related to later cognitive status. The growing body of work in the area indicates a strong thread of continuity in intellectual functioning extending from infancy onwards. The discovery of such continuites can be considered one of the major achievements of contemporary developmental psychology.

Although these are exciting initial findings, they throw into bold relief how little we still know about the nature of early cognition, its development course, and the qualities of mind that form the basis for the longitudinal relations observed. In this regard, this new work raises questions about (a) the cognitive processes tapped by the infant measures, (b) the psychometric adequacy of the infant measures, (c) the choice of measure used to assess outcome.

Cognitive Processes Assessed by Infant Measures. To better understand developmental continuities, it is essential to identify the processes tapped by the infant measures. Although data is sparse, we believe the following processes are likely to be important: speed of information processing, memory, representational skill, and perhaps motivational or child-rearing factors.

One possibility is that many of the infant measures tap short-term memory (Fagan & McGrath, 1981), an ability important in later cognitive performance. If this is the case, individual differences in any of the component processes of short-term memory, e.g., encoding, storage, or retrieval, could underpin the infant–childhood relations. Support for this possibility can be found in a recent report that a measure of visual recognition memory obtained at 7 months correlated with a measure of spatial memory obtained at 16 months (Colombo, Mitchell, Coldren, & Horowitz, 1989).

A second possibility is that the link lies in some general g-like factor related to speed of processing (Fagan, 1984). Deary (1988) notes that, historically, attempts to correlate speed of encoding with estimates of intelligence, although few in number, have been relatively successful. Evidence consistent with this possibility comes from studies indicating that faster habituation in infancy is related to a variety of later competencies, as well as from studies showing that infants at medical risk process information more slowly than normal infants (Rose, 1980, 1983; Rose et al., 1979, 1988; see also reviews by Bornstein & Sigman, 1986; Fagan & Singer, 1983).

A third possibility is that mental representation serves as the common thread linking the infant and childhood measures (Bornstein & Sigman, 1986). The formation of such representations would involve the extraction of salient features, commonalities, or invariances from the perceptual flux. Evidence consistent with this possibility comes from a study linking infants' habituation at 5 months to their representational competence at 13 months (Tamis-LeMonda & Bornstein, 1989). We have also considered our measure of cross-modal transfer as a measure of representational or symbolic competence (see, e.g., Rose, 1986; Rose et al., 1983). Here, the infant is asked to store a description of an object based on tactual information, and to match it to visual information about the same object. In other words, the infant must recognize tactual and visual correspondences at a level sufficiently abstract to allow for comprehension of object identity across the two modalities. This would seem to call for some central processing of the patterns of tactual and visual information.

A fourth possibility is that noncognitive factors, such as motivation or arousal, might underpin the longitudinal correlations (see Bornstein & Sigman, 1986; Sigman, 1988). If the infant measures simply reflect a proclivity to attend to new events, infants with low scores may simply be those who shun change rather than those whose memory is in any way impaired or those who are slower at processing information (see Berg & Sternberg, 1985). It should also be pointed out that individual differences in the individual's characteristic level of arousal could be involved. "The infant who is able to regulate states of arousal so as to attend effectively may maintain this capacity for self regulation so that attending and learning are easier in childhood" (Sigman, 1988, p. 513). If variations in the capability for self regulation were to remain stable, they could underpin stabilities between infant and childhood measures.

A fifth possibility is that consistency in child-rearing conditions may be a factor supporting the continuities in cognitive performance across age. However, a recent study by Tamis-LeMonda and Bornstein (1989) suggests that early cognitive continuities are at least partly independent of maternal stimulation.

Psychometric Considerations. In addition to identifying the processes involved in developmental continuities, more information on the psychometric properties of the infant measures is sorely needed. Many studies to date have used small samples, relatively restricted IQ ranges, and infant measures of unknown reliability. In fact, few have examined issues of long-term stability, short-term test–retest reliability, or internal consistency. This situation arose because the measures being used have been taken rather directly from experimental studies concerned with group performance. In adapting them for individual-difference research, psychometric considerations assume an importance they did not have in experimental work. Despite the need for psychometric examination of the new infant measures, little empirical work has yet been forthcoming.

Outcome Measures. Many of the prediction studies have used but a single type of outcome measure, generally a traditional intelligence test (but see DiLalla et al., 1990, for a notable exception). Whereas there is no doubt that intelligence tests provide a highly reliable estimate of global mental ability, they have some drawbacks. First, although made up tasks that are presumably unrelated, their various components are nearly always highly intercorrelated. Thus, they do not represent specific abilities, as demonstrated by the fact that they generally load highly on the first principal component that emerges in factor analytic studies (Detterman, 1987a, b; Jensen, 1987). Spearman (1927) speculated that this strong first principal component was due to a single underlying variable. In other words, a single ability would appear to determine performance on what are ostensibly very different tasks (Hunt, 1983). Others have suggested that the high loadings on a single factor are not a fundamental characteristic of intelligence as much as how it has been measured (e.g., Detterman, 1987a). In Detterman's conceptualization, intelligence can be thought of as consisting of components that (a) are relatively independent of one another, yet (b) when taken together account for most of the variance in IQ. Detterman has obtained empirical findings compatible with this conceptualization.

Second, factors derived from the popular factor-analytic approach have no psychological reality as components of intelligence. They are statistical abstractions and not a measure of any definable mental ability (Hunt, 1983). They do not identify an aspect of individual performance that would be important on theoretical grounds, such as memory strategies, inferential abilities, symbol manipulation, capacity factors, the representation of information, problem-solving strategies, etc. In contrast to traditional approaches, information-processing theorists seek to identify and study precisely such basic processing skills (Cooper & Regan, 1982). If we are to account for infant-to-child continuities, it will clearly be necessary to bring developmental and information-processing theorists together.

Clearly, much remains to be done in understanding the basis for the newly discovered developmental continuities in cognition. Most of the relations found, although not strong enough to be used as a basis for individual prediction, nevertheless have considerable theoretical significance. The results indicate that at least some of the roots of later cognition can be identified in infancy.

REFERENCES

Bayley, N. (1933). *The California First Year Mental Scale.* Berkeley, CA: University of California Press.
Bayley, N. (1958). Value and limitations of infant testing. *Children, 5,* 129–133.
Bayley, N. (1969). *Bayley Scales of Infant Development.* New York: Psychological Corporation.

Berg, C.A., & Sternberg, R.J. (1985). Response to novelty: Continuity versus discontinuity in the development course of intelligence. In. H.W. Reese (Ed.), *Child development and behavior* (Vol. 19, pp. 1–47). New York: Academic Press.

Binet, A. & Simon T. (1905). Methodes nouvelles pour le diagnostic du niveau intellectuel des anormaux. *L'Annee Psychologique, 11,* 191–244.

Bornstein, M.H., Pecheux, M.-G., & Lecuyer, R. (1988). Visual habituation in human infants: Development and rearing circumstances. *Psychological Research, 50,* 130–133.

Bornstein, M.H., & Sigman, M.D. (1986). Continuuity and mental development from infancy. *Child Development, 57,* 251–274.

Caron, A.J., & Caron, R.F. (1981). Processing of relational information as an index of infant risk. In S.L. Friedman & M. Sigman (Eds.), *Preterm birth and psychological development* (pp. 219–240). New York: Academic Press.

Caron, A.J., Caron, R.F., & Glass, P. (1983). Responsiveness to relational information as a measure of cognitive functioning in nonsuspect infants. In T. Field & A. Sostek (Eds.), *Infants born at risk: Physiological, perceptual and cognitive processes* (pp. 181–210). New York: Grune & Stratton.

Cattell, P. (1940) *The measurement of intelligence of infants and young children.* New York: Psychological Corporation.

Cattell, R.B. (1982). *The inheritance of personality and ability.* New York: Academic Press.

Cohen, L.B. (1981). Examination of habituation as a measure of aberrant infant development. In S.L. Friedman & M. Sigman (Eds.), *Preterm birth and psychological development* (pp. 240–254). New York: Academica Press.

Cohen, L.B., DeLoach, J.S., & Pearl, R.D. (1977). An examination of interference effects in infants' memory for faces. *Child Development, 48,* 88–96.

Cohen, S.E., & Parmelee, A.H. (1983). Prediction of five-year Stanford-Binet scores in preterm infants. *Child Development, 54,* 1242–1253.

Colombo, J. & Mitchell, D.W. (1990). Individual differences in early visual attention: Fixation time and information processing. In J. Colombo & J. Fagan (Eds.), *Individual differences in infancy: Reliability, stability, prediction* (pp. 193–227). Hillsdale, NJ: Erlbaum.

Colombo, J., Mitchell, D.W., Coldren, J.T., & Horowitz, F.D. (1989). Longitudinal correlates of infant visual behavior in the paired-comparison paradigm. *Intelligence, 13,* 33–42.

Colombo, J., Mitchell, D.W., & Horowitz, F.D. (1988). Infant visual behavior in the paired-comparison paradigm: Test-retest and attention-performance relations. *Child Development, 59,* 1198–1210.

Colombo, J., Mitchell, D.W., O'Brien, M., & Horowitz, F.D. (1987). The stability of visual habituation during the first year of life. *Child Development, 58,* 474–487.

Cooper, L.A., & Regan, D.T. (1982). Attention, perception and intelligence. In R.J. Sternberg (Ed.), *Handbook of human intelligence* (pp. 123–169). New York: Cambridge University Press.

Deary, I.J. (1988). Intelligence and encoding speed in infants, adults and children. *Cahier de Psychologie Cognitive/European Bulletin of Cognitive Psychology, 8,* 462–468.

Detterman, D.K. (1987a). Theoretical notions of intelligence and mental retardation. *American Journal of Mental Deficiency, 92, 2–11.*

Detterman, D.K. (1987b). What does reaction time tell us about intelligence? In P.A. Vernon (Ed.), *Speed of information processing and intelligence* (pp. 177–199). Norwood, NJ: Ablex Publishing Corp.

DiLalla, L.F., Thompson, L.A., Plomin, R., Phillips, K., Fagan, J.F., Haith, M.M., Cyphers, L.H., & Fulker, D.W. (1990). Infant predictors of preschool and adult IQ: A study of infant twins and their parents. *Developmental Psychology, 26,* 759–769.

Drillen, C.M., Thompson, A.J.M., & Burgoyne, K. (1980). Low birthweight children at early school age: A longitudinal study. *Developmental Medicine and Child Neurology, 22,* 26–47.

Escalona, S. (1982). Babies at double hazard: Early development of infants at biological and social risk. *Pediatrics, 70,* 670–676.

Fagan, J.F. (1973). Infants' delayed recognition memory and forgetting. *Jounral of Experimental Child Psychology, 16,* 424–450.

Fagan, J.F. (1974). Infant's recognition memory: The effects of length of familiarization and type of discrimination task. *Child Development, 45,* 351–356.

Fagan, J.F. (1977). Infant recognition memory: Studies in forgetting. *Child Development, 48,* 68–78.

Fagan, J.F. (1984). The relationship of novelty preference during infancy to later intelligence and later recognition memory. *Intelligence, 8,* 339–346.

Fagan, J.F., & McGrath, S.K. (1981). Infant recognition memory and later intelligence. *Intelligence, 5,* 121–130.

Fagan, J.F., & Montie, J.E. (1986). Identifying infants at risk for mental retardation: A cross validation study (Abstract). *Journal of Developmental and Behavioral Pediatrics, 7,* 199–200.

Fagan, J.F., Shepherd, P.A., & Montie, J.E. (1987). A screening test for infants at risk for mental retardation (Abstract). *Journal of Developmental and Behavioral Pediatrics, 8,* 118.

Fagan, J.F., & Singer, L.T. (1983). Infant recognition memory as a measure of intelligence. In. L.P. Lipsitt (Ed.), *Advances in infancy research* (Vol. 2, pp. 31–78). Norwood, NJ: Ablex Publishing Corp.

Fagan, J.F., Singer, L.T., Montie, J.E., & Shepherd, P.A. (1986). Selective screening device for the early detection of normal or delayed cognitive development in infants at risk for later mental retardation. *Pediatrics, 78,* 1021–1026.

Fantz, R.L. (1964). Visual experience in infants: Decreased attention to familiar patterns relative to novel ones. *Science, 146,* 668–670.

Gekoski, M.J., Fagen, J.W., & Pearlman, M.A. (1984). Early learning and memory in the preterm infant. *Infant Behavior and Development, 7,* 267–276.

Gesell, A., & Amatruda, C. (1954). *Developmental diagnosis.* New York: Holber.

Gottfried, A.W., Rose, S.A., & Bridger, W.H. (1977). Cross-modal transfer in human infants. *Child Development, 48,* 118–123.

Honzik, M.P., Macfarlane, J.W., & Allen, L. (1948). The stability of mental test performance between two and eighteen years. *Journal of Experimental Education, 18,* 309–324.

Hunt, E. (1983). On the nature of intelligence. *Science, 219,* 141–146.

Jacobson, S.W., Fein, G.G., Jacobson, J.L., Schwartz, P.M., & Dowler, J.K. (1985). The effect of intrauterine PCB exposure of visual recognition memory. *Child Development, 56,* 853–860.

Jensen, A.R. (1987). Individual differences in the Hick paradigm. In P.A. Vernon (Ed.), *Speed of information-processing and intelligence.* Norwood, NJ: Ablex Publishing Corp.

Kitchen, W.H., Ryan, M.M., Rickards, A., McDougall, A.B., Billson, F.A., Keir, E.H., & Nalor, F.D. (1980). A longitudinal study of very low birthweight infants: 4. An overview of performance at eight years of ages. *Developmental Medicine and Child Neurology, 22,* 172–188.

Kopp, C.B., & Kaler, S.R. (1989). Risk in infancy: Origins and implications. *American Psychologist, 44,* 224–230.

Kopp, C.B., & McCall, R.B. (1982). Predicting later mental performance for normal, at-risk, and handicapped infants. In P.B. Bates & O.G. Brin (Eds.), *Life-span development and behavior* (Vol. 4, pp. 33–61). New York: Academic Press.

Lewis, M., & Brooks-Gunn, J. (1981). Visual attention at three months as a predictor of cognitive functioning at two years. *Intelligence, 5,* 131–140.

McCall, R.B. (1979). The development of intellectual functioning in infancy and the prediction of later IQ. In J.D. Osofsky (Ed.)., *Handbook of infant development* (pp. 704–741). New York: Wiley.

McCall, R.B., Hogarty, P.S., & Hurlburt, N. (1972). Transitions in infant sensorimotor development and the prediction of childhood IQ. *American Psychologist, 27,* 728–748.

McCall, R.B., Kennedy, C.B., & Dodds, C. (1977). The interfering effect of distracting stimuli on the infant's memory. *Child Development, 48,* 79–87.

Miller, D.J., Ryan, E.B., Short, E.J., Ries, P.G., McGuire, M.D., & Culer, M.P. (1977). Relationships between early habituation and later cognitive performance in infancy. *Child Development, 48,* 658–661.

Miranda, S.B., & Fantz, R.L. (1974). Recognition memory in Down's syndrome and normal infants. *Child Development, 48,* 651–660.

O'Connor, J.J., Cohen, S., & Parmelee, A.H. (1984). Infant auditory discrimination in preterm and full-term infants as a predictor of 5-year intelligence. *Developmental Psychology, 20,* 159–165.

Piaget, J. (1954). *The construction of reality in the child.* New York: Basic Books.

Reynell, J.K. (1969). *The Reynell Developmental Language Scales.* Slough, UK: NFER.

Rose, D.H., Slater, A., & Perry, H. (1986). Prediction of childhood intelligence from habituation in early infancy. *Intelligence, 10,* 252–263.

Rose, S.A. (1977). Infants' transfer of response between two-dimensional and three-dimensional stimuli. *Child Development, 48,* 1086–1091.

Rose. S.A. (1980).Enhancing visual recognition memory in preterm infants. *Developmental Psychology, 16,* 85–92.

Rose, S.A. (1981). Developmental changes in infants' retention of visual stimuli. *Child Development, 52,* 227–233.

Rose, S.A. (1983). Differential rates of visual information processing in fullterm and preterm infants. *Child Development, 54,* 1189–1198.

Rose, S.A. (1986). Abstraction in infancy: Evidence from cross-modal and cross-dimension transfer. In L.P. Lipsitt & C. Rovee-Collier (Eds.), *Advances in infancy research* (Vol. 4, pp 218–220). Norwood, NJ: Ablex.

Rose, S.A. (1988). Shape retention in infancy: Visual integration of sequential information. *Child Development, 56,* 1161–1176.

Rose, S.A. (1993). *Relation between nutrition and information processing in infants born in India. Child Development,* in press.

Rose, S.A., & Feldman, J.F. (1987). Infant visual attention: Stability of individual differences from 6 to 8 months. *Developmental Psychology, 23,* 490–498.

Rose, S.A., Feldman, J.F., McCarton, C.M., & Wolfson, J. (1988). Information processing in seven-month-old infants as a function of risk status. *Child Development, 59,* 589–603.

Rose, S.A., Feldman, J.F., & Wallace, I.F. (1988). Individual differences in infant information processing: Reliability, stability, and prediction. *Child Development, 59,* 1177–1197.

Rose, S.A., Feldman, J.F., Wallace, I.F., & Cohen, P. (1991). Language: A partial link between infant attention and later intelligence. *Developmental Psychology, 27,* 798–805.

Rose, S.A., Feldman, J.F., Wallace, I.F., & McCarton, C.M. (1989). Infant visual attention: Relation to birth status and developmental outcome during the first five years. *Developmental Psychology, 25,* 560–576.

Rose, S.A., Gottfried, A.W., & Bridger, W.H. (1978). Cross-modal transfer in infants: Relationship to prematurity and socioeconomic background. *Developmental Psychology, 14,* 643–652.

Rose, S.A., Gottfried, A.W., & Bridger, W.H. (1979). Effects of haptic cues on visual recognition memory in full-term and preterm infants. *Infant Behavior and Development, 2,* 55–67.

Rose, S.A., Gottfried, A.W., & Bridger, W.H. (1981a). Cross-modal transfer and information processing by the sense of touch in infancy. *Developmental Psychology, 17,* 90–98.

Rose, S.A., Gottfried, A.W., & Bridger, W.H. (1981b). Cross-modal transfer in 6-month-old infants. *Developmental Psychology, 17,* 661–669.

Rose, S.A., Gottfried, A.W., & Bridger, W.H. (1983). Infant's cross-modal transfer from solid objects to their graphic representations. *Child Development, 54,* 686–694.

Rose, S.A., & Wallace, I.F. (1985a). Cross-modal and intra-modal transfer as predictors of mental development in fullterm and preterm infants. *Developmental Psychology, 21,* 949–962.

Rose, S.A., & Wallace, I.F. (1985b). Visual recognition memory: A predictor of later cognitive functioning in preterms. *Child Development, 56,* 843–852.

Ross, G. (1980). Categorization in 1- to 2-year olds. *Developmental Psychology, 16,* 391–396.

Rovee-Collier, C.K., Sullivan, N.W., Enright, M., Lucas, D., & Fagen, J.W. (1980). Reactivation in infant memory. *Science, 208,* 1159–1161.

Ruff, H.A. (1978). Infant recognition of the invariant form of objects. *Child Development, 49,* 293–306.

Ruff, H.A., McCarton, C., Kurtzberg, D., & Vaughan, H.G. (1984). Preterm infants' manipulative exploration of objects. *Child Development, 55,* 1166–1173.

Sherman, T. (1985). Categorization skills in infants. *Child Development, 56,* 1561–1573.

Singer, L.T., Drotar, D., Fagan, J.F., Devost, L., & Lake, R. (1983).The cognitive development of failure to thrive infants: Methodological issues and new approaches. In T. Field & A. Sostek (Eds.), *Infants born at risk: Physiological, perceptual, and cognitive processes* (pp. 222–242). New York: Grune & Stratton.

Sigman, M. (1976). Early development of preterm and fullterm infants: Exploratory behavior in eight-month-olds. *Child Development, 47,* 606–612.

Sigman, M. (1988). Infant attention: What processes are measured? *Cahier de Psychologie Cognitive/European Bulletin of Cognitive Psychology, 8,* 512–516.

Sigman, M., Cohen, E., Beckwith, L., & Parmelee, A.H. (1986). Infant attention in relation to intellectual abilities in childhood. *Developmental Psychology, 22,* 788-792.

Sigman, M., & Parmelee, A.H. (1974). Visual preferences of four-month-old premature and fullterm infants. *Child Development, 45,* 959–965.

Strauss, M. (1979). Abstraction of prototypical information by adults and 10-month-olds. *Journal of Experimental Psychology: Human Learning and Memory, 5,* 618–632.

Tamis-LeMonda, C. & Bornstein, M.H. (1989). Habituation and maternal encouragement of attention in infancy as predictors of toddler language, play, and representational competence. *Child Development, 60,* 738–751.

Yarrow, L.J., Klein, R.P., Lomonaco, & Morgan, G.A. (1975). Cognitive and motivational development in early childhood. In B.X. Friedlander, G.M. Sterritt, & G.E. Kirk (Eds.), *Exceptional infant* (Vol. 3, pp. 491–503). New York: Bruner/Mazel.

Chapter 3

Individual Differences in Visual-Cognitive Aging: Toward a Formal Model*

William J. Hoyer and Daniel J. Hannon

Syracuse University

The topic of this chapter concerns the description and explanation of individual differences in visual-cognitive aging. Our aim is to selectively review and evaluate the current status of empirical work and theory on visual-cognitive aging. Our second aim is to advocate a theoretically explicit approach to the description and explanation of visual-cognitive aging. It has been pointed out by a number of writers (e.g., Baltes, 1987; Light, 1991; Rybash, Hoyer, & Roodin, 1986; Salthouse, 1985b) that the field of cognitive aging has suffered from a lack of theoretical rigor. We evaluate recent work on the formalization of cognitive aging, and we consider the usefulness of a formal modeling approach to the study of age-related interindividual differences and intraindividual change in visual-cognitive aging. Since age-related changes in cognitive function are

---

* Preparation of this chapter was supported by grants RO1 AG 06041 and T32 AG 00185. We thank John Cerella and Dana J. Plude for their comments on an earlier draft.

typically attributed to general-purpose capacity or resource limitations, we attempt to apply recent developments in the modeling of attention to the study of age-related individual differences in visual-cognitive aging.

Points of Departure

Advances in our understanding of the nature of individual differences in intelligence and cognition necessarily depend on research efforts that represent a variety of methodological and theoretical approaches. For example, some of the important advances that have benefited our current understanding of individual differences in intelligence have involved exploration of the relative contributions of genetic and environmental influences (e.g., Detterman, Thompson, & Plomin, 1991; Plomin, Pederson, Nesselroade, & Bergeman, 1988); other productive approaches and lines of inquiry have focused on the specification of the information-processing components that comprise cognitive function, and the factor analytic description of the structure of intelligence. Interestingly, the scientific stories that are told about the nature of intelligence at any one of these levels are often quite discrepant with the accounts that unfold at different levels of analysis. Understanding the nature and the sources of individual differences in intelligence and cognition no doubt requires a multileveled attack.

In recent years, there has been tremendous excitement about the development of models that attempt to specify the functional architecture that underlies complex cognition. As Estes (1991) has pointed out, the term *cognitive architecture* gives emphasis to the importance of clear, explicit formulation at the level of *computation*, that is, the level at which the goals of cognition, as well as the internal and environmental constraints that make cognition possible, are specified. Until recently, very little effort has been expended on examining developmental change and individual differences in cognition from this perspective. Although only time will tell if this seemingly ambitious approach will have been of value to theory building, it is our view that recent developments in the formal modeling of cognition hold considerable promise (see Allport, 1989; Hintzman, 1990; McClelland, Rumelhart, & Hinton, 1986). We anticipate that these attempts to explicate cognitive architectures can be used to lend some theoretical precision to the study of cognitive aging, and that this approach will lead to important advances in our understanding of individual differences in cognitive aging (see also McKay & Burke, 1990; Salthouse, 1988a).

How do adults differ in terms of cognition and intelligence? What are the cognitive changes that occur as individuals grow older, and what mechanisms are responsible for age-related changes and differences in cognitive performance? And what is cognitive aging the aging of? These questions are highly complex due to the wide range of individual differences that can be observed for different aspects of cognitive function, and because of the many internal mechanisms and environmental factors that contribute to individual differences in cognition. Any attempt to organize the now vast literature on age-related individual differences in intelligence and cognitive performance requires consideration of a wide range of antecedents from neurobiological, to experiential, to environmental and contextual, along multiple measures representative of a wide variety of intellectual domains.

Shortcomings in the available literature are readily apparent. Cognitive aging researchers have given little attention to explicating the mechanisms that produce age-related interindividual differences, intraindividual change, and intraindividual differences along multiple measures. Perhaps what is most lacking are efforts to specify the connection between cognitive aging and brain aging. In most studies of cognitive aging, explanations of the results are offered without any assessment of the plausibility of the interpretation in terms of the neurophysiological mechanisms that might bear on the observed performance differences. Although the goal of precise specification of the linkages between neurobiological aging and behavioral aging seems futuristic, significant advances in the understanding of the connections between neurophysiological substrates and cognitive architecture are being made (e.g., McClelland, 1988; McNaughton & Morris, 1987; Posner, 1988; Posner, Inhoff, & Friedrich, 1987). Importantly for our purposes, this kind of work, as well as the "brain-style" computational approach it represents, holds considerable promise for the description and explanation of cognitive aging. If nothing else, this approach forces the theorist to be explicit, and discourages circular explanations of aging effects in terms of unverifiable constructs or unmeasured capacities (e.g., see Hoyer, 1990; Salthouse, 1988a,b). These issues are discussed later in the chapter; we begin with a brief overview of some of the main findings in cognitive aging.

Age-related Differences in Cognition

It is well known that, with aging, there are reliable declines in various kinds of cognitive function (e.g., Cerella, 1985; Light, 1991; Myerson, Hale, Wagstaff, Poon, & Smith, 1990; Rybash et al., 1986; Salthouse, 1985b, 1990). For example, in one survey, Salthouse (1985b) summarized the effects of age on performance across 54 studies of memory, reasoning, and spatial performance, and reported a median correlation of $-.36$ between chronological age and speed of cognitive performance.

Substantial age-related declines are frequently obtained on measures that appear to be basic components of high-level cognition. That is, the processes of stimulus identification (e.g., Madden, 1992), visual localization (Scialfa & Kline, 1988; Owsley, Ball, Sloane, Roenker, & Bruni, 1991), visual search and selectivity (Hoyer & Familant, 1987; Madden, 1986; Plude & Hoyer, 1986; Rabbitt, 1982), speed of mental rotation of visual objects (Berg, Hertzog, & Hunt, 1982; Sharps, 1990), perceptual closure (e.g., Frazier & Hoyer, 1992; Salthouse & Prill, 1987), vigilance and sustained visual attention (e.g., Davies,

Jones, & Taylor, 1984; Parasuraman, Nester, & Greenwood, 1989), visual-spatial analysis (Hoyer & Rybash, 1992; Kirasic, 1991; Salthouse, Babcock, Skovronek, Mitchell, & Palmon, 1990), and useful field of view (Owsley et al., 1991; Scialfa, Kline, & Lyman, 1987) all tend to be slower or otherwise less efficient in older adults as compared with younger adults. It is also generally reported that the magnitude of age-related differences in visual processing increases under conditions of increased stimulus degradation or noise (e.g., Cremer & Zeef, 1987), and as load-type manipulations (e.g., increased task complexity, display size) are imposed (e.g., Backman & Molander, 1986; Charness & Campbell, 1988; Madden, 1986; McDowd, 1986; McDowd & Craik, 1988; Plude & Hoyer, 1981, 1985, 1986; Rabbitt, 1982; Salthouse, 1988b). There are now several metaanalytic studies of the interactive effects of age and task complexity (see Cerella, 1985, 1990, 1991). In these analyses, the mean latencies of older adults in their 60s are plotted as a function of the mean latencies of younger adults in their early 20s, for the same experimental condition. Interestingly, simple types of linear or power functions with a near 0 intercept and a slope of between 1.2 and 2.0 yield highly accurate descriptions of the young–old comparisons across a wide range of task conditions. The reported r values generally exceed .9. Although it is well established that age-related declines are larger on some tasks than on others, Cerella (1985, 1990) and others (Hale, Myerson, & Wagstaff, 1987; Myerson et al., 1990) have interpreted the results of their metaanalyses as suggesting that most or all cognitive processes are equally age sensitive, and that cognitive aging is global. Compared to younger adults, older adults are simply slower on tasks that involve more processing steps or are otherwise more complex.

Age-related declines during the adult years are also well documented for many types of memory performance (see Hultsch & Dixon, 1990, Light, 1991, for comprehensive reviews). Age-related declines are particularly evident on measures of direct or explicit memory (Chiarello & Hoyer, 1988; Light & Singh, 1987; Mitchell, 1989), memory retrieval and naming (Albert, Heller, & Milberg, 1988), and working memory (Morris, Gick, & Craik, 1988; Reder, Wible, & Martin, 1986; Salthouse, Mitchell, Skovronek, & Babcock, 1989). Craik (1983) suggested that age deficits in memory depend on the extent to which the individual must self-initiate memory; small or negligible age differences are observed under conditions of contextual support for retrieval, such as in priming and implicing memory tasks (e.g., see Howard, 1988; Kihlstrom, Kaszniak, & Valdiserri, in press).

The pervasiveness and generality of age-related declines across a range of cognitive measures seems consistent with the equally pervasive observation of increased individual differences in complex cognitive performance with advancing age, especially in everyday situations. Although many visual-cognitive abilities show decline with increased age, the pattern of age-related change in performance is neither uniform nor orderly across individuals or tasks (e.g., see

Baltes, 1987; Hoyer, 1990). Interindividual diversity in cognitive performance is frequently reported to increase with aging (Botwinick & Thompson, 1968; Fozard, Thomas, & Waugh, 1976; Krauss, 1980), and there is also considerable intraindividual variability across tasks in older samples (e.g., Hertzog, 1985; Hoyer, 1974). Similarly, compared to younger individuals, older individuals show greater intraindividual differences across task domains, especially when skilled performance in a particular domain is contrasted with domain-general performance measures (Hoyer & Rybash, 1991; Salthouse, 1984, 1990). Thus, it is questionable whether the general pattern of decline that is commonly found across tasks and measures can be attributed to a global mechanism. However, some researchers maintain that observed increases in intraindividual and interindividual variability with age are entirely attributable to a simple mechanism, such as information loss or age-related general slowing, and not to differential aging of specific functions (e.g., Hale, Myerson, Smith, & Poon, 1988; Myerson et al., 1990). In order to clarify the nature of individual differences and the sources of the observed generality and diversity in cognitive performance, explicit models are needed. Researchers also need to consider the multidimensionality, mutlidirectionality, and multicausality of developmental data (Baltes, 1987; Baltes, Reese, & Lipsitt, 1980; Hoyer & Hooker, 1989). Most of our knowledge of visual cognitive aging is derived from cross-sectional data collections, but longitudinal assessments of age-related intraindividual change, interindividual differences, and intraindividual differences across multiple measures are needed to clarify these issues (Hertzog, 1985).

Sources of Individual Differences

The performance of individuals on visual-cognitive tasks depends on a variety of internal and external factors, including the speed and efficiency of the computations required to analyze and respond to the available information, and characteristics of the information being processed (e.g., its perceptual quality, familiarity, salience, and complexity). Although general slowing models, such as Cerella's (1990) overhead model, can account for a substantial portion of the variance in speeded cognitive performance across age groups and tasks, such models do not directly address the neurophysiological and experiential antecedents that affect individual performance. In this section, we briefly review the literature related to these two general sources of age-related interindividual and intraindividual differences in visual-cognitive performance.

Neurophysiological factors. Observed individual differences in visual cognition are in part associated with age-related changes in the neurophysiological mechanisms that control or limit the speed and efficiency of task-relevant performance. As discussed by Kosslyn, Flynn, Amsterdam, and Wang (1990), approaches to the study of individual differences should consider the computational constraints imposed by the neurophysiological mechanisms requisite to visual information processing. Increasingly, researchers are taking account of relevant neuroscience research in the formulation of cognitive models and hypotheses (Allport, 1989). With regard to aging of computational systems, there is compelling evidence to suggest a high level of parallel modular specialization of visual perceptual function. Some of the available data on visual-cognitive aging can be evaluated in light of neurophysiologically plausible models of computational vision. For example, Plude and Hoyer's (1986) findings that there are substantial age-related deficits in visual search performance, but only minor age differences in visual filtering (i.e., object recognition and identification without search or localization requirements) are consistent with recent work on the neurophysiology of vision suggesting that information about "what" and "where" is processed separately in the visual system (see Kosslyn, 1987; Treisman & Gormican, 1988). It has been reported that the neurons that represent an object's shape have relatively large receptive fields, and these neurons respond when the stimulus falls anywhere within a wide range of positions. Different visual mechanisms are responsible for the localization of objects in a display. Mishkin, Ungerleider, and Macko (1983) have shown that there are two independent visual processing subsystems at the neurophysiological level. One subsystem involves object recognition, and access to knowledge about the object such as its function and attributes. A second (and presumably independent) processing subsystem is involved in locating objects in space. In this case, the task is not to encode features or objects in order to access relevant semantic knowledge, but the task is to localize "where" things are.

Skill factors. It is well known that observed individual differences in the patterns of performance across tasks are related to the effects of accumulated knowledge or experience. In contrast to the parsimonious view that most if not all age-related declines in cognitive performance can be accounted for by an across-the-board slowing in the speed of mental computations, results of several recent studies show that magnitude of adult age differences in the speed and efficiency of visual information processing depends on the individual's prior experience relevant to the task domain (e.g., Charness & Campbell, 1988; Hannon & Hoyer, 1991; Salthouse, 1984). There is a growing body of evidence to suggest that cognitive proficiency in the later years can be maintained or even enhanced in well-practiced domains. Such maintenance or enhancement can be attributed to the efficiency of domain-specific processes and/or to the amount of contextual support (e.g., priming, cueing) available within familiar tasks. If general-purpose processing resources are more limited for older adults, or if the speed of each computational step is slower for older adults, or if some amount of information is lost at each processing step, then such limits will probably be most apparent in unpracticed tasks. In skilled or routine tasks, individuals have had the opportunity to organize domain-specific information in terms of prior knowledge, which probably serves to minimize computational demands or the number of processing steps required for response. Other factors may also contribute to individual differences in skilled and novel tasks, such as the attenuation of interference from distractors in familiar contexts, and criterion adjustments at encoding or object-level identification. Similarly, it may be useful to distinguish between new cognitive skills, and the more modest demands associated with carrying out overlearned, routine skills; the former typically show substantial age-related decline, and frequently no age differences are found when older adults are performing well-learned skills (e.g., see Hoyer, 1985; McKay & Burke, 1990).

Results suggesting functional dissociations across tasks appear to pose a challenge to the view that age-related declines can be explained in terms of a single, global mechanism, and to the implicit assumption that cognitive aging is largely domain-neutral. The distributed, interconnected nature of brain architecture also presents a challenge to single mechanism accounts. Although skilled tasks may simply require fewer time-consuming processing steps as compared to unpracticed tasks, a discrete mechanism that affects the speed of all or many mental computations is inconceivable. However, it is just as implausible to suggest a cognitive architecture consisting of fast and slow hard-wired processing modules that correspond to arbitrarily defined task operations. In light of neuroanatomical evidence, it is more likely that the patterns of activation and inhibition within the distributed networks associated with task performance are changed as a function of the individual's domain-relevant past experience. The usefulness of recently proposed network models of cognitive behavior that emphasize the distributed, interconnected nature of cognitive architecture is considered in the next section of this chapter.

Modeling age effects. Many models of cognitive aging are inadequate to deal with the sources of individual differences in the aging process. The study of cognitive aging has only recently been subjected to formal analyses that attempt to relate the phenomena of cognitive aging to neurobiological aging. Cerella (1990, 1991) and Salthouse (1988a) consider formal ways of conceptualizing aging in cognitive processes apart from the cognitive processes themselves. Age-related declines in cognitive abilities are attributed to global variables operating at a level closer to the neural architecture than cognitive theories that are based on intervening constructs (e.g., capacity). Although these model are not analytic regarding the antecedents of interindividual and intraindividual differences and, therefore, do not provide insights into questions of specific mechanisms, they do suggest that many of the findings across tasks are related to a common mechanism. Cerella (1990, 1991) developed what he termed an *overhead model* of the effects of aging in cognitive processing. In the overhead model, a cognitive task is considered to be a collection of discrete processing steps, each one requiring a finite and characteristic amount of time. The time required to perform the task is simply the sum of the times for computing each step in the task. Aging effects on processing are represented in a penalty function that adds an *overhead* to each step for the elderly as compared to the young. The model is expressed in the following equation:

$$L = \Sigma\ [\ I(i)\ +\ d(i)\ ],$$

where L is latency to perform the task I(i) is the time required for each step as a function of the step, d(i) is the penalty function assigning an additional amount of time to each processing step and i is an index to each step. These are summed over the total number of steps. For young subjects, $d(i) = 0$ for all i. The functions I(i) and d(i) may vary from task to task. These functions are also independent of each other which means that the values of I(i) are not influenced by d(i), and vice versa. This indicates that the number of processing steps required for computing a particular task is age invariant, but with age there is an additional overhead associated with each step. For relatively simple tasks involving only a few steps the effect of d(i) will be minimal. For more complex tasks involving many steps, the accumulated overhead will produce substantial age-related deficits. Implicit in this model is the assumption that a cognitive task is composed of discrete processing steps and that different individuals will use the same steps to perform the task.

In a secondary analysis of data for young and old subjects on various cognitive tasks, plots were made of old latency versus young latency. These plots were then fit by the model. Figure 1 shows the mean latency for the elderly on a given task as a function of the mean latency for the young on the same task. Each data point represents a different study of cognitive aging. The solid curve represents the fit of the overhead model. Based on the degree of fit between the data and the model, Cerella concluded that effects of aging on cognitive performance can be accurately modeled by an equation with a single free parameter. A simple form of the penalty function, $d(i) = c*i$, was sufficient to fit the data. This implies that a single global aging mechanism may underlie cognitive aging phenomena observed under a variety of tasks and conditions.

Another way of viewing the additional overhead incurred with age is in terms of an increase in the number of steps in the cognitive task. This could come about in a neural network that contains broken connections. As the number of broken connections that need to be bypassed increases, response time will also increase. The same basic processing steps are employed by both the elderly and the young, but the elderly have the additional burden of rerouting the processing sequence around areas of the network that are malfunctioning. Cerella (1990) dealt specifically with this idea. His analysis was based on a purely mathematical consideration of the time required for a signal to pass through a network of a certain length when some of the links between units have been attenuated or broken. Nothing was actually computed by this hypothetical network, and no simulations were actually performed. Through mathematical

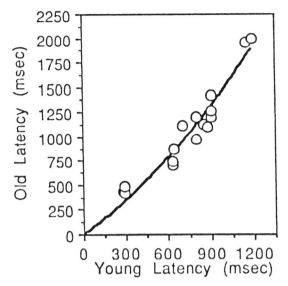

Figure 1.   **Hypothetical plot of latency data of elderly subjects as a function of the latency for young subjects on the same task. The solid line represents the overhead equation: L = Σ [l(i) + d(i)]. Each data point is a hypothetical pair of latencies from a different study of cognitive aging. Based on a plot from Cerella (1991).**

considerations of the hypothetical network, functions were generated that describe the latency of the network as a function of age-related slowing. As with the overhead model, good agreements between the model and the data were found. The main success of this model, therefore, was that a single parameter in a relatively low-level model that is somewhat neurally inspired was able to account for a large amount of the variance associated with aging across many studies and tasks. It was concluded that the effects of aging on cognition are best explained in terms of a lower-level mechanism common to all cognitive tasks rather than in terms of task-specific processes.

Salthouse (1988a) pointed out the distinction between product and process in cognition and viewed the effects of age in terms of a decline in general-purpose processing resources. Aging effects in cognition were conceptualized as a generalized age-related slowing of processing efficiency. There is no one locus of aging effects in a cognitive process, but rather the entire process is degraded in its performance. From this perspective, Salthouse developed a network spreading activation model to simulate the effects of aging on cognitive processes. Although it is claimed that many types of computational models will serve to demonstrate the effects, it was recognized that a network model has certain inherent properties that readily incorporate a generalized slowing

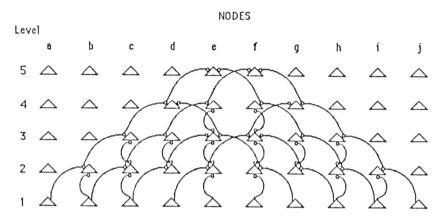

Figure 2.   Schematic diagram of network based on Salthouse (1988). Triangles represent individual nodes. Connections between nodes are indicated.

account of processing efficiency. Salthouse (1988a) proposed a multilayered model with inputs at the lowest end and connections between units at one layer with one or more units at higher layers. Figure 2 depicts one of the hypothetical network structures. Levels within the network are represented as rows in the diagram. Individual nodes are specified by their row and column identification. The connections between nodes are shown. With the exception of the input units, the connections are bidirectional, to incorporate top-down and bottom-up processing. The connections between units are linear and continuous, meaning that a unit computes the sum of its various inputs to determine its state of activation without upper or lower limits, and without discontinuities in the possible values it may hold. Only excitatory connections were specified in Salthouse's model.

The model updates the activity at each node on sequential time steps. The activity at each node is decayed by 10%, and the remaining activity is divided in two. Half remains at the unit and half of the rest is passed on, or propagated, to the connected units. For the purposes of the simulation, the activity in selected nodes, including both the amount of excitation and the time course of the activation, was taken as a measure of the model's performance. Only general aging effects are represented and the model didn't actually compute any type of cognitive task. Further, the nodes within the model were not assumed to correspond to neural-like structures and functions.

Salthouse considered three alternatives for incorporating the effects of aging into the model. One way was to limit the number of nodes that can be simultaneously active. In an implementation, after the activation of the nodes had been adjusted on a given time cycle, the weakest nodes would be turned down to zero. By restricting the number of nodes that can be active, the likelihood that any node would achieve its requisite state of activation is decreased in proportion to its dependence on the number of nodes that have been set to zero. Without sufficient input within a critical period of time, the activation level of a given node would decay. These two operations would serve to slow the rate of processing and reduce the efficiency of the network. The second method for representing aging effects was to limit the total amount of activation allowed in the network. This limits the ability of some nodes to reach certain critical states within critical amounts of time, and again speed and efficiency would be attenuated. The third method was to reduce the rate at which any node could propagate information. In an implementation this would have required waiting a specific number of time cycles before activation was transferred from one node to the next. Decay of activation of a node would occur on every time step. Of the three methods for incorporating aging effects, only the rate of propagation was actually implemented.

Salthouse highlighted several key features of his aging network. First, since the structure of the network remained intact while the rate of propagation was being limited, any behaviors of the overall network that were dependent on the structure should remain unchanged. That is, a particular node that is activated through a particular pattern of connections to other nodes will still rely on those nodes for its activation regardless of how slow the rate of propagation. The dynamics of the activation process will no doubt have changed. Second, slowing effects within the network were characterized as *graceful impairments*. The activation of any specific node was shown to reach its peak later in time with a diminished magnitude. This can be seen in Figure 3 for nodes at two different layers in the network. Log activation of a node is plotted as a function of time. Open symbols represent a fast rate, filled symbols a slow rate. All of the nodes are still functioning however, so "catastrophic" failures have not occurred, just gradual, generalized slowing. This slowing of the network is somewhat similar to the notion of graceful degradation used by McClelland et al. (1986). Figure 3 also shows that the deeper the node, the more pronounced are the shifts in time to reach peak activation in the node, and the greater the reduction in the magnitude of activation. This is claimed to be analogous to tasks of greater complexity requiring processing deeper into the network. Empirical evidence suggests that the more complex a task, the greater the observed age-related deficit (Cerella, Poon, & Williams, 1980; Charness & Campbell, 1988). Presumably, the slowdown in the network could result in the inability of some deep layer nodes to become active at all. This would be analogous to an inability to perform particular tasks.

Salthouse argued that the success of this model is in its fit with generalized aspects of cognitive aging. The aging effect is distributed throughout the network so all nodes are affected. The level of abstraction is lower than is usually postulated in studies of cognitive aging, but the lower level is necessary to model

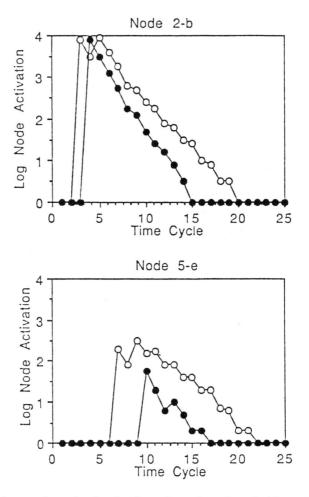

Figure 3. **Log node activation is plotted as a function of a time cycle for (a) node 2-b, and (b) node 5-e. Open symbols were obtained by updating the model on every time step, closed symbols for updating on every third time step. Adapted from Salthouse (1988).**

general age related slowing. The aging effect is now rather explicit in contrast to conventional approaches that invoke abstract properties such as limited capacity. Salthouse noted that while this method of modeling may be sufficient for describing some of the effects of aging on cognition, its necessity in this regard cannot be demonstrated. It is also the case that, in its current form, fundamental variables and parameters of the network cannot be distinguished from trivial ones since nothing is actually computed.

In addition to Salthouse's evaluation of the model, two additional points should be made. First, it may be misleading to study aging effects in a model that has not been designed or "trained" to do anything. Human beings gain knowledge and experience during the aging process. Models of human cognition, and of individual differences and change, need to incorporate these differences in knowledge and experience. We suggest that it would be more useful to apply the aging parameters to a realistic model after it is able to learn to perform some task. As an example, consider a parallel-distributed (PDP) network that has been trained to some criterion level on a particular task. In these models a pattern of connections between units builds up over repeated stimulations of the model and accumulated knowledge or experience is stored in the connections between the units (McClelland et al., 1986). If a general, across-the-board slowing parameter is applied to this network, the parameter will be applied after a distributed knowledge base has been established. The model, therefore, will have been given the proper developmental sequence for modeling cogniting aging. The behavior of the network still can be compared to the behavior obtained before the aging manipulation was applied. Perhaps the same pattern of results will occur as was found in the Salthouse model, but one is also likely to see an interaction of aging and experience not currently dealt with in this analysis of cognitive aging. It is necessary, therefore, to distinguish between networks that model slowing in experienced domains, versus slowing during training (Hintzman, 1990). In particular, the types of errors made, as well as the latency of the aged network, in response to novel and familiar stimuli can be determined and compared to empirical data. The behavior of the aged network to novel stimuli is analogous to performance on unfamiliar tasks by elderly subjects. Likewise, the behavior of the model in terms of processing familiar stimuli is analogous to performance of older adults on practiced tasks. This type of model is much more revealing about aging effects on cognitive function, particularly in regard to individual differences, than less specific models (e.g., Hannon & Hoyer, 1991).

A second point regarding Salthouse's model is that, while no claims are made about the actual computations of the nodes, it is asserted that they are simple computational units and that this model will have similar properties to parallel-distributed networks. One of the claims made about parallel distributed networks is that complex behavior can be modeled with relatively simple, neural-like computational units (e.g., McClelland et al., 1986). Information is distributed across the computational units, unlike models that represent information discretely at each node. Salthouse does not determine the relative simplicity of the nodes in his network by indicating their informational content. It is simply asserted that the units are performing a simple computational task. While it is true that the linear summation performed by each node is a simple calculation compared to the nonlinear functions used in other network models, this does not necessarily imply that the information being represented at the node by the computation is of a simple form. The similarity of Salthouse's model to a parallel-distributed network, and, therefore, the usefulness of the network for modeling cognitive processes at a level closer to the neural architecture, can be demonstrated only in a network that actually computes something.

It is worth noting that a distributed representation of information is not always advantageous in network models (Hintzman, 1990). The type of representation used should be dictated by the particular task considerations. It should also be noted that multiple layers in a network are not always necessary or desirable. In this particular example, there is no more computational power in the entire network than there is in the first two layers (see Rumelhart, Hinton, & McClelland, 1986). The additional layers do serve to illustrate the impact on the slowing of the network by showing how subsequent stages of the network are affected. But the presence of the extra layers beyond the second is not justified on any computational grounds, and therefore no insight is gained into the effects of slowing down the connections in a multilayered network in terms of the impact of the computations being performed. The current model is too simplistic to illustrate the real power of the many different kinds of network models being employed in other domains.

Most of the criticisms applied to Salthouse (1988a) also apply to the work of Cerella (1990, 1991). Collectively, these studies comprise the core of formal modeling efforts in cognitive aging. The criticisms of these studies center on underlying assumptions and not with the results as they are presented. The main criticism is that the models have been unrealistic in that they do not compute anything and that they do not realistically model aging, since aging affects performance during acquisition and may have different effects on the same task after acquisition than at different points in the acquisition process. Second, it should be cautioned that models of neural networks require more than a proposal of multiconnectedness. There is no way of knowing what is going on in the units of either network so the level of abstraction may have no relationship to the representation of neurophysiological mechanisms. Third, no provision was made in either model for understanding the effects of error rates and speed accuracy functions. This limitation was recognized by Cerella (1990). Fourth, the influence of experience and other individual differences are not represented. The study of individual differences and aging may shed some light on the mechanisms underlying cognition. By studying interindividual and intraindividual variability, alternate versions of specific mechanisms can be differentiated based on each one's ability to model these individualized effects.

In defense of these studies, it should be noted again that both of the models presented here have attempted to model age related processing independent of type of cognitive task. This was in an effo. t to understand cognitive aging in terms of a single, low-level, general mechanism. In so doing, they bring to light some important issues and represent a first step toward formal modeling of cognitive aging. Recently, McKay and Burke (1990) extended some of Salthouse's ideas to perception, production and memory for language. Their model incorporated an actual computation, and allowed the system the benefit of learning before it was aged. An additional mechanism was added in that practice effects and recency of use were able to counteract the degradations in performance caused by aging on some tasks. The McKay and Burke model shows the promise of this approach.

In an attempt to extend this approach further, we are focusing on visual selective attention. The work of Cerella (1991) showed that many different cognitive tasks plot along the same function. By exclusively dealing with visual selective attention, we isolate a portion of the curve and try to understand the relationship between the performance of old and young subjects. The study of attention is concerned with the nature of the limitations in processing information and with information selection processes (Allport, 1989). In the research on human visual information processing, the concept of attention has been used to refer to a variety of functions, including alertness and arousal, consciousness or awareness, span of comprehension, the selection of information for processing, and preparedness or expectancy (e.g., for a review see Parasuraman & Davies, 1984). The goal is to specify how individual differences in visual information processing can be incorporated into models of attentional mechanisms that affect what and how much information is processed.

A Formal Model of Visual Selective Attention

Although there is a substantial amount of research activity on the topic of visual selective attention and aging, particularly in regard to visual search tasks (McDowd & Craik, 1990; Madden, 1989; Plude & Hoyer, 1986; Rabbitt, 1982), there are no formal models of attentional processes and aging. A small number of formal models of attention have been developed (e.g., Shedden & Schneider, 1990; Sandon & Uhr, 1988; Sandon & Yanikoglu, 1990) but these do not address questions about the locus of individual differences. Recently, Cave and Wolfe (1990) have proposed a formal model of visual search that can be used to account for visual search data and that can be applied to the study of age-related individual differences in visual search. In this section a summary of some of the features and functions of this model are provided.

Cave and Wolfe (1990) offered a *modified feature integration theory* (MFIT) model that is an elaboration of the feature integration theory of Treisman (e.g., Treisman & Gelade, 1980). In the MFIT model, parallel processing of feature maps (i.e., maps of the visual field indicating the presence and position of the feature it encodes) and serial searches of visual field elements occur simultaneously, with the parallel processes guiding the serial mechanism to the most likely target among the field of display elements. In the parallel component, feature maps for each relevant dimension of the elements in the display hold a value for each particular element. Both bottom-up and top-down information are combined in the feature maps. The bottom-up information is in the form of a difference function. Each element in turn is compared to all of the other elements, and the differences along the feature dimension of a particular feature map are summed and distributed exponentially. Elements that are similar to many of the other elements in the display for a given feature will have a low bottom-up activation in the feature map. Likewise, the target element will tend to have a high bottom-up activation along the relevant feature dimensions. The top-down information is also represented in the form of a difference function, but the information is distributed linearly. The difference between the expected target and each element for a given feature map is computed. The total activation for a particular feature map equals the sum of the bottom-up and top-down activations. The sum of all of the maps gives a total activation value for each element in the visual display. A random noise value is then added to the total activation array.

The second component, the serial stage, determines if a given element is the target. Only one element at a time can be processed in this stage. Many of the details of the serial architecture have been left unspecified.

The parallel and serial components act simultaneously during visual search. All of the display elements are evaluated by the parallel mechanisms, continuously and simultaneously, along the dimensions of the feature maps. The signal from the elements is being continually updated. A random amount of noise is also continually added to the activation for each element. Over time, the effects of the noise become evenly distributed over all of the display elements. The signal from the distractor elements builds up slowly, since the activation for each element is low. The signal for the target element builds up quickly, since its activation is the highest. On each time cycle the serial stage chooses the element with the highest activation to process. Early in the search this may be a distractor if the noise level is high enough. After evaluating a distractor the serial stage eliminates it from further consideration. After awhile, the activation of the target will emerge and the serial component will be guided to it by the parallel component. Figure 4 is a plot of the activation level of each display element on subsequent time steps in an implementation of the model. As can be seen in the plot, if the chosen element on a given time step is not the target, its activity is suppressed. Eventually the target emerges as the most active display element.

This model is successful in describing several phenomena in the visual search literature. If the number of cycles required for the serial component to locate the target is used as the outcome measure, then the performance of the model can be directly compared to individual reaction times. The pop-out phenomenon is easily demonstrated. If the noise level is low relative to the signal, then the target element will have the highest activation from the beginning and will immediately draw the serial stage to it. Conjunctive search phenomena can also be shown. The activation of the target will not necessarily be the highest at the

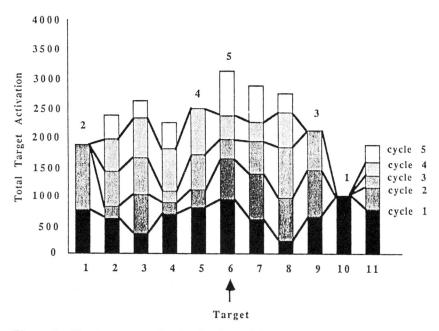

Figure 4. Total target activation is plotted for each element in the display. The target is indicating by the arrow. Time cycle is indicated by the shading pattern. The connections between the bars highlight the differences between elements on each time step. Adapted from Cave and Wolfe (1990).

outset since in any given feature map the target is similar to some of the distractors. As the number of elements increases it will take longer for the model to locate the target since the relative salience of the target to the distractors is diminished. However, the importance of one feature map (e.g., color) can be increased relative to other features. Top-down information serves to make the activation levels for all elements with the target color higher than other elements. In the serial component, therefore, the elements are evaluated in order with the correct color first. It can also be shown that elements that cannot be discriminated by the feature maps must be searched serially. For example, in this model distinctions between Ts and Ls cannot be made by the parallel component, and the result is a strictly serial search.

Compared to the feature integration theory of Treisman and Gelade (1980), a significant feature of the MFIT model is the effective use of the parallel component to guide the serial component. While the function of the parallel stage is fairly well established, the exact function of the serial stage is left unspecified. Since the serial stage is never "wrong," any errors must be a function of the poor signal to noise ratio coming from the parallel component.

Individual Differences and Selective Attention

One additional feature of the MFIT model of Cave and Wolfe (1990) is that the flexibility of this model allows for the modeling of individual differences in visual search. Cave and Wolfe used the noise parameter to account for the behavior of the model as a function of the number of elements in the display and also to represent individual differences in visual search. Empirical evidence from many visual search tasks show trial-to-trial variations in the slopes of the functions for plots of latency versus set size as well as inter-individual differences (Treisman & Gormican, 1988). In the model, the random noise function should also produce trial-to-trial variations. By varying the mean level of the noise function, it is also possible to represent interindividual variation. In this case, a single parameter, the noise function in the model, is able to account for interindividual differences. It is also the case that tasks that require a serial search from subjects also evoke serial searches from the model regardless of the noise level. When searching for L among T distractors, both subjects and the model perform the search serially (Wolfe, Cave, & Franzel, 1989). The parallel component of the model is not able to guide the serial component since detection of the difference between T and L is not possible at this stage. Regardless of the amount of noise, the serial component moves randomly among the different elements in the display until it finds the target. The noise parameter allows for the effective modeling of performance changes across trials, performance differences between individuals, and performance differences between tasks for the same subjects.

A further aspect of the MFIT model and the study of individual differences is in how the model deals with negative trials, that is, trials on which no target is present. An additional parameter is required to account for performance on negative probe trials. The empirical findings show that subjects do not need to search every element in the display before terminating the search on negative trials. As the number of items already evaluated by the serial stage increases, the likelihood of finding a target decreases. Somehow the serial component of the model must decide when to terminate the search. This can either be because the observer has searched too long and the probability of finding a target has now fallen too low, or that the overall activation level is too low and that no target is likely to be present. Given the average speed of the positive trials a time threshold can be set that, once reached, signals the end of the search and the conclusion that no target is present. Alternatively, an activation threshold can be set based on what is expected due to noise alone that can be used to determine if it is worth continuing the search. Since the serial stage operates on the most active element in the display, a comparison can be made between the activation level of the element currently being processed and the threshold. Using either method will end the search before all of the items have been processed. There is a great deal of variability between subjects on negative trials, more so than on positive trials (Wolfe et al., 1989). Different settings of the threshold, using either method yields similar behavior from the model. Similarly, the establishment of thresholds for terminating the search introduces errors in the model's behavior that are also seen on the empirical data. The model will tend to miss the target in some trials. The empirical evidence shows that subjects also tend to show misses (i.e., trials on which the target is present but is not detected) rather than false alarms (trials on which the target is not present but the subject signals that it is). (Note: False alarms do occur in the form of illusory conjunctions. On these trials, the display is presented briefly and subjects incorrectly combine features from different display elements into a precept of the target which is not actually present. See Treisman & Schmidt, 1982, for more details.)

The MFIT model has been successful at accounting for many of the phenomena of selective attention tasks (Cave & Wolfe, 1990), and we have highlighted how the model could be used to simulate individual differences. In light of the growing body of literature on adult age differences in visual selective attention, we attempt to directly compare the MFIT model to existing empirical data. Two recent studies by Plude and Doussard-Roosevelt (1989, 1990) have interpreted their findings in terms of the feature integration theory of Treisman and Gelade (1980), which is the basis for MFIT. These studies provide a preliminary evaluation of the MFIT model in terms of adult age deficits in visual selective attention.

The basic findings of Plude and Doussard-Roosevelt (1989) were that elderly subjects performed comparably to young subjects when the task involved identifying a target based on only one feature dimension. Subjects were asked to indicate the presence or absence of a red target element among a display of green distractors. This kind of display gives rise to the familiar pop-out phenomenon and the elderly subjects tested showed no deficits on this kind of task. Conjunctive searches, however, involve the detecting of a target based on two feature dimensions and this task proved much harder for the elderly than for their younger counterparts. The task may have involved searching for a green X among a field of red Xs and green Os. In order to establish the presence or absence of the target the subject must search the display for the joint combination of X and green. Conjunctive searches were harder than single feature based searches as more elements are added to the display for both young and old subjects but the elderly showed a differentially poorer performance.

These results were interpreted by the authors as being due to a deficit in spatial localization ability by the elderly subjects. According to the feature-integration theory, conjunctive searches require the alignment of feature maps and often an element-by-element search for the one element containing the correct conjunction of features. Although a single feature often pops out of the display and targets with single features can be detected without knowing their exact location, the conjunctive search requires correct localization in space for correct detection. The degraded performance of the elderly as compared to the young on conjunctive searches suggests, therefore, a deficit in spatial localization ability. A follow-up study by Plude and Doussard-Roosevelt (1990) showed that, when information about target location is provided to subjects, the differences between old and young subjects disappears and both types of subjects improve considerably. These collective results further imply that the independent parallel operations within each feature map are unaffected by the aging process and that the deficit is in the serial process of putting the features together.

The MFIT model offers a slightly different perspective on the deficits of the elderly on conjunctive searches. Recall that both top-down and bottom-up information is passed to the independent feature maps in this model. The bottom-up information acts to suppress similar items within a feature map and enhance dissimilar items. The top-down information uses knowledge of the target features to enhance display elements within a feature map that share the feature quality with the target over other elements. It is the top-down information that guides the MFIT model in conjunctive searches. Within this model a difficulty in performing conjunctive searches would be due to an inability to effectively utilize top-down information. A slight modification to the top-down component within the MFIT model that adjusts the strength of the component downward with age may provide a means for accounting for the differences between young and old subjects on conjunctive searches.

To test the validity of the MFIT model and this particular modification, more experiments are needed. The design of Plude and Doussard-Roosevelt (1989) incorporated color and shape differences that are fairly easy to discriminate. If the elderly are experiencing difficulty in using top-down information, this may show up if the discriminability of the target from the distractor elements along a given feature dimension is manipulated. For instance, different shades of red can be used rather than red and green, or different ellipses can be used rather than X and O. As discrimination is made more difficult the use of top-down information will become less effective, or will require a greater effort (i.e., knowing that the target is red is less useful when the other elements also look reddish and will require careful color matching if the information is to be used at all). If the deficit seen in the elderly performance on conjunctive searches is due to a decreased ability to use top-down information, their performance should be differentially affected by this manipulation.

Modeling Intraindividual Change and Interindividual Differences in Visual Search

There are a number of ways of incorporating age effects into a general model of visual search. First, the generalized slowing hypothesis proposed by Salthouse (1988) and by Cerella (1990) can be applied throughout the model. This manipulation would have its effect in terms of the dynamic development of activations in the feature maps. Whether a parallel distributed network is used to process each element or not, a generalized slowing would lead to different rates of processing. This would mean that, in addition to the noise, the relative strengths of activation of the elements would not necessarily reflect the underlying signal from the beginning. A certain amount of time would be needed for the signal to be fully processed, during which the serial component would still be processing the most active element. This model predicts that elderly will in general have to search more items in a display than younger subjects. The generalized slowing of propagation will have an interaction with the threshold as well. The error rate in the elderly would be expected to be higher if the threshold is not adjusted to allow for longer initial search times before termination or a lower activation level threshold. This interaction can be tested empirically to determine the proper range for both the slowing of propagation and the threshold.

Another method of implementing aging effects may be to make the noise parameter a function of age. The initial level can be set to reflect individual differences, but then can change with age. It may be impossible, however, to distinguish this type of manipulation from a generalized slowing. Both would lead to an increase of latency with age. Critical differences in error rate, as well as speed in performing different tasks, may play a key role in determining the plausibility of either mechanism. For instance, Salthouse (1988a) suggested that the difficulty of task should not increase as a function of age. That is, without considering practice effects, difficult tasks should remain difficult equally for different age groups. Increasing noise with age may, however, predict an increase in the apparent difficulty of a task as measured by the errors made by the model and time it takes to complete the task. The key to determining among possible aging mechanisms within a model may be in how they affect the performance of the model for different tasks as compared to empirical data.

It is certainly not the case that there can only be one parameter of the model that can be adjusted with age. The empirical literature confirms the generalized slowing of cognitive processes with age, but the implementation of slowing takes different forms in different parts of the system. For instance, both an increase of noise and a slowing of signal propagation may be incorporated in the visual search model. The amount of noise can be increased within specific feature maps reflecting a decrease in the integrity of the signal coming from them while a slowing of propagation can be distributed throughout the model. The interaction of these two parameters leads to many stable predictions, most notably, that some features may be more affected by age than others. Plude and Doussard-Roosevelt (1989) determined that the ability to use color as a feature is not affected by age. Many more feature dimensions need to be explored. By examining such a model and testing the predictions it makes, the mechanism underlying visual information processing can be further deduced.

The interaction between interindividual differences and interindividual change occurs frequently when different levels of skill or experience are possessed by subjects. There are also several ways to model age and skill interactions in visual search. Highly familiar tasks may involve a different or more efficient representation and this can be reflected in the elaboration or type of top-down information that is employed by the model. In light of McKay and Burke's model of opposing forces, familiarity with certain visual displays can be given an advantage over unfamiliar displays through the top-down information. If a parallel distributed network is used, skilled behavior can also be incorporated in the training of the model to perform certain tasks. The pattern of connections and weights between processing units would represent the domain knowledge. The strength of this representation would be in opposition to the aging factors in the model. This still does not address the question of how people maintain their abilities with age. It is certainly the case that processing strategies change to compensate for losses with age (e.g., Hoyer & Rybash, 1991; Reder, Wible, & Martin, 1986; Salthouse, 1984). More empirical research, guided by explicit or formal models is needed to understand these changes.

REFERENCES

Allport, A. (1989). Visual attention. In M.I. Posner (Ed.), *Foundations of cognitive science* (pp. 631–682). Cambridge, MA: MIT Press.

Albert, M.S., Heller, H.S., & Milberg, W. (1988). Changes in naming ability with age. *Psychology and Aging, 3*, 173–178.

Backman, L., & Molander, B. (1986). Effects of adult age and level of skill on the ability to cope with high-stress conditions in a precision sport. *Psychology and Aging, 1*, 334–336.

Baltes, P.B. (1987). Theoretical propositions of life-span developmental psychology: On the dynamics between growth and decline. *Developmental Psychology, 23, 611–626.*

Baltes, P.B., Reese, H.W., & Lipsitt, L.P. (1980). Life-span developmental psychology. *Annual Review of Psychology, 31*, 65–110.

Berg, C., Hertzog, C.K., & Hunt, E. (1982). Age differences in the speed of mental rotation. *Developmental Psychology, 18*, 95–107.

Botwinick, J., & Thompson, L.W. (1968). A research note on individual differences in reaction time in relation to age. *Journal of Genetic Psychology, 112*, 72–75.

Cave, C.R., & Wolfe, J.M. (1990). Modeling the role of parallel processing in visual search. *Cognitive Psychology, 22*, 255–271.

Cerella, J. (1985). Information processing rates in the elderly. *Psychological Bulletin, 98*, 67-83.

Cerella, J. (1990). Aging and information processing rate. In J. E. Birren & K.W. Schaie (Eds.), *Handbook of the psychology of aging* (3rd ed., pp. 201–221). New York: Academic Press.

Cerella, J. (1991). *Age-related slowing due to increased overhead in information processes.* Unpublished manuscript, Veterans Administration Outpatient Clinic, Boston.

Charness, N., & Campbell, J.I.D. (1988). Acquiring skill at mental calculation: A task decomposition. *Journal of Experimental Psychology: General, 117*, 115–129.
Chiarello, C., & Hoyer, W.J. (1988). Adult age differences in implicit and explicit memory. *Psychology and Aging, 3*, 358–366.
Craik, F.I.M. (1983). On the transfer of information from temporary to permanent memory. *Philosophical Transactions of the Royal Society of London, B302*, 341–359.
Cremer, R., & Zeef, E.J. (1987). What kid of noise increases with age? *Journal of Gerontology, 42*, 515–518.
Davies, D.R., Jones, D.M., & Taylor, A. (1984). Selective- and sustained-attention tasks: Individual and group differences. In R. Parasuraman & D.R. Davies (Eds.), *Varieties of attention* (pp. 395–447). New York: Academic Press.
Detterman, D.K., Thompson, L.A., & Plomin, R. (1991). Differences in heritability across groups differing in ability. *Behavior Genetics.*
Estes, W.K. (1991). Cognitive architectures: From the standpoint of an experimental psychologist. *Annual Review of Psychology, 42*, 1–28.
Fozard, J.L., Thomas, J.C., & Waugh, N.C. (1976). Effects of age and frequency of stimulus repetitions on two-choice reaction time. *Journal of Gerontology, 31*, 556–563.
Frazier, L.D., & Hoyer, W.J. (1992). Object recognition by component features: Adult age differences. *Experimental Aging Research, 18*, 9-14.
Hale, S., Myerson, J., Smith, G.A., & Poon, L.W. (1988). Age, variability, and speed: Between-subjects diversity. *Psychology and Aging, 3*, 407–410.
Hale, S., Myerson, J., & Wagstaff, D. (1987). General slowing of nonverbal information processing: Evidence for a power law. *Journal of Gerontology, 42*, 131–136.
Hannon, D. J. & Hoyer, W. J. (1991, November). *Aging and perceptual closure: An autoassociator model.* Paper presented at the meetings of the Gerontological Society of America, San Francisco, CA.
Herzog, C. (1985). An individual differences perspective. *Research on Aging, 7*, 7–45.
Hinton, G.E., McClelland, J.L., & Rumelhart, D.E. (1986). Distributed processing. In D.E. Rumelhart & J.L. McClelland (Eds.), *Parallel distributed processing* (Vol. 1, pp. 77–109). Cambridge, MA: MIT Press.
Hintzman, D.L. (1990). Human learning and memory: Connections and dissociations. *Annual Review of Psychology, 41*, 109–139.
Howard, D.V. (1988). Implicit and explicit assessment of cognitive aging. In M.L.Howe & C.J. Brainerd (Eds.), *Cognitive development in adulthood: Progress in cognitive development research* (pp. 3–33). New York: Springer-Verlag.
Hoyer, W.J. (1974). Aging as intraindividual change. *Developmental Psychology, 10*, 821–826.
Hoyer, W.J. (1985). Aging and the development of expert cognition. In T.M. Shlechter & M.P. Toglia (Eds.), *New directions in cognitive science* (pp. 69–87). Norwood, NJ: Ablex Publishing Corp.
Hoyer, W.J. (1990). Levels of knowledge utilization in visual information processing. In T.M. Hess (Ed.), *Aging and cognition: Knowledge organization and utilization* (pp. 387–409). Amsterdam: Elsevier.
Hoyer, W.J., & Familant, M.E. (1987). Adult age difference in the rate of processing expectancy information. *Cognitive Development, 2*, 57–70.

Hoyer, W.J., & Hooker, K. (1989). The psychology of adult development and aging: New approaches and methodologies in the developmental study of cognition and personality. In N.J. Osgood & A.H.L. Sontz (Eds.), *Science and practice of gerontology: A multidisciplinary guide* (pp. 29–54). New York: Greenwood Press.

Hoyer, W.J., & Rybash, J.M. (1991). How does knowledge help visual perception in everyday situations? In R.L. West & J.D. Sinnott (Eds.), *Everyday memory and aging: Current research and methodology* (pp. 79–98). New York: Springer-Verlag.

Hoyer, W.J., & Rybash, J.M. (1992). Age and visual field differences in computing visual-spatial relations. *Psychology and Aging, 7,* 339-342.

Hultsch, D.F., & Dixon, R.A. (1990). Learning and memory in aging. In J.E. Birren & K.W. Schaie (Eds.), *Handbook of the psychology of aging* (3rd ed., pp. 258–274). New York: Wiley.

Kirasic, K.C. (1991). Spatial cognition and behavior in young and elderly adults: Implications for learning new environments. *Psychology and Aging, 6,* 10–18.

Kosslyn, S.M. (1987). Seeing and imagining in the cerebral hemispheres: A computational approach. *Psychological Review, 94,* 148–175.

Kosslyn, S.M., Flynn, R.A., Amsterdam, J.B., & Wang, G. (1990). Components of high-level vision: A cognitive neuroscience analysis and accounts of neurological syndromes. *Cognition, 34,* 203–277.

Krauss, I.K. (1980). Between- and within-group comparisons in aging research. In L.W. Poon (Ed.), *Aging in the 1980s: Psychological issues* (pp. 542–551). Washington, DC: American Psychological Association.

Light, L.L. (1991). Memory and aging: Four hypotheses in search of data. *Annual Review of Psychology, 42,* 333–376.

Light, L.L., & Singh, A. (1987). Implicit and explicit memory in young and older adults. *Journal of Experimental Psychology: Learning, Memory, and Cognition, 13,* 531–541.

Madden, D.J. (1986). Adult age differences in the attentional capacity demands of visual search. *Cognitive Development, 1,* 335–363.

Madden, D.J. (1989). Adult age differences in the time course of visual attention. *Journal of Gerontology, 45,* P9–16.

Madden, D.J. (1992). Four to ten milliseconds per year: Age-related slowing of visual word identification. *Journal of Gerontology: Psychological Sciences, 47,* P59–P68.

McClelland, J.L. (1988). Connectionist models and psychological evidence. *Journal of Memory and Language, 27,* 107–123.

McClelland, J.L., Rumelhart, D.E., & Hinton, G.E. (1986). The appeal of parallel distributed processing. In D.E. Rumelhart & J.L. McClelland (Eds.), *Parallel distributed processing* (Vol. 1, pp. 3–44). Cambridge, MA: MIT Press.

McDowd, J.M. (1986). The effects of age and extended practice on divided attention performance. *Journal of Gerontology, 41,* 764–769.

McDowd, J.M., & Craik, F.I.M. (1988). Effects of aging and task difficulty on divided attention performance. *Journal of Experimental Psychology: Human Perception and Performance, 14,* 267–280.

McKay, D.G., & Burke, D.M. (1990). Cognition and aging: A theory of new learning and the use of old connections. In T.M. Hess (Ed.), *Aging and cognition: Knowledge organization and utilization* (pp. 213–264). Amsterdam: Elsevier.

McNaughton, B.L., & Morris, R.G.M. (1987). Hippocampal synaptic enhancement and information storage within a distributed memory system. *Trends in Neuroscience, 10*, 408–415.

Mishkin, M., Ungerleider, L.G., & Macko, K.A. (1983). Object vision and spatial vision: Two cortical pathways. *Trends in Neurosciences, 6*, 414–417.

Mitchell, D.B. (1989). How many memory systems? Evidence from aging. *Journal of Experimental Psychology: Learning, Memory, and Cognition, 15*, 31–49.

Morris, R.G., Gick, M.L., & Craik, F.I.M. (1988). Processing resources and age differences in working memory. *Memory and Cognition, 16*, 362–366.

Myerson, J., Hale, S., Wagstaff, D., Poon, L.W., & Smith, G.A. (1990). The information-loss model: A mathematical theory of age-related cognitive slowing. *Psychological Review, 97*, 475–487.

Owsley, C., Ball, K., Sloane, M.E., Roenker, D.L., & Bruni, J.R. (1991). Visual/ cognitive correlates of vehicle guidants in older drivers. *Psychology and Aging, 6*, 403–415.

Parasuraman, R., & Davies, D.R. (Eds.). (1984). *Varieties of attention.* New York: Academic Press.

Parasuraman, R., Nestor, P., & Greenwood, P. (1989). Sustained-attention in young and older adults. *Psychology and Aging, 4*, 339–345.

Plomin, R., Pedersen, N.L., Nesselroade, J.R., & Bergeman, C.S. (1988). Genetic influence on childhood family environment perceived retrospectively from the last half of the life span. *Developmental Psychology, 24*, 738–745.

Plude, D.J., & Doussard-Roosevelt, J.A. (1989). Aging, selective attention, and feature integration. *Psychology and Aging, 4*, 98–105.

Plude, D.J., & Doussard-Roosevelt, J.A. (1990). Aging and attention: Selectivity, capacity, and arousal. In E.A. Lovelace (Ed.), *Aging and cognition: Mental processes, self-awareness, and intervention* (pp. 97–133). Amsterdam: Elsevier.

Plude, D.J., & Hoyer, W.J. (1981). Adult age differences in visual search as a function of stimulus mapping and processing load. *Journal of Gerontology, 36*, 598–604.

Plude, D.J., & Hoyer, W.J. (1985). Attention and performance: Identifying and localizing age deficits. In N. Charness (Ed.), *Aging and human performance* (pp. 47–99). London: Wiley.

Plude, D.J., & Hoyer, W.J. (1986). Aging and the selectivity of visual information processing. *Psychology and Aging, 1*, 1–9.

Posner, M.I. (1988). Structures and functions of selective attention. In T. Boll & B.K. Bryant (Eds.), *Clinical neuropsychology and brain function.* Washington, DC: American Psychological Association.

Posner, M.I., Inhoff, A.W., & Friedrich, F.J. (1987). Isolating attentional systems: A cognitive anatomical analysis. *Psychobiology, 15*, 107–121.

Rabbitt, P.M.A. (1982). Visual search. In C.R. Puff (Ed.), *Handbook of research methods in human memory and cognition* (pp. 28–62). New York: Academic Press.

Reder, L.M., Wible, C., & Martin, J. (1986). Differential memory changes with age: Exact retrieval versus plausible inference. *Journal of Experimental Psychology: Learning, Memory, and Cognition, 12*, 72–81.

Rumelhart, D.E., Hinton, G.E., & McClelland, J.L. (1986). A general framework for parallel distributed processing. In D.E. Rumelhart & J.L. McClelland (Eds.), *Parallel distributed processing* (Vol. 1, pp. 45–76). Cambridge, MA: MIT Press.

Rybash, J.M., Hoyer, W.J., & Roodin, P.A. (1986). *Adult cognition and aging:*

Developmental changes in processing, knowing, and thinking. Elmsford, NY: Pergamon Press.

Salthouse, T.A. (1984). Effects of age and skill in typing. *Journal of Experimental Psychology: General, 113,* 345–371.

Salthouse, T.A. (1985a). Speed of behavior and its implications for cognition. In J.E. Birren & K.W. Schaie (Eds.), *Handbook of the psychology of aging* (2nd ed., pp. 400–426). New York: Van Nostrand Reinhold.

Salthouse, T.A. (1985b). *A theory of cognitive aging.* Amsterdam: North Holland.

Salthouse, T.A. (1988a). Initiating the formalization of theories of cognitive aging. *Psychology and Aging, 3,* 3–16.

Salthouse, T.A. (1988b). The role of processing resources in cognitive aging. In M.L. Howe & C.J. Brainerd (Eds.), *Cognitive development in adulthood* (pp. 185–239). New York: Springer-Verlag.

Salthouse, T.A. (1990). Cognitive competence and expertise in aging. In J.E. Birren & K.W. Schaie (Eds.), *Handbook of the psychology of aging* (3rd ed., pp. 310–319: New York: Academic Press.

Salthouse, T.A., Babcock, R.L., Skovronek, E., Mitchell, D.R.D., & Palmon, R. (1990). Age and experience effects in spatial visualization. *Developmental Psychology, 26,* 128–136.

Salthouse, T.A., Mitchell, D.R.D., Skovronek, E., & Babcock, R.L. (1989). Effects of adult age and working memory on reasoning and spatial abilities. *Journal of Experimental Psychology: Learning, Memory, and Cognition, 15,* 507–516.

Salthouse, T.A., & Prill, K.A. (1987). Effects of aging on perceptual closure. *American Journal of Psychology, 101,* 217–238.

Sandon, P.A. (1990). Simulating visual attention. *Journal of Cognitive Neuroscience, 2,* 213–231.

Sandon, P.A., & Yanikoglu, B.A. (1990). Visual search as constraint propagation. *Proceedings of the Cognitive Science Society* (pp. 574–581). Hillsdale, NJ: Erlbaum.

Schacter, D.L., Kihlstrom, J.F., Kaszniak, A.W., & Valdiserri, M. (in press). Preserved and impaired memory functions in older adults. In J. Cerella, W.J. Hoyer, J.M. Rybash, & M. Commons (Eds.), *Aging and visual information processing: Limits on loss.* New York: Academic Press.

Scialfa, C.T., & Kline, D.W. (1988). Effects of noise type and retinal eccentricity on age differences in identification and localization. *Journal of Gerontology: Psychological Sciences, 41,* 91–99.

Scialfa, C.T., Kline, D.W., & Lyman, B.J. (1987). Age differences in target identification as a function of retinal location and noise level: Examination of the useful field of view. *Psychology and Aging, 2,* 14–19.

Sharps, M.J. (1990). A developmental approach to visual cognition in the elderly. In T.M. Hess (Ed.), *Aging and cognition: Knowledge organization and utilization* (pp. 297–341). Amsterdam: Elsevier.

Shedden, J.M., & Schneider, W. (1990, August). *A connectionist model of attention enhancement and signal buffering.* Paper presented at the Cognitive Science Society, Ann Arbor, MI.

Treisman, A., & Gelade, G. (1980). A feature integration theory of attention. *Cognitive Psychology, 12*, 97–136.

Treisman, A., & Gormican, S. (1988). Feature analysis in early vision: Evidence from search asymetries. *Psychological Review, 95*, 15–48.

Treisman, A., & Schmidt, H. (1982). Illusory conjunctions in the perception of objects. *Cognitive Psychology, 14*, 107–141.

Uttal, W.R. (1990). On some two-way barriers between models and mechanisms. *Perception and Psychophysics, 48*, 188–203.

Wolfe, J.M., Cave, K.R., & Franzel, S.L. (1989). Guided search: An alternative to the feature integration model for visual search. *Journal of Experimental Psychology: Human Perception and Performance, 15*, 419–433.

Exceptionality

Chapter 4

Cognitive Differences among the Gifted: A Review and New Data*

Veronica J. Dark and Camilla Persson Benbow

Iowa State University

Some individuals in all cultures and historical periods have been recognized as *gifted* because they exhibit talents that are not evident in the majority of people (Grinder, 1985). Much of our hope for societal progress and for a better tomorrow has been invested in them and their superior abilities. To understand the reasoning abilities and problem-solving skills of such individuals could have far-reaching consequences, not the least of which may be the improvement of the problem-solving skills of those with lesser abilities. In this chapter, we review the literature on individual differences in cognition or intelligence with an emphasis on the literature derived from the study of gifted individuals.

The chapter is divided into six sections. In the first section, we set the stage

---

* We wish to thank David Lubinski for helpful comments regarding this chapter.

by briefly tracing the concept of giftedness from a *historical* perspective. The discussion borrows heavily from the work of Grinder (1985) and the interested reader is referred to that work for details. We then consider giftedness from four *current* perspectives: the psychometric perspective, the cognitive components perspective, the cognitive correlates perspective, and finally the neuropsychological perspective. Most of our own work has been conducted within the cognitive correlates perspective, and we describe a new experiment in that section. In the final section we draw some "general" conclusions.

GIFTEDNESS FROM AN HISTORICAL PERSPECTIVE

We begin by considering the concept of *giftedness*. How is it to be defined? Giftedness as a concept cannot be separated from its societal context. Each society has operationalized giftedness on the basis of the needs of that society (Grinder, 1985). In the earliest and most primitive cultures, gifted individuals were those astute in hunting and fishing. Such individuals were afforded the status of gods. As civilization developed, there was a change in the abilities that qualified individuals as gifted, but the relationship between giftedness and divinity remained intact. For example, the Greek philosophers were considered gifted because of their superior intellect. Yet their wisdom (i.e., their superior cognitive skills) was thought to be divinely inspired. Up through the Roman Empire, then, giftedness was a human quality that was venerated (Grinder, 1985).

In the Dark Ages and the Middle Ages, gifted individuals were less likely to be positively valued. It was unacceptable to have thoughts or capabilities that exceeded the narrow bounds of Christian dogma. Those who did were branded as heretical and were thought to be inspired by demons. Thus, gifted sages were labeled as witches and persecuted unmercifully (Grinder, 1985).

During the Renaissance, when reason was once again revered, the fate of gifted individuals did change for the better. Nevertheless, giftedness was not seen as an entirely positive trait. It was believed then that each individual was afforded a certain amount of mental energy. If this energy was used up too quickly, as in the case of gifted or precocious individuals, it would lead to insanity (Grinder, 1985). The negative stereotype of gifted individuals exemplified in the saying "early ripe, early rot" can be traced to this time period.

As a result of the work of Terman (Oden, 1968; Terman, 1925; Terman & Oden, 1947, 1959) and Hollingworth (1942), the negative stereotypes associated with giftedness were shown to be false, and more positive conceptualizations have again developed. The conception of giftedness itself has also changed, however. In the current literature, the focus is on potential rather than on accomplishment. Children are identified as gifted on the basis of their potential for talented or outstanding adult performance (e.g., Jackson & Butterfield, 1986; Grinder, 1985).

Viewing giftedness as potential for outstanding performance began with the work of Galton; the view was reinforced by Binet and the subsequent testing movement (Grinder, 1985). Today, as for the past 70 years, most children are identified as gifted because of their high scores on various intelligence, aptitude, or achievement tests. Thus, current views of giftedness are firmly embedded within the psychometric tradition of measuring intelligence. It is to this perspective that we now turn.

GIFTEDNESS FROM THE PSYCHOMETRIC PERSPECTIVE

The psychometric approach to intelligence concerns itself with the products of thought and individual differences in these products (Berk, 1989). Research typically examines how many factors constitute the construct of intelligence or how the identified factors are related in perhaps a hierarchical model. Some psychometrically oriented investigators have viewed intelligence as a solitary trait, g, and multiple specific factors (Spearman, 1904), while others viewed intelligence as separate aptitudes or abilities that varied in number (e.g., Thurstone, 1938; Guilford, 1967). Factor analysis has been and continues to be the primary statistical procedure used to elucidate the nature of intelligence and explain individual differences in test performance (see Carroll, 1989; Lohman, 1989, for state-of-the-art reviews of this work). A minor part of this extensive literature is based upon results with gifted individuals, a description of which is provided next.

Benbow, Stanley, Zonderman, and Kirk (1983) administered a battery of specific ability tests to a group of highly gifted adolescents and their parents. The adolescents had scored highly on the College Board Scholastic Aptitude Test (SAT) as either seventh or eighth graders. From their SAT performance, they were estimated to be in the top 1 in 1,000 of their age group in ability. In order to avoid test ceiling effects with such an able group, Benbow et al. selected tests designed for individuals several years older than the adolescent subjects. They also used some experimental tests. Results were factor analyzed separately for parents and students.

Individual differences in test performance among the exceptionally able could be accounted for by Vernon's (1950) hierarchical model or by Horn and Cattell's (1956) model of crystallized vs. fluid intelligence. There was also some evidence for g, especially among the parents. Pollins (1984) arrived at very similar conclusions with a different battery of tests and a similar sample of gifted youth, as did Benbow and Minor (1990) (described below). The results of these studies are in line with findings derived from studies of individuals not selected for high test scores (Lohman, 1989). It does not appear, therefore, that a different factor structure is needed to explain performance among the gifted (cf. Jackson & Butterfield, 1986). Rather, the performance of gifted youth is similar to that of persons several years older. The gifted youth are *precocious*.

Types of Talent

Although in the early 1970s it became evident that "special abilities failed either to predict educational outcomes better than general ability or to predict which students would profit from specialized educational interventions designed to match their particular patterns of abilities" (Lohman, 1989, p. 334; see also McNemar, 1964), a focus on specific talents rather than on high global IQ continues to be promoted within the field of gifted children (e.g., Feldhusen, 1989; Gagne, 1985; Gardner, 1983; Stanley, 1984). Part of the reason is that specific abilities improve prediction when samples are restricted in general ability, as in the case of the gifted (Thorndike, 1986). Another part of the reason stems from the arguments for seven separate intelligences put forth by Howard Gardner (1983) in the influential book *Frames of Mind*. Knowledge of specific abilities is also useful information for guidance (Tyler, 1986).

Mathematical and verbal talent are perhaps the two most widely researched specific abilities in the gifted literature. Benbow and Minor (1990) investigated whether, in fact, mathematical and verbal talent should be viewed as distinct abilities. They administered a battery of specific ability tests (designed to tap each of Thurstone's, 1938, Primary Mental Abilities) to highly verbally or highly mathematically precocious 12–14-year-olds. The verbally precocious youth were in the top 1 in 10,000 of children their age in verbal reasoning ability, while the mathematically precocious were in the top 1 in 10,000 in mathematical reasoning ability.

Results of the factor analysis confirmed that the two forms of giftedness were distinct. Verbally precocious students scored more highly on verbal and general knowledge types of tests, while mathematically precocious students scored more highly on tests of nonverbal reasoning, spatial ability, and memory. The factor analyses of these students' test scores yielded not only a verbal and a nonverbal factor, as had been found previously, but also a speed factor. (Some of the tests were highly speeded.) Interestingly, the mathematically talented students scored higher on the speed factor.

Colangelo and Kerr (1990) studied high school students who obtained perfect scores on one of the subjects of the American College Testing (ACT) Assessment. Receiving a perfect score in one domain did not assure comparable high performance in the other academic areas. Indeed, almost one-fourth of those with perfect scores in one domain did *not* score at or above the 95th percentile on the ACT composite score. The data support the assertion that there are distinct academic talents.

Lubinski and Humphreys (1990), moreover, conducted a broadly based analysis of mathematical giftedness using a different paradigm. Using the Project Talent database, they examined the generality of mathematical talent. That is, they asked whether mathematically talented individuals also excelled in other nonquantitative areas, and whether there was something unique about mathematical talent. Mathematically gifted students were found to be superior across a wide range of cognitive abilities. Mathematical talent was intimately related to general intelligence, yet there was somewhat more mathematical specificity within the gifted population than in the general population. Specifically, there was nonlinearity of regressions at the high end of the distribution of mathematical ability.

Gender Differences

Our final topic in this section concerns gender differences. Studies within the psychometric tradition have revealed gender differences in mathematical talent but not in overall ability (Benbow, 1988; Benbow & Stanley, 1980, 1981, 1983). Further, gender differences are consistently observed in both *level* and *variability* on this parameter; that is, males display larger means *and* variances on tests of mathematical reasoning. As a result of both of these differences, an inordinate proportion of males to females are found at the upper tail on distributions of several tests of mathematical talent, like SAT-M (Benbow, 1988). Lubinski and Humphreys (1990) present similar evidence and, in addition, show that males tend to display more dispersion on a variety of intellectual variables, even on variables for which females have higher means. With respect to measures of intellectual ability, Lubinski and Humphreys suggest that there are probably different determinants for gender differences in the means and variances (see also Eysenck & Kamin, 1981).

Conclusions Concerning the Psychometric Perspective

Two general conclusions are supported by studies conducted with the psychometric approach to intelligence. First, differences between the highly able and the general population are quantitative rather than qualitative in nature. The gifted exhibit abilities that are typical of individuals several years older. The structure of or relationships among their talents conform to models developed to explain individual differences in general intelligence among the general population. Second, there is evidence in support of distinct separate talents, as well as for the construct g.

GIFTEDNESS FROM THE COGNITIVE COMPONENTS PERSPECTIVE

Although the studies reviewed in the previous section tell us about the structure of intelligence in the gifted, they do not provide an explanation for why or how individual differences occur. The studies do not describe the "workings of the mind." The cognitive approach to intelligence attempts to address this area. Although the cognitive approach is not without its own shortcomings (Keating, 1984), it offers a solution to why individuals show performance differences on psychometric tests: Individuals differ in terms of the structure of their information-processing systems (e.g., memory capacity or speed of operation) and/or its contents. The contents can be further divided into knowledge concerned with processes (i.e., strategies, plans, and procedures) and knowledge concerned with facts (i.e., declarative knowledge). To use a rough computer analogy, individuals can differ in mental hardware, software, or in their database (cf. Hunt, 1978). These distinctions are fuzzy in that there may be interactions (e.g., speed may depend upon the type of data), but they provide a useful heuristic for organizing the literature.

Except for our own research, the studies to be discussed in this section and the next were not, for the most part, designed as research on giftedness per se. Thus, they do not necessarily adopt the definition of *giftedness* used by psychometricians. For example, some investigators have studied experts in various domains, like chess or physics. Such experts might not be labeled as *gifted* in the psychometric sense of the word. This methodological difference should be kept in mind when generalizing or comparing results.

With that caveat, we turn first to the question of whether there are "software" and database differences between gifted and other individuals. We explore what studies in cognitive psychology have revealed about gifted learners. This literature has been referred to as the *cognitive components approach* to intelligence (e.g., Pellegrino & Glaser, 1979). In the section that follows, we discuss the *cognitive correlates approach*, which is more directed towards the differences in mental "hardware."

The cognitive components approach is basically a 'top-down' analysis of individual problem statements or test items. The purpose of such task decomposition is to investigate the relationship between individual differences in test performance and individual differences in domain-specific knowledge. Indeed, the investigation of prior knowledge and strategies that students employ are considered critical areas of research in teaching and learning mathematics (Romberg & Carpenter, 1986). Romberg and Carpenter (1986) concluded that cognitive components "research appears to have the greatest potential for understanding how mathematics is learned" (p. 853). They suggested that the identification of strategies used by "expert learners" in mathematics will allow the development of programs designed to help less skilled individuals. Presumably, the same logic is applicable in a variety of domains.

The gifted are characterized as, and perhaps even defined by, having a wealth of general knowledge (Feldhusen & Kolloff, 1986; Lubinski & Humphreys, 1990; Parke, 1989). That is, they have large databases. We will not consider further differences in the databases per se. Rather, the question is whether the large database allows the development of more abstract problem representations and the use of more mature strategies.

Differences in Problem Representation

Research comparing experts to novices, young children to older children or adults, and children with learning problems to average-ability children has shown that an important influence on skilled performance is the knowledge people bring to a task (Rabinowitz & Glaser, 1985). Thus, Chi, Glaser, and Rees (1982) postulated that high intelligence is the possession of a large body of accessible and usable knowledge. In support of this view, domain-specific knowledge has been shown to have significant influence on cognitive skills in baseball (Chiesi, Spilich, & Voss, 1979), in bridge (Charness, 1979), in chess (deGroot, 1965; Chase & Simon, 1973a,b; Chi, 1978), among computer programmers (Jeffries, Turner, Polson, & Atwood, 1981; McKeithen, Reitman, Reuter, & Hirtle, 1981), in electronics (Egan & Schwartz, 1979), among Go players (Reitman, 1976), among Gomoku players (Eisenstadt & Kareev, 1975), in mathematics (Paige & Simon, 1966), among musicians (Sloboda, 1976), in physics (Chi, Feltovich, & Glaser, 1981; Simon & Simon, 1978), in political science (Voss, Fincher-Kiefer, Greene, & Post, 1986), and in medical diagnosis (Lesgold, 1984). According to these studies, the knowledge of experts tends to be contained in large, higher order chunks (comprised of principles, strategies, functions, and sequences), whereas knowledge of novices is limited to smaller, lower order chunks (e.g., information on structure, color, proximity). Therefore, for less intelligent learners, the problem representation is in close correspondence with the literal details of the problem, while for the most intelligent learners, the representation also contains derived inferences and abstractions (e.g., underlying principles).

Chi et al. (1982) proposed that problem-solving difficulties of novices should be attributed to inadequacies of their knowledge bases (and as a result, their problem representations) rather than limitations in either the structure of their cognitive systems or their processing capabilities (e.g., inability to detect important cues in the problem statement). In other words, novices are limited by their inability to infer further knowledge from the literal cues contained in a problem statement. For experts, however, inferences during problem solving are readily generated from their knowledge structures. Krutetskii (1976) and Silver (1979) similarly reported that skilled problem solvers attend to the problem's structural characteristics, while less skilled problem solvers attend to surface details.

Although domain-specific knowledge may be one key to problem solving, it does *not* predict the exceptional performance of gifted students on tests that tap content that is unfamiliar to them. Declarative knowledge can not explain high scores on the SAT-M, for example, of seventh graders who have not even taken a course entitled algebra or geometry. Such children have been shown to lack even basic knowledge of algebra: In special mathematics programs designed for high-scoring youth on the SAT-M (Benbow, Napolski, & Glass, 1990), most of the highly able participants must begin their studies with Algebra I (T. VanderZyl, personal communication, September 1990).

It is possible that these students invented their own mathematics to solve what is for them novel problems on the SAT-M, just as children have been found to invent addition strategies before they are formally taught (Resnick, 1980). Another possibility, however, is that general problem-solving skills are an emergent feature of the large general database that is characteristic of gifted children; that is, general strategic (procedural) knowledge may allow gifted children to perform at high levels. Greeno noted: "All problem solving is based on knowledge. A person may not have learned exactly what to do in a specific problem situation, but whatever the person is able to do requires some knowledge, even if that knowledge is in the form of general strategies for analyzing situations and attempting solutions" (1980, p. 10).

Dark and Benbow (1990) examined whether mathematically talented youth with no formal training in algebra approached mathematical problems in a qualitatively different way then verbally talented youth, average-ability youth, and college students. Subjects were asked to express in equation format the relationships expressed in a sentence. They were also asked to break a complex problem into its basic components and then, somewhat later, to recall the problems. There were two types of statements in the complex problems: Some statements expressed an assignment proposition in which a numerical value is assigned to a variable; other statements expressed a relation proposition in which numeric relationships between two variables are expressed. Relational propositions are more difficult to process than assignment propositions in the college population (e.g., Clement, Lochhead, & Monk, 1980; Mayer, 1982; Soloway, Lochhead, & Clement, 1982).

The college students in Dark and Benbow (1990), with few exceptions, had taken college-level math courses and thus, we assumed, had the appropriate declarative knowledge to actually solve the problems. None of the youth had had formal training in algebra. Subjects were never asked to actually solve the problems, however, only to analyze them. Our intent was to probe the problem representations to determine whether and how the representations of the mathematically talented were different.

The average-ability youth performed less well than the other groups on all tasks. The mathematically talented students were indeed better than the other groups in writing equations expressing complex relationships, but not in writing equations representing simple relationships. Mathematically talented youth were no better than verbally talented students or college students at breaking the problem into its components and recalling the problem statements. Moreover, relational propositions were harder than assignment propositions for the mathematically talented students, just as they were for the other groups. Thus, there was no support for qualitative differences in understanding and representing mathematical information.

Gifted children, both verbally and mathematically gifted, and college students appeared to have similar problem representations, although they differed in terms of declarative knowledge. We suggest, along with Krutetskii (1976), Silver (1979), and Greeno (1980), that gifted individuals are able to perform well even on novel tasks as the result of general problem-solving skills. Just as domain-specific knowledge has been shown to allow inference and more abstract representations of problems in a domain, a large knowledge base encompassing many domains may allow the development of more general skills.

Differences in Strategy and Metacognitive Components

Sternberg (1981, 1982, 1986) has been a strong advocate of the proposition that differences between skilled and nonskilled learners are metacognitive, or strategic. He has repeatedly rejected the notion that to be smart is to be fast. Rather, what is critical for superior intellectual functioning is how effort or time is allocated. Efficient metacomponents (i.e., control processes that are often referred to as executive, planning, or monitoring processes) are prevalent in intellectual functioning and are the key to successful problem solving.

Gifted students tend to allocate most of their time to the planning or "metacognitive" phase of problem solving (Sternberg, 1981). Thus, even though they tend to be more rapid in reaching a solution to a problem compared to individuals with average abilities, gifted students spend more time up front, deciding just what the problem is that needs to be solved, organizing and selecting relevant information, and selecting appropriate solution strategies. They also spend more time than average-ability students encoding the information contained in the problem statement (Sternberg, 1981), although the extra time may not be up front with difficult problems (Gitomer, Curtis, Glaser, & Lensky, 1987). Consequently, gifted students spend less time on local, problem-specific, lower level planning. Less able persons show the reverse pattern, emphasizing local rather than global planning.

The literature comparing experts and novices also supports strategic and metacognitive differences in problem solving. Simon and Simon (1978), for example, reported differences in the solution process of experts and novices. The expert's strategy is to work forward from the variables in the problem, successively generating the equations that can be solved from the given information. The novice, in contrast, starts with an equation containing the unknown of the problem. If it contains a variable that is not among the givens, then the novice selects another equation to solve for it, and so on. In the same vein, Schoenfeld (1983) noted, when comparing expert and novice problem solvers, that experts appear to have "vigilant managers" that carefully monitor problem-solving performance and strive for efficiency and accuracy.

Unlike many of his fellow cognitive-components researchers, Sternberg downplays the importance of knowledge: Amount of knowledge is not as important for expertise or high intelligence as being able to learn from experience (Sternberg, 1986). Basically, Sternberg views intelligence as a measure of one's ability to deal with novelty and then to automatize information processing. To investigate this process of learning within context, as Sternberg calls it, Sternberg and colleagues have studied performance on insight problems. An example of an insight problem is: In a drawer with 100 blue and 50 brown socks, what is the minimum number of socks you must pull out to insure that you obtain a matching pair? (The answer is 3.)

Gifted students exhibit superior performance on such insight problems compared to nongifted students (Davidson, 1986; Sternberg & Davidson, 1983). They do so at least partly because they are less often misled by irrelevant information contained in insight problem statements (e.g., the number of socks in the drawer). Training of average-ability students with strategies for solving insight problems improves their performance, whereas training effects are less marked for gifted students. Moreover, supplying nongifted children with the insights needed to solve a problem improved their performance; similar assistance had no effect on gifted students' performance. It appears, then, that gifted students spontaneously recognize productive problem-solving strategies or relevant information in a problem, while average-ability students do so only after training (Sternberg, 1986).

Further evidence that metacognitive knowledge may limit intellectual functioning can be found in the work of Borkowski and Peck (1986) and Pressley, Borkowski, and Sullivan (1985). When an impoverished metamemorial (metacognitive) structure was developed by presenting children with a novel situation in which the information about appropriate strategies was vague or with a situation in which the children had to use a poorly trained strategy, the subjects had difficulty in understanding the instructions. That is, when the knowledge necessary for specific strategy implementation was missing, intellectual functioning was compromised (Borkowski & Peck, 1986).

Gifted children exhibit superior metamemorial knowledge compared to average-ability students: They know more strategies for retrieving information, they know that embedding to be remembered words into a story enhances their probability of recall, they know that type of memory test would affect performance, and so forth (Borkowski & Peck, 1986). Because gifted students were not superior in their ability to invent appropriate strategies for solving a problem, these data further support the conclusion that knowledge of a variety of general problem-solving strategies may empower the individual faced with novel tasks, such as when a seventh-grade student is asked to take the SAT. Thus, gifted students can solve some of the problems on the SAT, not because of the content taught in their mathematics classes up to that time or because they can invent specific new strategies, but rather because of the many general problem-solving strategies they have mastered.

The above interpretation of the fact that gifted students handle solving novel problems so well is consistent with results from studies of aptitude–treatment interactions in classroom learning (Snow & Yalow, 1982). The most consistent finding in that literature has been that academic performance differences between more and less intelligent students are most strongly evident in programs that require students to organize their own learning and fill in instructional gaps.

Conclusions from the Cognitive Components Perspective

The cognitive components approach is concerned with knowledge—both declarative knowledge and knowledge of procedures or strategies. Skilled compared to unskilled learners have greater knowledge. They have access to a greater number of problem-solving strategies and, in the case of experts, can infer even further knowledge from the problem characteristics or their representations of the problems. They are also better able to identify relevant information contained in a problem. When solving problems, they tend to allocate most of their time and effort "up front" in the planning or metacognitive phase. Thus, as Jackson and Butterfield (1986) concluded in their review, "the rapidly growing new literature on metacognition and giftedness suggests that superordinate processes regulating task analysis and self-management of problem-solving behavior may be important components differentiating gifted from average performance" (p. 176).

It is not necessary to appeal to qualitative differences in explaining the superior metacognitive function of gifted individuals. Rather, gifted children simply appear to function as individuals several years older. The processing differences between the gifted and the average-ability child are quantitative in nature, just like the differences between the average-ability child and the mentally retarded child (Jackson & Butterfield, 1986).

GIFTEDNESS FROM THE COGNITIVE
CORRELATES PERSPECTIVE

Although research from the cognitive components perspective has revealed much about the processes associated with extreme skill or talent, our own work has used primarily the cognitive correlates approach to studying individual differences. In this section we (a) outline the cognitive correlates approach, (b) briefly and selectively describe the extant literature, (c) describe our own prior work, and (d) report the results of a new experiment that demonstrates the usefulness of the approach in expanding our knowledge of intelligence in general and giftedness in particular.

Intuition suggests not only that more intelligent people know more, but that they are in some way more alert to information in the environment (Hunt, 1978). The apparent relationship between ability and speed was also noted by early psychologists (e.g., DuBois, 1932; Thurstone, 1937; McFarland, 1930). By using information-processing theory as the guiding framework, Hunt and colleagues began to break this general speed factor into a set of *mechanistic* (or strategy free) cognitive processes that were correlated with performance on psychometric tests (Hunt, 1978, 1983; Hunt, Frost, & Lunneborg, 1973; Hunt, Lunneborg, & Lewis, 1975). The hope was that understanding differences at the most basic level of information processing would lead to better understanding of differences in complex reasoning tasks and ultimately to the development of *theory-driven* measures of intelligence (e.g., Hunt et al., 1973).

One of the main components of information-processing theories is a description of memory. In the typical information-processing model, two memory states (or stages) are described: working memory (short-term or active memory) and long-term memory. In a generic information-processing system, environmental stimuli can activate long-term memory representations (concepts) into working memory. The activated representations can be maintained in working memory or transformed in some way. The results of working-memory processing can become encoded into long-term memory.

By the mid-1970s, various laboratory tasks had been developed to measure the effect of environmental manipulations (e.g., stimulus presentation rate) on encoding, maintaining, and transforming information within and between the two memory states. Hunt (1978; Hunt et al., 1975) observed that some of these tasks did not depend upon general knowledge or upon selection of an appropriate strategy, factors associated with giftedness within the cognitive correlates literature. Rather, they reflected the operations of very basic components of the information-processing system. Hunt and colleagues (e.g., Hunt et al., 1973, 1975) reported reliable relationships between performance on these tasks and performance on psychometric tests, leading Hunt (1978, 1983) to suggest that there was a *mechanistic* component of intelligence.

Hunt's hypothesis relating performance on very simple tasks to the construct of intelligence followed in the tradition of Galton (1869), over 100 years earlier. They were in direct contrast to theories, like that of Jensen (1970), stating that more able individuals, as measured by psychometric tests, would not differ from less able individuals on basic, perceptual processes involving registration, holding, and retrieving of simple information (Level I processes). By showing a relationship between very basic processing and psychometric intelligence, the cognitive correlates literature has, in a sense, vindicated Galton.

The Cognitive Correlates Literature

Contemporary cognitive correlates research began with the work of Hunt et al. (1973). The subjects were university students who were either high or low in verbal ability and either high or low in quantitative ability, as defined by the Washington Pre-College Test. The students performed a variety of basic information-processing tasks including (but not limited to) digit span, memory search, continuous paired-associates, and letter matching. Comparisons among the resulting groups suggested that the more verbally able were better (a) in accessing long-term memory (i.e., in encoding long-term memory information into working memory), (b) in maintaining the temporal order of items in working memory, and (c) in scanning through working memory. The more quantitatively able, on the other hand, showed more resistance to interference once information was encoded into working memory.

Numerous other researchers working within the cognitive correlates approach extended the initial findings of Hunt et al. (1973). Because different components of the information-processing system are reflected in different tasks, our selective description of the extant literature will be organized by task.

Span. Span tasks are those that require immediate reproduction of a short series of items (usually digits) in the order in which they were presented. From an information-processing view, simple forward span tasks have been used as indicators of the capacity of working memory or of its buffers. Forward span performance has also been interpreted as reflecting the capacity to maintain linear (temporal) orderings among stimuli (e.g., Anderson, 1983). The cognitive functions tapped by backward span tasks are more complex (cf. Bachelder & Denny, 1977a,b). Thus, they have not been widely used within the cognitive correlates research.

Although span tasks are assumed to measure verbal ability on psychometric tests of intelligence (e.g., Wechsler, 1974), cognitive correlates data relating forward span to ability are somewhat inconsistent. Using college students as subjects, Hunt et al. (1973) reported no difference in digit span as a function of quantitative ability; Chiang and Atkinson (1976) found no relationship between digit span and SAT-V or SAT-M; and Daneman and Carpenter (1980) found no reliable relationship between word span and SAT-V in college students. Das and Siu (1989), however, found that word span was related to reading ability in children. Schofield and Ashman (1986) found a reliable correlation between WISC-R performance and forward digit span in fifth- and sixth-grade children. And Jackson and Myers (1982) reported a positive relationship between span and reading ability in preschoolers. Thus, the pattern suggests that span performance is predictive of verbal ability with children and/or with samples showing greater variability in ability.

Memory search. The memory search task, introduced by S. Sternberg (1965), has been used to measure the speed with which information already encoded into working memory can be accessed. On each trial, the subject encodes a set of from one to six digits into working memory. A single digit is then displayed, and the subject indicates whether or not the digit was part of the memory set. Typically, there is a linear increase in response time as a function of memory set size. The slope of the line is interpreted as the amount of time needed to "search" each item and, thus, is a measure of the ability to manipulate information in working memory.

Hunt et al. (1973) reported that faster search time was related to higher verbal ability among college students, but Chiang and Atkinson (1976) found no relationship between search speed and SAT-V or SAT-M in a sample of male and female students. When they conditionalized performance on gender, however, they found increased speed was related to higher SAT-V in males and to lower SAT-V in females. Studies with children have shown faster search speed among the more intellectually able (e.g., Keating & Bobbitt, 1978) and among normal-ability children in comparison to less-able children (e.g., Harris & Fleer, 1974).

Verification. Another measure of the ability to manipulate information in working memory is the sentence–picture verification task. Originally it was assumed to measure the speed with which a proposition held in working memory could be matched against the environment. A simple proposition (e.g., STAR ABOVE PLUS) is followed by a picture of a star above a plus or of a plus above a star. The subject responds true or false depending on whether the picture matches the sentence.

Response time is generally related to verbal ability (e.g., Hunt et al., 1975; Spiegal & Bryant, 1978; Lansman, Donaldson, Hunt, & Yantis, 1982; Palmer, MacLeod, Hunt, & Davidson, 1985) and increases as the linguistic complexity of the sentence increases (e.g., STAR NOT BELOW PLUS). MacLeod, Hunt, and Mathews (1978), however, identified a subgroup of subjects who appeared to use pictoral rather than propositional representations in working memory. Their performance was related to spatial ability and not verbal ability. The possible influence of strategy in this task complicates the interpretation of performance in terms of basic information-processing characteristics.

Lexical decision and matching. Several related tasks have been used to measure *long-term memory access*, defined as the speed with which long-term memory representations can be activated into working memory. The tasks fall into two classes depending upon whether the dependent variable is the speed of a response or a difference score derived from two speed measures. Lexical decision and category matching represent the former class. In the lexical decision task, letter strings are presented and the subject indicates, usually via a button press, whether the string forms a word (e.g., FLOME or FLAME). Faster decisions are associated with higher reading ability among children (Carr, 1981) and college students (Palmer et al., 1985). In category matching, the subject indicates whether a stimulus is an instance of a given category, two stimuli are instances of the same category, or two instances are identical on some dimension. For the most part, faster responses are related to higher verbal or reading ability in both college students (e.g., Hunt, Davidson, & Lansman, 1981; M.D. Jackson & McClelland, 1978; but see Hogaboam & Pellegrino, 1978) and children (Ford & Keating, 1981; Goldberg, Schwartz, & Stewart, 1977).

Variations of the matching task introduced by Posner and colleagues (Posner, Boies, Eichelman, & Taylor, 1969; Posner & Mitchell, 1967) represent the second class of task used to investigate long-term memory access. *Speed of access* is defined as the difference between two speeded responses. In the standard version of the task, subjects first judge whether a series of stimulus pairs match in terms of physical identity (e.g., A A) and then whether a series of pairs match in terms of name identity (e.g., A a). The difference in judgment time for the *same* stimuli under the two instruction conditions (name minus physical) is interpreted as an index of how long it takes to retrieve the name of the stimuli from long-term memory into working memory (Posner et al., 1969).

Although there are statistical problems associated with such difference scores (Donaldson, 1983), the procedure allows an examination of long-term memory access while controlling for general speed differences between groups (Campione & Brown, 1978). Higher verbal ability is associated with smaller differences between conditions among college students (Hunt et al., 1975; M.D. Jackson, 1980).[1] More intelligent children are less slowed by the switch from physical to name identity than are less intelligent children (Keating & Bobbitt, 1978).

Continuous paired associates. In the continuous paired-associate task, the subject attempts to remember a set of stimulus–response pairs in an ongoing sequence of test–study trials. Each pair is presented once for study. At some latter time, the stimulus term is presented and the subject attempts to recall the response term. Immediately after it is tested, the stimulus term is paired with a new response term, which the subject must then remember until the next test. Although different components of the task can be distinguished (Atkinson & Shiffrin, 1968), the task involves manipulation of information in working memory via the formation and maintenance of temporary associations. Hunt et al. (1973) reported that college students higher in quantitative ability showed less forgetting of the associations. Except for our own research described below, we know of no other individual differences research using the task, perhaps because it is not related to verbal ability, the focus of most of the literature.

---

[1] Lansman et al. (1982) reported that the difference was more related to clerical perceptual speed than to verbal ability. The difference score reported by Lansman et al. was the difference in the time to respond "yes" to pairs matching on name only, minus the time to respond "yes" to physically matching pairs under name matching instructions. Such a difference score would represent lexical access (according to the subtraction method) only if there is no difference in the physical processing of the pairs and if the name code is not accessed for the physically matching pairs. Either or both of these assumptions may be wrong.

A Weakness in the Cognitive Correlates Literature

The cognitive correlates literature shows indeed that individual differences in performance on very simple tasks are correlated with performance on more complex ability tests. Except for the original study by Hunt et al. (1973), however, the cognitive correlates approach has generally been used to compare groups differing along one ability dimension, usually verbal ability. Because psychometrically defined verbal ability is strongly related to general ability (e.g., Carroll, 1989; Humphreys, 1962; Lavin, 1965; McNemar, 1964), it is unclear from most of the cognitive correlates literature whether the measured differences reflect specific verbal ability or a more general ability.

As described earlier, the psychometric literature suggests that intelligence is comprised of separate abilities, all of which share a general ability factor. Just as Hunt et al. (1973) were correct 20 years ago in suggesting that our understanding of psychometric abilities could be furthered by considering underlying cognitive processes, we suggest that it is time to increase our understanding of the cognitive correlates of intelligence by considering how the identified processes relate to different psychometrically defined ability profiles. That is, it is time for the cognitive correlates approach to address the question of specific versus general abilities.

Mathematical and verbal ability share a great deal of common variance but also have psychometrically distinct components of intelligence (e.g., Benbow & Minor, 1990; Gardner, 1983; Lubinski & Humphreys, 1990). Because of the distinct components, they may be correlated with different patterns of basic information-processing skills. We argue that comparisons among differentially gifted individuals allow separation of general and specific abilities and will help define the nature of the specific abilities. Our logic is similar to that of Jackson and Butterfield (1986), who have argued for the need to determine similarities and differences between idiot savants and "normally" gifted individuals. The results of such comparisons would better delimit just what comprises the ability being examined. Research designs that show a positive relationship between performance on an information-processing task and a specific psychometrically defined ability while showing no relationship with general ability or another specific factor make a stronger case that the identified relationship is a component of the ability of interest.

Cognitive Correlates in the Extremely Talented

We began our cognitive correlates research (Dark & Benbow, 1990) with the same four groups of subjects described earlier: verbally precocious youth, mathematically precocious youth, average-ability youth, and college students. The extant cognitive correlates literature suggested that verbal ability was related to performance on working-memory tasks. We conceptualized our research within the information-processing model of Baddeley and Hitch (1974; Baddeley, 1986). The model breaks working memory into three subcomponents: a central executive and two buffer systems, one for verbal information and one for spatial information. We asked whether the performance differences on simple tasks were attributable to differences in capacity of the buffers or differences in the ability of the executive system to manipulate information, or both. We chose a span task to measure the former and a continuous-paired associate task to measure the latter. We used two types of stimuli (digits and locations in a matrix) in each task so that we could tap the functioning of each of the buffers.

On both tasks, the gifted youth performed better than the average-ability youth and more like the older college students (cf. Cohn, Carlson, & Jensen, 1985); that is, the gifted appeared to be "precocious." On both tasks and with both types of stimuli, the mathematically talented youth performed at a higher level than their verbally talented counterparts. This latter finding was somewhat unexpected. The literature suggested a relationship between mathematical ability and the ability to handle spatial information (e.g., Burnett, Lane, & Dratt, 1979; McGee, 1979). Thus, we had anticipated that mathematically talented youth would outperform verbally talented youth with the spatial location stimuli. Because the digits functioned only as stimuli to be named in our tasks, and because digits would be represented in the verbal buffer in the Baddeley and Hitch (1974) model, we had anticipated that any difference with the digit stimuli would favor the verbally talented. Yet the opposite was found.

Dark and Benbow (1991) further examined performance on span and continuous-paired associate tasks, but they included word and letter stimuli in the former task and letter stimuli in the latter task. They also included a lexical-decision task to examine access to long-term memory. By contrasting performance among youth who were (a) mathematically precocious, or (b) verbally precocious, or (c) both mathematically and verbally precocious, we attempted to determine whether differences were associated with specific or general ability.

Enhanced *digit* span continued to be associated with mathematical precocity, but enhanced *word* span was associated with verbal precocity. Because type of stimulus was important to span-task performance, we interpreted better performance in terms of compactness of the representations rather than as differences in storage capacity (cf. Dempster, 1981, 1985). Performance on the continuous paired-associate task was not as affected by a change in stimulus type and was yet again associated with mathematical precocity. We concluded that a general ability to manipulate information in working memory was a component of mathematical talent, but we did note that word stimuli had not been included in the continuous paired-associate task. Performance on the lexical-decision task was associated with verbal precocity, and thus confirmed the assertion in the literature that fast access to long-term memory was a component of verbal ability (e.g., Ford & Keating, 1981; Hunt et al., 1973, 1975).

We find the fact that individual differences in performance on very simple working-memory tasks varies as a function of type of stimulus to be extremely interesting. With familiar material, at least, the contents of working memory are activated long-term memory representations. The differences in span performance as a function of stimulus can, therefore, be "explained" by appealing to individual differences in the compactness (or cohesiveness) of long-term memory units.

The knowledge portion of long-term memory is often conceptualized in terms of a highly interlinked network of semantic units (e.g., Collins & Loftus, 1975). The importance to performance of specific knowledge has been pointed out repeatedly in the literature (e.g., Chi et al., 1982); it has been assumed that the breadth of the interconnections is important. Our data suggest, at least for precocious children, that there may also be differences in the knowledge "units" themselves: Digits may have more compact representations in the network for mathematically precocious youth, and words may have more compact representations for verbally precocious youth. The more compact the representation, the more items can be maintained in working memory at one time, as reflected in span performance. Note that the explanation relies on quantitative differences along a dimension of compactness.

If there are differences in working-memory capacity for digits and words as a function of differences in the compactness of the long-term memory representations, might there also be differences in the speed with which the representations can be activated into working memory? As noted above, an often made generalization from the cognitive correlates literature is that fast access to long-term memory is associated with high verbal ability. The data, however, are derived from tasks using words or letters. In the experiment reported in the next section, we examined the possibility that individual differences in the speed of accessing long-term memory are related to the type of stimulus by using a variation of the Posner matching task described earlier.

Some New Data

As indicated earlier, Posner's name-match minus physical-match difference score is often used as a measure of the speed with which long-term memory can be accessed. The logic is based on the subtraction method (Donders, 1868/1969). If the subject responds to the same pair of stimuli under two instruction conditions, differences in reaction time can*not* be attributed to differences in the physical properties of the stimulus that might affect perceptual encoding. Similarly, if the same choice (yes or no) is made and executed for the pair under both instruction sets, reaction time differences can*not* be attributed to decision or motor components. Logically, the *only* difference between the two situations is the nature of the instructions. In the Posner task it is that the name is required for the name match. Thus, reaction time differences should reflect only the speed with which the name can be accessed.

In the study to be described, we used digit rather than letter stimuli. Case can not be manipulated for digits as it can for letters, so we were not able to precisely mimic the standard procedure in the present experiment. We did follow the logic of the subtraction method, however. Our stimuli were digits (numerals, e.g., 3) and number words (e.g., THREE). On each trial, the subject saw one of four types of pairs: digit–digit, digit–word, word–digit, or word–word. In the first half of the experiment, the pairs were judged as matching in terms of physical identity (e.g., 3 3 is a matching pair). In the second half, they were judged in terms of name identity (e.g., 3 three is a matching pair). The difference in response time between the two instruction conditions was then computed separately for digit–digit and word–word pairs and for "yes" and "no" responses.

Method. Forty-three[2] 13- or 14-year-old students (14 girls and 29 boys) who had just finished either seventh or eighth grade participated in the experiment. The students were attending a summer program for highly gifted youth. To qualify for the program, the youth must have scored as a seventh grader at the level of college-bound high school senior males on either the mathematics portion of the SAT (SAT-M $\geq$ 500) or the verbal portion (SAT-V $\leq$ 430). Students with the most extreme SAT-M and SAT-V scores were recruited as subjects from two sessions during one summer. Although students were expected to participate in research projects as part of their educational experience and in return for a financial subsidy to the program, individual participation was voluntary.

On the basis of their SAT-M performance, each youth was classed as either extremely mathematically gifted or less extremely mathematically gifted (SAT-M $\geq$ 590 and < 590, respectively). On the basis of SAT-V performance, each youth was classed as either extremely verbally gifted or less extremely verbally gifted (SAT-V $\geq$ 490 and < 490, respectively). The terms *extreme* and *less extreme* are used as descriptors, rather than *high* and *low*, as a reminder that all the participants were highly gifted youth. The extreme math, extreme verbal group (MV) was comprised of 10 students (all boys). The extreme math, less extreme verbal group (Mv) was comprised of 15 students (14 boys, 1 girl). The less extreme math, extreme verbal group (mV) was comprised of 12 students (5 boys, 7 girls). The less extreme math, less extreme verbal group (mv) was comprised of 6 students (all girls). The average SAT-M and SAT-V scores for each group are presented in Table 1.

---

[2] The data from an additional subject were discarded because the subject's mean latency was over four standard deviations slower than the mean of the group as a whole.

Table 1.   Average SAT-M and SAT-V for Each of the Four Groups

| | Group[a] | | | | | | | |
| | MV | | Mv | | mV | | mv | |
	Mean	SD	Mean	SD	Mean	SD	Mean	SD
SAT-M	650	71	643	43	428	100	511	75
SAT-V	532	41	400	31	526	44	426	59

[a]Capital letters denote extreme ability, and lower case letters denote less extreme ability.

Stimulus presentation and response recording were controlled by an Apple II computer equipped with a Timemaster II clockcard and a Zenith (ZVM121) monochrome monitor. The computer operated under the APT software package (Foltz & Poltrock, 1985).

Each trial began with a plus-sign ready signal for 500 ms, followed by a 1000-ms blank and then the stimulus pair. The pair remained on the screen until the subject's response. Items used in the pairs were six digits (0,1,2,3,4,5) and the words comprising the digit names (zero, one, two, three, four, and five).

Instructions stated that the subject should as quickly as possible, but without making errors, press the right key (labeled "yes") if the items matched and press the left key (labeled "no") if they did not match. After 20 practice trials, subjects completed 72 trials under physical-match instructions. Eighteen digit–digit pairs and 18 word–word pairs required a "yes" response, because the two stimuli in the pair were physically the same (e.g., 1 1, or two two). The "no" trials consisted of different digits, different words, or a word and a digit. In the latter case, the digit and word could refer to the same number or a different number (e.g., 1 one, two 3). When different numbers were referenced in a pair, the two numbers always differed by one.

After completing the physical-match trials, the subject received name-match instructions in which "yes" responses were also required when the stimuli had the same name (e.g., 2 two). There were 18 practice trials and 96 experimental trials. Of the 48 "yes" trials, there were 12 digit–digit pars, 12 word–word pairs, 12 word–digit pairs, and 12 digit–word pairs. The "no" trials were similarly distributed.

Results. Only latencies for correct responses were included in the analyses. An alpha of .05 was used.

Subjects were faster overall in responding to digit pairs (620 msec) than to word pairs (702 msec) [$F(1,39) = 111.58$, $MS_e = 1,171$], but there were no reliable differences associated with mathematical or verbal ability. Although the difference was small and did not vary with ability, there was a tendency for higher overall accuracy with digits (98% correct) than with words (97%) [$F(1,39) = 3.49$, $MS_e = .0010$, $.05 < p < .10$]. The faster and more accurate responses to digit than word pairs is likely the result of differences in perceptual complexity.

In the matching task, performance under name-matching instructions for a given stimulus pair is assumed to reflect all the same processes as performance under the physical-matching instructions with the additional step of retrieving the name of each item from long-term memory. For each subject, therefore, the response latency for word–word and digit–digit pairs under physical-matching instructions was subtracted from the corresponding latency under name-matching instructions. (Word–digit and digit–word pairs were not included in the analysis.) Performance was separately computed for "yes" and "no" responses. The average of the difference scores for each group are presented in Table 2.

The responses to digit pairs were examined via an analysis of variance with type of response (yes vs. no) as a within-subject factor and mathematical extremity and verbal extremity as between-subject factors. There was a reliable main effect of type of response [$F(1,39) = 4.45$] and a reliable Type of Response x Mathematical Extremity interaction [$F(1,39) = 5.19$, $MS_e = 4{,}030$ for both Fs]. The interaction between Mathematical Extremity and Verbal Extremity approached reliability [$F(1,39) = 3.13$, $MS_e = 8{,}625$, $.05 < p < .10$].

Examination of the word pairs via a similar analysis also showed a reliable main effect of type of response [$F(1,39) = 5.00$] and a reliable Type of Response x Verbal Extremity interaction [$F(1,39) = 5.48$, $MS_e = 12{,}800$ for both Fs]. The main effect of Verbal Extremity approached reliability [$F(1,39) = 3.97$, $MS_e = 15{,}084$, $p = .05$].

The results suggest that verbal ability is related to the speed with which word stimuli activate their long-term memory representations, while mathematical ability is related to the speed with which digits activate their representations. Although the confound between gender and mathematical extremity in the sample does not allow an unambiguous interpretation of the results in terms of ability–activation relationships, confidence in the interpretation is strengthened by examining the partial correlations between SAT-M and SAT-V and the four

Table 2. Average Group Latency Difference (in Msec) for Yes and No Responses to Digit and Word Pairs With the Change in Instructions from Physical Match to Name Match

Type of Pair and Response	Group[a] MV Mean	SD	Mv Mean	SD	mV Mean	SD	mv Mean	SD
Digit								
Yes	35	65	74	64	57	113	39	42
No	28	47	76	87	134	93	89	71
Word								
Yes	56	39	44	50	44	69	46	57
No	−1	145	166	181	95	157	160	100

[a]Capital letters denote extreme ability, and lower-case letters denote less extreme ability.

Table 3. Partial Correlations Between the Difference Scores and SAT-M and SAT-V Controlling for Gender and Simple Correlations with Gender for Each Combination of Type of Response and Type of Pair

Type of Pair and Response	SAT-M[a]	SAT-V[a]	Gender[b]
Digit			
Yes	−.164	−.087	−.178
No	−.343*	.014	.167
Word			
Yes	.203	.103	−.043
No	−.043	−.293*	.063

[a]Partial correlations controlling for gender. df = 39
[b]Simple correlations. N = 43
*p < .05

latency differences while controlling for gender. The partial correlations are shown in Table 3, along with the simple correlation with gender. As in the analyses of variance, the only reliable relationships were between SAT-M and the digit-no difference and between SAT-V and the word-no difference. Sex was not reliably related to any difference score.

Discussion. Hunt et al. (1973, 1975) reported that enhanced long-term memory access, as reflected in the name-matching minus physical-matching score, was a component of verbal ability. Hunt's subjects were contrasted only on verbal ability, however, and letters were used as stimuli. We found no relationship between verbal or mathematical ability and the difference score for "yes" responses with either digit–digit or word–word pairs. The fact that *all* yes responses in the current study were to physically identical pairs may have contributed to the lack of differences. There were, however, clear and informative differences between groups in the response to the "no" pairs. The results showed differential performance by the groups as a function of type of stimulus similar to the pattern reported by Dark and Benbow: Verbally precocious youth appeared to have faster access to long-term memory with word pairs, whereas mathematically precocious youth appeared to have faster access to long-term memory with digit pairs.

In combination with the span results of Dark and Benbow (1991), the current results highlight the complexity of factors affecting human performance in even very basic tasks. As already discussed, word representations are more compact and more easily activated into working memory in individuals who are extremely verbally talented. In contrast, digit representations are more compact and more easily activated into working memory in individuals who are extremely mathematically talented.

Conclusions from the Cognitive Correlates Perspective

The cognitive correlates literature supports the suggestion of Hunt et al. (1973) that individual differences on complex intellectual tasks, like those employed on psychometric tests, can be meaningfully related to differences in basic information processing. For the most part, the cognitive correlates literature is concerned with quantitative differences in performance. The selected tasks are so simple that performance differences are assumed to reflect differences in speed or efficiency; qualitative differences in processing should not be possible. Because of this, the cognitive correlates perspective confirms the conclusions drawn from the other perspectives that giftedness is a matter of degree.

The cognitive correlates literature suggested that verbally talented individuals are more efficient in certain kinds of working-memory operations. Indeed they are, but the recent identification of the role of type of stimulus in our work with gifted children, suggests the need for caution in making generalizations. In some simple information-processing cognitive tasks (e.g., those assumed to reflect working-memory capacity and access to long-term memory), the relationship between intellectual ability and performance appears to depend upon the compactness of the long-term memory representation. Performance on other tasks (like continuous paired-associates, which is assumed to reflect the ability to update and monitor working memory) may, in contrast, reflect abilities that are not dependent on characteristics of the long-term memory representations: Regardless of type of stimulus, the mathematically talented performed at a higher level. The data clearly indicate the need for a more precisely developed models of both long-term memory and working memory. In this regard, the newer connectionist models with distributed representations may prove to be useful (e.g., McClelland & Rumelhart, 1985; Masson, 1990).

GIFTEDNESS FROM A NEUROPSYCHOLOGICAL PERSPECTIVE

In the prior section, we reviewed the literature on individual differences in basic information-processing abilities, what might be called mental "hardware." In this final section before the summary, we review the literature on individual differences in cerebral hemispheric asymmetry. This literature examines differences in cognitive functioning that derive from a biological perspective. In a sense, it is the literature on individual differences in biological "hardware," or "wetware."

The human brain is split into two parts, the left and right hemispheres, with the corpus callosum, a nerve fiber, connecting the two hemispheres and allowing them to communicate (Springer & Deutsch, 1985). Work with split-brain patients, individuals who have had the corpus callosum cut, and with clinical and nonclinical populations has revealed that the two hemispheres are specialized for different functions and processes. The left hemisphere is specialized for language production, is analytical and sequential in its processing of information, and is compartmentalized for the various modalities (Semrud-Clikeman & Hynd, 1990). The right hemisphere, on the other hand, is specialized for nonverbal abilities (e.g., spatial ability or judging emotions) and the distribution of attention across space (e.g., Kosslyn, 1987), is more holistic in its processing of information, and integrates information across modalities.

Although it has been suggested that there are independent streams of consciousness in each hemisphere (Sperry, 1966), in normal cognitive functioning the right and left hemisphere appear to work together so that the dichotomies presented above are not that clear-cut (Hellige, 1990). For example, the right hemisphere aids in verbal comprehension and in the understanding of humor, as well as in other aspects of language (Gardner, Brownell, Wapner, & Michelow, 1983).

Recent evidence suggests that individual differences in hemispheric asymmetry might be related to individual differences in cognitive ability and style, as well as in social skills (e.g., Benbow, 1986; Hellige, 1990; Lewis & Harris, 1988, 1990; O'Boyle & Benbow, 1990b; O'Boyle & Hellige, 1989; Semrud-Clikeman & Hynd, 1990). Specifically, the relationship between patterns of brain organization and individual differences in cognitive ability can be found in the literatures on dyslexia (for a review see O'Boyle & Hellige, 1989; Hynd & Semrud-Clikeman, 1989), gender differences (e.g., McGlone, 1978, 1980), and nonverbal forms of learning disabilities (e.g., difficulties with social skills, prosody, spatial orientation, problem solving and the recognition of nonverbal cues—Semrud-Clikeman & Hynd, 1990).

A rather recent development in the brain/individual differences literature concerns the intellectually gifted. Intellectually precocious children have been found to be more frequently left-handed than their parents and siblings, average-ability students, and the modestly gifted (Benbow, 1986; Benbow & Benbow, 1984).[3] Benbow and Benbow (1984) and Benbow (1986), therefore, proposed that bilaterality or enhanced right hemispheric functioning may be associated with extreme intellectual precocity. (The specialization of cognitive functions in the right and left hemispheres tend to be more diffuse in left than right handers—Bradshaw & Nettleton, 1983.)

---

[3] A recent newsflash in *Science News* ("Doubt cast," 1990) reported that the results of a new study by Wiley and Goldstein at Duke University had cast doubt on our findings of increased left-handedness among extremely precocious youth. The study, however, was seriously flawed. The sample size was too small to examine a characteristic occurring in 7%–10% of the general population. It is also not clear that they used an appropriate control group.

Benbow and Benbow (1987) presented data from the visual domain that were consistent with such a view. The data were obtained by simulating, via a computer, tachistoscopic presentation of stimuli (verbal and spatial) to each visual field and measuring response times. O'Boyle and Benbow (1990a) explored the idea further. Intellectually gifted and average-ability subjects (12- to 14-year-olds) performed a verbal dichotic listening task (Hellige & Wong, 1983) and a free-vision chimeric face task (Levy, Heller, Banich, & Burton, 1983a,b). As expected from the literature, average-ability students showed a right ear/left hemispheric advantage for the ostensibly verbal dichotic listening task, while for the chimeric face task (a task involving the judging of emotions), they showed the expected right hemisphere bias. The intellectually gifted subjects exhibited a different pattern, however. Gifted subjects failed to show the usual left hemisphere advantage in dichotic listening; that is, both hemispheres were equally effective in dealing with the linguistic stimuli. (Parenthetically, Hunt et al., 1975, found a similar trend among their high-verbal college students.) In the free-vision chimeric face task, the gifted youth also exhibited a right hemisphere bias, but the bias was appreciably stronger by a magnitude of four. Most interesting was the finding that the higher the SAT score, the greater the right hemispheric bias in the gifted group.

O'Boyle and Benbow (1990a) concluded that the results were consistent with the view that the right hemisphere of the intellectually precocious may be particularly engaged during cognitive processing. Support for this controversial hypothesis was subsequently obtained in a study examining differences at the physiological level. O'Boyle, Alexander, and Benbow (1991) conducted a preliminary electroencephalographic (EEG) investigation to determine if the pattern of hemispheric activation characterizing mathematically precocious boys is different from that of average-ability boys. Alpha activity at four brain sites was monitored.

At baseline (looking at a blank slide) the left hemisphere of the precocious boys was more active than that of the average-ability boys. In the chimeric face task there was a switch, and the right hemisphere was markedly more active than the left among the mathematically gifted boys, while the left hemisphere was somewhat more active among average-ability boys. In a verbal task (noun/verb determination), the right hemisphere was again somewhat more active than the left in the mathematically gifted boys, with the opposite pattern found for the average-ability boys. Thus, the electrophysiological data corroborate, in principle, the behavioral findings of O'Boyle and Benbow (1990a). Although limited to boys and to mathematical giftedness, the results support the hypothesis that enhanced right hemisphere processing is a correlate in intellectual precocity.

In this context, it is interesting to note that some of the characteristics used to describe intellectually talented students (see Parke, 1989) are also thought to characterize the cognitive functions or contributions of the right hemisphere (e.g., see things holistically, deep comprehension, advanced moral reasoning, and humor). Similarly, the suggestion of the cognitive components literature that gifted individual are better at handling novel tasks fits the hypothesis: The right hemisphere is thought to be better at dealing with novelty than the left hemisphere (Semrud-Clikeman & Hynd, 1990).

Conclusions from the Neuropsychological Perspective

In summary, there is evidence that the organization of cognitive functions within the left and right hemispheres in the intellectually precocious differs from individuals with average abilities. The intellectually precocious exhibit enhanced right hemispheric functioning. Is this difference a quantitative or qualitative difference? For tasks in which a right hemisphere bias is expected, the difference can be seen as one of degree. College students show more right bias on the chimeric faces task than do children. Thus, the right bias is developmentally more mature. The same cannot be said for the lack of a left hemisphere bias on the verbal tasks, however. College students show a left bias, just as do average-ability youth.

The ontogeny of the difference in brain organization between gifted and average-ability youth cannot be determined from our data. It would be interesting, however, to see if any of the cognitive processing attributes that characterize the gifted can in some way be explained by their different organization of functions within the two cerebral hemispheres. Of specific interest would be differences that vary with specific ability and/or with gender. That is a future direction of our research.

GENERAL CONCLUSIONS

We have reviewed an extremely wide range of studies addressing giftedness from four different perspectives and have indicated conclusions that can be drawn from each perspective. On the basis of our review, there is one conclusion that is clearly evident from all perspectives except, perhaps, the neuropsychological perspective: The differences between gifted and average individuals are quantitative rather than qualitative. In the individual conclusions we stated that: (a) gifted performance is described by the same factor structure on psychometric tests, (b) gifted youth appear to use more mature strategies in solving problems, and (c) gifted youth are faster and more accurate on very simple tasks.

Although others have pointed out that giftedness is the result of quantitative differences (e.g., Jackson & Butterfield, 1986), it is not a universally accepted generalization (e.g., Shore & Dover, 1987; Sternberg, 1981). One might argue, for example, that strategy differences between gifted and average-ability children are qualitative. We would agree, except for the additional finding that the strategies employed by gifted youth are similar to those of older individuals.

The difference in strategies is better viewed as a difference in maturity: Gifted children seem to be developmentally precocious.

The data of Keating and Schaefer (1975) clarify what we mean. Gifted children are likely to differ from average-ability children of the same age in terms of Piagetian stage of development. Yet, they do follow the same sequence of stages, but at a faster rate—they are precocious, not qualitatively different. Our own data comparing college students, gifted youth, and average-ability youth corroborate the "precocity" argument. The performance of gifted youth was more similar on all tasks to the college students than the average-ability, age-level peers.

Another generalization that we would like to make is derived from two of the perspectives. The psychometric and cognitive correlate perspectives both supported the distinction between mathematical and verbal talent. Different psychometric tests contribute to the definition of mathematical and verbal giftedness: Mathematical talent is psychometrically related to spatial and nonverbal reasoning, memory, and speed, whereas verbal talent is psycho-metrically related to general knowledge and vocabulary (Benbow & Minor, 1990). Moreover, individuals psychometrically defined as verbally talented versus mathematically talented show different patterns of performance on very simple information-processing tasks: Mathematical talent is associated with enhanced ability to maintain and update information in working memory, with enhanced digit span, and with faster encoding of digits from long-term memory to working memory; verbal talent is associated with enhanced word span and with faster encoding of words from long-term memory.

The fact that enhanced span and speed of encoding are stimulus dependent suggests differences in the efficiency (or compactness) of the stimulus representations as a function of talent. This is an intriguing finding, especially because digits and words are very familiar to essentially all individuals. Perhaps in the future we will be able to determine how/why such differences develop.

In another vein, our literature review suggests that, as a result of domain-specific knowledge, experts and novices differ in how they form problem representations. Our own work, however, suggested that the mathematically and verbally talented comprehend story problems in a similar fashion, but that the mathematically talented *are* better at generating equations representing complex relationships. If generating complex equations requires active manipulation of digit representations in working memory, then the cognitive components data fit nicely with the cognitive correlates data.

Mentioned up to this point are differences in information-processing characteristics between gifted and average-ability students. There may also be differences in their biological hardware. It appears that intellectual precocity is associated with enhanced right hemisphere functioning. Intellectually precocious children do *not* show a left hemisphere bias in at least some verbal tasks (dichotic listening) and they show an extreme right hemisphere bias on some nonverbal tasks (chimeric faces). EEG research shows a similar pattern, but that research has so far been limited to mathematically precocious boys. Thus, differences between mathematical and verbal talent cannot be addressed at present.

Our generalizations thus far have been descriptive. Are there any practical conclusions to be drawn from our review of the literature? We believe that there are some. Research from the cognitive components perspective has not focused on giftedness per se as much as on skilled versus unskilled learning. As a result, it provides the most practical information: Skilled performers use different strategies in solving problems. How and why the different strategies develop is not clear; but expert strategies *can* be identified, and, more importantly, others can be trained in their use. Such training has been shown to be helpful (e.g., Davidson, 1986; Sternberg, 1986; cf. Romberg & Carpenter, 1986).

In conclusion, this volume is intended to highlight the contribution of research with various specific populations to the understanding of intelligence and cognition in general. The generalizations outlined above illustrate what, in our opinion, we have learned. The "knowledge" that we have gained is mostly descriptive, however. From our examination of individuals at the high end of the distribution, we have gleaned a better description of the characteristics associated with various abilities. But we have yet to gain insight into the how and the why. How is it that mathematically talented youth are better able to update associations in working memory? Why are the representations of words more compact for the verbally talented? Why do intellectually precocious children show enhanced functioning of the right hemisphere? Which, if either, came first, the talent or the processing difference? We have asserted that gifted youth are not qualitatively different from average-ability youth, but is that true for adults? Is there a qualitatively different stage of reasoning that gifted adults attain that is not attained by the average-ability adult (cf. Arlin, 1975)? These are important questions that may or may not be answerable by further research. We will, however, assume that they are and continue our investigations.

REFERENCES

Anderson, J.R. (1983). *The architecture of cognition.* Cambridge, MA: Harvard University Press.
Arlin, P.K. (1975). Cognitive development in adulthood: A fifth stage. *Developmental Psychology, 11*, 602–606.
Atkinson, R.C., & Shiffrin, R.M. (1968). Human memory: A proposed system and its control processes. In K.W. Spence & J.T. Spence (Eds.), *The Psychology of learning and motivation: Advances in research and theory* (Vol. 2, pp. 89–195). New York: Academic Press.
Bachelder, B.L., & Denny, M.R. (1977a). A theory of intelligence: I. Span and the complexity of stimulus control. *Intelligence, 1*, 127–150.

Bachelder, B.L., & Denny, M.R. (1977b). A theory of intelligence: II. The role of span in a variety of intellectual tasks. *Intelligence, 1*, 237–256.

Baddeley, A.D. (1986). *Working memory*. Oxford: Clarendon Press.

Baddeley, A.D., & Hitch, G. (1974). Working memory. In G. Bower (Ed.), *Recent advances in learning and motivation* (pp. 47–89). London: Academic Press.

Benbow, C.P. (1986). Physiological correlates of extreme intellectual precocity. *Neuropsychologia, 24*, 719–725.

Benbow, C.P. (1988). Neuropsychological perspectives on mathematical talent. In L.K. Obler & D. Fein (Eds.), *The exceptional brain: Neuropsychology of talent and special abilities* (pp. 48–69). New York: Gilford Press.

Benbow, C.P., & Benbow, R.M. (1984). Biological correlates of high mathematical reading ability. *Progress in Brain Research, 61*, 469–490.

Benbow, C.P., & Benbow, R.M. (1987). Extreme mathematical talent: Hormonal induced ability? In D. Ottoson (Ed.), *Duality and unity of the brain* (pp. 147–157). New York: MacMillan.

Benbow, C.P., & Minor, L.L. (1990). Cognitive profiles of verbally and mathematically precocious students: Implications for identification of the gifted. *Gifted Child Quarterly, 34*, 21–26.

Benbow, C.P., Napolski, A.J., & Glass, L.W. (1990). CY-TAG (Challenges for Youth-Talented and Gifted): An opportunity offered by SMPY and Iowa State University. *Illinois Council of Gifted Journal, 9*, 1–3.

Benbow, C.P., & Stanley, J.C. (1980). Sex differences in mathematical ability: Fact or artifact? *Science, 210*, 1262–1264.

Benbow, C.P., & Stanley, J.C. (1981). Mathematical ability: Is sex a factor? *Science, 212*, 118–119.

Benbow, C.P., & Stanley, J.C. (1983). Sex differences in mathematical reasoning ability: More facts. *Science, 222*, 1029–1031.

Benbow, C.P., Stanley, J.C., Zonderman, A.B., & Kirk, M.K. (1983). Structure of intelligence in intellectually precocious individuals and their parents. *Intelligence, 7*, 129–152.

Berk, L.A. (1989). *Child development*. Boston, MA: Allyn & Bacon.

Borkowski, J.G., & Peck, V.A. (1986). Causes and consequences of metamemory in gifted children. In R.J. Sternberg & J.E. Davidson (Eds.), *Conceptions of giftedness* (pp. 182–200). Cambridge, UK: Cambridge University Press.

Bradshaw, J.L., & Nettleton, N.C. (1983). *Human cerebral asymmetry*. Englewood Cliffs, NJ: Prentice-Hall.

Burnett, S.A., Lane, D.M., & Dratt, L.M. (1979). Spatial visualization and sex differences in quantitative ability. *Intelligence, 3*, 345–354.

Campione, J.C., & Brown, A.L. (1978). Toward a theory of intelligence: Contributions from research with retarded children. *Intelligence, 2*, 279–304.

Carr, T.H. (1981). Building theories of reading ability: On the relation between individual differences and cognitive skills and reading comprehension. *Cognition, 9*, 73–114.

Carroll, J.B. (1989). Factor analysis since Spearman: Where do we stand? What do we know? In R. Kanfer, P.L. Ackerman, & R. Cudeck (Eds.), *Abilities, motivation, and methodology* (pp. 43–67). Hillsdale, NJ: Erlbaum.

Clement, J., Lochhead, J., & Monk, G.S. (1980). Translation difficulties in learning mathematics. *American Mathematical Monthly, 88*, 286–290.

Charness, N. (1979). Components of skill in bridge. *Canadian Journal of Psychology, 33*, 1–50.

Chase, W.G., & Simon, H.A. (1973a). The mind's eye in chess. In W.G. Chase (Ed.), *Visual information processing* (pp. 215–281). New York: Academic Press.

Chase, W.G., & Simon, H.A. (1973b). Perception in chess. *Cognitive Psychology, 4*, 55–81.

Chi, M.T.H. (1978). Knowledge structures and memory development. In R.S. Siegler (Ed.), *Children's thinking: What develops?* (pp. 73–96). Hillsdale, NJ: Erlbaum.

Chi, M.T.H., Feltovich, P., & Glaser, R. (1981). Categorization and representation of physics problems by experts and novices. *Cognitive Science, 5*, 121–152.

Chi, M.T.H., Glaser, R., & Rees, E. (1982). Expertise in problem-solving. In R.J. Sternberg (Ed.), *Advances in the psychology of human intelligence* (Vol. 1, pp. 7–75). Hillsdale, NJ: Erlbaum.

Chiang, A., & Atkinson, R.C. (1976). Individual differences and interrelationships among a select set of cognitive skills. *Memory & Cognition, 4*, 661–672.

Chiesi, H., Spilich, G.J., & Voss, J.F. (1979). Acquisition of domain-related information in relation to high and low domain knowledge. *Journal of Verbal Learning and Verbal Behavior, 18*, 257–283.

Cohn, S.J., Carlson, J., & Jensen, A. (1985). Speed of information processing in academically gifted youth. *Personality and Individual Differences, 6*, 621–629.

Colangelo, N., & Kerr, B.A. (1990). Extreme academic talent: Profiles of perfect scores. *Journal of Educational Psychology, 82*, 404–409.

Collins, A.M., & Loftus, E.F. (1975). A spreading activation theory of semantic processing. *Psychological Review, 82*, 407–428.

Daneman, M., & Carpenter, P.A. (1980). Individual differences in working memory and reading. *Journal of Verbal Learning and Verbal Behavior, 19*, 450–466.

Dark, V.J., & Benbow, C.P. (1990). Enhanced problem translation and short-term memory: Components of mathematical talent. *Journal of Educational Psychology, 82*, 420–429.

Dark, V.J., & Benbow, C.P. (1991). Differential enhancement of working memory with mathematical versus precocity. *Journal of Educational Psychology, 83*, 48–60.

Das, J.P., & Siu, I. (1989). Good and poor readers' word naming time, memory span, and story recall. *The Journal of Experimental Education, 57*, 101–114.

Davidson, J.E. (1986). The role of insight in giftedness. In R.J. Sternberg & J.E. Davidson (Eds.), *Conceptions of giftedness* (pp. 201–222). Cambridge, UK: Cambridge University Press.

deGroot, A. (1965). *Thought and choice in chess*. The Hague: Mouton.

Dempster, F.N. (1981). Memory span: Sources of individual and developmental differences. *Psychological Bulletin, 89*, 63–100.

Dempster, F.N. (1985). Short-term memory development in childhood and adolescence. In C.J. Brainerd & M. Pressley (Eds.), *Basic processes in memory development* (pp. 208–248). New York: Springer—Verlag.

Donaldson, G. (1983). Confirmatory factor analysis models of information processing stages: An alternative to difference scores. *Psychological Bulletin, 94*, 143–151.

Donders, F.C. (1969). On the speed of mental processes (W.G. Koster, Trans.). *Acta Psychologica, 30*, 412–431. (Original work published 1868)

Doubt cast on biology of giftedness. (1990). *Science News, 138*, 124.

DuBois, P.H. (1932). A speed factor in mental tests. *Archives of Psychology, 141*, 5–38.

Egan, D.E., & Schwartz, B. (1979). Chunking in recall of symbolic drawings. *Memory & Cognition, 7*, 149–158.

Eisenstadt, M., & Kareev, Y. (1975). Aspects of human problem-solving: The use of internal representation. In D.A. Norman & D.E. Rumelhart (Eds.), *Explorations in cognition*. San Francisco: Freeman.

Eysenck, H.J., & Kamin, L. (1981). *The intelligence controversy*. New York: Wiley.

Feldhusen, J.F. (1989). Synthesis of research on gifted youth. *Educational Leadership, 46*, 6–11.

Feldhusen, J.F., & Kolloff, P.B. (1986). The Purdue Three-Stage Enrichment Model for Gifted Education at the elementary level. In J.S. Renzulli (Ed.), *Systems and models for developing programs for the gifted and talented* (pp. 126–152). Mansfield, CT: Creative Learning Press.

Foltz, G.S., & Poltrock, S.E. (1985). *Apple Pascal tester version II (APT II): An experiment development system* [Software manual]. Austin: TX: Authors.

Ford, M.E., & Keating, D.P. (1981). Developmental and individual differences in long-term memory retrieval: Process and organization. *Child Development, 52*, 234–241.

Gagne, F. (1985). Giftedness and talent. *Gifted Child Quarterly, 29*, 103–112.

Galton, F. (1869). *Hereditary genius*. London: Macmillon.

Gardner, H. (1983). *Frames of mind*. New York: Basic Books.

Gardner, H., Brownell, H.H., Wapner, W., & Michelow, D. (1983). The role of the right hemisphere n the processing of complex linguistic materials. In E. Perecman (Ed.), *Cognitive processing in the right hemisphere* (pp. 169–191). New York: Academic Press.

Gitomer, D.H., Curtis, M.E., Glaser, R., & Lensky, D.B. (1987). Processing differences as a function of item difficulty in verbal analogy performance. *Journal of Educational Psychology, 79*, 212–219.

Goldberg, R.A., Schwartz, S., & Stewart, M. (1977). Individual differences in cognitive processes. *Journal of Educational Psychology, 69*, 9–14.

Greeno, J.G. (1980). Trends in the theory of knowledge for problem-solving. In D.T. Tuma & F. Reif (Eds.), *Problem-solving and education: Issues in teaching and research*. Hillsdale, NJ: Erlbaum.

Grinder, R.E. (1985). The gifted in our midst: By their divine deeds, neuroses, and mental tests scores we have known them. In F.D. Horowitz & M. O'Brien (Eds.), *The gifted and talented: Developmental perspectives* (pp. 5–36). Washington, DC: American Psychological Association.

Guilford, J.P. (1967). *The nature of human intelligence*. New York: McGraw-Hill.

Harris, G.J., & Fleer, P.B. (1974). High speed memory scanning in mental retardates: Evidence for a central processing deficit. *Journal of Experimental Child Psychology, 17*, 452–459.

Hellige, J.B. (1990). Hemispheric asymmetry. *Annual Review of Psychology, 41*, 55–80.

Hellige, J.B., & Wong, T.M. (1983). Hemisphere-specific interference in dichotic listening: Task variables and individual differences. *Journal of Experimental Psychology: General, 112*, 218–239.

Hogaboam, T.W., & Pellegrino, J.W. (1978). Hunting for individual differences in cognitive processes: Verbal ability and semantic processing of pictures and words. *Memory & Cognition, 6*, 189–193.

Hollingworth, L.S. (1942). *Children above 180 IQ Stanford-Binet: Origin and development.* New York: World Book.

Horn, J.C., & Cattell, R.B. (1966). Refinement and test of the theory of fluid and crystallized ability intelligences. *Journal of Educational Psychology, 58*, 120–136.

Humphreys, L.G. (1962). The organization of human abilities. *American Psychologist, 17*, 475–483.

Hunt, E. (1978). Mechanics of verbal ability. *Psychological Review, 85*, 109–130.

Hunt, E. (1983). On the nature of intelligence. *Science, 219*, 141–146.

Hunt, E., Davidson, J., & Lansman, M. (1981). Individual differences in long-term memory access. *Memory & Cognition, 9*, 599–608.

Hunt, E.G., Frost, N., & Lunneborg, C.L. (1973). Individual differences in cognition: A new approach to intelligence. In G. Bower (Ed.), *Learning and motivation* (Vol. 7, pp. 87–122). New York: Academic Press.

Hunt, E., Lunneborg, C., & Lewis, J. (1975). What does it mean to be high verbal? *Cognitive Psychology, 7*, 181–193.

Hynd, G.W., & Semrud-Clikeman, M. (1989). Dyslexia and brain morphology. *Psychological Bulletin, 106*, 447–482.

Jackson, M.D. (1980). Further evidence for a relationship between memory access and reading ability. *Journal of Verbal Learning and Verbal Behavior, 19*, 683–694.

Jackson, M.D., & McClelland, J.L. (1979). Processing determinants of reading speed. *Journal of Experimental Psychology: General, 108*, 151–181.

Jackson, N.E., & Butterfield, E.C. (1986). A conception of giftedness designed to promote research. In R.J. Sternberg & J.E. Davidson (Eds.), *Conceptions of giftedness* (pp. 151–181). Cambridge, UK: Cambridge University Press.

Jackson, N.E., & Myers, M.G. (1982). Letter naming time, digit span, and precocious reading achievement. *Intelligence, 6*, 311–329.

Jeffries, R., Turner, A.T., Polson, P.G., & Atwood, M.E. (1981). Processes involved in designing software. In J.R. Anderson (Ed.), *Cognitive skills and their acquisition* (pp. 255–283). Hillsdale, NJ: Erlbaum.

Jensen, A.R. (1970). Hierarchical theories of mental ability. In B. Dockrell (Ed.), *On intelligence* (pp. 119–190). Toronto: Ontario Institute for Studies in Education.

Keating, D.P. (1984). The emperor's new clothes: The "new look" in intelligence research. In R.J. Sternberg (Ed.), *Advances in the psychology of human intelligence* (Vol. 2, pp. 1–46). Hillsdale, NJ: Erlbaum.

Keating, D.P., & Bobbitt, B.L. (1978). Individual and developmental differences in cognitive processing components of mental ability. *Child Development, 49*, 155–167.

Keating, D.P., & Schaefer, R.A. (1975). Ability and sex differences in the acquisition of formal operations. *Developmental Psychology, 11*, 531–532.

Kosslyn, S.H. (1987). Seeing and imagining in the cerebral hemispheres: A computational approach. *Psychological Review, 94*, 148–175.

Krutetskii, V.A. (1976). *The psychology of mathematical abilities in school children.* Chicago: University of Chicago Press.

Lansman, M., Donaldson, G., Hunt, E., & Yantis, S. (1982). Ability factors and cognitive processes. *Intelligence, 6*, 347–386.

Lavin, D.E. (1965). *The prediction of academic performance*. New York: Russel Sage.

Lesgold, A.M. (1984). Acquiring expertise. In J.R. Anderson & S.M. Kosslyn (Eds.), *Tutorials in learning and memory* (pp. 31–60). San Francisco: Freeman.

Levy, J., Heller, W., Banich, M., & Burton, L. (1983a). Are variations among right-handed individuals in perceptual asymmetries caused by characteristic arousal differences between the hemispheres? *Journal of Experimental Psychology: Human Perception and Performance, 9*, 329–359.

Levy, J., Heller, W., Banich, M., & Burton, L. (1983b). Asymmetry of perception in free-viewing of chimeric faces. *Brain and Cognition, 2*, 404–419.

Lewis, R.S., & Harris, L.J. (1988). The relationship between cerebral lateralization and cognitive ability: Suggested criteria for empirical tests. *Brain and Cognition, 8*, 275–290.

Lewis, R.S., & Harris, L.J. (1990). Handedness, sex and spatial ability. In S. Coren (Ed.), *Left-handedness: Behavioral implications and anomalies* (pp. 319–342). Amsterdam: North-Holland.

Lohman, D.F. (1989). Human intelligence: An introduction to advances in theory and research. *Review of Educational Research, 59*, 333–373.

Lubinski, D., & Humphreys, L.G. (1990). A broadly based analysis of mathematical giftedness. *Intelligence, 14*, 327–355.

MacLeod, C.M., Hunt, E.B., & Mathews, N.N. (1978). Individual differences in the verification of sentence-picture relationships. *Journal of Verbal Learning and Verbal Behavior, 17*, 493–507.

Masson, M.E.J. (1990). A distributed memory model of context effects in word identification. In D. Besner & G.W. Humphreys (Eds.), *Basic processes in reading: Visual word recognition* (pp. 233–263). Hillsdale, NJ: Erlbaum.

Mayer, R.E. (1982). Memory for algebra story problems. *Journal of Educational Psychology, 74*, 199–216.

McClelland, J.L., & Rumelhart, D.E. (1985). Distributed memory and the representation of general and specific information. *Journal of Experimental Psychology: General, 114*, 159–188.

McFarland, R.A. (1930). An experimental study of the relationship between speed and mental ability. *Journal of General Psychology, 3*, 67–97.

McGee, M.G. (1979). Human spatial abilities: Psychometric studies and environmental, genetic, hormonal, and neurological influences. *Psychological Bulletin, 86*, 889–918.

McGlone, J. (1978). Sex differences in functional brain asymmetry. *Cortex, 14*, 122–128.

McGlone, J. (1980). Sex differences in human brain activity: A critical review. *The Behavioral and Brain Sciences, 3*, 215–263.

McKeithen, K.B., Reitman, J.S., Rueter, H.H., & Hirtle, S. (1981). Knowledge organization and skilled differences in computer programming. *Cognitive Psychology, 13*, 307–325.

McNemar, Q. (1964). Lost: Our intelligence? Why? *American Psychologist, 19*, 871–882.

O'Boyle, M.W., Alexander, J., & Benbow, C.P. (1991). Enhanced right hemisphere activation in the mathematically precocious: A preliminary EEG investigation. *Brain and Cognition, 17*, 138–153.

O'Boyle, M.W., & Benbow, C.P. (1990a). Enhanced right hemisphere involvement during cognitive processing may relate to intellectual precocity. *Neuropsychologia, 28*, 211–216.

O'Boyle, M.W., & Benbow, C.P. (1990b). Handedness and its relationship to ability and talent. In S. Coren (Ed.), *Left-handedness* (pp. 343–372). North Holland: Elsevier.

O'Boyle, M.W., & Hellige, J.B. (1989). Hemispheric asymmetry and individual differences in cognition. *Learning and Individual Differences, 1,* 7–35.

Oden, M.H. (1968). The fulfillment of promise: 40 year follow up of the Terman gifted group. *Genetic Psychology Monographs, 17,* 3–93.

Paige, J.M., & Simon, H.A. (1966). Cognitive processes in solving algebra word problems. In B. Kleinmuntz (Ed.), *Problem solving* (pp. 51–148). New York: Wiley.

Palmer, J., MacLeod, C.M., Hunt, E., & Davidson, J.E. (1985). Information processing correlates of reading. *Journal of Memory and Language, 24,* 59–88.

Parke, B.N. (1989). *Gifted students in regular classrooms.* Boston, MA: Allyn & Bacon.

Pellegrino, J.W., & Glaser, R. (1979). Cognitive correlates and components in the analysis of individual differences. *Intelligence, 3,* 187–214.

Pollins, L.D. (1984). *The construct validity of the Scholastic Aptitude Test for young gifted students.* Unpublished doctoral dissertation, Duke University.

Posner, M.I., Boies, S.J., Eichelman, W.H., & Taylor, R.L. (1969). Retention of visual and name codes of single letters. *Journal of Experimental Psychology Monograph, 79,* 1–16.

Posner, M.I., & Mitchell, R. (1967). A chronometric analysis of classification. *Psychological Review, 74,* 392–409.

Pressley, M., Borkowski, J.G., & Sullivan, J.T. (1985). Children's metamemory and the teaching of memory strategies. In D.T. Forest-Pressley, D. Mackinnon, & T.G. Waller (Eds.), *Metacognition, cognition, and human performance.* San Diego, CA: Academic Press.

Rabinowitz, M., & Glaser, R. (1985). Cognitive structure and process in highly competent performance. In F.D. Horowitz & M. O'Brien (Eds.), *The gifted and talented: Developmental perspectives* (pp. 75–98). Washington, DC: American Psychological Association.

Reitman, J. (1976). Skilled perception in Go: Deducing memory structures from inter-response times. *Cognitive Psychology, 8,* 336–356.

Resnick, L.B. (1980). The role of invention in the development of mathematical competence. In H.R. Spuwe & H. Spada (Eds.), *Developmental models of thinking* (pp. 213–244). New York: Academic Press.

Romberg, T.A., & Carpenter, T.P. (1986). Research on teaching and learning mathematics: Two disciplines of scientific inquiry. In M.C. Wittrock (Ed.), *Handbook of research on teaching* (pp. 850–873). New York: MacMillan.

Schoenfeld, A.H. (1983). The wild, wild, wild, wild, wild world of problem-solving. *For the Learning of Mathematics, 3,* 40–47.

Schofield, N.J., & Ashman, A.F. (1986). The relationship between digit span and cognitive processing across ability groups. *Intelligence, 10,* 59–73.

Semrud-Clikeman, M., & Hynd, G.W. (1990). Right hemispheric dysfunction in nonverbal learning disabilities: Social, academic, and adaptive functioning in adults and children. *Psychological Bulletin, 107,* 196–209.

Shore, B.M., & Dover, A.C. (1987). Metacognition, intelligence, and giftedness. *Gifted Child Quarterly, 31,* 37–39.

Silver, E.A. (1979). Student perceptions of relatedness among mathematical verbal problems. *Journal for Research in Mathematics Education, 10*, 195–210.

Simon, D.P., & Simon, H.A. (1978). Individual differences in solving physics problems. In R. Siegler (Ed.), *Children's thinking: What develops?* (pp. 325–348). Hillsdale, NJ: Erlbaum.

Sloboda, J.A. (1976). Visual perception of musical notation. *Quarterly Journal of Experimental Psychology, 28*, 1–16.

Snow, R.E., & Yalow, E. (1982). Education and intelligence. In R.S. Sternberg (Ed.), *Handbook of human intelligence* (pp. 493–585). Cambridge, UK: Cambridge University Press.

Soloway, E., Lochhead, J., & Clement, J. (1982). Does computer programming enhance problem solving ability? Some positive evidence on algebra word problems. In R.J. Seidel, R.E. Anderson, & B. Hunter (Eds.), *Computer literacy* (pp. 171–185). New York: Academic Press.

Spearman, C. (1904). "General intelligence" objectively determined and measured. *Applied Journal of Psychology, 15*, 201–293.

Sperry, R.W. (1966). Brain bisection and consciousness. In J. Eccles (Ed.), *Brain and conscious experience* (pp. 298–313). New York: Springer-Verlag.

Spiegal, M.R., & Bryant, N.D. (1978). Is speed of processing information related to intelligence and achievement? *Journal of Educational Psychology, 70*, 904–910.

Springer, S.P., & Deutsch, G. (1985). *Left brain, right brain.* New York: Freeman.

Stanley, J.C. (1984). Use of general and specific aptitude measures in identification: Some principles and certain cautions. *Gifted Child Quarterly, 28*, 177–180.

Sternberg, R.J. (1981). A componential theory of intellectual giftedness. *Gifted Child Quarterly, 25*, 86–93.

Sternberg, R.J. (1982). Lies we live by: Misapplication of tests in identifying the gifted. *Gifted Child Quarterly, 26*, 156–161.

Sternberg, R.J. (1986). Triarchic theory of intellectual giftedness. In R.J. Sternberg & J.E. Davidson (Eds.), *Conceptions of giftedness* (pp. 223–243). Cambridge, UK: Cambridge University Press.

Sternberg, R.J., & Davidson, J. (1983). Insight in the gifted. *Educational Psychologist, 18*, 51–57.

Sternberg, S. (1965). High speed scanning in human memory. *Science, 153*, 652–654.

Terman, L.M. (1925). Mental and physical traits of a thousand gifted children. *Genetic studies of genius* (Vol. 1). Palo Alto: CA: Stanford University Press.

Terman, L.M., & Oden, M.H. (1947). The gifted child grows up: Twenty-five years follow-up of a superior group. *Genetic studies of genius* (Vol. 4). Palo Alto, CA: Stanford University Press.

Thorndike, R.L. (1986). The role of general ability in prediction. *Journal of Vocational Behavior, 29*, 332–339.

Thurstone, L.L. (1937). Ability, motivation, and speed. *Psychometrika, 2*, 249–254.

Thurstone, L.L. (1938). *Primary mental abilities.* Chicago: University of Chicago Press.

Tyler, L. (1986). Back to Spearman? *Journal of Vocational Behavior, 29*, 445–450.

Vernon, P.E. (1950). *The structure of human abilities.* London: Methucn.

Voss, J.F., Fincher-Kiefer, R.H., Greene, T.R., & Post, T.A. (1986). Individual differences in performance: The contrastive approach to knowledge. In R.J. Sternberg (Ed.), *Advances in the psychology of human intelligence* (Vol. 3, pp. 297–334). Hillsdale, NJ: Erlbaum.

Wechsler, D. (1974). *Manual for the Wechsler Intelligence Scale for Children—Revised.* New York: The Psychological Corporation.

Chapter 5

Individual Differences in Cognition Among Learning Disabled Children: Intelligence, Memory, Perception, and Language

Lynne V. Feagans
Ann Merriwether

In a recent review on individual differences, Richard Snow (1986) commented:

> Individual differences among students present a pervasive and profound problem to educators. At the outset of instruction in any topic, students of any age and in any culture will differ from one another in various intellectual and psychomotor abilities and skills in both general and specialized prior knowledge, interest and motives, and in personal styles of thought and work during learning. These differences in turn, appear directly related to differences in the students' learning progress. (p. 1029)

This statement is particularly true for learning disabled children, because the overriding characteristic of their learning profile is variable performance within children across different academic areas as well as variability across children in their performance in different areas. Although almost every article on learning disabilities comments on this heterogeneity within and across children, most of the research has focused on the examination of differences between normal and learning disabled children (Feagans & McKinney, 1991).

The following review will try to exclude research that only documents group differences and instead focus on research that helps us to understand the variability among learning disabled children with respect to their cognitive abilities. Research on both intra- and interindividual differences will be reviewed with some attention to the few longitudinal studies that address whether these intra- and interindividual differences are stable over time.

There are many facets of cognition that could be examined. This chapter will focus on four major aspects of cognition that have been particularly important in understanding the functioning of learning disabled children. These characteristics have been linked to the academic problems that learning disabled children have, and most studies have found that learning disabled children, as a whole, do not perform as well as normally achieving children on the measures that tap these cognitive processes. Although these group differences are interesting, it is more important to understand what proportion of learning disabled children have poorer performance on the cognitive components and whether their performance is stable over time.

INTELLIGENCE

IQ Tests

Although many if not all of the cognitive abilities to be discussed in this chapter could fit under the rubric of *intelligence,* this section will be restricted to the use of intelligence as measured by standardized IQ tests. Since learning disabilities are most often identified as a discrepancy between IQ and Achievement (Braden & Weiss, 1988), and because, initially, scatter among the subtests of intelligence tests was used to diagnose learning disabilities (Bannatyne, 1974), the use of intelligence tests has been central to diagnosis and remediation strategies. Although it was originally thought that most learning disabled children had average to above-average intelligence, as measured by IQ tests, recent research has found that, although some learning disabled children score well on intelligence tests, the usual LD child scores from 5 to 10 points below average (Feagans & McKinney, 1981).

The focus on subtest scatter of IQ tests has been widely used since the inception of standardized IQ tests, especially the Wechsler Intelligence Scales for Children (Wechsler, 1974). Wechsler (1958) himself suggested that spread between the lowest and highest subtest scores might indicate particular problems. It was thought that an exaggerated pattern of strengths and weaknesses across the subtests of the Wechsler scales may suggest an uneven pattern of development, one of the hallmarks of a learning disability (Gallagher, 1966). For instance, Bannatyne (1974) categorized the subtests on the WISC-R into four groupings, representing spatial ability, verbal conceptualization ability, sequencing ability, and acquired knowledge. Especially important for Bannatyne was the poor performance of learning disabled children on sequencing ability, which was believed to be central to the problems of many learning disabled children. Although clinically many IQ tests have been used in this way, there is little evidence that patterns of performance across subtests of an IQ test predict learning disabilities (Bryan & Bryan, 1978; Feagans & McKinney, 1981).

A number of other studies that have merely examined the pattern of performance across subtests on IQ have indicated that the pattern of performance by normal and learning disabled children is remarkably similar (Huelsman, 1970; Kender, 1972). In one study of WISC-R performance (Feagans & McKinney, 1981), the authors examined 58 learning disabled and 58 normally achieving first-, second-, and third-grade children. Overall, the LD children performed more poorly than normally achieving children, but profile analysis indicated that the pattern of scores was remarkably similar. Two other common indices of subtest scatter were employed. One index was a 15-point discrepancy between verbal and performance IQ (Black, 1974; Holroyd & Wright, 1965). Eight LD and 13 non-LD students had discrepancies of this magnitude or greater. Another common index of scatter is the difference between the highest and lowest scale scores earned on the subtests of the WISC-R (Kaufman, 1976). The mean discrepancy scale scores for LD and non-LD children was the same at about 7.5. This was very similar to the average discrepancy found in a large population of 2200 children on the WISC-R (Kaufman, 1976). A statistical test of variability among within-cell variances (O'Brien, 1978) revealed that LD children were actually more homogeneous with less variability than normally achieving students.

Richman (1983) examined whether a discrepancy between verbal and performance IQ would predict reading problems. He studied 88 children who had a verbal IQ at least 15 points below their performance IQ. Only with the addition of a more process-related test was he able to identify children with reading problems. A further study supported these results with 75 children. Many of these children with low verbal IQ obtained excellent reading scores. Richman concludes, "Although many children with a verbal deficit do display reading disability, the present results indicate that a considerable proportion of these children read at or above grade level. Diagnostic interpretation of WISC Verbal, Performance, or Full Scale IQs for LV/HP children can be a misleading index of reading expectations. . . . Thus, the results suggest caution in the use of the verbal-performance discrepancy for providing reading expectations of individual children" (p. 99).

In summary, although there has been an attempt to understand individual differences among LD children and between LD and normally achieving children, only consistent mean differences in IQ level have been systematically found. The examination of subtest scatter within IQ tests has not produced major differences between normal and learning disabled children. More process-oriented approaches to intelligence have recently been pursued and may offer more promising information about the cognitive abilities of learning disabled children.

Alternative Views of Intelligence

In contrast to the psychometric view of intelligence, some theorists have proposed very different approaches to defining and understanding intelligence. Gardner (1983) has attempted to redefine current conceptions of intelligence by discarding the notion of an underlying general intelligence and replacing this with a framework consisting of a number of relatively independent multiple intelligences. Gardner (1983) defines *intelligence* as "the ability to solve problems, or create products, that are valued within one or more cultural settings" (p. X). Gardner outlines a specific set of criteria for establishing the existence of an intelligence and then goes on to describe seven intelligences.

The first two intelligences Gardner (1983) describes are related to but not completely dependent on the oral and auditory capabilities. The first intelligence Gardner (1983) discusses is linguistic. He suggests that the core operations of linguistic intelligence include a sensitivity to: the meaning of words, to word order, and even to the "sounds, rhythms, inflections, and meters of words" (p. 177). He also describes the way language is most generally used such as rhetorically, to recall information, to explain concepts, and actually to use language to reflect back on language. This kind of intelligence seems quite central to some of the problems learning disabled children have and will be discussed in the language section of this chapter. The second intelligence Gardner describes is musical intelligence. The components that make up musical intelligence include rhythm, pitch, and timbre.

Gardner (1983) identifies three intelligences as being related to the manipulation of objects in the environment. The first is logical mathematical intelligence, which is modeled after the theoretical framework of Piaget. Children, according to Piaget, acquire knowledge through acting on the world. Through their actions and interactions with the world children acquire such concepts as object permanence (the knowledge that objects continue to exist even when one cannot see them). Children progress through a series of stages, acquiring the ability to internalize their actions on the world, and ultimately acquiring the ability to reason about the hypothetical and test hypotheses of logical mathematical concepts. The second object-related intelligence is spatial intelligence. According to Gardner (1983), the following capabilities are important to spatial intelligence: "to perceive the visual world accurately, to perform transformations and modifications upon one's initial perceptions, and to be able to recreate aspects of one's visual experience, even in the absence of relevant physical stimuli" (p. 239). Again, this kind of intelligence has been implicated in learning disabilities. The third object related intelligence is bodily kinesthetic intelligence, which includes components like control of fine and gross motor skills, a sense of timing, and the ability to manipulate objects.

Finally, Gardner (1983) outlines the personal intelligences. This description includes both *intrapersonal intelligence,* which is knowledge about one's own internal emotional state, and *interpersonal intelligence,* which is knowledge of, and the ability to predict, other people's desires, moods, and intentions.

Gardner's (1983) framework offers an alternative to the traditional view of intelligence applied to the study of LD children. Recent research on subtypes of LD children has focused on the heterogeneous nature of the LD population. A model of intelligence based on the idea of multiple intelligences rather than a single general intelligence would seem to be more consistent with the current view of heterogeneous subtypes of LD children.

Another alternative to the psychometric approach is that of Sternberg (1984). Sternberg has developed a triarchic theory of intelligence made up of three subtheories. The first subtheory is contextual intelligence, viewed within its naturally occurring setting. Thus ability is characterized by handling everyday problems in the context of everyday living. The second subtheory is described by Sternberg as two-faceted. It involves the ability to handle novelty in both understanding an unfamiliar task and then completing that task. The second facet is concerned with the ability to automatize information processing. Information processing consists of *executive processes,* which are global processes involved in planning, monitoring, and revising information-processing strategies. There are also *automatic processes,* which do not require conscious attention and resources. Automatic processes are local rather than global and deal with very familiar tasks. Novel tasks require global executive processes, but as expertise develops tasks can be processed locally by automatic processes. The third subtheory is componential. Sternberg's (1984) description of a *component* is "an elementary information process that operates on an internal representation of objects or symbols" (p. 281). Sternberg (1984) describes three types of components. *Metacomponents* are described as executive components responsible for planning monitoring and decision making. Metacomponents direct the other types of components. *Performance components* are responsible for executing tasks such as encoding information and making a response. *Knowledge acquisition components* are involved in learning new information. Knowledge acquisition components are involved in selective encoding, which is described as encoding only relevant stimuli and disregarding irrelevant stimuli. Knowledge acquisition components are also involved in combining information selectively and comparing new information to existing information.

Sternberg and Wagner (1982) have applied this framework to a discussion of learning disabled children. Sternberg and Wagner suggested that learning disabled children may experience problems in automatization of information-processing components, particularly in the area of phonetic encoding. Sternberg and Wagner suggest that, over the normal course of reading development, information processing becomes more automatic and requires less attention and information processing resources. Learning disabled children experience a failure in this automatization process, and for them, reading is a task that requires a great deal of attention and information-processing resources. Sternberg and Wagner compare their position with other views of learning disability and acknowledge that their view is in conflict with the position of Ceci. Briefly, Ceci (1983) believes learning disabled children do not have problems with automatic processing but with purposive processing (Ceci's work will be discussed later in this chapter).

Intelligence viewed as Sternberg (1984) and Gardner (1983) view it is more compatible with the view that learning disabled children exhibit a pattern of strengths and weaknesses that are more conceptually based and less based on psychometrically designed subtests of an overall intelligence. Further work in this area is needed before its usefulness in conceptualizing the individual differences between and within LD children is validated.

MEMORY

Memory certainly can be considered a part of intelligence as conceived in many theories of intelligence. It will be separated out in this review because memory deficits have received much attention in the literature on learning disabilities. There is still controversy about the kind of memory problems that children with learning disabilities exhibit. This is probably the case because most researchers have studied one kind of memory problem without assessing other possible problems or the researchers have focused on a particular type of LD child, thus excluding children with different kinds of memory deficits. A number of major theoretical approaches have dominated the research on memory is learning disabilities. Each will be reviewed briefly, and then the little research on multimemory problems will be presented.

Strategy Deficits

The original work by Atkinson and Shiffrin (1968) made a distinction between *memory structures,* such as the sensory register, short-term memory and long term memory; and *control processes,* such as rehearsal and categorization, which were considered strategies for remembering. This kind of conceptualization of memory was also embodied in the work of Flavell (Flavell, Beach, & Chinsky, 1966), who distinguished between competence and performance in memory ability. According to these researchers some children exhibited a production deficiency because they were unable to use their underlying ability due to possible performance and strategy parameters. It has been demonstrated by a number of researchers that many LD children do not have problems in memory structure but do have problems with control processes or have a production deficiency (Torgesen, 1977; Torgesen & Goldman, 1977; Wong, 1980). This hypothesis that learning disabled children are "inactive learners" and do not spontaneously use strategies has been a compelling explanation for many of the performance deficits exhibited by learning disabled children.

The original research on strategy demonstrated the utility of the approach, but most of the research concentrated on the monolithic learning disabled child who had a strategy problem. More recent work has focused on a more multidimensional approach to strategy deficits. Wong, Wong, and Foth (1977) examined the performance of good and poor readers, both with and without cues, for recall. The experimenters examined the effects of cues on the clustering behavior of the children as well as whether time affected performance. Fourth- and fifth-grade poor and good readers were used in the study. The procedure involved four conditions. In the cued condition subjects were told at the time of presentation that a list of words could be categorized and that they were to recall them by category. For the no-cue condition, subjects were not told about category or to recall the words in any way. In the timed condition, subjects were given 90 seconds to learn the words, while in the untimed condition they were given a maximum of 180 seconds to learn the words. Study behavior during the learning period was observed for signs of self-testing, grouping, and verbalization.

The results of the study (Wong et al., 1977) indicated that good readers recalled more in both and cued/timed and cued/untimed conditions than did the poor readers in either condition. Good readers also verbalized more than poor readers during the learning period. When compared to the poor readers, good readers also spontaneously clustered items more frequently in the no-cue conditions. The experimenters concluded that poor readers have problems using verbal rehearsal. Good readers were able to use their study time to rehearse the items verbally, while poor readers seemed to have difficulty using such a strategy. Wong et al. intentionally eliminated subjects who scored poorly on the digit span of the WISC. The experimenters felt subjects with poor memory span would confound the results of a study designed to investigate memory organization. However, by eliminating subjects in this way, important subgroups may have been underrepresented in the study. Thus, this research may not be completely representative of the heterogeneous population of learning disabled children.

In a related study, Wong (1977) showed that, when items were not easily categorized, many of the differences between good and poor readers disappeared. Using an identical procedure Wong instead chose words that did not clearly fall into categories. Again, the subjects were good and poor readers in the fourth and fifth grades. The results indicated no differences between groups on recall scores or clustering in the cued conditions, and no differences in study behaviors between groups. Wong noted that, when the benefit of using easily categorized words is eliminated, strategy use by good readers was not as effective and differences between groups were reduced. Because there were no differences in the basic memory capabilities of the two groups, some other factor such as knowledge about strategy was influencing task performance. Since group differences essentially disappeared under conditions where effective strategy use was diminished, Wong interpreted these results as supporting a performance/production deficit, as originally suggested by Flavell et al. (1966).

Torgesen (1977) also suggested a performance explanation of memory deficits in reading disabled children by characterizing these children as "inactive learners." Torgesen examined category recall and ordered recall for reading disabled and normally achieving children (with a mean age of approximately 9 years). The stimuli in the category recall condition were pictures of common objects divided evenly into four categories. The stimuli in the ordered recall condition were pictures of common objects. Children were first familiarized with the category recall task. Then, on each trial, they were presented with an array of pictures and allowed to study them for a specific period. Following the study period, there was a free recall task. On the ordered recall task, the children were again familiarized with the task, after which they were allowed to study the pictures. Following this study period the children were required to recall the pictures in the order of presentation. During the practice trial of the second session the children were trained in recall strategies. For the category recall, they were taught how to group the pictures and how to use self-testing. For the ordered recall, they were instructed in cumulative rehearsal. Study behavior during all learning periods was observed for evidence of clustering, self-testing, verbalization, and off-task behavior.

Results on the uninstructed condition indicated significant differences favoring good readers on both category and ordered recall; clustering during the learning period, but not during the recall period; and the amount of verbalization. However, in the instructed condition, no significant differences arose between poor and good readers on either category or ordered recall. Furthermore, study behavior in the instructed condition improved for both groups with a very significant reduction in off-task behavior for the poor readers. Again, a production deficiency was implicated by Torgesen in his conclusions: "I suggest that a third variable, the efficient and organized management of cognitive resources, can be a crucial factor contributing to individual differences on both experimental memory tasks and the attainment of reading skills" (Torgesen, 1977, p. 577).

More recent research has demonstrated that memory deficits experienced by LD children may not be the result of a simple strategy problem like self-verbalization, but in fact are the result of more complex interactions. In subsequent research, Wong (1980) showed that LD children have problems making inferences and using implied information as an aid in recall. In the first of two studies, second- and sixth-grade LD and normally achieving children were presented stimuli under two conditions: explicit and implicit. In the explicit condition the stimuli were read to the children and contained sentences with consequences. In the implicit condition the sentences were the same, but the consequences were not read. An example was a sentence like: "My brother fell down on the playground (and skinned his knee)" (Wong, 1980, p. 31). In recall, subjects were cued with the consequence and one word from the sentence (like playground). While the results indicated no between-group differences in the explicit condition, normal children recalled more sentences in the implicit condition than did LD children, again suggesting no underlying differences in memory capacity.

Wong (1980) conducted a second experiment to examine the possibility that the difference in the implicit condition could be reduced if LD children were made aware of the implied information. In this study, second- and sixth-grade children identified as LD were tested. While no explicit condition was employed, the implicit condition was altered, so that subjects were required to generate the implicit consequence for each sentence during presentation. The recall scores of these subjects were significantly higher when compared with the scores in the implicit condition of the LD subjects in the first experiment.

Wong (1982) further demonstrated that LD children differ from normal and gifted children on cue selection to aid in recall. In this experiment, subjects were gifted LD and normally achieving children. The subjects were given cards with a Japanese folktale divided into separate ideas. Subjects were instructed to select 12 cues which they thought would aid them in recall of the story. There were two conditions: experience in recall (children recalled the stimuli once), and no experience in recall. The results showed that all children who were in the experience group chose cues that were judged to be more salient. The most interesting differences suggested that LD children were less exhaustive in their checking behavior and used self-checking less than normal and gifted subjects.

These experiments (Wong, 1980, 1982) demonstrated that LD children have other strategy problems in recall tasks. Wong (1980) showed that LD children did not use implied information as an aid in recall and were not proficient at selecting cues to aid in later recall (Wong, 1982). The results of both of these experiments were particularly important, because both used recall tasks that were more realistic than those commonly used in memory experiments.

Unfortunately, both experiments also indicated that the memory problems of LD children were not limited to a single strategy but encompassed a number of limitations on access and use of strategic devices.

Further studies have shown that very little instruction in the use of strategies can improve recall for learning disabled children. Torgesen and Goldman (1977) used an ordered recall task to examine study behaviors and recall scores in second grade poor and good readers. Each child was shown an array of pictures, and the experimenter pointed to them in succession. The child was required to point to the pictures in the same order in a new array after a 15-second interval. The results indicated that the normal reader group had higher scores and verbalized more than did the poor reader group. The task was then repeated, but subjects were required to name the pictures during presentation and during recall. The results showed significant improvements in the poor readers' scores and significantly more verbalization. Lewis and Kass (1982) used a similar experimental design with learning disabled and normally achieving children. They also found that simply requiring LD children to verbalize items to be recalled improved recall scores considerably so that they were indistinguishable from normally achieving children.

Additional Performance Factors that Affect Memory Performance

Another area of memory research that has focused on performance deficits has been Ceci's (1983, 1984) work on semantic processing. Ceci examined the semantic processing characteristics of normal and language/learning disabled children and postulated a two-process model of semantic processing. Ceci made a distinction between automatic semantic and purposive semantic processing. *Automatic semantic processing* was an unconscious spontaneous extraction of the meaning of the stimulus. *Purposive semantic processing* involved deliberate planned activity to encode information using the meaning of a stimulus. These two processes were similar to the last two subtheories of the Sternberg framework (Sternberg, 1984). Ceci conducted two studies of long-term memory to examine differences in automatic and purposive semantic processing between LD and normally achieving children.

The first study (Ceci, 1983) examined automatic and purposive processing of auditory stimuli with 10-year-old LD children, 4-year-old normal children, and 10-year-old normal children. Subjects were presented with a tape-recorded "prime" such as "Here is an animal," followed by a slide. For the related prime condition, the slide would be an animal, while for the unrelated prime stimuli the slide would be something other than an animal. There was also a neutral prime condition: "Here is something you know." The distribution of slides was set up to create two processing conditions: automatic or purposive. In automatic processing, 50% of the slides were neutral prime slide pairs. Of the remaining slides, 20% were related prime slides and 80% were unrelated prime slides. In the purposive processing condition, again 50% of the slides were neutral prime pairs, and of the remaining slide pairs 80% were related prime pairs and 20% were unrelated prime slide pairs. In the related condition the primes were thought to excite pathways of the nervous system unconsciously. This would result in time benefits. Reaction times across the three groups were compared. A cost/benefit analysis was conducted comparing reaction time across the three groups of subjects. This revealed that there were no differences in automatic processing. There were no costs to the unrelated primes, but there were time benefits to all groups on the related prime slide pairs. However, in the purposive condition, the normal 10-year-olds evidenced both costs and benefits, while the other two groups showed only a benefit pattern. Ceci interpreted this as evidence that the normal 10-year-olds were consciously attending to the primes as aids.

The second study in Ceci's (1983) experiment was added to compare the demands placed on working memory capacity by the two kinds of semantic processing. It was similar to the first study, except that, while responding to the slides, the subject had to press a button whenever a tone was heard. It was expected that this task would interfere with purposive processing but not with automatic processing. The same subjects were used and as expected the tone affected only the normal 10-year-olds in the purposive condition.

In a related study with a different methodology, Ceci (1984) again demon- strated differences in purposive semantic processing between LD and normally achieving children. Ceci presented 7-, 10-, and 13-year-old children with words arranged in ordered lists. Words in some positions were semantically related, while others were not. The results for the younger LD children indicated that automatic processing was stronger in recall than purposive processing. This same pattern was evident for the normal children but purposive processing began at an earlier age. Again the results supported the two-process model of semantic processing and suggested that LD children have problems with purposive semantic processing.

A recent model of long-term memory has been proposed by Brainerd, Howe, and Kingma (1982). This model proposed that memory can be divided into two events: storage and retrieval. Performance on memory tasks was divided into three possible states: an unmemorized state, an intermediate memory state, and a memorized state. These researchers suggested that two processes were involved in the retrieval of information out of long-term memory: heuristic retrieval and algorithmic retrieval. *Heuristic retrieval* was described as auto- matic processing which was content free, while *algorithmic retrieval* was a controlled item-specific process. Recall in the intermediate memory state was associated with a heuristic retrieval strategy, while recall in the memorized state was associated with algorithmic retrieval. Howe, O'Sullivan, Brainerd, and Kingma (1989) applied this model to memory research with learning disabled children. They examined a large sample of both second-grade and sixth-grade LD children, and a matched sample of normally achieving controls. Subjects

were divided into groups and were given lists of words that were either unrelated
or grouped into categories. After being given a distracter task to eliminate short-
term memory effects, subjects were asked to recall the words. Subjects were
either in a free-recall condition or a cued-recall condition where they were given
the category title as a cue. According to the authors, normally achieving subjects
made better use of category as an aid in both storage and retrieval. The use of
cueing resulted in larger improvements in storage and recall, especially for the
sixth-grade children and for the normally achieving group overall. There were
developmental differences, in general, favoring older children in both storage
and retrieval. The study reported that more consistent gains were made by the
normally achieving group. Based on the long-term memory model developed by
Brainerd, Howe, and Kingma, they concluded that the difficulty for LD children
seemed to be in algorithmic retrieval (the more deliberate and controlled
retrieval skills). This is consistent with the findings of Ceci, who found
differences in purposive rather than automatic semantic processing. Howe et al.
also found that in heuristic retrieval differences favored the LD subjects. The
results of Ceci's work and those of Howe et al. are in conflict with the position of
Sternberg and Wagner (1982). Sternberg and Wagner suggest that learning
disabled children have deficits in the area of automatic processing, while Ceci
and Howe et al. find no such deficits in automatic processing but do find deficits
in the area of more purposive processing. Sternberg and Wagner note the
discrepancy between their framework and some of Ceci's (1982) findings and
suggest that Ceci's subject sample may be more generally disabled than other
samples. The idea that sampling differences may account for differences in
reported results is very likely considering the heterogeneous nature of learning
disabled children. It may be that some learning disabled subtypes have deficits
in automatic processing while others have deficits in more purposive processing.

This body of research suggests that while there may not be differences
between LD children and normal children in capacity (Lewis & Kass, 1982;
Torgesen, 1977; Wong, 1977), there are differences in the use of strategies. LD
subjects do not seem to be aware of strategies. For example, Torgesen states:
"Overall the results indicated that a major factor in the deficient recall of the
children in the reading disabled group was their lack of application of efficient
mnemonic strategies" (Torgesen, 1977, p. 576). Torgesen and Goldman state: "a
greater number of poor readers seemed to have almost no idea that any special
strategy would be useful" (Torgesen & Goldman, 1977, p. 58).

Metamemory

Theories of metamemory have also been applied to understanding memory
deficits in learning disabled children. Simply put, *metamemory* has been
defined as "knowing about knowing" (Brown, 1975). Metamemory has been
discussed at length by Flavell and Wellman (1977). They suggested that

metamemory includes "sensitivity" (that is, knowing when planned activities are necessary to aid in later recall). They also suggested three kinds of factors that influence performance on memory tasks. These included the memory characteristics of the person, which involved knowledge about memory capacity and about the kinds of tasks in which one was proficient. The second factor influencing memory performance involved task variables such as the relatedness of the material to be recalled and the length of the material. The last factor addressed by Flavell and Wellman was the strategies one has available to use on a particular memory task. Metamemory included understanding about these variables and understanding their interaction. Metamemory consisted of knowing the limitations of one's own memory, knowing what tasks were easy or hard, knowing when to use various strategies, and having a repertoire of strategies to use. It would seem that at least part of the problem with LD children involves knowledge about strategies. This problem, however, could extend into other areas of metamemory such as awareness of person variables.

Only a small amount of research has investigated LD children's metamemory understanding. Torgesen (1979) examined the differences between good and poor readers on their understanding of memory problems. The subjects were 30 good and poor readers (identified as having normal intelligence but significant reading problems) of approximately 9 years of age. They were tested using a questionnaire that included questions on memory ability, understanding of task difficulty, and generating solutions to various memory problems. The results supplied a considerable amount of information on the metamemory characteristics of LD children. Poor readers did not generate as many solutions to memory problems, and their solutions were not as planned. More good readers described verbal rehearsal as a strategy they used, and more of the good readers thought of themselves as good rememberers. Both groups seemed to be able to evaluate simple tasks as to which was easier. However, since memory performance was not actually evaluated, the relationship between memory and metamemory could not be examined.

Trepanier and Casale (1982) conducted a similar investigation using two different age groups. The subjects were 50 children identified as learning disabled, and 50 normal children. Both groups of children were divided into two age groups, old (10–15 years), and young (6–9). The experimenters used a design similar to that of Torgesen. Subjects were interviewed on eight metamemory questions concerning memory capacity, evaluation of the relative difficulty of memory tasks, and knowledge about various strategies. The results indicated that the younger LD group was not accurate on memory estimation. Both LD groups could evaluate the relative difficulty of simple tasks, but could not explain their evaluations. The experimenters concluded that the metamemory development of LD children paralleled that of normal children but proceeded more slowly. While this statement may be correct, the age divisions used seemed to be too wide for any real developmental differences to be demonstrated. It would be better to look for developmental differences across narrower age groupings. Again memory was not examined in relationship to metamemory awareness, so it is difficult to predict the usefulness of the information gained.

The literature reviewed so far suggests that intraindividual differences among the subcomponents of memory are apparent. Learning disabled children did not use strategies, did not seem to be aware of strategies in general, were inaccurate in estimating memory capacity, and did not engage in planned solutions to memory problems. The LD children examined in the research discussed above did not seem to be impaired in basic memory ability and were able to evaluate simple memory tasks.

Memory Subtypes

More recent research in the area of learning disabilities has put forth the idea that LD children are a heterogeneous population composed of subgroups with a profile of strengths and weaknesses. Instead of a simple performance deficit in the area of strategy use, it has been shown that LD children experience a range of deficits and strengths. Some LD children may have "production deficiencies" in memory skills and be inactive learners, but others may have deficits in underlying memory competence (Speece, 1987; Swanson, 1988). In addition, memory research has been conducted that examines one specific memory subgroup of LD children (Torgesen, 1988).

The specific subtype research conducted by Torgesen (1988) suggested another possible performance explanation for deficits on memory tasks. In a series of studies, Torgesen and his colleagues identified and subsequently investigated the abilities of one subgroup of LD children. Torgesen identified a small group of LD children who had problems with the retention of briefly presented verbal material. Torgesen examined performance on a battery of tasks between LD children who evidenced this specific memory deficit, LD children who did not have this memory deficit, and a group of normally achieving children. Using a battery of memory tasks Torgesen found that this subgroup was not impaired in memory universally, but performed as well as the other LD group on tasks such as semantic encoding and recognition memory. Interestingly, Torgesen suggested that "only a small proportion of performance deficits" of the LD poor memory children could be explained by inefficient strategy use (Torgesen, 1988, p. 608). Instead Torgesen proposed that this deficit was the result of a deficit in the use of phonological coding. In support of this idea, this subgroup also had problems with word identification and spelling, in addition to problems with immediate recall of verbal material, thus this specific subtype supports Sternberg and Wagner's (1984) notion that learning disabled children have problems at the automatic level.

Swanson (1988) examined a battery of memory tasks to determine a profile of strengths and weaknesses for subgroups of LD children. In addition, Swanson wanted to determine the kinds of memory deficits that were found more globally in the LD population as well as those that only occurred for certain subgroups. Swanson's hypotheses about memory performance rested on the idea that memory capabilities were divided into structural resources (which consist of prior knowledge) and a central processing unit. Structural resources were difficult to modify, while central processing ability was more flexible and could be modified to meet task demands. Swanson administered a battery of memory tasks to 50 LD children and 25 matched controls. Among the tasks given were a semantic orienting task designed to assess "the ability to access structural resources" (Swanson, 1988, p. 353); a sentence elaboration task, which was designed to assess the ability to assess structural resources; an effortful encoding task, which was expected to assess central processing demands; and a digit span task to examine short-term memory span. Swanson reported that the LD sample universally had difficulty accessing structural resources in comparison to controls but also evidenced profiles of strengths and deficits that were specific to each subgroup. Using cluster analysis, Swanson identified eight memory subtypes. Subtype 1 was characterized as having normal access to structural resources but had problems with central processing monitoring. Subtype 2 was characterized as deficient in both accessing structural resources and central processing capacity. However, this group was also characterized as proficient in "allocating resources between central and secondary items during low effort encoding" (Swanson, 1988, p. 353). Subtype 3 was characterized as "primarily deficient in accessing structural resources." This was the largest subtype and as such was compared to the control sample. Subtype 3 was found to be deficient in comparison to the control group in a variety of ways including "short term memory operations, resource depletion, and allocating central processing capacity" (Swanson, 1988, p. 353). Subgroup 4 had a memory ability profile similar to the control group evidencing strengths in the areas of "maintaining resources for secondary recall during elaborative encoding" (Swanson, 1988, p. 353), and on elaboration and organizational skills. Subtype 5 was characterized as having good short-term memory ability and as being good on low effort tasks. However this subtype was also characterized as poor on elaborative encoding tasks which Swanson related to resource depletion during those tasks. Subtype 6 was characterized as strong on retrieval ability but weak on elaboration and central processing capacity. Subtype 7 was characterized as strong on recalling secondary information but deficient on recalling primary information. Subtype 8 was characterized as strong on retrieval organization but deficient in central processing. This research suggests that LD children, while having an overall deficiency in accessing past knowledge, may have very different memory abilities. Some LD children may have deficits due to performance factors which may be correctable while other LD children may have deficits in underlying capacity which may be less correctable. Caution must be applied in the interpretation of the Swanson clusters, given the small sample size and the large number of clusters chosen to be interpreted.

Speece (1987), in contrast to Swanson, approached memory ability by examining information processing subtypes of LD children. Speece used a battery of information-processing tasks to examine both LD children and a control sample of normally achieving children. Among the tasks used was a sustained attention task, which assessed children's ability to monitor incoming auditory information against a visual array; an encoding task, which examined both semantic (similar meaning) and phonetic encoding; a short-term memory task; a long-term memory organizational task, which examined children's category clustering ability; and speed of recoding. Subjects also received the Woodcock Reading Mastery Test to assess reading abilities. Speece used cluster analysis and identified six LD subgroups. All groups evidenced deficits in speed of recoding, and four of the six clusters also had deficits on short-term memory. Subgroup 1 was characterized as particularly deficient on the short-term memory task. This subgroup was somewhat better at the sustained attention and memory organization tasks. Subgroup 2 was extremely deficient at the speed of recoding task and also had difficulty with semantic encoding. This subgroup was relatively strong on memory organization. Subgroup 3 had extremely low sustained attention but was relatively strong on phonetic encoding. Speece also reported that children in this group had more difficulty on tasks involving digits as compared to tasks involving words. Subgroup 4 was proficient on the sustained attention task but evidenced difficulty on both encoding and speed of recoding. Subgroup 5 was similar to the fourth subgroup but had lower scores on sustained attention and had better speed of recoding scores. Speece reported that this subgroup had relatively no information-processing strengths. Subgroup 6 was good at semantic encoding but had difficulties with the memory organization task. The reading task Speece used failed to differentiate the subgroups identified. Speece suggested that the reading task might be tapping into a more global reading ability while the information processing tasks assessed a number of discreet abilities. Even though Speece's reading measure failed to validate the existence of the subgroups identified, this may simply mean that deficits in many areas of information processing translate into an overall deficit in reading. More sensitive reading measures might be used on future research to validate subtypes.

Both Speece and Swanson found subgroups that had higher percentages of females than were found in the LD population. For instance, Speece's first subgroup had a higher percentage of females. This subgroup was deficient on short-term memory. Swanson's subgroups also had varying percentages of males and females, but overall Swanson's sample was composed of half male and half female subjects. This is atypical in comparison to most LD samples, which generally have a 3 to 1 male to female ratio. However the results of both articles are provocative and suggest future subgroup research should examine possible sex differences in memory abilities.

While much of the memory research reviewed here supported the hypothesis that LD children were inactive learners, more recent research paints a more complicated picture of interindividual differences among LD children. LD children must be considered as a heterogeneous population with a variety of strengths and weaknesses. Some children may have "production deficiencies" that may be more correctable, others may have difficulties in underlying memory competence.

PERCEPTION

Although this review will not present a lengthy review of perception, this area of cognition was central to the initial work in the identification and remediation of learning disabilities (Frostig, 1972; Frostig & Horne, 1964). This initial work postulated that many children with learning disabilities had visual/perceptual problems at the root of their reading problems. Boder (1970) described these perceptual problems as one of the three main subtypes of learning disabilities. Many of the original interventions for such children relied on practice in perceptual motor skills. Unfortunately, many of the children's perceptual skills improved without a concomitant increase in reading ability. Perceptual interventions and programs fell into disrepute in the 1970s and early 1980s, but has received more careful attention recently, because it has been evident that some form of perceptual impairment is implicated in learning disabilities.

A review of learning disabilities subtyping research across domains of functioning has revealed a visual perceptual subtype in almost every study (Feagans & McKinney, 1991; Lyon & Watson, 1981; Satz & Morris, 1980). In addition, some recent studies examining visual perceptual skills have found that only some, but not all, reading disabled children have visual deficits. Kavale (1982) did a metaanalysis of 161 studies and identified eight different visual constructs measured in the studies. He reported that the two constructs most related to reading were visual memory and visual discrimination, even when IQ was controlled.

A criticism of much of this research has also been that there is little evidence that there is stability of perceptual deficits, and that many children who display them may be merely immature and grow out of this deficit. One of the few studies done longitudinally examined the stability of perceptual deficits from childhood into adulthood. Spreen and Haaf (1986) identified different kinds of subtypes of learning disabilities in childhood from IQ and achievement tests, as well as sentence repetition and right–left orientation tasks. Both learning disabled children and normal children were included in the study. In the initial cluster analysis there appeared to be a visual spatial cluster, and this same cluster was stable into adulthood.

One of the prevailing problems in visual perceptual research with children who are learning disabled is the lack of a theoretical framework to guide research. One framework that has been applied to this area has been that of Gibson (1979). Gibson developed a controversial theory of direct visual perception. This theory rests on the idea that the environment is rich in information, and that perception is based on the pick-up of this information. The visual system does not need to embellish incoming stimulation for perception to occur. Surfaces in the environment structure the light reaching the visual system and as the perceiver moves about, or simply looks about, certain constancies are picked up. The perceiver is able to make use of this invariant information. An example would be linear texture (which a perceiver can utilize to detect distance relationships). Eleanor Gibson has adapted this framework to the development progression of visual perception and theorized that, over the course of development, children learn to attend to this invariant information.

Gibson, Gibson, Pick, and Osser (1962) extended the idea of picking up invariant information in the environment to the development of discrimination of graphic symbols. In a study of normally achieving children, they plotted the progression over development of visual discrimination of graphic symbols. They developed a set of letter-like forms equivalent in construction to real letters but without cultural meaning. Gibson et al. then generated an array of error types by transforming the letter-like forms in four ways: rotating or reversing the forms, transforming straight lines to curves or curves to straight lines, changing the perspective, and inserting breaks or closes. All these transformations, with the exception of the perspective transformation, are critical for discriminating between English letters.

Children in the study ranged in age from 4 to 8 years and were asked to select, from an array, only forms that exactly matched a target form. The results showed that all ages had few errors on the break and close transformations. Younger children evidenced more difficulty than older children on the line-to-curve and the curve-to-line transformations, although errors still persisted in the older age groups. Younger children also evidenced more difficulty on the rotation and reversal transformations, and older children made very few errors of this kind. Perspective transformation errors remained high in all age groups.

The results supported the experimenter's predictions. Children learn to attend to the invariant information in the environment and this ability is then extended to the pick-up of critical information in graphic symbols. Break and close transformations are important for visual discrimination of objects in the real environment and are developed early. This is consistent with the results of the study; even the youngest groups made few errors of this type. Line-to-curve and curve-to-line transformations, as well as reversal and rotation transformations, are not as important in the visual discrimination of objects in the environment.

A rotated car is still a car. However, these transformations are important for discriminating letters. For example, a *b* reversed is a *d*. Thus children learn to attend to these transformations as they are exposed to letters. This is also evident in the results of Gibson et al., where the youngest children had difficulty with these transformations but the older children, who had more exposure to graphic symbols, did not have difficulty. Perspective transformations are not critical for distinguishing real objects in the environment, nor are perspective transformations critical for discriminating between letters. Again, the results are consistent; this error remains high across all age groups. This experiment is valuable to the study of visual discrimination skills of children with learning disabilities, because the normal course of development has been plotted.

Based on the results of these studies and extending the work of Gibson et al. (1962), Feagans and Merriwether (1990) investigated visual discrimination of letterlike forms in children who were learning disabled. Learning disabled children and normally achieving controls were given the letterlike forms task developed by Gibson et al. These children were in the higher age range, in comparison to the groups studied by Gibson et al., and most had little difficulty with the transformation errors. However, there was a small group of both learning disabled and normally achieving children who did have difficulty with the line-to-curve transformations. The children in this high-error group (both learning disabled and normally achieving) had difficulty on the performance subtest of the WISC-R. Achievement measures also indicated that this high-error subtype had lower scores on reading recognition and reading comprehension over a three year period. A follow-up was conducted when the children were 12, and there were significant differences between the high-error subtype and low-error children in reading, specifically word identification and word attack skills.

In summary, it does appear that a small number of learning disabled children do have specific perceptual deficits, mainly in the visual discrimination area. The evidence suggests that these deficits do persist over time and are linked to reading ability over time.

LANGUAGE AND DISCOURSE PROCESSES

Language disorders are said to constitute one of the major problems associated with learning disabilities (Myklebust, 1971). The association between a reading disability and a linguistic deficit has been attributed to Rabinovitch (1959), who noted that many children with reading problems also had expressive language problems (Richman, 1983). Marge (1972) estimated that at least 50% of children with learning disabilities had some language disorder. In a recent study of 242 children with learning disabilities between 8 and 12 years of age, it was found that 90% of them had a language problem as measured by the Test of Language

Development (Hammill & Newcomer, 1982). In the recent proceedings from a national conference on learning disabilities, five topics were deemed central to this disability. One was language disorders.

Even though it is clear that language is an important descriptive marker of learning disabilities, there is much controversy about whether language problems are the result of some larger cognitive deficit or are specific language related deficits. Beyond this there are controversies about what kind of language is affected and whether these deficits are causally linked to the problems learning disabled children find with reading and other school-related tasks (Feagans, 1983; Tallal, 1988).

One of the problems with much of the research is that it merely documents differences in language functioning between normal and learning disabled children. Even more than the literature on memory and intelligence, the research on language has been group-differences oriented, without regard to individual differences across different language skills and with almost no information of the stability of deficits across time. Even fewer studies have linked the language problems to school deficits in reading and other tasks.

In this section of the chapter, we will try to review the few studies that address some of the issues in individual differences. Thus, the large body of literature that documents group differences between normal and learning disabled children on basic language measures will not be reviewed here. These can be found elsewhere (Donahue, 1986; Feagans, 1983; Tallal, 1988). Instead, an emphasis will be placed on examining individual differences in language beyond the sentence level at the discourse level.

Language, Narratives, and Communication

Theoretically, language can be described as existing at three levels of abstractness (Carnap, 1964). The most abstract level is the syntactic level, which includes the formal relationships that words or phrases have to each other in a sentence. For instance, the relationship of the subject to the verb in a sentence is a syntactic relationship, independent of the meaning of this relationship. The second level is semantics and is often dependent on syntax. Semantics interprets the syntactic relationships by imposing meaning on the words in the sentences. Thus, semantic information is combined with the syntactic relationships to form the set of possible meanings of an isolated sentence. The exact meaning of a word, sentence, or text cannot be interpreted correctly without including the least abstract level, but probably the most complex level, pragmatics. Pragmatics includes the nonlinguistic and contextual factors that operate to interpret the intent and use of the language beyond the syntax and semantics.

Isolating various levels of language has been an important endeavor in understanding normal language development, but it may be less important in understanding the critical processes that are involved in learning disabilities. As has been discussed in the previous parts of the chapter, this disability is multifaceted and is defined by the academic, usually reading, failure of the children in the pragmatic context of school.

Language which is beyond the sentence level at the discourse and narrative level is the language that is used in everyday life by the child. The understanding of discourse requires knowledge about the relationship of the meaning of one sentence to another as well as the organization of the larger unit of the topic. Language at this level cannot be divorced easily from memory and other cognitive processes without careful examination. Language at this level has been found to be more of a problem for learning disabled children in comparison to problems in syntax and semantics (Donahue, 1986; Feagans, 1983; Worden, 1986).

This chapter will focus on two skills beyond the sentence level: narrative skills and communication skills. The first is narrative skill. *Narrative skills* are defined as "those abilities which allow for the understanding and exchange of event-structured material" (Feagans, 1983). Narrative skills in the form of storytelling ability and script ability have generated the greatest interest in the last 10 years. A number of cognitive psychologists have been interested in mapping out what has been called a *story grammar*, which describes the structure of the story with its various elements (Stein & Glenn, 1979). Skill with narratives requires knowledge about the introduction, setting information, character descriptions, event sequences, plot sequences, and resolutions of conflict. In addition, some event-based material could be characterized as a script, rather than a story. *Scripts* are sequences of actions that form common everyday events such as grocery shopping, eating a meal, or going to a birthday party (Schank & Abelson, 1977). Knowledge of such scripts seems to be a prerequisite for even the simplest of the tasks children face in school. Many textbooks and lessons in school assume children are familiar with such scripts of grocery shopping or a birthday party. Therefore, the text of a story can omit elaboration or detail when describing a familiar event sequence (Pace & Feagans, 1984).

In addition to narrative skills, communication skills include the exchange of narrative information, but the success of the ventured interaction depends on the skills of both parties in the interaction. These skills require a certain level of linguistic proficiency by school-age children, but they also require understanding the competence of the listener and the shared knowledge between the listener and speaker (Feagans, 1983). Children with poor communication skills will indeed have a difficult time obtaining the information needed in school, particularly in the early elementary years, when much information is obtained by the question/answer format of the classroom.

Intraindividual Variability in Narrative Ability

Although differences in storytelling ability have been found between normal and learning disabled children, the focus of this section is on the differential abilities across the different skills of understanding and producing narratives. Learning disabled children have more subtle deficits than other disabled children because of their near-normal overall cognitive abilities. Thus, it is important to understand which areas of functioning are strengths and which are weaknesses.

Basic knowledge about the structure of stories has been attributed to children as young as 5 years of age (Stein & Glenn, 1979). It could be hypothesized that young or learning disabled children have a somewhat undifferentiated story schema, such that their knowledge of the important elements of a story and the sequencing of a story are poor. A series of studies has been conducted to explore this possibility. The first study that tried to examine the various processes in narrative ability for good and poor readers was by Smiley, Oakley, Worthem, Campione, and Brown (1977). In this study children were given fairy tales to read or listen to, and then they were asked to recall the story. As expected, the good readers produced more information than the poor readers, but in addition the good readers also produced proportionately more of the important aspects of their story in their recall than poor readers. These results were found in both the auditory and visual presentation modes, indicating that similar processes are involved in both reading and listening. The results from this study were striking, because the poor readers' listening performance was later compared to first- and third-graders' performance, indicating that the junior-high poor readers performed like first graders in their sensitivity to the importance of the structural units in the stories.

Hansen (1978) used propositional analysis (Kintsch, 1974) to examine the story recall of 17 LD and 17 normal fifth- and sixth-grade children. The narrative stories used were oral reading stories from the Durrell Analysis of Reading Difficulty. After practice with the first-grade story, each child was asked to read each of the stories aloud and then afterward to orally retell the story. The questions associated with the stories on the Durrell were then asked. Significant differences favoring the normal children were found on the answers to the questions for both reading selections. In addition, although the normal children told a greater proportion of correct propositions in their retells than LD children, an even greater difference between the groups was obtained when the analysis examined the proportion of main ideas versus details in their retells. The propositions were divided into superordinate (main ideas) and subordinate (details) units. Learning disabled children had a much lower proportion of main ideas but the same proportion of details as normal children. Correlations between the proportion of proportions recalled and the scores on the questions were highly significant (.50 to .77), indicating considerable overlap in these abilities.

Additional studies were designed to test whether children with learning disabilities were deficient in story recall. Weaver and Dickinson (1982) presented children with stories derived from the Stein and Glenn (1979) grammar. They found that the recall patterns for both groups were highly similar. However there were subtle differences in the recall. Learning disabled children produced fewer elaborations of major story events; and although they did not misunderstand the story, they often added new information and left out relevant information. Although they explain these results by appealing to a linguistic deficiency hypothesis, it could also be the case that the children had memory or comprehension problems that were confounded in the experiment. No test of the children's understanding of the story was assessed.

In order to control for comprehension of the story and memory problems, Feagans and Short (1984) examined the narrative skills in one of the few longitudinal studies of learning disabled and normally achieving children. In order to insure that children's performance on the narrative tasks was not due to poor memory or a lack of understanding of the basic story structure, both a comprehension and production task were employed. They presented 63 LD and 63 non-LD 6- and 7-year-old children with script-like narratives about a grocery store. Half of the stories contained theme information in the beginning, and half did not. A miniature grocery story was placed in front of the children, and the entire script-like story was read to the children. The children were required to act out the script with the props provided. If they did not act out the story correctly, or if they did so incompletely, they were read the story again until perfect enactment was achieved. The grocery store was then covered up, and the children were asked to tell the story in their own words. The task was given to most of the children over a 3-year period, with different stories being used each year. Surprisingly, there were no real differences between the learning disabled and normally achieving groups on the comprehension of the scripts. Findings did reveal large differences in the paraphrases, with normally achieving children paraphrasing more of the event units, using more complex sentences and words and fewer nonreferential pronouns. Unlike the previous research, there did not appear to be any differences between the groups on whether theme information helped them organize their narratives or sequencing events within the stories.

This study suggested that, besides differences in the actual development of the story schemata, differential flexibility or willingness to utilize these skills to retrieve a narrative may also account for possible differences between learning disabled and normal children. This deficit associated with an otherwise competent child has been called a *production deficiency* (Flavell, 1977) in contrast to a *mediational deficiency*. It has been hypothesized to derive from the lack of appropriate strategies to retrieve information or a lack of reflective abstraction about the nature of strategies to be employed. It has been shown that normal children learn to use their schematic knowledge to aid recall of story narratives, and this study supports the notion that learning disabled children may not do this in the same effective way.

Feagans and Short (1984) also suggest that learning disabled children may have stored the memory for the story more motorically and nonverbally than the normally achieving children. Thus verbally paraphrasing the story might require translation between nonverbal and verbal memory for the learning disabled children and not so for the normally achieving children. This hypothesis has been used to explain performance by some low-income children also (Feagans & Farran, 1981).

A study by Wong and Wilson (1981) bolsters this strategy hypothesis. They presented children with organized versus scrambled passages to study, and then the children were asked how the passages were different. Learning disabled children were less able to verbally say why the passages were different and were less likely subsequently to spontaneously reorganize the disorganized passages. Yet, with little training in strategy, the learning disabled children were easily able to overcome their deficiency. Wong and Wilson argue that the learning disabled children had the rudimentary knowledge of the story structure but were unable to employ strategies to use this knowledge. In a related study, Wong (1982) had subjects read through 59 story units from the Brown and Smiley (1977) stories and select 12 to serve as potential retrieval cues. Results indicated that learning disabled children were not less organized, but that they were less exhaustive in considering the whole list and less likely to check over their selected list of cues. Paris and Myers (1981) found that poor readers were less aware of their own noncomprehension when reading stories. Thus these studies suggest that learning disabled children have fewer strategies to spontaneously use in discourse tasks and may be less aware of their own behavior during reading.

In a final study (Newcomer, Barenbaum, & Nodine, 1988), learning disabled, low-achieving and normally achieving children were presented with the tasks of telling and writing a story. Using categories drawn from Stein and Glenn (1982), they scored the stories for complexity. Although there were some differences among the groups, the results were more impressive with respect to the similarities in comparison to the differences. Learning disabled children produced fewer stories but the stories they produced were just as complex. Only younger children showed differences between the oral and written mode.

The results from these studies with respect to narrative skills suggest that learning disabled children do not have serious deficits in story structure or the organization of the narrative, but that they do have problems with the production of narratives and often do not use optimal strategies to produce their best performance. Research is lacking in consistency of subject population and only one of the studies shows consistency of the results over time.

Intraindividual Variability in Communication

Communication is a broad category of ability that could include both verbal and nonverbal ability to interact with another in conveying and receiving information. The skills required include, not only the ones used for narratives, but also social and emotional skills that allow the person to be sensitive to the partner in the communication. In general, communication skill requires both the social skills to negotiate the interaction and the cognitive and linguistic skills to use language effectively (Feagans, 1983; Donahue, 1986).

Most of the studies of learning disabled children's communication have been examined using the referential communication paradigm (Glucksburg & Krauss, 1967). Usually a prespecified set of materials with prespecified attributes must be communicated to another person, who is naive about the relevant attributes. Other less structured tasks have also been used, but few studies have employed naturalistic observation of communication skill in learning disabled children.

A number of studies in the early eighties suggested that learning disabled children have significant problems in communicating information to another. The exact nature of the children's difficulties, and the explanations for this problem in communication, have ranged widely. This may be due to different theoretical orientations, but also to the diverse nature of the children used in the studies.

In one of the first studies (Donahue, Pearl, & Bryan, 1980), differences between learning disabled and normal children's competence as a listener were assessed. The children were learning disabled and normally achieving children drawn from first through eighth grade and asked to pick a target picture from a set of four pictures based on the verbal description given by an adult confederate. The children were told to ask for more information or clarification if the message was judged to be inadequate. Both learning disabled and normal children were able to detect adequate and inadequate messages equally well, but the learning disabled children were less likely than normal children to request clarification under the inadequate condition and thus were less likely to pick the correct picture. In a follow-up of this study (Donahue, 1984), the inactive learner hypothesis was tested by trying to train learning disabled children using strategies to try to improve their performance on the task. Unfortunately, the intervention failed to improve performance.

A similar study was conducted by Spekman (1981) in which fifth-grade pairs containing a learning disabled and normal child, as well as two normal children, were used to evaluate skill in the listener and speaker role in a referential communication task. The speaker was required to communicate to the listener how to arrange a set of 16 blocks into prespecified geometric designs. Each partner in the pair played both speaker and listener. Learning disabled children and normal children performed the same in the listener role, including asking relevant questions. This is different from the Donahue et al. (1980) results, but this may be due to age differences or task difficulty differences. In addition the Donahue et al. study used children from a private school, where identification as learning disabled was done by the investigators. Results from the Spekman study also revealed large differences between the groups in the ability to communicate information effectively. Learning disabled speakers gave less task-relevant information to the listener, and overall the dyads containing a learning disabled child as speaker had less success in completing the task correctly.

Support for a specific deficit in communication of information was found in a study by Noel (1980). Nine- and 11-year-old children, both learning disabled and normal children, were asked to communicate information about a set of six pictures. The clarity of these descriptions was evaluated in a subsequent listener task. In this listener role learning disabled and normal children did not differ in the ability to select the correct picture from the descriptions generated by the learning disabled and normal children. However, the descriptive communications produced by the normal children yielded more correct responses by both groups of children than those produced by the learning disabled children.

One of the criticisms that could be made about the studies just described was that the listener task and speaker task were not of equal difficulty, and that the task specificity restricted the kinds of responses that the children could make. In addition, none of the studies were longitudinal in nature, nor did they assess whether the skill of communicating was linked to any real-world task in school. These issues were addressed in the next study.

Feagans and Short (1986) examined 6- and 7-year-old learning disabled and normal children over a 3-year period, collecting information each year about achievement and assessing the children's ability to perform on a communication task each year. Children were shown an attractive wooden puzzle box that contained a series of knobs, each of which could be moved in two directions. Hidden on the side of the box was a small plexiglass container which had an M&M candy inside. Children were read a set of instructions about how to move the knobs, and in what order, in order to get the M&M inside. If the child failed to follow the directions correctly, the directions were read again until the child succeeded. After complete comprehension of the instructions was demonstrated by finding the M&M, the child was asked to tell a naive puppet everything that needed to be known about how to open the box. The child then tried to recount the six steps. After the child's initial attempt to tell these steps, the puppet feigned noncomprehension and asked for the steps one at a time. After the child's attempt to describe a step, the puppet would ask for a rephrase, either by nonverbally touching the wrong knob or by verbally saying "I don't know." This resulted in three verbal and three nonverbal requests for reformulations.

Learning disabled children performed more poorly on all three parts of the task, the listener portion, the speaker portion, and the rephrase portion. Learning disabled children took longer to learn how to open the box, and although they communicated all six steps in the speaker role, they communicated less information about each step. On the rephrase portion of the task, Year 3 results indicated a dramatic increase in the normal children's ability to reformulate information upon verbal request. This was not true for the learning disabled children.

The results of this study lend some support for the "production deficiency" hypothesis, but it appears that the results point to a more complicated interpretation. Since LD children took longer to learn how to open the box, they showed some comprehension deficits as well as production deficits. The comprehension may be due to verbal memory problems. In addition, LD children may not have the same strategies as normal children for obtaining information during the listener portion of the task, and they may not store the same kind of information. For instance, LD children may have relied on perceptual/motor memory to store information about the six steps. Thus trying to retrieve the information and translating it into verbal communication would be more difficult.

The relationship of these skills to reading has been little addressed. Feagans and Short (1986) did perform regression analysis, using the major variables from the referential communication task to predict reading achievement and IQ over 3 years. The results indicated that the speaker task was the best predictor of reading for the learning disabled children, but that the task variables were not good predictors of IQ for the LD children. On the other hand IQ was a better predictor of reading for the normal children. This supports the notion that different processes may be implicated in poor reading for learning disabled versus normally achieving children.

More informal communication tasks have also been used to understand the conversational communication of learning disabled children. In one study (Bryan, Donahue, Pearl, & Strum, 1981), children in second and fourth grade were asked to interview a classmate about favorite movies and TV programs, as though they were a talk show host. Results indicated that learning disabled children were less effective in getting children to talk about these topics. They used fewer questions and were less skilled at initiating and sustaining dialogue. The guests of LD children were less likely to elaborate on topics. A further study (Donahue & Bryan, 1983) explored the use of modeling in improving the skills of children. Before each interview, each host listened to one of two audiotaped models: The intervention model consisted of a dialogue in which a child interviewer produced frequent open-ended questions, conversational devices, and contingent comments and questions. The control audiotape was merely a monologue. This intervention did improve the level of performance of the learning disabled host so that they performed like normally achieving children in this situation. These findings do support the inactive learner hypothesis, because such a brief intervention changed behavior so radically.

Subgroups or Interindividual Variability

Variability across different language domains within individual children did not initially produce important information about learning disabled children. Some attempts to categorize different kinds of language skills in learning disabled children have resulted in taxonomies (Kirk, McCarthy, & Kirk, 1968; Wiig, Lapointe, & Semel, 1977). Tests like the Illinois Test of Psycholinguistic Abilities were developed from a theoretical model of learning disabilities but have been shown to be of questionable reliability and validity in the identification, remediation, and prediction of learning problems (Hammill & Larsen, 1974).

More recently a number of studies have used Q factor analysis and Cluster analysis to group children together who have similar profiles of performance across a number of different variables. These studies have almost invariably identified a subgroup of children who have language difficulty, and this is often the largest single subgroup (McKinney & Feagans, in press; Doehring & Hoshko, 1977; Watson, Goldgar, & Ryschon, 1983; Satz & Morris, 1980; Lyon & Watson, 1981). Although these studies were interesting, all were exploratory in nature, did not have a priori profiles defined, and were not theoretically driven. No attempt was made to validate the subgroups, although Lyon and Watson (1981) did find that the language clusters were the ones that showed the poorest reading achievement. These studies were also not designed to examine a large battery of language measures but were more designed to use a battery of global measures, including IQ, achievement, and other cognitive variables.

Recently, Feagans and Appelbaum (1986) examined a number of language measures obtained in a group of 55 LD and 66 normally achieving 6- and 7-year-old children. They included six language variables: two tapped syntactic ability, two tapped word and vocabulary knowledge, and two tapped narrative skill. This study had a theoretical focus and predicted that children who were relatively impaired in narrative skill in comparison to the other skills would perform most poorly on reading tasks. Cluster analyses of the learning disabled children revealed that the hypothesis was supported. Those children who were superior in narrative abilities relative to the others had the best reading scores over 3 years. Those who were in the cluster with superior syntactic and vocabulary skills relative to narrative skills were most impaired in reading over 3 years, even though the superior syntax vocabulary subgroups had generally higher IQs. Forecasting normally achieving children into these clusters resulted in a poor fit, with most of them fitting into the good prognostic subgroups.

Much more work is needed on examining different subgroups of children on language measures before there is any definitive answer about the different kinds of narrative and communication deficits that appear in different subgroups of learning disabled children. It does appear that attention needs to focus on the narrative and communication area since these seem most related to problems seen in school and seem especially related to reading deficits.

CONCLUSIONS

The literature reviewed reveals that learning disabled children have been found to have some patterns of strengths and weaknesses within domains, and that there appear to be different subgroups of learning disabled children within and across some domains in the cognitive areas. A consistent pattern of results in the memory and language domain support a production deficiency hypothesis for some learning disabled children. The children appear to comprehend material fairly well and have the basic cognitive ability for remembering well but they do not employ efficient strategies spontaneously in situations that demand it for good performance (Torgesen & Licht, 1983). Because most of the studies did not examine subtypes across learning disabled children, or the studies only recruited children with a memory or language deficit, there is no ready estimate of the proportion of learning disabled children to which this generalization should apply.

The literature on intelligence and perception is much less likely to propose the inactive learner hypothesis to explain the pattern of performance. The results in these areas indicate that learning disabled children may have less skill overall in cognitive tasks, like those on an IQ test, and that at least some learning disabled children may have a perceptual discrimination deficit.

Clearly what is needed is intensive research with a large number of well identified learning disabled children; research which would focus on many domains in an attempt to understand the different kinds of processes involved as well as to identify consistent subtypes that could be tied to specific interventions efforts. In addition the subtype research needs to focus on the link between patterns of performance in basic cognitive processes and school performance. The causal link between these two is often elusive, and until patterns of performance are causally linked to poor school performance, our intervention efforts for learning disabled children will continue to be less effective than is needed.

REFERENCES

Atkinson, R.C., & Shiffrin, R.M. (1968). Human memory: A proposed system and its control processes. In K.W. Spence & J.T. Spence (Eds.), *The psychology of learning and motivation: Advances in research and theory* (Vol. 2). New York: Academic Press.

Bannatyne, A. (1974). Diagnosis: A note on recategorization of the WICZ scaled scores. *Journal of Learning Disabilities, 7,* 272–274.

Black, F.W. (1974). WISC verbal-performance discrepancies as indicators of neurological dysfunction in pediatric patients. *Journal of Clinical Psychology, 30,* 165–167.

Boder, E. (1970). Developmental dyslexia: A new diagnostic approach based on the identification of three subtypes. *Journal of School Health, 40,* 289–290.

Braden, J.P., & Weiss, L. (1988). Effects of simple differences versus regression discrepancy methods: An empirical study. *Journal of School Psychology, 26,* 133–142.

Brainerd, C.J., Howe, M.L., & Kingma, J. (1982). An identifiable model of two-stage learning. *Journal of Mathematical Psychology, 26,* 263–293.

Brown, A.L. (1975). The development of memory: Knowing, knowing about knowing, and knowing how to know. In H.W. Reese (Ed.), *Advances in Child Development and Behavior* (Vol. 10). New York: Academic Press.

Brown, A.L., & Smiley, S.S. (1977). Rating the importance of structural units of prose passages. A problem of metacognitive development. *Child Development, 48*, 1–8.

Bryan, T.H., & Bryan, J.H. (Eds.). (1978). *Understanding learning disabilities* (2nd ed.). Sherman Oaks, CA: Alfred.

Bryan, T.H., Donahue, M., Pearl, R., & Strum, C. (1981). Learning disabled children's conversational skills. *Learning Disability Quarterly, 4*, 250–259.

Carnap, R. (1964). Foundations of logic and mathematics. In J.A. Fodor & J.J. Katz (Eds.), *The structure of language: Readings in the philosophy of language* (pp. 419–436). Englewood Cliffs, NJ: Prentice-Hall.

Ceci, S.J. (1982). Extracting meaning from stimuli: Automatic and purposive processing of the language-based learning disabled. *Topics in Learning and Learning Disabilities, 2*, 46–53.

Ceci, S.J. (1983). Automatic and purposive semantic processing characteristics of normal and language/learning disabled children. *Developmental psychology, 19*, 427–439.

Ceci, S.J. (1984). A developmental study of learning disabilities and memory. *Journal of Experimental Child Psychology, 38*, 352–371.

Doehring, D.G., & Hoshko, I.M. (1977). Classification of reading problems by the Q-technique of factor analyses. *Cortex, 13*, 281–294.

Donahue, M. (1984). Learning disabled children's conversational competence: An attempt to activate the inactive listener. *Applied Psycholingusitics, 5*, 21–35.

Donahue, M. (1986). Linguistic and communicative development in learning-disabled children. In S.J. Ceci (Ed.), *Handbook of cognitive, social, and neuropsychological aspects of learning disabilities* (pp. 263–289). Hillsdale, NJ: Erlbaum.

Donahue, M., & Bryan, T. (1983). Conversational skills and modeling in learning disabled boys. *Applied Psycholinguistics, 4*, 251–278.

Donahue, M., Pearl, R., & Bryan, T. (1980). Learning disabled children's conversational competence: Responses to inadequate messages. *Journal of Applied Psycholinguistics, 1*, 387–403.

Feagans, L.V. (1983). Discourse processes in learning disabled children. In J.D. McKinney & L.V. Feagans (Eds.), *Current topics in learning disabilities* (pp. 87–115). Norwood, NJ: Ablex Publishing Corp.

Feagans, L.V., & Appelbaum, M.I. (1986). Validation of language subtypes in learning disabled children. *Journal of Educational Psychology, 78*, 1–7.

Feagans, L.V., & Farran, D.C. (1981). How demonstrated comprehension can get muddled in production. *Developmental Psychology, 17*, 718–727.

Feagans, L.V., & McKinney, J.D. (1981). Pattern of exceptionality across domains in learning disabled children. *Journal of Applied Developmental Psychology, 1*(4), 313–328.

Feagans, L.V., & Short, E.J. (1984). Developmental differences in the comprehension and production of narratives by reading-disabled and normally achieving children. *Child Development, 55*, 1727–1736.

Feagans, L.V., & Short, E.J. (1986). Referential communication and reading performance in learning disabled children over a 3-year period. *Developmental Psychology, 22*, 177–183.

Feagans, L.V., & Merriwether, A. (1990). Visual discrimination of letter-like forms and its relationship over time to achievement in children with learning disabilities. *Journal of Learning Disabilities, 23,* 417–425.

Feagans, L.V., & McKinney, J.D. (1991). Subtypes of learning disabilities: A review. In L.V. Feagans, E.J. Short, & L. Meltzer (Eds.), *Subtypes of learning disabilities: Theoretical perspectives and research* (pp. 3–31). Hillsdale, NJ: Erlbaum.

Flavell, J.H. (1977). *Cognitive development.* Englewood Cliffs, NJ: Prentice-Hall.

Flavell, J.H., Beach, D.R., & Chinsky, J.M. (1966). Spontaneous verbal rehearsal in a memory task as a function of age. *Child Development, 37,* 284–299.

Flavell, J.H., & Wellman, H.M. (1977). Metamemory. In R.V. Kail & J.W. Hagen (Eds.), *Perspectives on the development of memory and cognition.* Hillsdale, NJ: Erlbaum.

Frostig, M. (1972). Visual perception, integrative functions and academic learning. *Journal of Learning Disabilities, 5,* 1–8.

Frostig, M., & Horne, D. (1964). *The Frostig program for the development of visual perception: Teacher's guide.* Chicago: Follet.

Gallagher, J.J. (1966). Children with developmental imbalances: A psychoeducational definition. In W.M. Cruickshank (Ed.), *The teacher of brain injured children.* Syracuse, NY: Syracuse University Press.

Gardner, H. (1983). *Frames of mind: The theory of multiple intelligences.* New York: Basic Books.

Gibson, E.J., Gibson, J.J., Pick, A.D., & Osser, H. (1962). A developmental study of the discrimination of letter-like forms. *Journal of Comparative and Physiological Psychology, 55,* 897–906.

Gibson, J.J. (1979). *The ecological approach to visual perception.* Hillsdale, NJ: Erlbaum.

Glucksburg, S., & Krauss, R.M. (1967). What do people say after they have learned to talk? Studies of the development of referential communication. *Merrill Palmer Quarterly, 13,* 309–316.

Hammill, D.D., & Larsen, S.C. (1974). The effectiveness of psycholinguistic training. *Exceptional Children, 41,* 5–14.

Hammill, D.D., & Newcomer, P.L. (1982). *Test of language development: Intermediate.* Austin, TX: PRO-ED.

Hansen, C.L. (1978). Story retelling used with average and learning disabled readers as a measure of reading comprehension. *Learning Disability Quarterly, 1,* 62–69.

Holroyd, J., & Wright, F. (1965). Neurological implications of WISC verbal-performance discrepancies in a psychiatric setting. *Journal of Consulting Psychology, 29,* 206–212.

Howe, M.L., O'Sullivan, J.T., Brainerd, C.J., & Kingma, J. (1989). Localizing the development of ability differences in organized memory. *Contemporary Educational Psychology, 14,* 336–356.

Huelsman, C.R. (1970). The WISC subtest syndrome for disabled readers. *Perceptual and Motor Skills, 30,* 535–550.

Kaufman, A.S. (1976). A new approach to the interpretation of test scatter on the WISC-R. *Journal of Learning Disabilities, 9,* 160–168.

Kavale, K. (1982). Meta-analysis of the relationship between visual perceptual skills and reading achievement. *Journal of Learning Disabilities, 15,* 42–51.

Kender, J.P. (1972). Is there really a WISC profile for poor readers? *Journal of Learning Disabilities, 5,* 397–401.

Kintsch, W. (1974). *The representation of meaning in memory.* Hillsdale, NJ: Erlbaum.

Kirk, S.T., McCarthy, J., & Kirk, W. (1968). *Illinois Test of Psycholinguistics Abilities* (rev. ed.). Urbana: University of Illinois Press.

Lewis, R.B., & Kass, C.E. (1982). Labeling and recall in learning disabled students. *Journal of Learning Disabilities, 15,* 238–241.

Lyon, R., & Watson, B. (1981). Empirically derived subgroups of learning disabled readers: Diagnostic characteristics. *Journal of Learning Disabilities, 14,* 256–261.

Marge, M. (1972). The general problem of language disabilities in children. In J.V. Irwin & M. Marge (Eds.), *Principles of childhood language disabilities* (pp. 75–98). Englewood Cliffs, NJ: Prentice-Hall.

Myklebust, H.R. (Ed.). (1971). *Progress in learning disabilities* (Vol. 2). New York: Grune & Stratton.

Newcomer, P.L., Barenbaum, E.M., & Nodine, B.F. (1988). Comparison of the story production of LD, normally achieving, and low-achieving children under two modes of production. *Learning Disability Quarterly, 11,* 82–96.

Noel, M.M. (1980). Referential communication abilities of learning disabled children. *Learning Disability Quarterly, 3,* 70–75.

O'Brien, R.G. (1978). Robust techniques for testing heterogeneity of variance effects in factorial designs. *Psychometrika, 43,* 327–342.

Pace, A., & Feagans, L. (1984). Knowledge and language: Children's ability to use and communicate what they know about everyday experiences. In L. Feagans, C. Garvey, & R. Golinkoff (Eds.), *The origins and growth of communication* (pp. 268–280). Norwood, NJ: Ablex.

Paris, S.G., & Myers, M. (1981). Comprehension monitoring: Memory and study strategies of good and poor readers. *Journal of Reading Behavior, 13,* 5–22.

Rabinovitch, R.D. (1959). Reading and learning disabilities. In S. Aneti (Ed.), *American handbook of psychiatry.* New York: Basic Books.

Richman, L.C. (1983). Language-learning disability: Issues, research, and future directions. *Advances in Developmental and Behavioral Pediatrics, 4,* 87–107.

Satz, P., & Morris, R. (1980). Learning disability subtypes: A review. In F.J. Pirozzolo & M.C. Wittrock (Eds.), *Neuropsychological and cognitive processes in reading* (pp. 109–141). New York: Academic Press.

Schank, R.C., & Abelson, R.P. (1977). *Scripts, plans, goals, and understanding: An inquiry into human knowledge structures.* Hillsdale, NJ: Erlbaum.

Smiley, S.S., Oakley, D.D., Worthen, D., Campione, J.C., & Brown, A.L. (1977). Recall of thematically relevant material by adolescent good and poor readers as a function of written versus oral presentation. *Journal of Educational Psychology, 69,* 381–389.

Snow, R. (1986). Individual differences and the design of educational programs. *American Psychologist, 41,* 1029–1039.

Speece, D.L. (1987). Information processing subtypes of learning disabled readers. *Learning Disabilities Research, 2,* 91–102.

Spekman, N. (1981). Dyadic verbal communication abilities of learning disabled and normally achieving fourth and fifth grade boys. *Learning Disability Quarterly, 4,* 139–151.

Spreen, O., & Haaf, R.G. (1986). Empirically derived learning disability subtypes: A replication attempt and longitudinal patterns over 15 years. *Journal of Learning Disabilities, 19,* 170–179.

Stein, N.L., & Glenn, C.G. (1979). An analysis of story comprehension in elementary school children. In R.O. Freedle (Ed.), *New directions in discourse processing* (Vol. 2). Norwood, NJ: Ablex Publishing Corp.

Stein, N.L., & Glenn, C.G. (1982). Children's concept of time: The development of a story schemata. In W. Friedman (Ed.), *The developmental psychology of time* (pp. 255–282). New York: Academic Press.

Sternberg, R.J. (1984). Towards a triarchic theory of human intelligence. *The Behavior and Brain Sciences, 7,* 269–290.

Sternberg, R.J., & Wagner, R.K. (1982). Automatization failure in learning disabilities. *Topics in Learning and Learning Disabilities, 2,* 1–11.

Swanson, H.L. (1988). Memory subtype in learning disabled readers. *Learning Disability Quarterly, 11,* 342–357.

Tallal, P. (1988). Developmental language disorders. In J.F. Kavanaugh & T.J. Truss (Eds.), *Learning disabilities: Proceedings of the national conference* (pp. 181–272). Parkton, MD: York Press.

Torgesen, J.K. (1977). Memorization processes in reading-disabled children. *Journal of Educational Psychology, 69,* 571–578.

Torgesen, J.K. (1979). Factors related to poor performance on memory tasks in reading disabled children. *Learning Disabilities Quarterly, 2,* 17–23.

Torgesen, J.K. (1988). Studies of children with learning disabilities who perform poorly on memory span tasks. *Journal of Learning Disabilities, 21,* 605–612.

Torgesen, J.K., & Goldman, T. (1977). Verbal rehearsal and short-term memory in reading-disabled children. *Child Development, 48,* 56–60.

Torgesen, J.K., & Licht, B.G. (1983). The learning disabled child as an inactive learner: Retrospect and prospects. In J.D. McKinney & L. Feagans (Eds.), *Current topics in learning disabilities* (pp. 3–31). Norwood, NJ: Ablex Publishing Corp.

Trepanier, M.L., & Casale, C.M. (1982). Metamemory development in learning disabled children. In W.M. Cruickshank & E. Tash (Eds.), *Academics and beyond* (Vol. 4). New York: Syracuse University Press.

Watson, B.V., Goldgar, D.E., & Ryschon, K.L. (1983). Subtypes of reading disability. *Journal of Clinical Neuropsychology, 5,* 377–399.

Weaver, P.A., & Dickinson, D.K. (1982). Scratching below the surface structure: Exploring the usefulness of story grammars. *Discourse Processes, 5,* 225–243.

Wechsler, D. (1958). *The measurement and appraisal of adult intelligence* (4th ed.). Baltimore, MD: Williams and Wilkins.

Wechsler, D. (1974). *Wechsler Intelligence Scale for Children - Revised.* Cleveland, OH: Psychological Corporation.

Wiig, E.H., Lapointe, C., & Semel, E.M. (1977). Relationships among language processing and production abilities of learning disabled adolescents. *Journal of Learning Disabilities, 10,* 292–299.

Wong, B.Y.L. (1977). The effects of directive cues on the organization of memory and recall in good and poor readers. *The Journal of Educational Research, 72,* 32–38.

Wong, B.Y.L. (1980). Activating the inactive learner: Use of questions/prompts to enhance comprehension and retention of implied information in learning disabled children. *Learning Disabilities Quarterly, 3,* 29–37.

Wong, B.Y.L. (1982). Strategic behaviors in selecting retrieval cues in gifted, normal achieving and learning disabled children. *Journal of Learning Disabilities, 15,* 33–37.

Wong, B.Y.L., & Jones, W. (1982). Increasing metacognition in learning-disabled and normally-achieving students through self-questioning training. *Learning Disability Quarterly, 5,* 228–240.

Wong, B.Y.L., & Wilson, M. (1981). *Investigating awareness of and teaching passage organization.* Unpublished manuscript.

Wong, B.Y.L., Wong, R., & Foth, D. (1977). Recall and clustering of verbal materials among normal and poor readers. *Bulletin of the Psychonomic Society, 10,* 375–378.

Worden, P.E. (1986). Prose comprehension and recall in disabled learners. In S.J. Ceci (Ed.), *Handbook of cognitive, social, and neuropsychological aspects of learning disabilities* (pp. 241–261). Hillsdale, NJ: Erlbaum.

Biological Approaches

Biological and Psychometric Intelligence: Testing An Animal Model In Humans With Positron Emission Tomography

Richard J. Haier
Benjamin V. Siegel, Jr.
Frank M. Crinella*
Monte S. Buchsbaum

Department of Psychiatry and Human Behavior
University of California, Irvine

The continuing search for a biological basis for intelligence has been a long and controversial one. Lashley (1929) was a pioneer in the field, studying the effects of brain lesions on cognitive function in the rat. More recently, Thompson, Crinella, and Yu (1990) published the findings of their own lesion studies in the

---

* State Developmental Research Institutes Costa Mesa, California

rat, and, based on these elaborate studies, they have developed a model of the biological basis of intelligence.

Until recently, lesion studies or studies of brain-injured humans have been the primary means by which the neuroanatomical basis of intelligence could be studied. In the past few years, the development of a brain imaging technology, positron emission tomography (PET), has allowed us to study regional brain metabolism during cognition in normal human subjects.

It is reasonable to surmise that some of the same structures important for problem solving and intelligence in the rat may be important in humans. These structures would also be activated during a problem-solving task, or their activity might correlate with performance on the task, and this could be detected with PET. Using PET and autoradiography, Blin, Ray, Chase and Piercey (1991) have demonstrated a close correspondence between human and rat brain glucose metabolism.

The purpose of this chapter is to summarize the work of Thompson, Crinella, and Yu and to report if the brain areas they identified as important in intelligence and problem solving in the rat are the same regions where metabolic rate changes with learning and/or correlates with intelligence in humans.

RAT BRAIN LESION STUDIES BY THOMPSON ET AL. (1990)

For each of 50 brain sites, a group of about 7 weanling (21- to 25-day-old) rats underwent lesion surgery. A control group of 75 animals underwent sham surgery. Following a 3-week recovery period, the groups of animals began training on a test battery, consisting of varying combinations of tests, including three climbing detour problems, eight puzzle box problems, visual and inclined discrimination habits, and a maze learning task. The intention of the investigators was to test, as thoroughly as possible, a wide variety of problem-solving tasks of which rats are capable. Subsequent to testing, the animals were sacrificed and lesion location was verified by histological examination of the brain.

Brain regions where lesions impaired performance on a test were assumed to be integral to the learning of that type of task. Lesions in eight regions caused significant impairment in performance on all tasks and were defined as being part of a nonspecific mechanism, a mechanism for biological g. These were ventrolateral thalamus, pontine reticular formation, dorsal caudatoputamen, globus pallidus, substantia nigra, ventral tegmental area, median raphe, and superior colliculus (illustrated in our human brain sterotaxic templates shown Figure 1; substantia nigra, ventral tegmental areas, and median raphe were too small for PET analysis, so they were not included in illustrations).

For all 75 sham-operated and 349 test animals combined, a factor analysis was done on performance on the different learning tests. Performance scores were based on error scores for detour tests, black-white discrimination, three-cul maze, and inclined plane, based on response latency for detours, and based on the frequency of foot shocks required to induce animals to leave the start box in discrimination and maze tests. Two factors were extracted, accounting for 97% of the common factor variance, with the first factor representing 91% and the second representing 6% of the variance.

Thompson et al. (1990, pp. 138–141) believe that the first factor is the equivalent g in the white rat, primarily because the test with the highest loading on that factor is the detour test, the test which is most similar to complex g-loaded tests of human intelligence.

Next (1990, p. 145), they determined the factor loading for each lesion, and each lesion whose factor loading with the first, or g, factor was >.20 was thought to be important. Six regions met this criterion: superior colliculus, posterior cingulate cortex, dorsal hippocampus, posterolateral hypothalamus, parietal cortex, and occipitotemporal cortex (illustrated in our human brain stereotaxic templates shown in Figures 1 & 2).Thompson et al. consider these structures to part of the mechanism of a psychometric g, as opposed to the biological g determined by brain lesions that significantly affected performance on all tasks. Note that only the superior colliculus was found to be part of the mechanisms for both biological and psychometric g.

They argue (1990, pp. 157–151) that biological g represents a measure of capacity for survival and adaptation because lesions to those structures grossly impair the ability to solve many kinds of problems. On the other hand, they argue that psychometric g measures abilities analogous to those on a conventional IQ test, which do not necessarily equate to survival capacity, because lesions to those structures each correlate with performance on only a few complex individual tests of cognitive ability.

POSITRON EMISSION TOMOGRAPHIC STUDIES OF PROBLEM SOLVING AND LEARNING IN HUMANS

Positron emission tomography (PET) with [18]fluro-2-deoxyglucose (FDG) is a relatively new brain imaging-tool. The scanning procedure starts after a subject receives an intravenous injection of FDG. Over an approximately 35-minute uptake period, the FDG is taken up and metabolically trapped by brain cells which normally take up glucose, the primary source of energy for brain cells. During that period, it is useful to engage the experimental subject in a task, which we have our subjects perform in an uptake room, separate from the PET scanner. The task determines, to a great degree, the pattern of regional brain glucose use, based on the brain regions important for task performance. After the 35-minute glucose uptake period, the patient is moved to the PET scanner. The PET scanner measures the radiation emitted as gamma rays when the positron from the 18F decay collides with an electron. Our scanner is able to measure, with a resolution of approximately 7.6mm, the concentration of FDG (or any other positron emitting substance) in the brain. The cognitive processes occurring during the execution of complex tasks, such as those used to measure intelligence, may be highly variable over short intervals. The relatively long uptake period of FDG (35 minutes) minimizes the moment-to-moment variation that might complicate the results of studies using blood flow techniques that assess functional activity over only 20–40 seconds.

We have completed two PET studies of intelligence and learning. Scan procedure and analysis of brain regions of interest were performed in the same manner as in previous studies (Buchsbaum et al., 1989), with two exceptions. One exception was that in order to study intelligence, we had the subjects perform complex cognitive tasks during the FDG uptake period (see below). Also, because of the interest in the role of the cerebellum in learning proposed by R.F. Thompson (Thompson, 1990), and because of Thompson et al.'s finding of general learning impairments in rats with lesions to the pontine reticular formation, we located regions of interest in the pons and cerebellum not studied in other projects (see Haier et al., 1992, for method).

In one study of eight normal volunteers (Haier et al., 1988; Haier, LaFalase, Katz, & Buchsbaum, submitted), we correlated regional brain glucose metabolic rate with performance on a g-loaded test of intelligence, the Raven's Advanced Progressive Matrices (RAPM), which was performed during the FDG uptake period. Inverse correlations between RAPM score and glucose metabolic rate (GMR) in cortical and subcortical areas (see Table 2) were interpreted as evidence that more intelligence people use their brains more efficiently than less intelligence ones (see also Haier, in press). Two other PET studies (Berent et al., 1988; Parks et al., 1988) also report inverse correlations between brain function and performance on complex tasks.

In the second study of another eight normals (Haier, Siegel, et al., 1992), we looked for within-individual changes in brain glucose use when performing a visuospatial/motor task (the Tetris computer game) for the first time and then after 4 to 8 weeks of practice (30–45 minutes per day). The Tetris game requires the subject, using the right hand on a computer keyboard, to rotate and move objects, consisting of four square blocks in various configurations, in such a fashion as to try to create a solid wall of blocks. The objects move downward from the top of the screen, and as the game progresses, if performance is good, their speed increases. This task was chosen because it is difficult enough so that marked and continuous improvement is shown over the practice sessions.

Results showed a general decrease in GMR in cortical areas after practice. Following significant interactions by ANOVA, 2-tailed t-tests on cortical areas showed significant relative GMR decreases with practice in the left postcentral and the left angular gyrus. A significant increase in relative GMR was in the right occipital cortex area 18.

Numerous areas showed significant decreases in GMR for medial and subcortical areas including parts of the cingulate gyrus, precuneus, putamen, and cerebellum. For relative GMR, significant decreases were in some cingulate and cerebellum areas after learning but increases occurred in areas of the right precuneus and the right hippocampus. There are also significant correlations between Tetris score and relative GMR in several areas (see Table 2).

SIMILARITIES AND DIFFERENCES BETWEEN HUMAN PET AND RAT LESION DATA

There are fundamental difficulties with comparing the results of a study measuring the performance of lesioned rats on relatively simple tasks to those of studies of regional glucose use in the brains of intact humans performing complex tasks. The lesion study purports to find brain regions whose intactness is essential to learning. Analogously, glucose metabolic rate may increase in a brain region during learning if the functioning of that region is necessary for learning. But regional GMR may also increase in structures that are not necessary for learning if those structures are just one of many possible learning strategies or if the structure is (inefficiently) activated despite its lack of essential involvement in learning. So regions where lesions impair learning (the sites of biological *g*) in the rat might be the same brain areas where there are changes in GMR with learning in the human PET studies. In Table 1, we compare the results of our PET studies to the rat brain studies of Thompson et al. (1990) based on this analogy.

We are only reporting and discussing relative glucose metabolic rate in this comparison to the rat data. Whole brain mean glucose metabolic rate accounts for most of the variance in regional glucose metabolic rate and is thus of limited usefulness in studying regional hypotheses. The relative GMR eliminates this source of variance by dividing GMR within each region by whole brain GMR.

The factor analysis of task performance in rats with varying lesion locations in the study by Thompson et al. purports to identify those brain regions where damage would cause impairment but not complete loss of cognitive performance. Although no improvements in task performance after lesioning were noted, in PET studies of normal controls negative correlations between GMR and performance may be meaningful. In Haier et al. (1988), we have discussed how a positive correlation between task performance and GMR in patients with brain pathology (as found by Berent et al., 1988, and by Chase et al., 1984) might occur in the same regions where a negative correlation would occur in normal controls. A positive correlation between regional GMR and performance in brain-damaged patients probably reflects low GMR in an injured brain structure that is necessary for task performance. In a group of normal subjects, a negative correlation might occur because the use of too many circuits within this same, essential structure may reflect a poor or confused cognitive strategy. On the other hand, a positive correlation in normal subjects might suggest that a

Table 1.   Regions implicated in biological intelligence by Thompson, Crinella, and Yu's rat brain lesion studies and by Haier et al. PET studies[1] and using group comparisons (t-tests)[2]

Thompson et al.'s Biological g	Naive vs. Practiced Tetris relative GMR
Ventrolateral thalamus	Not implicated
Dorsal caudatoputamen	Not implicated
Globus pallidus	Not implicated
Substantia nigra	Not tested
Ventral tegmental area	Not tested
Median raphe	Not tested
Superior colliculus	Not implicated
Not implicated	Postcentral gyrus (L: +)
Not implicated	Angular gyrus (L: +)
Not implicated	Occipital cortex, area 18 (R: +)
Not implicated	Cingulate gyrus (L: + & − , R: +)
Not implicated	Superior frontal gyrus, medial aspect (L: +)
Not implicated	Precuneus (R: −)
Not implicated	Cerebellar cortex (L & R: +)
Not implicated	Hippocampus (R: −)

[1]Analogous regions are included on each line. (See Figures 1 and 2.) Areas not tested by PET were too small for the resolution of our scanner.

[2]" + " indicates that naive minus practiced GMR was significantly greater than zero by 2-tailed t-test, while " − " indicates a difference significantly less than zero. Thompson, Crinella, and Yu (1990) found only one direction of change, impairment with lesion. "R" means the finding was on the right side, and "L" means it was on the left. Thompson et al.'s studies were bilateral.

structure is part of a good cognitive strategy, such that the more the structure is used (activated), the better the performance.

Analogous to the rat brain lesion factor analyses the PET studies examine psychometric g with correlation methods and the correlations of task performance with regional GMR. Regions determined to be important in the biological basis of intelligence by these methods are listed in Table 2. Not nearly enough human subjects have completed PET for factor analyses.

Because regional brain anatomy is different in the rat than it is in humans, in Tables 1 and 2, we are considering regions to be analogous if they are in the same general brain structure. For instance, any part of the cingulate gyrus in humans was considered to be analogous to posterior cingulate in the rat, and any part the hippocampus in humans was considered to be analogous to the dorsal hippocampus in the rat.

Unfortunately, even with the inclusion of all analogous structures, 33 of the 50 regions lesioned by Thompson et al. were too small to allow measurement of GMR in our PET studies. These include primarily small brainstem structures (e.g., central gray, interpedunculocentral tegmental ara), some thalamic nuclei

Table 2.   Regions implicated in psychometric intelligence by Thompson, Crinella, and Yu's rat brain lesion studies and by Haier et al. PET studies using correlational techniques[1]

Thompson et al. Psychometric g	Correlations of Tetris score with relative GMR	Correlations of RAPM score with relative GMR
Superior colliculus	Sup. colliculus (R, −)	Not implicated
Posterior cingulate cortex	Not implicated	Cingulate gy. (R, −) Ant. cing. g. (R, −)
Dorsal hippocampus	Not implicated	Not implicated
Occipitotemporal cortex	Inferior temporal cortex (L, −)	Posterior temporal cortex (L, +) and Area 17 occipital cortex (L, −)
Posterolateral hypothalamus	Not tested	Not tested
Not implicated	Superior frontal gyrus (L, +)	Inferior frontal gyrus (L, +)
Not implicated	Posterior rectal gyrus (R, +)	Medial frontal gyrus (L, +)
Not implicated	Putamen (L, +) Caudate (L, +)	Putamen (R, +)
Not implicated	Not implicated	Fusiform gyrus (R, +)
Not implicated	Not implicated	Frontal lobe white matter (R, +)
Not implicated	Not implicated	Paracentral gy. (R, +)
Not implicated	Cerebellar vermis (R, −)	Not implicated

[1]" + " indicates a positive correlation between GMR and task performance, while a " − " signifies a negative correlation. Only positive correlations were considered meaningful in the rat brain lesion study. "R" refers to a structure on the right side, while "L" refers to a left-sided structure. Thompson et al.'s studies were bilateral.

(e.g., habenular nuclei, parafascicular region), and subregions of the hypothalamus (e.g., mammillary bodies, subthalamus). Seventeen areas remain for comparison with human PET data.

Some of the rat brain structures lesioned by Thompson et al. (1990) include several stereotaxic regions of the human brain localized by our PET studies that might be considered analogous. For example, dorsal caudatoputamen (rat studies) is comparable to left and right caudate nucleus, left and right putamen, and left and right posterior putamen (PET studies). We have elected to include analyses of each of these regions separately, although we recognize that this increases the possibility of type I statistical error, because these analyses allow more exact localization of structures involved in the biological basis of intelligence.

Because they were not discussed by Thompson et al. (1990), laterality issues (left vs. right hemisphere) are not addressed here, although they may be of importance in the biological basis of intelligence.

BIOLOGICAL INTELLIGENCE

Three of the 8 brain regions implicated in biological *g* by Thompson, Crinella, and Yu: the substantia nigra, ventral tegmental area, and median raphe were too small to accurately measure FDG uptake with our scanner. Thus our study cannot adequately assess the importance of these particular structures in intelligence. Of the five remaining, measurable structures: dorsal caudtoputamen (caudate and putamen in human PET studies), pontine reticular formation (posterior pons in PET studies), globus pallidus, ventrolateral thalamus (lateral thalamus in PET studies), and superior colliculus, none showed changes in

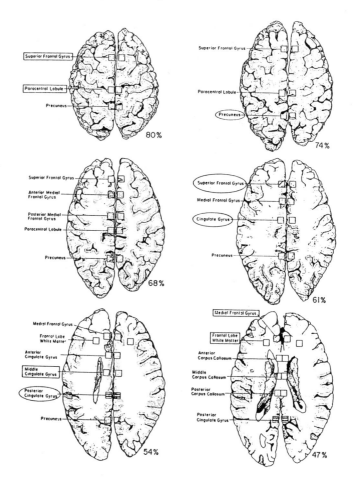

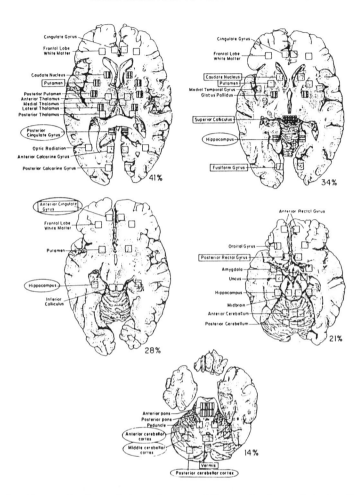

Figure 1.   Human brain region analogues of the rat brain regions implicated by Thompson et al. (1990) in biological and psychometric *g*. Regions implicated in biological *g* are indicated by vertical lines. Those implicated in psychometric *g* are indicated by horizontal lines. And the superior colliculus, which is implicated in both, is indicated by cross hatching. Area names surrounded by a box indicate a significant correlation between relative GMR and either RAPM or tetris score. Area names surrounded by an ellipse indicate a significant t-test between naive and practiced tetris scans. No distinction is made between right and left hemisphere findings. Posterolateral hypothalamus (implicated in psychometric *g*), pontine reticular formation, substantia nigra, ventral tegmental area, and median raphe (implicated in biological *g*) were all too small for resolution by our PET scanner, so they are not included in the figure or in our analyses. Percentage indicates percentage of head height above the canthomeatal line for each slice based on the Matsui and Hirano (1978) atlas.

relative GMR between the first and the second Tetris scan. There were significant correlations between Tetris game performance and relative GMR in putamen, caudate, and some areas of the superior colliculus (Figure 1); there also is the significant correlation between RAPM score and relative GMR in the putamen (analogous to part of the rat dorsal caudatoputamen (Figure 1).

PSYCHOMETRIC INTELLIGENCE

Only one of 6 regions identified by Thompson et al. (1990) as important in psychometric g was too small for resolution with our PET scanner, the posterolateral hypothalamus. Of the other 5 regions, two, the superior colliculus and temporal cortex, showed a significant correlation between relative GMR and Tetris performance (Figures 1 and 2). While posterior cingulate cortex and occipitotemporal cortex were associated with psychometric g in the rat, middle and anterior cingulate and temporal and occipital cortical relative GMR correlated with RAPM performance. Relative GMR in the anterior cingulate cortex was significantly higher during the first than the second Tetris scan (Figure 1).

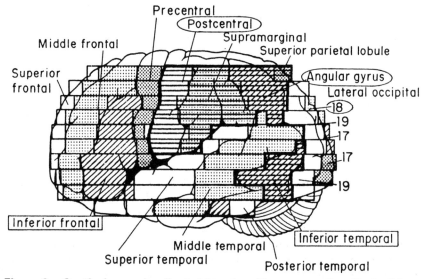

Figure 2. Cortical areas implicated in rat and human studies. Each of four segments in each of the four major lobes are shaded and labeled. Horizontal lines over shading indicate areas implicated in psychometric g according to rat lesion data. Area names surrounded by a box indicate a significant correlation between relative GMR and either RAPM or tetris score. Area names surrounded by an ellipse indicate a significant t-test between naive and practiced tetris scans.

CONCLUSIONS

This chapter compares the results of studies using two useful means of studying the biological basis of intelligence. Although the methodologies are much different, several regions, the occipitotemporal cortex, parietal cortex, cingulate gyrus, hippocampus, putamen, and superior colliculus, were implicated both in rat lesion studies and in one or both of our human studies with PET as being related to task performance. Additionally, two regions not implicated in intelligence by the lesion studies were implicated by both PET studies: lateral and medial frontal cortex, and five areas were implicated by one or the other PET study: cerebellum, paracentral gyrus, precuneus, fusiform gyrus, and frontal lobe white matter. Thus, the regions that were implicated by PET studies and not by rat lesion studies were in the frontal lobe, medial pariental and temporal cortices, and cerebellum. Analogous regions lesioned by Thompson et al., but not implicated in biological or psychometric g, were frontocingulate cortex, ventral frontal cortex and dorsal frontal cortex in the frontal lobe, septofornix area and entorhinosubicular area in temporal cortex, and cerebellum.

Thirty-seven of the 50 rat brain areas studied by Thompson et al. were not implicated in biological or psychometric g. Eight are large enough for measurement of GMR with our PET scanner (frontocingulate cortex, dorsal frontal cortex, ventral frontal cortex, amygdala, anterior thalamus, inferior colliculus, and cerebellum). Of those eight, four also were not implicated by PET studies (anterior thalamus, medial thalamus, inferior colliculus, and amygdala). The four that were implicated are: frontocingulate cortex, dorsal frontal cortex, ventral frontal cortex, and cerebellum. Of the thirteen rat brain structures implicated in either biological or psychometric g, nine were large enough for PET; six of these were implicated by one or both PET studies. Thus, overall, there were 17 areas studied in both PET and rat data; 10 areas were congruent and seven areas were not (see Table 3). This is not statistically significant.

The differences between the results of the studies may be due to the fundamental difference in design of the two studies, as discussed. Another complicating issue is that there may be differences in the sites of intelligence in rats and humans. For example, Thompson et al. (1990, pp. 159–160) have pointed out that frontal lobe structures are phylogentically new, and that during evolution, this region may have acquired some of the functions of the dorsal caudatoputamen (which has dense connections with prefrontal cortex). The power of the comparison is further limited by the larger number of rat areas too small for reliable PET determinations in humans. There is also a bias in that there are more testable PET areas for psychometric than for biological g rat areas.

The studies of Vietnam veterans with penetrating head wounds by Grafman and his colleagues (Grafman, Salazar, Weingartner, Vance, & Amin, 1986;

Table 3.   Summary of congruence between rat and human studies biological and psychometric g combined

	Human Data	
	number of areas implicated	number of areas not implicated
Rat Data		
areas implicated	6	3
areas not implicated	4	4

Grafman et al., 1988) correlating lesion size and location assessed by computerized tomography (CT) scans with measures of cognitive ability are similar in method to rat brain lesion studies. Those human studies found that premorbid intelligence and lesion size were better predictors of postmorbid intelligence than was the site of brain injury. Thus these studies call into question the existence of sites of biological g in man.

Given the number of regions analyzed in our PET studies, it is noteworthy that four of nine general regions whose GMR was found to correlate with task performance were common to the two PET studies (lateral frontal cortex, medial frontal cortex, lateral temporal cortex, and striatum).

Numerous studies suggest that cingulate cortex is involved in the filtering of sensory input and of cognitive processes, and that increased efficiency of this filtering after learning decreases GMR in those regions and increases task performance (see LaBerge, 1990). Increased electrical potentials in the cingulate cortex have also been associated with learning in animal models (Gabriel & Orona, 1982; Gabriel & Sparenborg, 1986). The superior colliculus has not previously been associated with intelligence, however, the convergence of our findings with those of Thompson et al. (1990) suggests that this region may also be an important site of cognitive processes or of their organization. The hippocampus has been widely implicated as important in learning (Berger, 1984; Thompson, 1990), and the posterior cerebral cortex is thought to be important in abstract reasoning (Luria, 1973).

The findings of our PET studies of intelligence do not directly address the conceptual differences between two main psychometrically based theories of intelligence. Detterman (1987) has hypothesized that there are several *independent* factors underlying different kinds of cognitive abilities that, taken together, account for what is measured in tests of general intelligence (see also Kranzler & Jensen, 1991). Carroll (1991), on the other hand, has argued that there is one underlying general factor, g, which accounts for at least some of the variance in performance on any kind of test of cognitive ability. A PET study done examining brain metabolic changes with simple tasks, each measuring a different kind of cognitive ability, might give results that would support one of these theories. If performance on each task correlated with metabolic activity (analogous to psychometric g) in a different brain structure or structures, it would suggest that the different cognitive abilities are located in different parts of the brain. If instead there were brain structures whose GMR correlated with performance on all of the kinds of cognitive tasks (or a g factor from the tasks), it would suggest that there are one or more brain regions which are involved in all kinds of cognitive abilities, and that there is a general factor underlying intelligence.

Our study demonstrates the potential usefulness of PET as a technique for bridging the gap between the animal literature and human studies concerned with the biological basis of intelligence. Our findings, while tentative, suggest that the putamen, superior colliculus, hippocampus, frontal lobe regions, posterior cerebral cortex, and cingulate gyrus are involved in learning and intelligence and deserve attention in future human and animal studies.

REFERENCES

Berent, S., Giordani, B., Lehtinen, S., Markel, D., Penney, J.B., Buchtel, H.A., Starosta-Rubinstein, S., Hichwa, R. & Young, A.B. (1988). Positron emission tomographic scan investigations of Huntington's Disease: Cerebral metabolic correlates of cognitive function. *Annals of Neurology, 23,* 541–546.

Berger, T.W. (1984). Long-term potentiation of hippocampal synaptic transmission affects the rate of behavioral learning. *Science, 224,* 627–630.

Blin, J., Ray, C.A., Chase, T.N., & Piercey, M.F. (1991). Regional cerebral glucose metabolism compared in rodents and humans. *Brain Research, 568,* 215–222.

Buchsbaum, M.S., Gillin, J.C., Wu, J., Hazlett, E., Sicotte, N., Dupont, R.M., & Bunney, W.E., Jr. (1989). Regional cerebral glucose metabolic rate in human sleep assessed by positron emission tomography. *Archives of Neurology, 41,* 1244–1247.

Carroll, J.B. (1991). No demonstration that g is not unitary, but there's more to the story: Comment on Kranzler & Jensen. *Intelligence, 15,* 423–436.

Detterman, D. (1987). Theoretical notions of intelligence and mental retardation. *American Journal of Mental Deficiency, 92,* 2–11.

Gabriel, M., & Orona, E. (1982). Parallel and serial processes of the prefrontal and cingulate cortical systems during behavioral learning. *Brain Research Bulletin, 8,* 781–785.

Gabriel, M., & Sparenborg, S. (1986). Anterior thalamic discriminative neuronal response enhanced during learning in rabbits with subicular and cingulate cortical lesions. *Brain Research, 384,* 195–198.

Grafman, J., Salazar, A., Weingartner, H., Vance, S., & Amin, D. (1986). The relationship of brain-tissue loss volume and lesion location to cognitive deficit. *The Journal of Neuroscience, 6,* 301–307.

Grafman, J., Jonas, B.S., Martin, A., Salazar, A.M., Weingartner, H., Ludlow, C., Smutok, M.A., & Vance, S.C. (1988). Intellectual function following penetrating head injury in Vietnam veterans. *Brain, 111,* 169–184.

Haier, R.J. (in press). Cerebral glucose metabolism and intelligence. In A. Vernon (Ed.), *The biological basis of intelligence.*

Haier, R.J., LaFalase, J., Katz, M., & Buchsbaum, M.S. (1992). *Brain efficiency and intelligence: Inverse correlations between cerebral glucose metabolic rate and abstract reasoning.* Manuscript submitted for publication.

Haier, R.J., Siegel, B.V., MacLachlan, A., Soderling, E., Lottenberg, S., & Buchsbaum, M.S. (1992). Regional glucose metabolic changes after learning a complex visuospatial/motor task: A positron emission tomographic study. *Brain Research, 570,* 134–143.

Haier, R.J., Siegel, B.V., Nuechterlein, K.H., Hazlett, E., Wu, J.C., Paek, J., Browning, H.L., & Buchsbaum, M.S. (1988). Cortical glucose metabolic rate correlates of abstract reasoning and attention studied with positron emission tomography. *Intelligence, 12,* 199–217.

Kranzler, J.H., & Jensen, A.R. (1991). The nature of psychometric *g*: Unitary process or a number of independent processes? *Intelligence, 15,* 397–422.

Laberge, D. (1990). Thalamic and cortical mechanisms of attention suggested by recent positron emission tomographic experiments. *Journal of Neuroscience, 10,* 613–619.

Lashley, K.S. (1929). *Brain mechanisms and intelligence: A quantitative study of injuries to the brain.* New York and London: Hafner.

Luria, A.R. (1973). *The working brain. An introduction to neuropsychology.* London: Penguin.

Matsui, T., & Hirano, A. (1978). *An atlas of the human brain for computerized tomograpy.* Tokyo: Igaku-Shoin.

Parks, R.W., Loewenstein, D.A., Dodrill, K.L., Barker, W.W., Yoshii, F., Chang, J.Y., Emran, A., Apicella, A., Sheramata, W., & Duara, R. (1988). Cerebral metabolic effects of a verbal fluency test: A PET scan study. *Journal of Clinical and Experimental Neuropsychology, 10,* 565–575.

Roland, P.E., Meyer, E., Shibasaki, T., Yamamoto, Y.L., & Thompson, C.J. (1982). Regional cerebral blood flow changes in cortex and basal ganglia during voluntary movements in normal human volunteers. *Journal of Neurophysiology, 48,* 467–480.

Thompson, R., Crinella, F.M., & Yu, J. (1990). *Brain mechanisms in problem solving and intelligence.* New York and London: Plenum Press.

Thompson, R.F. (1990). Neural mechanisms of classical conditioning in mammals. *Philosophical Transactions of the Royal Society of London B, 329,* 161–170.

Chapter 7

Intelligence and Neural Efficiency

Philip A. Vernon

Department of Psychology
University of Western Ontario

Biological approaches to the study of human intelligence have generated some of the most exciting, yet, at the same time, some of the most neglected results in recent years. In this chapter, three such approaches—involving the measurement of averaged evoked potentials, cerebral glucose metabolic rate, and nerve conduction velocity—are discussed and related to a neural efficiency model of intelligence. Ties between the biological approaches and recent work on the relationship between psychometric intelligence and speed of information processing—a behavioral manifestation of neural efficiency—are also described. It is concluded that work in this area has produced a considerable amount of valuable information concerning the underlying contributors to, and causes of, individual differences in intelligence and mental abilities.

AVERAGED EVOKED POTENTIAL RESEARCH

Following a number of investigations of relationships between intelligence and spontaneous EEGs (e.g., Ellingson, 1966; Giannitrapani, 1969; Vogel & Broverman, 1964, 1966), the results of which tended to be inconclusive (Gale & Edwards, 1983), researchers such as Ertl (Chalke & Ertl, 1965; Ertl & Schafer, 1969) began to study various parameters of evoked potentials and their correlations with measures of intelligence. Evoked potentials, as their name implies, are measures of the electrical activity of the brain in response to (or evoked by) some external stimulus: typically a light flash or an auditory stimulus such as a beep or a click. Over a large number of trials, random fluctuations in each individual potential can be smoothed out, yielding an averaged evoked potential (AEP), whose latency (indicating how quickly the brain responds to the external stimulus) and amplitude (indicating the amount of electrocortical activity the stimulus evokes) are the primary parameters of interest.

In Ertl and Schafer (1969), for example, multiple measures of intelligence (Wechsler Intelligence Scale for Children, Primary Mental Abilities Test, and Otis) were administered to 573 primary school children from Grades 2 to 8 and correlated with the latencies of the children's AEPs to visual stimuli. Correlations were generally negative (ranging from .10 to $-.35$), and were higher for later (average $r = -.34$) than for earlier (average $r = -.18$) components, indicating that the brains of the higher IQ children responded more rapidly than those of the lower IQ children. Based on these results, Ertl and Schafer (1969) concluded that AEPs "could be the key to understanding the biological substrate of individual differences in behavioral intelligence" (p. 422): a prediction that has received some support from subsequent research.

Ertl's findings stimulated considerable interest and activity: a number of other AEP-intelligence studies following his pioneering work (e.g., Gucker, 1973; Plum, 1968; Rhodes, Dustman, & Beck, 1969; Shucard & Horn, 1972, 1973; Weinberg, 1969). In each of these, significant correlations between measures of intelligence and latencies and/or amplitudes of AEPs to visual stimuli were reported, most of about the same magnitude as those obtained by Ertl and Schafer (1969). Subsequently, Schafer (Schafer & Marcus, 1973; Schafer, 1979, 1982) proposed a construct of *neural adaptability* to account for the finding that higher IQ subjects tended, not only to show higher amplitude AEPs to random (or unexpected) stimuli than lower IQ subjects, but also to show *lower* amplitude AEPs to self-generated (or expected) stimuli. Neural adaptability indicated that the brains of persons of higher intelligence could more efficiently regulate and make use of their limited neural resources. An index of neural adaptability correlated .66 with the Wechsler Adult Intelligence Scale (WAIS) scores of 79 high IQ subjects (Schafer, 1982) and .31 with g factor scores in a sample of severely retarded adults (Jensen, Schafer, & Crinella, 1981).

Since 1980, much AEP-intelligence research has focused on what has become known as the "string measure" (A.E. Hendrickson, 1982; D.E. Hendrickson,

1982; Hendrickson & Hendrickson, 1980), which is essentially the length of the contour perimeter of an AEP waveform. If unexpected stimuli elicit AEPs from higher IQ subjects which have shorter latencies and larger amplitudes than those of lower IQ subjects, on average, then, the Hendricksons reasoned, their AEP waveforms, if "stretched out," would be longer. Positive correlations are therefore predicted between IQ scores and the string measure and, with some exceptions (e.g., Sandman & Barron, 1986; Shagrass, Roemer, Straunanis & Josiassen, 1981), these have been found. D.E. Hendrickson (1982), for example, reported a correlation of .72 between WAIS IQs and the string measure (from AEPs to auditory stimuli) in a sample of 219 adolescents. In the same year, Blinkhorn and Hendrickson (1982) reported a correlation of .45 between the string measures and Advanced Raven Matrices scores of 33 undergraduates. Corrected for restriction of range in IQ, this correlation might be as large as .71 but, offsetting this to some extent, was the finding of no correlation between the AEP measures and tests of verbal analogies and divergent thinking.

Besides the Hendricksons, other researchers have reported generally positive results with the string measure. Eysenck and Barrett (1984), for example, re-analyzed D.E. Hendrickson's (1982) data and reported a correlation of $-.83$ between WAIS full-scale IQs and a composite AEP measure derived from the string measure and a measure of intraindividual variability in waveform complexity. The composite AEP measure also loaded .77 on the general factor when entered into a factor analysis with the 11 WAIS subtests. Haier, Robinson, Braden, and Williams (1983) reported correlations between Advanced Raven Matrices scores and the string measures of AEPs obtained under different conditions of stimulus intensity. The highest correlation ($r = .50$) was obtained in the highest intensity condition. Haier et al. (1983) also found that N140-P200 amplitudes of the AEPs were even more highly correlated with the Raven than was the string measure: with correlations as high as .69. More recently, Caryl and Fraser (1985) reported a correlation of .80 between Advanced Raven scores and string measures in a sample of 10 students, and Stough, Nettelbeck, and Cooper (1990) reported correlations as high as .86 (after correction for restriction of range and for test reliability) between string measures and WAIS IQ scores among 20 undergraduates. No significant correlations were found between string measures and Advanced Raven scores in this latter study: Stough et al. (1990) suggests that this may be attributable to the very restricted range in Raven scores that existed in their sample.

The Hendricksons have proposed a very detailed, albeit somewhat specula-tive, neurophysiological model to account for their AEP-intelligence correlations (A.E. Hendrickson, 1982; Vernon, 1985), whereby distinct patterns of electrical pulses are elicited by different sensory stimuli and stimulate the release of what they term *engram RNA*. Errors in the transmission of the pulses may result in engram RNA being released too soon or too late, and, to the Hendricksons, the probability of the occurrence of such errors forms the biological basis of individual differences in intelligence. Some support for their model comes from

Deary, Hendrickson, and Burns (1987), who first describe the importance of calcium ions in facilitating pulse-transmission and go on to report a correlation of .488 between serum calcium level and Mini-Mental Health Questionnaire scores among 20 subjects diagnosed as having Alzheimer-type senile dementia.

In sum, the above brief overview of AEP-intelligence studies leaves little doubt that a number of AEP parameters are moderately to highly correlated with a variety of psychometric measures of intelligence. Readers interested in this area will find a more comprehensive review in Deary and Caryl (1993). The AEP work is important both for having demonstrated that performance on intelligence tests can be related to a basic physiological measure—elicited by stimuli no more complex than a flash of light or a click, and demanding little more of subjects than that they stay awake and attentive—and for providing the groundwork to an understanding of intelligence in terms of the speed and efficiency with which the brain and neural systems operate.

CEREBRAL GLUCOSE METABOLISM RESEARCH

Work that builds upon the foundation provided by AEP research has investigated relationships between intelligence test performance and cerebral glucose metabolic rates. The latter are measured by *positron emission tomography* (PET) scans of the brain, which map the concentration of a positron-emitting radionuclide (typically fluorodeoxyglucose F18) that has been intravenously administered to subjects and which is taken up into different regions of the brain over about a half-hour period. Those regions of the bran that have been active during the uptake period (e.g., as a result of the subject being involved in some task that demands cognitive activity) will show the greatest amount of glucose metabolism (like any other organ, when the brain is active, it consumes energy and has to compensate for this by metabolizing glucose); mathematical models exist that can convert the PET scan-measured isotope concentrations into estimates of *glucose metabolic rates* (GMRs).

Haier, Siegel, Nuechterlein, Hazlett, Wu, Paek, Browning, and Buchsbaum (1988) engaged 30 normal male subjects in either a continuous performance task (CPT), involving the recognition of visually degraded numerical stimuli, or the Advanced Raven Matrices during the isotope uptake period and reported two main results of interest. First, the eight subjects who had been involved with the Raven Matrices showed greater relative GMRs than the CPT subjects in five different regions of the brain, all but one being a posterior region. Thus, subjects upon whom the greatest cognitive demands were placed (i.e., the Raven subjects) showed, as expected, the greatest amount of glucose metabolism. Second, within the Raven subjects, high *negative* correlations between Raven scores and absolute GMRs were found, ranging from −.44 to −.84. The sign of these correlations indicates that subjects who obtained the highest Raven scores consumed the *least* amount of energy. This is in accord with the AEP and neural adaptability work described above: providing additional support for the notion that the brains of more intelligent persons operate more efficiently than those of persons of lower intelligence.

It is unfortunate that Haier et al.'s (1988) Raven sample only contained eight subjects. This is attributable to the considerable expense associated with purchasing and operating the equipment necessary for PET scans: Haier (1990) states that an eight-subject PET scan study may cost as much as $20,000. At the same time, another PET study (Parks, Loewenstein, Dodrill, Barker, Yoshii, Chang, Emran, Apicella, Sheramata, & Duara, 1988) yielded very similar results, suggesting that Haier et al.'s findings are replicable and reliable. In Parks et al. (1988), 16 normal subjects yielded negative correlations of $-.54$, $-.50$, and $-.54$ between relative GMRs in the frontal, temporal, and parietal regions of the cortex, respectively, and performance on a verbal fluency test that subjects were engaged in during the isotope uptake period.

Other PET studies have investigated the relationship between intelligence test performance and cerebral GMRs obtained from subjects who were at rest, that is, not engaged in any kind of task, during the uptake period. Chase, Fedio, Foster, Brooks, Di Chiro, and Mansi (1984), for example, reported correlations of .61, .56, and .68 between overall cerebral GMRs and the Verbal, Performance, and Full-Scale WAIS IQs, respectively, of a sample containing 17 Alzheimer patients and 5 normal controls whose eyes were patched and ears plugged during isotope uptake. The positive sign of these correlations is not necessarily incompatible with the negative correlations reported by Haier et al. (1988) and Parks et al. (1988): It may simply indicate that the subjects in Chase et al.'s sample who obtained the highest IQ scores (i.e., those without Alzheimer's disease) were more mentally alert and spontaneously engaged in more cognitive activity even when "at rest" than the lower scoring subjects. Chase et al. (1984) also reported that their subjects' Verbal IQ scores were most highly correlated with their left hemisphere GMRs ($r = .68$) and that Performance IQs were most highly correlated with right hemisphere GMRs ($r = .61$). Unfortunately, no information is provided about the magnitude of Verbal IQ-right hemisphere correlations or Performance IQ-left hemisphere correlations, so it is impossible to evaluate how important these findings may be in implicating the use of PET scans to identify specific regions of the brain that may be involved when subjects perform different types of tests.

Other PET scan studies involving subjects with some type of dementia include Alavi, Ferris, Wolf, Reivich, Farkas, Dann, Christman, MacGregor, and Fowler (1980)—who reported that the cerebral GMRs of six senile dementia subjects were approximately 20% to 30% lower than those of four age-matched normal controls, whose cerebral GMRs were in turn some 50% lower than those of eight young normal subjects—and a number of studies have reported a similar decline in the cerebral GMRs of Alzheimer patients (e.g., Benson, 1982; Benson, Metter, Kuhl, & Phelps, 1982; de Leon, Ferris, George, Christman, Fowler, Gentes, Reisberg, Gee, Emmerich, Yonekura, Brodie, Kricheff, &

Wolf, 1983; Martin, Brouwers, Lalonde, Cox, Teleska, Fedio, Foster, & Chase, 1986).

The use of PET scans to measure the cerebral GMRs of persons involved in different cognitive tasks may well represent one of the most promising directions for future research of biological correlates of intelligence to pursue. Even though many of the PET studies reported to date have employed small samples, there can be little doubt that this is a powerful methodology with the potential to reveal much about the physiological basis of individual differences in intelligence. As has been noted, a PET scan study is an expensive proposition, which may deter some who might otherwise be interested in using the technique. Haier (1990), however, makes the point that intelligence researchers could collaborate with existing brain imaging teams and argues that the contributions that PET is capable of making to our understanding of the nature of mental abilities are too important to allow financial considerations to prevent their realization. As he states: "Sooner or later, however, all psychology research leads into the human brain. . . . Every psychology department faculty should be plotting a strategy for access to brain imaging and major neuroscience collaborations" (p. 373).

NERVE CONDUCTION VELOCITY

Nerve conduction velocity (NCV) is a measure of the speed with which electrical impulses are transmitted along nerve fibers and across synapses. It is, therefore, a pure physiological measure involving absolutely no cognitive activity. Reed (1984), however, hypothesized that individual differences in NCV are attributable to genetic variation in the structure and amount of transmission proteins and, in turn, may be related to (and set limits on) information-processing rates and intelligence. Studies that have investigated this intriguing hypothesis have yielded mixed results: two (Vernon & Mori, 1989, 1992) reporting moderate correlations between NCV, IQ scores, and a variety of reaction time (RT) measures of speed of information processing; two others (Barrett, Daum, & Eysenck, 1990; Reed & Jensen, 1991) reporting no significant IQ-NCV correlations. (Of historical interest: Travis, 1928, reported a correlation of .87 between a measure of mental ability and speed of nerve impulse conduction through the patellar reflex arc; Travis and Hunter, 1928, obtained a correlation of the same magnitude between the same variables in a different sample; and Rounds, 1928, reported correlations between performance on a variety of mental tests and latent time in the Achilles tendon that ranged between .21 and .51. Two other studies of this era—Travis & Young, 1930; Whitehorn, Lundholm, & Gardner, 1930, failed to replicate these results.)

In Vernon and Mori (1989, 1992), 85 undergraduates were administered the Multidimensional Aptitude Battery (MAB; Jackson, 1983), a group test of intelligence patterned after and highly correlated with the WAIS-R (Jackson, 1984); a battery of 12 RT tests, measuring speed of scanning or processing

Table 1.   Correlations among first unrotated (general) factors extracted
from IQ, RT, and NCV measures

	IQ	RT	NCV
IQ	1	− .44	.42
RT		1	− .28
NCV			1

information in short-term memory (STM), speed of retrieval of information from long-term memory, and the extent to which subjects could store one type of information in STM while simultaneously processing other types of information (see Vernon, Nador, & Kantor, 1985a, for a fuller description of these tests); and conduction velocities were recorded from three different segments of the median nerve of their arms. Since readers may be unfamiliar with NCV methodology, the procedure used by Vernon and Mori (1989, 1992) will be described in some detail. Differences among the NCV–intelligence correlations obtained by different investigators may in some part be attributable to procedural differences.

To measure NCV, the median nerve in each subject's right arm was given supramaximal stimulation, at a rate of one stimulation per second, for a duration of .2 milliseconds, via a surface electrode applied to the wrist. Prior to stimulation, subjects' arms were encased in heating pads which, via an attached thermistor, maintained the arm's skin temperature between 32 and 35 degrees Celsius. This is necessary, because NCV is quite susceptible to minor changes in temperature. Saline solution-soaked recording electrodes were attached at one of three points: the fingers, the elbow, or the axilla. Reference electrodes were employed to partial out any extraneous electrical activity that might be present in the system, and a ground, placed between the stimulating and recording electrodes, was employed to remove any surface electrical activity. Stimulation was generated by a DISA 1500 digital EMG system, and subjects' sensory nerve action potentials were averaged cumulatively by an online averager across series of eight responses. Latencies were measured from the baseline to the peak of the first negative deflection of each averaged potential. The distance between the stimulating and recording electrodes was also measured, allowing an estimate of velocity to be computed. Subjects were administered as many trials as were needed to yield eight "clean" averaged potentials and velocities: four from the wrist to the finger, and two each from the wrist to the elbow and the wrist to the axilla. Each NCV test session lasted approximately 45 minutes.

Intercorrelations among the 10 MAB subtests, among the 12 RT tests and among the 8 NCV measures were each subjected to principal factor analyses, yielding three general (i.e., first unrotated) factors which accounted for 44%, 66%, and 59% of the variance, respectively. Correlations between these factors are presented in Table 1 (zero-order correlations) and Table 2 (partial correlations controlling for age [above the main diagonal] or for sex [below the main diagonal]). Referring to Table 1, it can be seen that higher intelligence is

Table 2. Partial correlations among first unrotated factors extracted from IQ, RT, and NCV measures controlling for age (above main diagonal) and sex (below main diagonal)

	IQ	RT	NCV
IQ	1	−.46	.41
RT	−.43	1	−.29
NCV	.42	−.28	1

associated with faster information-processing speed ($r = -.44$), as has been found in previous studies, and to approximately the same degree with faster nerve conduction velocity ($r = .42$). RTs and NCV are themselves correlated −.28. As reported in Table 2, none of these correlations changes appreciably after controlling either for age or for sex.

In Table 3, the loadings of each of the 10 subtests of the MAB on their general factor are reported, alongside which are their zero-order correlations with the general NCV factor. As can be seen, both the loadings and the correlations vary somewhat and it is of particular interest that there is a positive correlation ($r = .44$) between the two. That is, those subtests that load more highly on the general intelligence (or g) factor tend to be more highly correlated with NCV. Previous work (Jensen, 1987a) has reported a positive correlation ($r = .60$) between the g-loadings of the subtests of the Wechsler and these subtests' heritabilites. The present results extend this by showing that the degree to which a subtest measures general intelligence is positively related to that subtest's correlation with a basic physiological property.

Barrett et al. (1990) measured sensory nerve action potentials from the median nerves (wrist to finger) of 44 adult subjects, and found no significant correlations between NCV and Advanced Raven Matrices scores. Correlations

Table 3. Factor loadings of MAB subtests on first unrotated factor and correlations with first unrotated NCV factor

Subtest[1]	Factor-loading	Correlation with NCV
INFO	.81	.283
COMP	.73	.363
ARITH	.68	.356
SIMS	.75	.288
VOCAB	.77	.241
DIGSYM	.39	.181
PICO	.56	.296
SPAT	.60	.258
PICARR	.52	.311
OBJAS	.68	.324

[1]Subtest names, in the order they appear, are Information, Comprehension, Arithmetic, Similarities, Vocabulary, Digit Symbol, Picture Completion, Spatial, Picture Arrangement, and Object Assembly.

were found, however, between intelligence and the within-subject standard deviations of NCV across trials: combining variability measures from the right and left hands yielded a multiple R with Raven scores of approximately .50. This finding is puzzling, because intertrial variability of NCV is usually small or nonexistent unless only maximal or submaximal (rather than supramaximal) stimulation has been used (supramaximal stimulation is required to ensure that all nerve fibers are firing) or some other variable(s) such as temperature fluctuations has interfered with the recording process. Whatever the reason, the fact that intertrial variability in NCV was found at all indicates that Barrett et al. (1990) and Vernon and Mori (1989, 1992) used different methods to measure NCV, and that the results of these two studies should not necessarily be viewed as contradictory.

The third recent NCV study (Reed & Jensen, 1991), conducted with 200 male college students, also failed to find any significant correlation between median nerve NCV and Advanced Raven Matrices scores. Procedural differences between this study and Vernon and Mori's (1989) appear less pronounced, although Reed and Jensen did not maintain their subjects' arm temperatures at a constant level (but controlled for temperature statistically) and other differences between the methods used to measure NCV in the two studies do exist. Clearly, the relationship (if any) between NCV and intelligence requires further study and attempts at replication. In this regard, I (Vernon & Mori, 1992) have recently tested an additional sample of 88 university students using the same equipment and procedures as Vernon and Mori (1989) did. These subjects' NCVs correlate .48 with their MAB full-scale IQ scores and $-.18$ with their RTs (IQ and RTs correlate $-.45$). It is to be hoped that other investigators will attempt to replicate these results which, given that the median nerve is in the *peripheral* nervous system, will be of considerable interest if they prove to be reliable.

THE NEURAL EFFICIENCY MODEL OF INTELLIGENCE

The results of the work described above, drawn from studies of averaged evoked potentials, cerebral glucose metabolic rates, and nerve conduction velocity, converge on what may be termed a *neural efficiency model* of intelligence. In this model, individual differences in intelligence test performance are understood as being largely attributable to differences in the speed and efficiency with which the requisite neurophysiological processes that occur during such performance are executed. Thus, the brains of persons of higher intelligence show greater neural adaptability, which Schafer (1979, 1982) describes as an efficient use of limited neural resources, and consume less energy during performance of complex reasoning problems (Haier et al., 1988; Parks et al., 1988) than the brains of persons of lower intelligence. In addition, there is some evidence that the greater efficiency of the neural system of higher IQ persons extends into the peripheral nervous system: faster NCV in the median nerve of the arm being positively associated with IQ scores in one recent study (Vernon & Mori, 1989), and this result appearing to be replicated when the same procedure for measuring NCV is adopted (Vernon & Mori, 1992).

What structural properties of the brain might underlie these manifestations of more efficient functioning that are hypothesized to contribute to individual differences in intelligence? Willerman and Raz (1987) suggest that the number, organization, and degree of interconnectedness of cortical cell analyzers, and the size and number of association and commissural nerve fibers in cortical white matter (which, respectively, interconnect neurones within and between the two hemispheres), may be fundamental to intelligence. As they state:

> The association and commissural fibers would seem especially relevant to intelligence because they probably represent important neurological underpinnings for educing relations and correlates, or more simply put, making connections between disparate cognitive elements and applying them to new problems...it seems reasonable to propose the theory that intelligent people have a greater number of cortical elements arranged in some hierarchical order which permits finer analysis of signals. (p. 9)

Willerman and Raz (1987) also discuss a number of biochemical factors that may contribute to individual differences in neurotransmission and intelligence. Such factors are also considered by Weiss (1984), and Naylor, Callaway, and Halliday (1993) provide a comprehensive review of biochemical correlates of human information-processing. Most recently, Willerman, Schultz, Rutledge, and Bigler (1991) used magnetic resonance imaging to measure in vivo brain size. They report a significant difference between the brain sizes of 40 high- and average-IQ university students, after controlling for differences in height and weight, with a point-biserial correlation of .40. An in-depth review of head and brain size and other physical correlates of intelligence is provided by Jensen and Sinha (1993). Taken together, it would seem that preliminary steps, at least, have been taken toward identifying the underlying physical and physiological factors that contribute to the functional efficiency of the brain.

INTELLIGENCE AND SPEED
OF INFORMATION PROCESSING

Additional information pertinent to the neural efficiency model of intelligence is provided by recent work on the relationship between intelligence and speed of information processing. Detailed overviews of this work are provided elsewhere (e.g., Vernon, 1987), and only a few key findings will be summarized here.

First, individual RT or speed-of-processing measures, be they simple responses to lights on a panel or more complex measures requiring retrieval of verbal or spatial information from long-term memory, mostly seem to correlate between approximately $-.20$ to $-.40$ with IQ scores (Vernon, 1990a): higher intelligence being associated with faster, or shorter, RTs. One exception to this generalization is Eysenck's "Odd-Man-Out" test, a relatively complex RT task performed on Jensen's Hick apparatus, which has shown correlations with intelligence of $-.483$ (Frearson, Barrett, & Eysenck, 1988) and $-.62$ (Frearson & Eysenck, 1986).

Second, studies that have employed different versions of information-processing tasks, designed to vary in complexity, have shown that the more complex versions correlate more highly with intelligence than do the less complex versions. This result occurs even when the different versions of the RT tests are all relatively simple: Jensen (1987b) reports average correlations of $-.19$, $-.21$, $-.24$, and $-.26$ between IQ scores and RTs obtained in four conditions of increasing complexity in the Hick paradigm, in the most complex condition of which mean RTs rarely exceed about 400 milliseconds. It also occurs when quite complex information-processing tasks (with mean RTs of the order of 900 to 1000 milliseconds) are employed (Vernon & Weese, 1991). Moreover, a very strong relationship ($r = .97$) has been reported between the relative complexity of a number of RT measures and the degree to which the measures discriminate between groups differing in mean IQ (Vernon, Nador, & Kantor, 1985b).

More complex RT tasks are expected to correlate more highly with intelligence, because, almost by definition, they impose increasing information-processing demands and thus more closely approximate the types of cognitive activity elicited by intelligence test items. Speed-of-processing is proposed to be a property of the working-memory system that allows it to cope with the information-processing demands of mental tasks despite its limited storage capacity and its inability to store information for more than a short period of time in the absence of continued rehearsal. As tasks move upward along a continuum of complexity, ranging from simple RT tests at one end, to more complex RT tests in the middle, to highly complex problem-solving tasks at the other end, speed-of-processing becomes increasingly important and is one determinant of a person's ability to perform the task(s) successfully. In this sense, then, speed of information processing can be viewed as a behavioral manifestation of neural efficiency: It is a property that allows the brain to make the most efficient use of its limited-capacity information-processing system.

Third, studies that have employed multiple measures of speed of information processing have reported quite sizeable multiple correlations between these and intelligence test scores. Vernon (1990a), for example, summarizes six studies in which multiple Rs from the regression of IQ scores onto five or more speed-of-processing tests range from .366 to .737. Similarly, composite general intelligence and general speed-of-processing factors, derived from batteries of IQ and RT tests, respectively, correlate between $-.260$ and $-.673$ (Vernon, 1989a). Thus, speed of information processing may account for as much as 50% of the variance in intelligence.

Fourth, although performance on RT tests is a behavioral (rather than a biological) manifestation of neural efficiency, there is evidence relating individual differences in speed-of-processing to underlying biological mechanisms. McGue, Bouchard, Lykken, and Feuer (1984), for example, using data from the Minnesota Study of Twins Reared Apart, reported that factor scores on an overall speed of response factor had a heritability of .46. Comparable results were reported by Ho, Baker, and Decker (1988), who found heritabilities of .52 and .49 for a rapid automatic naming task and the Colorado perceptual speed task, respectively, and by Vernon (1989b), who found a heritability of .49 for a general speed-of-processing factor derived from a battery of 11 measures. In both McGue et al. (1984) and Vernon (1989b), moreover, positive correlations exist between the heritability of the different RT tests that they administered and the degree to which these tests correlated with intelligence (r = .48 and .61, respectively). Similar to the relationship between the g-loading of MAB subtests and the tests' correlations with NCV reported above, in these studies the more g-loaded a RT test, the higher that test's heritability. Finally, using multivariate biometrical analyses, Ho et al. (1988) reported genetic correlations of approximately .42 between each of their information-processing tests and IQ, and Baker, Vernon, and Ho (1991) report genetic correlations of 1.0 and .92 between RTs and Verbal and Performance IQ scores, respectively. These correlations indicate that "speed and IQ may share some common biological mechanisms" (Ho et al., 1988, p. 258) and, indeed, significant correlations have been reported between a number of AEP parameters and measures of speed-of-processing (e.g., Donchin & Lindsley, 1966; Dustman, 1965; Kutas, McCarthy, & Donchin, 1977; Morrell & Morrell, 1966; Zhang, Caryl, & Deary, 1989a,b) and, as noted above, between RTs and NCV (Vernon & Mori, 1989, 1992).

CONCLUSIONS

In sum, considerable progress has been made in the identification of biological correlates of intelligence and information processing. It bears noting, too, that the work described in this chapter by no means represents an exhaustive summary of all that has been accomplished in this area: a recent book (Vernon, 1993) provides a broader overview. Further advances seem highly likely as more researchers begin to pursue this line of inquiry and as continuing technological developments make the requisite equipment increasingly accessible.

As more is learned about the underlying biological correlates of, and contributors to, individual differences in mental abilities, it will become increasingly necessary for theories of intelligence to accommodate them. Measures of biological processes also have considerable assessment potential which remains to be realized: Unlike traditional IQ tests they can, for example, be administered in the same manner to subjects of virtually any age and level of mental ability and they surely must come close to being as culture fair as is possible (Vernon, 1990b). What are needed at present are continued attempts at replication—particularly of the PET scan and NCV studies—and studies that look at the relationship between intelligence and multiple biological/physiological measures: an appropriately weighted combination of which may be anticipated to account for a sizeable proportion of the variance.

REFERENCES

Alavi, A., Ferris, S., Wolf, A., Reivich, M., Farkas, T., Dann, R., Christman, D., MacGregor, R.R., & Fowler, J. (1980). Determination of cerebral metabolism in senile dementia using F-18 deoxyglucose metabolism and positron emission tomography. *Journal of Nuclear Medicine, 21,* 21.

Baker, L.A., Vernon, P.A., & Ho, H.Z. (1991). The genetic correlation between intelligence and speed of information-processing. *Behavior Genetics, 21,* 351–367.

Barrett, P.T., Daum, I., & Eysenck, H.J. (1990). Sensory nerve conduction and intelligence: a methodological study. *Journal of Psychophysiology, 4,* 1–13.

Benson, D.F. (1982). The use of positron emission scanning techniques in the diagnosis of Alzheimer's disease. In S. Corkin, K.L. Davis, J.H. Growdon, E. Vodin, & R.J. Wurtman (Eds.), *Alzheimer's disease: A review of progress in research* (pp. 79–82). New York: Raven Press.

Benson, D.F., Metter, E.J., Kuhl, D.E., & Phelps, M.E. (1982). Positron computed tomography in neurobehavioral problems. In A. Kertesz (Ed.), *Localization in neuropsychology* (pp. 121–139). New York: Academic Press.

Blinkhorn, S.F., & Hendrickson, D.E. (1982). Averaged evoked responses and psychometric intelligence. *Nature, 295,* 596–597.

Caryl, P.G., & Fraser, I.C. (1985, September). *The Hendrickson string length and intelligence—a replication.* Paper presented at the Psychophysiology Society Scottish Conference, Edinburgh.

Chalke, F., & Ertl, J. (1965). Evoked potentials and intelligence. *Life Science, 4,* 1319–1322.

Chase, T.N., Fedio, P., Foster, N.L., Brooks, R., Di Chiro, G., & Mansi, L. (1984). Wechsler Adult Intelligence Scale performance: Cortical localization by fluorodeoxyglucose F18-positron emission tomography. *Archives of Neurology, 41,* 1244–1247.

Deary, I.J., & Caryl, P.G. (1993). Intelligence, EEG and evoked potentials. In P.A. Vernon (Ed.), *Biological approaches to the study of human intelligence.* Norwood, NJ: Ablex Publishing Corp.

Deary, I.J., Hendrickson, A.E., & Burns, A. (1987). Serum calcium levels in Alzheimer's disease: A finding and an aetiological hypothesis. *Personality and Individual Differences, 8,* 75–80.

de Leon, M.J., Ferris, S.H., George, A.E., Christman, D.R., Fowler, J.S., Gentes, C., Reisberg, B., Gee, B., Emmerich, M., Yonekura, Y., Brodie, J., Kricheff, I.I., & Wolf, A.P. (1983). Positron emission tomographic studies of aging and Alzheimer disease. *American Journal of Neuroradiology, 4,* 568–571.

Donchin, E., & Lindsley, D.B. (1966). Average evoked potentials and reaction times to visual stimuli. *Electroencephalography and Clinical Neurophysiology, 20*, 217–223.

Dustman, R.E. (1965). Phase of alpha brain waves, reaction time, and visually evoked potentials. *Electroencephalography and Clinical Neurophysiology, 18*, 433–440.

Ellingson, R.J. (1966). Relationship between EEG and test intelligence: A commentary. *Psychological Bulletin, 65*, 91–98.

Ertl, J.P., & Schafer, E.W.P. (1969). Brain response correlates of psychometric intelligence. *Nature, 223*, 421–422.

Eysenck, H.J., & Barrett, P. (1984). Psychophysiology and the measurement of intelligence. In C.R. Reynolds & V. Willson (Eds.), *Methodological and statistical advances in the study of individual differences*. New York: Plenum Press.

Frearson, W., Barrett, P., & Eysenck, H.J. (1988). Intelligence, reaction time and the effects of smoking. *Personality and Individual Differences, 9*, 497–517.

Frearson, W.M., & Eysenck, H.J. (1986). Intelligence, reaction time (RT) and a new 'odd-man-out' RT paradigm. *Personality and Individual Differences, 7*, 807–817.

Gale, A., & Edwards, J.A. (1983). Cortical correlates of intelligence. In A. Gale & J.A. Edwards (Eds.), *Physiological correlates of human behaviour. Vol. 3: Individual differences and psychopathology*. London: Academic Press.

Giannitrapani, D. (1969). EEG average frequency and intelligence. *Electroencephalography and Clinical Neurophysiology, 27*, 480–486.

Gucker, D.K. (1973). Correlating visual evoked potentials with psychometric intelligence: Variation in technique. *Perceptual and Motor Skills, 37*, 189–190.

Haier, R.J. (1990). The end of intelligence research. *Intelligence, 14*, 371–374.

Haier, R.J., Robinson, D.L., Braden, W., & Williams, D. (1983). Electrical potentials of the cerebral cortex and psychometric intelligence. *Personality and Individual Differences, 4*, 591–599.

Haier, R.J., Siegel, B.V., Nuechterlein, K.H., Hazlett, E., Wu, J.C., Paek, J., Browning, H.L., & Buchsbaum, M.S. (1988). Cortical glucose metabolic rate correlates of abstract reasoning and attention studied with Positron Emission Tomography. *Intelligence, 12*, 199–217.

Hendrickson, A.E. (1982). The biological basis of intelligence. Part I: Theory. In H.J. Eysenck (Ed.), *A model for intelligence*. Berlin: Springer-Verlag.

Hendrickson, D.E. (1982). The biological basis of intelligence. Part II: Measurement. In H.J. Eysenck (Ed.), *A model for intelligence*. Berlin: Springer-Verlag.

Hendrickson, D.E., & Hendirckson, A.E. (1980). The biological basis of individual differences in intelligence. *Personality and Individual Differences, 1*, 3–33.

Ho, H.Z., Baker, L., & Decker, S.N. (1988). Covariation between intelligence and speed-of-processing: Genetic and environmental influences. *Behavior Genetics, 18*, 247–261.

Jackson, D.N. (1983). *Multidimensional Aptitude Battery*. Port Huron, MI: Research Psychologists Press.

Jackson, D.N. (1984). *Multidimensional Aptitude Battery manual*. Port Huron, MI: Research Psychologists Press.

Jensen, A.R. (1987a). The g beyond factor analysis. In J.C. Conoley, J.A. Glover, & R.R. Ronning (Eds.), *The influence of cognitive psychology on testing and measurement*. Hillsdale, NJ: Erlbaum.

Jensen, A.R. (1987b). Individual differences in the Hick paradigm. In P.A. Vernon (Ed.), *Speed of information-processing and intelligence*. Norwood, NJ: Ablex Publishing Corp.

Jensen, A.R., Schafer, E.W.P., & Crinella, F.M. (1981). Reaction time, evoked brain potentials, and psychometric g in the severely retarded. *Intelligence, 5*, 179–197.

Jensen, A.R., & Sinha, S.N. (1993). Physical correlates of human intelligence. In P.A. Vernon (Ed.), *Biological approaches to the study of human intelligence*. Norwood, NJ: Ablex Publishing Corp.

Kutas, M., McCarthy, G., & Donchin, E. (1977). Augmenting mental chronometry: The P300 as a measure of stimulus evaluation time. *Science, 197*, 792–795.

Martin, A., Brouwers, P., Lalonde, F., Cox, C., Teleska, P., Fedio, P., Foster, N.L., & Chase, T.N. (1986). Towards a behavioral typology of Alzheimer patients. *Journal of Clinical and Experimental Neuropsychology, 8*, 594–610.

McGue, M., Bouchard, T.J., Jr., Lykken, D.T., & Feuer, D. (1984). Information processing abilities in twins reared apart. *Intelligence, 8*, 239–258.

Morrell, L.K., & Morrell, F. (1966). Evoked potentials and reaction times: A study of intra-individual variability. *Electroencephalography and Clinical Neurophysiology, 20*, 567–575.

Naylor, H., Cailaway, E., & Halliday, R. (1993). Biochemical correlates of human information processing. In P.A. Vernon (Ed.), *Biological approaches to the study of human intelligence*. Norwood, NJ: Ablex Publishing Corp.

Parks, R.W., Loewenstein, D.A., Dodrill, K.L., Barker, W.W., Yoshii, F., Chang, J.Y., Emran, A., Apicella, A., Sheramata, W.A., & Duara, R. (1988). Cerebral metabolic effects of a verbal fluency test: A PET scan study. *Journal of Clinical and Experimental Neuropsychology, 10*, 565–575.

Plum, A. (1968). *Visual evoked responses: Their relationship to intelligence*. Unpublished doctoral dissertation, University of Florida, Gainseville.

Reed, T.E. (1984). Mechanism for heritability of intelligence. *Nature, 311*, 417.

Reed, T.E., & Jensen, A.R. (1991). Arm nerve conduction velocity (NCV), brain NCV, reaction time, and intelligence. *Intelligence, 15*, 33–47.

Rhodes, L.E., Dustman, R.E., & Beck, E.C. (1969). The visual evoked response: A comparison of bright and dull children. *Electroencephalography and Clinical Neurophysiology, 27*, 364–372.

Rounds, G.H. (1928). Is the latent time in the Achilles tendon reflex a criterion of speed in mental reactions? *Archives of Psychology*, No. 95.

Sandman, C.A., & Barron, J.L. (1986). Parameters of the event-related potential are related to functioning in the mentally retarded. *International Journal of Neuroscience, 29*, 37–44.

Schafer, E.W.P. (1979). Cognitive neural adaptability: A biological basis for individual differences in intelligence. *Psychophysiology, 16*, 199.

Schafer, E.W.P. (1982). Neural adaptability: A biological determinant of behavioral intelligence. *International Journal of Neuroscience, 17*, 183–191.

Schafer, E.W.P., & Marcus, M.M. (1973). Self-stimulation alters human sensory brain responses. *Science, 181*, 175–177.

Shagrass, C., Roemer, R.A., Straumanis, J.J., & Josiassen, R.C. (1981). Intelligence as a factor in evoked potential studies of psychopathology - 1. Comparison of low and high IQ subjects. *Biological Psychiatry, 16*, 1007–1030.

Shucard, D.W., & Horn, J.L. (1972). Evoked cortical potentials and measurement of human abilities. *Journal of Comparative and Physiological Psychology, 78*, 59–68.

Shucard, D.W., & Horn, J.L. (1973). Evoked potential amplitude change related to intelligence and arousal. *Psychophysiology, 10*, 445–452.

Stough, C.K.K., Nettelbeck, T., & Cooper, C.J. (1990). Evoked brain potentials, string length and intelligence. *Personality and Individual Differences, 11*, 401–406.

Travis, L.E. (1928). The correlation between intelligence and speed in conduction of the nerve impulse in a reflex arc. *Science, 67*, 41–43.

Travis, L.E., & Hunter, T.A. (1928). The relation between 'intelligence' and reflex conduction rate. *Journal of Experimental Psychology, 11*, 342–354.

Travis, L.E., & Young, C.W. (1930). The relations of electromyographically measured reflex times in the patellar and achilles reflexes to certain physical measurements and to intelligence. *Journal of General Psychology, 3*, 374–400.

Vernon, P.A. (1985). Individual differences in general cognitive ability. In L.C. Hartlage & C.F. Telzrow (Eds.), *The neuropsychology of individual differences*. New York: Plenum.

Vernon, P.A. (1987). *Speed of information-processing and intelligence*. Norwood, NJ: Ablex Publishing Corp.

Vernon, P.A. (1989a). The generality of g. *Personality and Individual Differences, 10*, 803–804.

Vernon, P.A. (1989b). The heritability of measures of speed of information-processing. *Personality and Individual Differences, 10*, 573–576.

Vernon, P.A. (1990a). An overview of chronometric measures of intelligence. *School Psychology Review, 19*, 399–410.

Vernon, P.A. (1990b). The use of biological measures to estimate behavioral intelligence. *Educational Psychologist, 25*, 293–304.

Vernon, P.A. (Ed.). (1993). *Biological approaches to the study of human intelligence*. Norwood, NJ: Ablex Publishing Corp.

Vernon, P.A., & Mori, M. (1989). Intelligence, reaction times, and nerve conduction velocity. *Behavior Genetics* (abstracts), *19*, 779.

Vernon, P.A., & Mori, M. (1992). Intelligence, reaction times, and peripheral nerve conduction velocity. *Intelligence, 16*, 273–288.

Vernon, P.A., Nador, S., & Kantor, L. (1985a). Reaction times and speed-of-processing: Their relationship to timed and untimed measures of intelligence. *Intelligence, 9*, 357–374.

Vernon, P.A., Nador, S., & Kantor, L. (1985b). Group differences in intelligence and speed of information-processing. *Intelligence, 9*, 137–148.

Vernon, P.A., & Weese, S.E. (1991, April). *The effect of task complexity on the relationship between intelligence and speed of information-processing*. Paper presented at the Annual Meeting of the American Educational Research Association, Chicago.

Vogel, W., & Broverman, D.M. (1964). Relationship between EEG and test intelligence: A critical review. *Psychological Bulletin, 62*, 132–144.

Vogel, W., & Broverman, D.M. (1966). A reply to "Relationship between EEG and test intelligence: A commentary." *Psychological Bulletin, 65*, 99–109.

Weinberg, H. (1969). Correlation of frequency spectra of averaged visual evoked potentials and verbal intelligence. *Nature, 224*, 813–815.

Weiss, V. (1984). Psychometric intelligence correlates with interindividual different rates of lipid peroxidation. *Biomedica Biochemica Acta, 43*, 755–763.

Whitehorn, J.C., Lundholm, H., & Gardner, G.E. (1930). Concerning the alleged correlation of intelligence with knee jerk reflex time. *Journal of Experimental Psychology, 13*, 293–295.

Willerman, L., & Raz, N. (1987, June). *Implications of research on auditory recognition masking for a theory of intelligence.* Paper presented at the 3rd meeting of the International Society for the Study of Individual Differences, Toronto.

Willerman, L., Schultz, R., Rutledge, J.N., & Bigler, E. (1991). *In vivo* brain size and intelligence. *Intelligence, 15*, 223–228.

Zhang, Y., Caryl, P.G., & Deary, I.J. (1989a). Evoked potential correlates of inspection time. *Personality and Individual Differences, 10*, 379–384.

Zhang, Y., Caryl, P.G., & Deary, I.J. (1989b). Evoked potentials, inspection time, and intelligence. *Personality and Individual Differences, 10*, 1079–1094.

Chapter 8

Individual Differences in the Predominant Direction of Gaze Shift in Relation to Cognitive Function—A Metaanalysis*

Lee Friedman and John T. Kenny

*Department of Psychiatry,
Case Western Reserve University School of Medicine
Cleveland, OH*

INTRODUCTION

The idea that the lateral direction of gaze shift during information processing might be related to individual differences in cognitive style, or preferred cognitive mode, was first proposed by Day (1964). Since then, a substantial literature has accumulated relating an individual's predominant direction of gaze shift to his or her cognitive functioning. The basic assumptions which underlie

* The authors would like to thank the many researchers in this area that we needed to contact to complete the metaanalysis: Paul Bakan, John Stern, Bruce Dunn, Howard Ehrlichman, Merrill Hiscock, Blair Johnson, Patricia Salt, Bob Zenhausern, Brian Mullen, John Limber, and Wayne

this literature are: (a) that cortical brain function is lateralized so that, for example, the left hemisphere is predominantly involved in verbal processing, whereas the right hemisphere is predominantly involved in spatial processing; (b) that ipsilateral stimulation of the frontal eye fields (FEF) causes a con-tralateral saccade; (c) that cognitive tasks which require reflection can cause a "spill-over" of excitation in the cortex, and that this "spill-over" can stimulate the FEF and cause a contralateral saccade; and (d) that people can be divided into those who predominantly move their eyes to the left (*left-movers*) and those who predominantly move their eyes to the right (*right-movers*) upon reflection. These four assumptions have led investigators to hypothesize that individuals who are right-movers predominantly employ the left hemisphere during cognition, and that individuals who are left-movers predominantly use the right hemisphere during cognition. We shall refer to this hypothesis as the *individual differences hypothesis*. As we shall see, the verbal/spatial distinction is only one of several commonly invoked in this literature. We note in passing that, in addition to the individual differences hypothesis, there is a large body of work on the *question type hypothesis*, which proposes that Ss move their eyes to the left when reflecting on questions that activate the right hemisphere, and vice versa (Kinsbourne, 1972). Since the theme of the current volume is individual differences in relation to cognition, we review only the former hypothesis. Excellent reviews of the question type hypothesis are available (Ehrlichman & Weinberger, 1978; Ehrlichman, 1984; Hiscock, 1986; Charlton, Bakan, & Moretti, 1989).

As indicated above in assumption 1, lateralization of brain function is presumed. The verbal (left hemisphere) / nonverbal (right hemisphere) distinc-tion is one of several cognitive constructs invoked in order to examine the relationship between lateralized brain functioning and lateral eye movements. The nature and strength of the data supporting the lateralization of these constructs varies. A brief overview of the validation research for the major constructs will follow.

Verbal vs. Nonverbal or Visuospatial. There is a substantial body of data in support of the idea that lesions of the left hemisphere are more often associated with a verbal deficit and lesions of the right hemisphere are more often associated with a nonverbal deficit (for reviews, see Milner, 1971; Levy, 1974; Bradshaw & Nettleton, 1983; Alexander, Benson, & Stuss, 1989). Also, patients with dyslexia have been found to have abnormal brain morphology in the left hemisphere (for review, see Hynd & Semrud-Clikeman, 1989).

In neurologically intact subjects, studies of spatial recognition performance with tachistoscopic displays directed to either the left visual field (right

Weitan. Usually, our efforts to obtain the necessary data were successful. In the few cases where we failed, we thank those researchers for trying. We appreciate the burden of searching for old data. Gregory Sherrad was of immense help in the accumulation and management of the literature. We wish to thank John Jesberger and Laura Knutson for editorial assistance.

hemisphere) or right visual field (left hemisphere) also support the notion that the left hemisphere is more proficient at verbal recognition and the right hemisphere is more proficient at spatial recognition (Kimura, 1969; Levy, 1974). Finally, a number of studies of regional cerebral blood flow (rCBF), either with the Xe[133] technique or with positron emission tomography (PET) have indicated that verbal tasks activate the left hemisphere and spatial tasks the right (Risberg, Halsey, Wills, & Wilson, 1975; Carmon, Lavy, Gordon, & Portnoy, 1975; Reivich & Gur, 1985; Posner, Peterson, Fox, & Raichle, 1988). While there is considerable support for the notion of lateralization of verbal vs. visual/spatial functions, highly complex spatial tasks are more likely to require both hemispheres (Bradshaw & Nettleton, 1983).

Analytic vs. Holistic/Global. The analytic/holistic distinction hypothesizes that "the minor [right] hemisphere is seen to organize and treat data in terms of complex wholes, being in effect a synthesizer with a predisposition for viewing the total rather than the parts. The left hemisphere sequentially analyzes input, abstracting out the relevant details" (p. 132). (Nebes, 1978; also see Bradshaw & Nettleton, 1983). Studies with split-brain (commissurotomized) patients have found that the right hemisphere is much better than the left in tasks that require the formation of a visual gestalt (Levy-Agresti & Sperry, 1968; Nebes, 1978). Some lesion studies have suggested that patients with unilateral right hemisphere lesions perform relatively more poorly on tasks that require a pictorial visual discrimination than on tasks that require an analytical discrimination (Levy, 1974), although Semenza, Denes, D'Urso, Romano, and Montorsi (1978) found no difference between patients with left or right hemisphere lesions on type of strategy (analytic vs. global) when copying designs.

In normal subjects, Natale (1977) provides evidence that the left hemisphere is superior on tasks of auditory sequential analysis of rhythm and suggests that a central auditory analyzer of rhythms is in the left hemisphere, although Lezak (1983) has reviewed evidence of right hemisphere involvement in the analysis of tone quality and rhythm of speech. Bradshaw and Sherlock (1982) performed a tachistoscopic visual discrimination task in which, for the same stimuli, subjects were either required to attend to the spatial relationships, independent of detail (holistic condition), or to the shape of certain discrete features (analytic condition). There was a left visual field–right hemisphere advantage in the holistic condition, and a right field advantage for the analytic condition. Van Kleek (1989) metaanalyzed a number of similar tachistoscopic studies in normal subjects, which tested for a left vs. right visual field difference in the perception of global versus detailed information and found evidence that a left hemisphere/local, right hemisphere/global specialization does in fact exist.

Visceral Perception. The research literature on brain lateralization and visceral perception, although not as extensive as for the verbal/nonverbal and analytic/holistic constructs, appears to be consistent across different contexts in suggesting that autonomic perception may be mediated by the right rather than left hemisphere. Walker and Sandman (1979) recorded visual evoked potentials during periods of fast, midrange, and slow heart rates and found a greater detectable difference in magnitude of visual evoked potentials during these heart beat conditions for the right hemisphere than for the left hemisphere. In a follow-up investigation (Walker & Sandman 1982), right hemispheric visual evoked potentials recorded during systolic and diastolic blood pressure differed significantly, whereas there was no difference for the left hemisphere. Stimuli presented to the right and left visual fields were found to elicit anticipatory heart rate acceleration only for stimuli presented in the left visual field (right hemisphere). For a more detailed review of this topic, consult the review of Katkin (1985).

Field-Independence/Field-Dependence. When a vertical rod is viewed within a tilted square frame in an otherwise blacked-out environment, there is a tendency to misperceive the rod as tilted due to the influence of the frame. Stable individual differences in this tendency, termed "field-dependence", have been documented (Witkin & Asch, 1948). Several studies have presented evidence that the left hemisphere processes in a field-independent mode, and the right hemisphere processes in a field-dependent mode. For example, Cohen, Berent, and Silverman (1973) administered the Rod-and-Frame test to female psychiatric patients before and after delivery of a single electroconvulsive shock treatment to either the left or right hemisphere. Following treatment, all 12 patients receiving left hemispheric shock, and with presumably reduced efficiency of this hemisphere, showed greater field dependence. By contrast, all 12 patients receiving right hemispheric shock showed increased field independence, presumably as a result of increased influence of the left hemisphere. In another study, field-independent females were found to perform significantly worse than field-dependent females on a verbal (left hemisphere) but not on a visuospatial (right hemisphere) task (Berent & Silverman, 1973). Russo and Vignolo (1967) found that patients with left hemispheric lesions and aphasia performed significantly worse on a test of field independence (the Gottschalt Hidden Figures Test, which requires "field independence" to detect the figures hidden in the "field") than those with right hemispheric lesions.

The FEF and Contralateral Saccades. Zee (1986) has recently reviewed the evidence with respect to assumption 2: Ipsilateral activation, including microstimulation, of the FEF does lead to a contralateral saccade. In particular, in monkeys the FEF contains a subpopulation of neurons that discharge before voluntary saccades. Finally, acute lesions of the FEF create a transient defect in the ability to generate contralateral saccades.

Spill-Over Hypothesis. One of the criticisms that Ehrlichman and Weinberger (1978) raise regarding the "lateral eye movement–cognitive process association" is that, if cognitive activity causes hemispheric activation, there is no evidence or explanation as to how this "spills over" to the FEF. However, Charlton et al. (1989) marshall some evidence in support of the spill-over hypothesis. For example, the FEF has the appropriate anatomical connections consistent with the spill-over hypothesis, particularly from primary and secondary association cortical areas (Crowne, 1983). Moreover, activation of the FEF, as indicated by increased rCBF, has been noted during visual and auditory discrimination tasks, naming of visually exposed items, and listening to verbal commands with eyes closed (Roland, 1984). Even more to the point, increases in rCBF in the FEF are frequently asymmetrical. For example, when subjects judge the slopes of lines and when attention is turned towards nonverbal auditory signals, the right FEF was activated more than the left. Similarly, Gur et al. (1983) measured regional cerebral glucose metabolism in the FEF and found a higher metabolism in the left FEF when subjects performed a verbal task and higher metabolism in the right FEF when subjects performed a spatial task.

Conclusions from Traditional Reviews. The "individual differences hypothesis" has been carefully reviewed several times. The earlier review of Ehrlichman and Weinberger (1978) concluded that individual differences in lateral eye movement patterns and their cognitive correlates provide little support for the hemispheric asymmetry model. Among the reasons cited by these reviewers for reaching this conclusion was the failure of many studies to find statistically significant differences between left-movers and right-movers on cognitive variables. In a later review, Ehrlichman (1984) indicated that a clear pattern of results in studies of the individual differences hypothesis had not emerged, in part, because attempts to replicate prior studies had failed. In a similar vein, Hiscock (1986) states that "the correlational approach to the study of LEMS [lateral eye movements] has generated many speculations about the neural basis for differences among humans, but few reliable facts." The most recent comprehensive reviewers (Charlton et al., 1989) restricted themselves to studies based on the verbal vs. visual/spatial cognitive construct, since "the two variables which are most noted for demonstrating hemispheric asymmetry in the [hemispheric] specialization literature are spatial and verbal tasks." They concluded that, although there are some discrepancies in the literature, overall, results from both the WAIS-based and verbal task type studies appear to support the hemispheric interpretation, but that results from studies employing non-WAIS-based spatial tasks alone were much more equivocal, with some studies supporting the hemispheric asymmetry hypothesis and others failing to confirm these findings.

The use of metaanalysis to summarize results of separate reports has been steadily increasing (Mann, 1990), as the power of the technique has become increasingly evident. There have been several recent developments in meta-analytic techniques (for review and discussion, see Hedges & Olkin, 1985; Bangert-Drowns, 1986; Becker, 1987; Hunter & Schmidt, 1990). We have chosen the methods proposed by Hedges and Olkin (1985) as implemented in the software package *DSTAT* by Blair T. Johnson (1989), since these techniques appear to be less subject to current criticism by metaanalytic experts (Bangert-Drowns, 1986; Becker, 1987; Johnson, 1989), as compared to the "tests of combined significance" approach (Rosenthal, 1978). In the present review, effect sizes (known as *d values*) are calculated for individual studies in order to determine whether differences between left-movers and right-movers on cognition-related variables are consistent with any of a set of hypotheses regarding the differential role of the two cerebral hemispheres. Composite effect sizes and confidence intervals are presented to summarize the studies. Statistics are presented which address the extent to which the results of the studies are homogeneous. The influence of independent variables (such as the gender of the subjects or the criteria by which left-movers and right-movers are classified) on study outcomes is assessed with techniques analogous to ANOVA in primary-level studies (Hedges & Olkin, 1985; Johnson, 1989). Studies that are outliers are identified. An assessment of "publication bias" (Light & Pillemer, 1984; Mullen, 1989) in this literature is also presented. (Publication bias refers to the situation in which nonsignificant studies with small sample sizes are not reported, whereas studies with large samples, regardless of statistical significance, are reported, as are statistically significant studies with small samples.) In our presentation of the meta-analysis, we have followed the form of two meta-analyses (Kite & Johnson, 1988; Johnson & Eagly, 1989) recently published in major APA journals.

STUDY CHARACTERISTICS

Gender as a Potential Modifier of Study Outcome. One hypothesis regarding sex differences in cerebral laterality proposes that males have a greater degree of hemispheric specialization and are therefore more dependent on their left hemisphere for language and their right for spatial abilities (Maccoby & Jacklin, 1974; Butler, 1984; but see Buffrey & Gray, 1972, for a diametrically opposite theory). Lesion evidence in support of the concept of males being more lateralized was provided by Landsdell (1961), who reported that males exhibited more profound decrements than females on verbal tests of proverbs following left temporal lobectomy, presumably because they depended more heavily on the left hemisphere for language. Conversely, females with left hemispheric lesions showed a greater decline in performance than males on a test of design preference, which is presumably mediated by the right hemisphere (Lansdell, 1962). This is consistent with the notion that females have some of their spatial capability in the left hemisphere whereas males have all of their spatial capability in the right hemisphere. McGlone and Kertesz (1973) found that males with right hemispheric lesions showed a greater impairment or spatial tasks than females with right hemispheric lesions (Block Design, Raven's Colored Progressive Matrices). It has also been suggested that males are more prone to develop aphasia secondary to left hemispheric lesions (McGlone, 1977). However, Kertesz and Benke (1989) question the latter finding, since, in their study, females became aphasic after left-hemisphere lesions as often as men when the data were corrected for sex differences in the incidence of infarcts. Also, Brown and Grober (1983) found no sex differences in the rate of aphasia after left hemisphere cerebrovascular incidents over most of the lifespan.

There are some studies in normal subjects that have also indicated sex differences in cerebral laterality (for reviews, see Buffrey & Gray, 1972; Bryden, 1979). For example, Lake and Bryden (1976) concluded that men were more highly lateralized than women based on a dichotic listening task. According to Butler (1984), electroencephalographic (EEG) studies have supported the notion that men are more highly lateralized. However, one study has found that blood flow to the cerebral hemispheres is more lateralized in *women* than men (Gur et al., 1982). Despite inconsistencies, these data suggested the need to examine the potential influence of sex differences as a moderator variable on lateral eye movements in the meta-analysis.

Left-Mover/Right-Mover Classification Criteria as a Potential Modifier of Study Outcome. Two reviews have summarized the data on the reliability of both detection of lateral eye movements and the classification of an individual subject's preferential direction of gaze shift (Ehrlichman & Weinberger, 1978; Hiscock, 1986). Both reviewers concluded that, in general, both measurement and classification are "reasonably reliable" (Ehrlichman & Weinberger, 1978) and "quite satisfactory" (Hiscock, 1986).

In reviewing the distributional characteristics of lateral eye movements, Ehrlichman and Weinberger (1978) present evidence that the distribution is not bimodal, as would be predicted if one assumes that the population is comprised solely of right- versus left-movers. Rather, the distribution appears to be multimodal, with modal points at the extremes. Thus, subjects are on a continuum, ranging from the extreme right through a mixture of both right and left (bimodals) to extreme left. Therefore any typology of right- versus left-mover will need to utilize some criteria of inclusion. Although some studies have classified subjects as left-movers if the majority of the lateral eye movements was to the left, and vice versa, most studies use a 70% criteria in an effort to obtain relatively pure groups. The potential influence of this variable on study outcome is assessed in this meta-analysis.

METHODS

Sample of Studies. Most of the studies were identified by examining the reference lists of three major reviews of this area (Ehrlichman & Weinberger, 1978; Ehrlichman, 1984; Charlton et al., 1989). In addition, computerized literature searches were conducted using Medline and PsychLit. The following key words were employed: *lateral eye movements* and *cognition*; *lateral eye movements* and *intelligence; lateral eye movements* and *cerebral dominance.*

Dissertation Abstracts were searched, and bibliographies of located studies were examined. Finally, two experts in this area, Drs. Paul Bakan and Howard Ehrlichman, were contacted by phone. For cases in which the data were available both as dissertations and publications, the publication was chosen, unless the data were not fully described (e.g., Hiscock 1975, 1977).

The Structure of Included Studies. To be included in our meta-analysis, studies had to: (a) *Divide Ss into left-movers and right-movers.* A number of papers characterized subjects along a continuum based on, for example, the number of left eye movements, and correlated this number with the score on a cognitive variable. We did not include these correlational studies, since the data were in a markedly different form compared to the papers that dichotomized *S*s as left- or right-movers. Also, a number of studies included a group of "bimovers" who did not meet the criterion for left- or right-movers. In such cases, the data on bimovers were ignored, and the data on left- versus right-movers was extracted for computation of effect size. (b) *Compare these groups on some cognition-related measure.* Papers which examined personality, emotional, and biological indices were not included. In cases where there was some question regarding the cognitive nature of the hypothetical construct, we deferred to the author's opinion. (c) *Not have wide and irreconcilable inconsistencies in the reported statistical information* (1 report). (d) *Provide enough information to be entered into a formal meta-analysis.* With respect to this last point, it should be mentioned that we made a considerable effort to obtain useful information from every study. The DSTAT software package (Johnson, 1989) provides extremely flexible tools for recovery of effect size data from a variety of reported statistics, including F-tests, t-tests, Chi-Square, means and standard deviations, and p-values. These tools also allow for the reconstruction or extraction of the statistic of interest from a more complicated design. In a number of cases, when more information about a study was needed or when raw data was needed, authors were contacted by phone (see acknowledgments).

Effect Sizes. For each hypothesis tested, i.e., each cognitive construct and each operational definition, within each study, effect sizes (g, defined as the difference between two means divided by the pooled standard deviation) were computed in most cases from reported means and standard deviations or from F or t statistics. In several cases effect sizes were computed based on the proportion of *S*s in a given category, or in the absence of any more detailed information, from a reported p-value. Studies which provided no numerical information but only indicated that the results were not significant were excluded from the meta-analysis, since an estimate of the effect size was not calculable. The resulting effect size, or g, was corrected for bias due to sample size, a bias that is found especially with small samples (Hedges & Olkin, 1985)—the resulting variable was termed d. The direction of the effect size was positive if it supported the author's hypothesized relationship between the ability of left-movers vs. right-movers on the cognitive variable of interest. We did not impose our own expectations for effect direction on these studies, since we did not feel that such an imposition was justified.

Table 1 lists all the hypothesis tests evaluated along with their effect size (*d*) and direction. Sixteen of 29 studies reported more than one hypothesis test. As has been pointed out (Bangert-Drowns, 1986; Hunter & Schmidt, 1990; Rosenthal & Rubin, 1986; Mullen, 1989), multiple effect sizes calculated from a given study are not statistically independent observations, since they may have resulted from evaluation of the same set of subjects, by the same investigators, in the same experimental situation. For this reason, all metaanalytic work, with one important exception (see below), was performed at the level of a study, and derived effect sizes within a study were averaged (Bangert-Drowns, 1986; Hunter & Schmidt, 1990).

To assess the composite effect size, a *weighted mean effect size*, computed by weighting each effect by the reciprocal of its variance, was calculated (Hedges & Olkin, 1985). The homogeneity of groups of effect sizes (Qwi) was computed according to the method of Hedges and Olkin (1985)—a computation that takes into account each study's effect size as well as the sample sizes in the left-mover and right-mover groups.

Independent Variables. Most of the studies defined left-movers and right-movers on the basis of either a majority of eye movements in a given direction (51%, six studies) or 70% or more (18 studies). A determination was made of whether the studies that used 51% had different effect sizes than those that employed 70% or more. The potential for published reports to have different outcomes than unpublished theses was also examined. The year of publication was evaluated as a continuous variable regressed on effect size using special methods developed for metaanalysis (Hedges & Olkin, 1985, Johnson, 1989).

Gender effects were evaluated by performing a subsidiary metaanalysis. Studies that included only males were coded as group 1. The single study that included only females was coded as group 2. Studies which provided data separately for males and/or females were re-analyzed, and the data were entered into one or both groups. A categorical analysis comparing studies with all males with those containing all females was then conducted to evaluate gender effects.

Several variables that we had intended to assess as outcome moderators did not have sufficient variability across studies to warrant assessment as categorical models. We had intended to compare studies in terms of the method of recording eye movements. However, 26 of the 29 studies used visual inspection, two used videotape, and one used electro-oculography. With only two studies in a category, any comparisons would be very unreliable. Similarly, we coded whether studies used exclusively right-handed Ss, exclusively left-handed Ss, or both, since there is evidence that left-handers are less lateralized (Levy, 1974). Twenty-four studies employed only right-handed Ss, none studied only left-

Table 1.   Summary of Individual Hypothesis Tests in the Metaanalysis

Authors	Year	Reported P-Value	Effect size (d)[1]	N	Cognitive Construct (Code[2])	Operational Definition	Hemisphericity
Bakan	1969	.05	+.81	35	Analytic vs. Intuitive/Global (1)	Hard vs. Soft Major	Left vs. Right
		.05	+.63	41	Analytic vs. Intuitive/Global (1)	Math vs. Verbal SAT Scores	Left vs. Right
		NS	+.51	42	Image Clarity (2)	Self Rated Image Clarity	Right vs. Left
Bakan & Shotland	1969	.025	+.63	49	Visual Attention Interference (4)	Stroop Interference Test	Left
		.01	+.81	49	Reading Speed (2)	Reading Names of Colors	Left
Ogle	1971	NS	+.33	48	Interference (4)	Stroop Interference Test	Left
		.05	+.54	48	Silent Reading Speed (2)	Silent Reading Speed	Left
		.025	+.56	48	Oral Reading Speed (2)	Oral Reading Speed	Left
		NS	+.08	48	Silent Reading Comprehension (2)	Silent Reading Comprehension	Left
		NS	+.29	48	Oral Reading Comprehension (2)	Oral Reading Comprehension	Left
		NS	+.30	48	Comprehension in Speeded Task (2)	Comprehension in Speeded Task	Left
		.05	+.79	48	Sensory Modality (4)	Auditory/Visual/Audio-Visual Modes	Left vs. Right
		.005	+.88	48	Silent Reading Speed (2)	Fixations	Left
		.005	+.56	48	Silent Reading Speed (2)	Regressions	Left
		.02	+.84	48	Silent Reading Speed (2)	Pure Fixations	Left
		.05	+1.74	48	Silent Reading Speed (2)	Pause Durations	Left
		NS	+.04	48	Oral Reading Speed (2)	Fixations	Left
		NS	+.02	48	Oral Reading Speed (2)	Regressions	Left
		NS	+.08	48	Oral Reading Speed (2)	Pure Fixations	Left
		.005	+1.35	48	Oral Reading Speed (2)	Pause Durations	Left

Table 1. Summary of Individual Hypothesis Tests in the Metaanalysis (continued)

Authors	Year	Reported P-Value	Effect size (d)[1]	N	Cognitive Construct (Code[2])	Operational Definition	Hemisphericity
Barnat	1972	NS	+.04	95	Analytic Processing (1)	Embedded Figures Test	Left
		*	−.16	59	Analytic Processing (1)	Embedded Figures Test	Left
		NS	+.06	95	Tough Mindedness (−9)	Kuder Mechanical Interest	Left
		NS	+.01	95	Tough Mindedness (−9)	Kuder Computational Interest	Left
		NS	+.12	95	Tough Mindedness (−9)	Kuder Scientific Interest	Left
		NS	−.10	95	Tough Mindedness (−9)	Kuder Clerical Interest	Left
		NS	−.06	95	Tender Mindedness (1)	Kuder Artistic Interest	Right
		NS	−.10	95	Tender Mindedness (1)	Kuder Literary Interest	Right
		NS	+.12	95	Secondary Process (4)	Rorschach F+%	Left
		NS	+.15	95	Secondary Process (4)	Rorschach Lambda	Left
		NS	−.06	95	Secondary Process (4)	Rorschach D %	Left
		NS	−.23	95	Secondary Process (4)	Rorschach Dd %	Left
		NS	−.19	95	Primary Process (4)	Rorschach W %	Right
		NS	−.06	95	Primary Process (4)	Hold Primary Process Summary	Right
Harnad	1972	.05	+.70	32	Visual Imagery (2)	Self Report Visual Imagery	Right
		.01	+.93	32	Aesthetic Interests (4)	Engages in Artistic Activity	Right
		.005	+1.44	20	Creativity (4)	Remote Associates Test	Right
		NS	+.74	20	Aesthetic Responsivity (4)	Neutral Response to Emotional Prose	Right
Weitan & Etaugh	1973	.05	+.88	18	Verbal/Analytic vs Perceptual Motor (−9)	Concept Identification vs. Inverted Alphabet Print	Left vs. Right
		NS	+.50	18	Perceptual-Motor (4)	Inverted Alphabet Print	Right
		.05	+1.02	15	Math vs. Verbal Aptitude (−9)	Math vs. Verbal SAT Scores	Left vs. Right
		*	+.97	14	Rational vs. Subjective (4)	Science vs. Humanities	Left vs. Right

Table 1. Summary of Individual Hypothesis Tests in the Metaanalysis (continued)

Authors	Year	Reported P-Value	Effect size (d)¹	N	Cognitive Construct (Code²)	Operational Definition	Hemisphericity
Gur et al.	1975	.05	+.73	43	Seating Preference (4)	Right vs. Left Side Seating Choice	Left vs. Right
Hiscock	1975	NS	−.37	37	Visual Spatial (2)	Mental Object Manipulation	Right
		NS	−.36	37	Verbal (2)	Quick Word Test	Left
		NS	−.42	37	Verbal (2)	IQ Verbal Scale	Left
		NS	−.36	37	Imagery (−9)	IQ Imagery Scale	Right
Crouch	1976	.05	+.45	78	Verbal vs. Visual/Holistic (−9)	Verbal vs. Facial Cues	Left vs. Right
Combs et al.	1977	*	+.93	24	Analytic vs. Intuitive (1)	Language vs. Art Majors	Left vs. Right
Hoffman & Kagan	1977	NS	+.14	48	Field Dependence (1)	Analytic Index	Right
Huang & Byrne	1978	.025	+2.07	16	Narrow vs. Broad Categorizers (4)	Pettigrews C-W Scale	Left vs. Right
Moretti	1978	NS	+.34	53	Verbal Comprehension (2)	Verbal Comprehension Factor—WAIS IQ	Left
		NS	+.08	53	Perceptual Organization (2)	Perceptual Organization Factor—WAIS IQ	Right
Tucker & Suib	1978	.001	+1.66	60	Verbal vs. Visual Spatial (2)	Verbal vs. Performance IQ	Left vs. Right
MaCallum	1979	NS	−.30	36	Simultaneous Minus Successive (4)	Simultaneous Minus Successive Tests	Right-Left
		NS	+.37	36	Simultaneous Processing (4)	Simultaneous Tests	Right
		NS	−.26	36	Successive Processing (4)	Successive Tests	Left
Ray et al.	1979	*	+.27	133	Spatial/Horizontality (2)	Water Jar Task	Right

Table 1. Summary of Individual Hypothesis Tests in the Metaanalysis (continued)

Authors	Year	Reported P-Value	Effect size (d)[1]	N	Cognitive Construct (Code[2])	Operational Definition	Hemisphericity
Stan & Spanos	1979	.05	−.45	10	Nonanalytic Attending (−9)	Tellegren Atkinson Questionnaire	Right
		NS	−.59	6	Nonanalytic Attending (1)	Attending to Nonsense Syllables	Right
		.05	+1.45	6	Nonanalytic Attending (1)	Self Rated Attention Depth	Right
Baldinger	1980	NS	+.33	64	Verbal Fluency (2)	Produce Word Beginnings	Left
		.01	+.69	64	Verbal Fluency (2)	Produce Word Endings	Left
		.01	+.68	64	Verbal Fluency (2)	Produce Word Beginnings/Word Endings	Left
		NS	+.28	64	Vocabulary (2)	WAIS Vocabulary Subtest	Left
		.01	+.68	64	Verbal Closure (2)	Identifying Scrambled Words	Left
		NS	+.00	64	Spatial/Nonverbal Processing (2)	WAIS Block Design Subtest	Right
		NS	−.21	64	Spatial/Nonverbal Processing (2)	Shape Memory Test	Right
		NS	−.32	64	Spatial/Nonverbal Processing (2)	Map Memory Test	Right
Spanos et al.	1980	*	+.71	52	Imaginative Absorption (−9)	Tellegren Atkinson Questionnaire	Right
		NS	−.37	52	Mental Imagery Vividness (2)	Betts Mental Imagery Questionnaire	Right
		NS	+.37	52	Verbalizers vs. Visualizers (2)	Verbal/Visual Questionnaire	Left vs. Right
		NS	−.08	52	Gestalt Visual Closure (2)	Thurstone Gestalt Closure Test	Right

Table 1. Summary of Individual Hypothesis Tests in the Metaanalysis (continued)

Authors	Year	Reported P-Value	Effect size (d)[1]	N	Cognitive Construct (Code[2])	Operational Definition	Hemisphericity
Walton	1980	*	+.74	30	Nonverbal Processing (2)	Facial Recognition Test	Right
		*	−.14	30	Verbal Processing (2)	Abstract Word Definitions	Left
		*	+.41	30	Facial Recognition Speed (2)	Facial Recognition Latency	Right
		*	+.61	30	Facial Recognition Duration (2)	Facial Recognition Time Spent	Right
		*	+.08	30	Abstract Word Definition Speed (2)	Abstract Word Definition Latency	Left
		*	+.40	30	Nonverbal vs. Verbal Processing (2)	Facial vs. Word Definition	Right vs. Left
Katz & Salt	1981	.001	+1.52	25	Analytic (1)	Hard Majors	Left
		.008	+1.06	25	Intuitive/Global (1)	Soft Majors	Right
		.10	+.51	25	Verbal Skills (2)	SAT Verbal Scale Scores	Left
		.10	+.51	25	Adjectives/Feeling Quality (2)	Use of Adjectives	Right
Toombs	1982	.05	+1.12	58	Verbal Recall (2)	Nonsense Word Recall	Left
		.05	+.61	58	Nonverbal Recall (2)	Facial Recall	Right
Jean	1982	.006	+.75	87	Facial Recognition (1)	Reaction time, tachistoscopic display	Right
Pierro & Goldberger	1982	NS	+.33	35	Field Dependence (1)	Rod and Frame Test	Right
Domangue	1984	.04	−.30	70	Nonverbal Sensitivity (2)	Profile Nonverbal Sensitivity	Right
Hantas et al.	1984	.001	+1.88	20	Visceral Perception (3)	Heart Beat Detection	Right
Montgomery & Jones	1984	.05	+.75	39	Visceral Perception (3)	Heart Beat Detection	Right

Table 1. Summary of Individual Hypothesis Tests in the Metaanalysis (continued)

Authors	Year	Reported P-Value	Effect size (d)[1]	N	Cognitive Construct (Code[2])	Operational Definition	Hemisphericity
Reed	1987	NS	+.35	49	Visceral Perception (3)	Heart Beat Detection	Right
Dunn et al.[3]	1989	*	−.94	48	Analytic vs. Holistic (1)	Sentence vs. Pictorial Inferenceses	Left vs. Right
		NS	−.36	38	Complex Inferential Reasoning (1)	Logical Syllogisms	Left
		NS	+.35	38	Syllogistic Memory (1)	Memory for Syllogisms	Left

[1]Effect sizes are positive if the results were in the expected or hypothesized direction with respect to the relationship between hemisphericity and the left-mover/right-mover individual difference dichotomy. They are corrected for sample size according to Hedges and Olkin (1985).

[2]A construct was coded "1" if it referred to the "analytic vs. global/intuitive/non-analytic" dimension, "2" if it referred to the "verbal vs. visual/spatial/non-verbal" dimension, "3" if it referred to visceral perception, "4" if it did not refer to 1, 2 or 3 and "−9" if it was potentially confounded, such as "analytic vs. spatial."

[3]Hypotheses test for Dunn et al., which we obtained from data provided to us by Dr. Dunn. Unfortunately, data for 1 additional hypothesis, concerning memory for sentence vs. pictorial inferences, were not available.

*Statistical significance not provided in original report.

handed Ss, two studied a mixture, and in four studies the data were not indicated. Also, we coded the types of Ss included as either normals or patients. All of the studies reported herein were conducted on normal Ss.

For meta-analysis of the moderating effect of cognitive construct, each hypothesis was categorized as either pertaining to the *analytic vs. global/ intuitive/nonanalytic* dimension (code 1), the *verbal vs. visual/spatial/nonverbal* dimension (code 2), the *visceral perception* dimension (code 3), and *other* (code 4). Hypotheses that were potentially confounded, such as *analytic vs. spatial*, were coded as -9, and were not included in the test of the effect of construct. As is evident in Table 1, multiple hypotheses within a study might pertain to different constructs. Thus, the effect of construct could not be tested at the level of a study. Rather, all the hypotheses within a study that pertained to the same construct were averaged and entered as an entity into the categorical meta-analysis.

Publication Bias, the File Drawer Problem and Fail-Safe Numbers. We made a considerable effort to obtain unpublished theses as well as published reports. An assessment of publication bias, or in the present case, "report-bias," was made through the use of a funnel plot (Light & Pillemer, 1984; Mullen, 1989), which plots effect size on the abscissa and sample size on the ordinate. The law of large numbers predicts that the larger studies will be most representative of the true population effects. Studies with smaller samples should be randomly scattered about the central effect size of the larger studies, with scatter increasing as study size decreases, thus creating an inverted funnel appearance. Report bias is evident if the lower left portion of this inverted funnel is missing, indicating that small studies with nonsignificant results are not as frequently reported as small studies with significant results. It is certainly possible that nonsignificant studies exist in scientists' files and have not been reported anywhere. This has been referred to as the *file-drawer problem* (Rosenthal, 1979). Orwin (1983) has developed a method for determining the number of studies with null effects in file drawers somewhere that would be required to reduce the overall effect size to a negligible level. In the present case, we chose .1 as our negligible target effect size, following the example of Hunter and Schmidt (1990).

RESULTS

Each hypothesis test included in the metaanalysis is listed in Table 1. There are a total of 94. Note the high degree of variability in hypothetical constructs and operational definitions. There were 45 hypotheses relevant to the verbal vs. visual/spatial dimension, 17 relevant to the analytic vs. global/intuitive/ non-analytic dimension, 3 that concerned visceral perception, 19 that were in the "other," class and 10 that were confounded (-9).

Of the 94 hypothesis tests, no p-value was reported for 12. Of the 82 remaining hypotheses, 46, or 56.1%, were reported to be nonsignificant.

Overall Analysis. For meta-analysis, the effect sizes within a study were averaged. The effect sizes of the 29 studies in the meta-analysis are listed in Table 2. Five papers (17.2%) reported an effect opposite to the hypothesis, 1 paper (3.3%) reported no effect, and 23 (76.7%) reported effects in support of the hypothesis. Eight (27.6%) of the positive effect sizes were in the small range (0.1 to 0.35), 3 (10.3%) were in the moderate range (0.36 - 0.65) and 12 (41.4%) were in the large to very large range (above 0.65). The average uncorrected effect size, or g, was 0.56, the average corrected effect size, d, was 0.55, and the weighted mean effect size was 0.41 (Table 3), which would fall into the moderate (0.5) to small (0.2) range (Cohen, 1988). As noted in the Table 3, the 95% confidence limits around this composite effect size do not include 0, and thus it may be concluded that, overall, studies that have compared left-movers to right-movers on cognitive variables have found differences in the predicted direction. However, before this conclusion is accepted, the homogeneity of the effect sizes must be considered.

Homogeneity Test. For all 29 studies combined, Qwi was highly significant, indicating marked inhomogeneity (Table 3). According to Johnson (1989), the first step in accounting for nonhomogeneity is to test the effects of independent categorical and continuous variables in an effort to determine if study outcomes are homogeneous within levels of an independent variable. Another approach is to sequentially remove outliners until homogeneity is achieved.

Tests of Categorical and Continuous Models. The results of the categorical model tests are presented in Table 4 for the cognitive dimension, and in Table 5 for the eye movement classification criterion, published versus unpublished studies, and gender. The largest effects were seen for the visceral perception dimension, followed by the "other" category, then the verbal vs. visual/spatial dimension, and finally the analytic vs. global/intuitive/holistic dimension. These differences were not statistically significant, however. The difference in effect size between studies that used a 51% criterion and those that used a 70% or larger criterion was negligible. As expected, published studies had larger effect sizes than unpublished studies, but this difference was also not statistically significant. Finally, contrary to expectation, studies with only women had larger effects than studies with only men, although, once again, this difference was not significant. Thus, our categorical analyses were not able to account for any significant variation in effect size. There was no evidence of a linear year- of-publication effect (regression effect = 0.53, df = 1, p = 0.47), and removal of a linear year-of-publication factor did not enhance effect size homogeneity (Q-E = 75.8, df = 27, p < 0.0001).

Outlier Analysis. Outliers were removed successively until homogeneity was achieved (Table 3). The three studies with the largest effect size and the study with the second from the lowest (negative) effect size were marked as outliers.

Table 2.   List of Reports Included in the Metaanalysis Ordered by Effect Size

Authors	Year	Effect Size[1] & Direction	Sample[2] Size	Associated[3] p-value	Cognitive Construct	Coded Variables[4]
Hiscock	1975	-.38	37	0.253	Verbal vs. Visual/Spatial Processing	1/100/3/2/1
Domangue	1984	-.30	70	0.209	Nonverbal Sensitivity	1/100./1/2/1
Hoffman et al.	1977	-.14	48	0.626	Field Dependence	1/45.8/1/2/1
McCallum	1979	-.06	36	0.860	Simultaneous vs. Successive Processing	2/-9/1/-9/2
Barnat	1972	-.03	92	0.884	Tough vs. Tendermindedness	2/50./1/-8/1
Dunn et al.	1989	.00	41	0.990	Analytic vs. Holistic Reasoning	1/50./1/1/1
Spanos et al.	1980	.16	52	0.570	Verbal vs. Visual Imagery	1/51.9/1/2/1
Stan and Spanos	1979	.16	7	0.818	Nonanalytic Attention	2/49./1/2/1
Moretti	1978	.19	53	0.488	Verbal vs. Visual/Spatial Intelligence	2/52.8/1/2/1
Baldinger	1980	.27	64	0.288	Verbal vs. Nonverbal Processing	2/50./1/2/1
Ray et al.	1979	.27	133	0.117	Spatial Processing	1/37.59/1/-9/1
Pierro and Goldberger	1982	.33	35	0.332	Field Dependence	1/44.2/1/2/2
Reed	1987	.35	49	0.221	Visceral Perception	2/100./1/2/1
Walton	1980	.35	30	0.343	Verbal vs. Nonverbal Processing	2/100./1/2/1
Crouch	1976	.45	78	0.050	Verbal vs. Visual/Holistic	1/44.9/1/1/1
Ogle	1971	.56	48	0.057	Reading Speed	2/50./1/1/2
Bakan	1969	.65	39	0.047	Analytic vs. Intuitive/Global Processing	1/60.9/1/1/2
Bakan and Shotland	1969	.72	49	0.015	Visual Attention	1/59.2/1/-9/2
Gur et al.	1975	.74	43	0.020	Classroom Seating Preference	1/55.4/1/2/2
Montgomery and Jones	1984	.75	39	0.023	Visceral Perception	1/100./2/-9/1
Jean	1982	.75	87	0.001	Facial Processing	2/52.8/1/2/1
Weitan and Etaugh	1973	.85	16	0.101	Verbal/Analytic vs. Perceptual Motor	1/-9/1/2/-9
Toombs	1982	.86	58	0.002	Verbal vs. Nonverbal Memory	1/-9/1/2/2
Katz and Salt	1981	.90	25	0.031	Analytic vs. Intuitive/Global Processing	1/64./1/1/2

Table 2. List of Reports Included in the Metaanalysis Ordered by Effect Size (continued)

Authors	Year	Effect Size[1] & Direction	Sample[2] Size	Associated[3] p-value	Cognitive Construct	Coded Variables[4]
Combs et al.	1977	.93	24	0.030	Analytic vs. Intuitive Processing	1/46.9/2/1/2
Harnad	1972	.96	26	0.021	Visual Imagery and Aesthetic Responsivity	1/−9/1/2/2
Tucker and Suib	1978	1.66	60	0.000	Verbal vs. Visual/Spatial Processing	1/50./1/2/2
Hantas et al.	1984	1.88	20	0.000	Visceral Perception	1/100.1/2/1
Huang and Byrne	1978	2.07	16	0.001	Narrow vs. Broad Categorization	1/0./1/2/1

[1]Effect sizes are positive if the results were in the expected or hypothesized direction with respect to the relationship between hemisphericity and the left-mover/right-mover individual difference dichotomy. They are corrected for sample size according to Hedges and Olkin (1985). In cases where a report contained multiple relevant hypotheses, the effect sizes listed are an average (Hunter and Schmidt, 1990).

[2]In cases where different hypotheses within a study were associated with different Ns, sample size listed is an average.

[3]These p-values correspond to the corrected effect sizes (Johnson, 1989) and are all two-tailed.

[4]The first coded variable is the format of the report (1 = published, 2 = unpublished thesis), the second variable is the percent of subjects that were male, the third variable is the method of measuring eye movements (1 = visual inspection, 2 = video tape, 3 = electrooculogram), the fourth variable refers to the criteria used to classify subjects as left or right movers based on the percent of eye movements in a given direction (1 = 51%, 2 = 70% or more; −8 = 66.6% as criteria—this study was not included in the analysis of this variable), the fifth variable is coded 1 if the data were included in the categorical analysis of a sex effect (studies with 100% male, studies with 0% male and studies which provided data separately for the sexes) and coded 2 if the study could not be included in the sex effect test. In all cases, a −9 means that the data were not available.

Table 3.   Composite Effect Sizes Before and After Outlier Removal

	Mean Weighted Effect Size (d[1+])	95% Confidence Limits	P-value[1]	Homogeneity Statistic (Qwi) Value	df	p-value[2]
All 29 Studies:	+0.4137	+0.30/+0.52	.0000	72.51	28	0.0000
With 4 Outlying Studies Removed:[3]	+0.3768	+0.26/+0.49	.0000	32.13	24	0.1239

[1] Two-tailed p-value corresponding to each effect size. The value is based on the total sample sizes for all studies.

[2] Statistical significance indicates rejection of homogeneity.

[3] Four was the minimum number of outlying studies that could be removed to first achieve homogeneity. The four outlying studies, in order of largest outlier to smallest are: Tucker and Suib, 1978 (d = +1.66); Domangue, 1984 (d = −0.30); Hantas et al., 1984 (d = +1.88); and Huang and Byrne, 1978 (d = +2.07). Removal of 4/29 studies corresponds to 13.8%.

Table 4. Tests of Cognitive Construct as a Moderator of Study Effect Size

Constructs	n	Mean weighted effect size (d_{i+})[1]	95% CI for d_{i+} Lower	Upper	Homogeneity within class (qwi)[2]	Between class effect (Q_B)
						2.84 ns
Analytic vs. Global/Intuitive/Non-analytic:	9	+0.34	−0.13	+0.55	17.69*	
Verbal vs. Visual/Spatial/Non-Analytic:	14	+0.38	+0.23	+0.53	40.59**	
Visceral Perception:	3	+0.72	+0.32	+1.11	6.3 ns	
Other	8	+0.42	+0.20	+0.64	17.8*	

[1]Effect sizes are positive if the results were in the expected or hypothesized direction with respect to the relationship between hemisphericity and the left mover/right mover individual difference dichotomy.
[2]Significance indicates a rejection of homogeneity.
*p < .05. **p < .001.
*ns - not significant.

Table 5.   Tests of Categorical Models for Study Effect Sizes

Variable and Class	Between-class effect (Q_B)	n	Mean weighted effect size (d_{i+})[1]	95% CI for d_{i+} Lower	Upper	Homogeniety within class (Qwi)[2]
Studies which used a 51% Unidirectional Criteria to Distinguish "Mover" Groups vs. Studies which Used a 70% (or more) Criteria:	0.03					
50%:		6	+0.50	+0.24	+0.76	4.03
70%:		18	+0.47	+0.32	+0.62	58.33**
Published vs. Unpublished Reports:	0.61					
Published:		20	+0.45	+0.31	+0.59	59.36**
Unpublished:		9	+0.36	+0.18	+0.53	12.54
Studies of Men vs. Studies of Women:	0.29					
Men Only:		15	+0.22	+0.04	+0.39	27.90*
Women Only:		10	+0.29	+0.07	+0.51	16.47

[1]Effect sizes are positive if the results were in the expected or hypothesized direction with respect to the relationship between hemisphericity and the left mover/right mover individual difference dichotomy.
[2]Significance indicates a rejection of homogeneity.
*p < .05., ** p < .001.

Funnel Plot
Effect Size by Sample Size

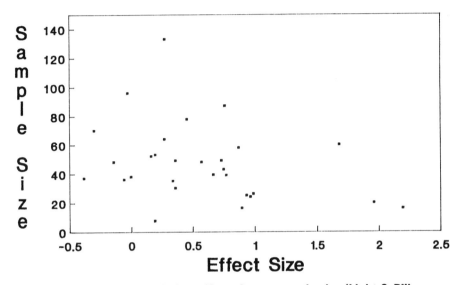

Figure 1.   **Funnel plot relating effect size to sample size (Light & Pillemer, 1984). This type of plot is used to assess the presence of report bias. The rough approximation to an inverted funnel is consistent with the absence of report bias—large sample studies more closely approximate the weighted mean effect size, and small sample studies vary around this central tendency.**

(In addition to effect size, sample size is considered in determining outliers in this analysis.) With these studies removed, the composite effect size was 0.38, and the set of studies was not inhomogeneous. The difference between the composite effect size before and after outlier removal was a negligible 0.03.

Report Bias and Fail Safe Analysis. A funnel plot of the 29 studies in the metaanalysis is presented in Figure 1. In the absence of publication bias, the plot would look like an inverted funnel. In the presence of publication bias, the funnel would be missing its lower left (small effect size, small sample size) corner. The plot does have the shape of an inverted funnel, without a missing lower left quadrant, as would be expected in the absence of report bias. Orwin's (1983) analysis reveals that there would have to be 91 unreported studies with null effects to bring the overall composite effect size to a negligible 0.1. There is no statistical model by which to assess the probability that this is the case, and so the reader will have to reach his own conclusion. In our view, it seems unlikely that there are that many unreported studies with null effects.

DISCUSSION

The main finding of this meta-analysis is that overall, there is a moderate to small effect size associated with the differences between left-movers and right-movers on cognitive variables. Homogeneity of the set of effect sizes can be achieved by removing only four outlying studies (less than 15%), but even after removal of outliers, the composite effect size is not substantially changed. There is no evidence of report bias in this literature, and it is unlikely that there are enough unreported studies to seriously call into question the presence of an effect.

The clear evidence in support of the individual difference hypothesis is not consistent with the traditional reviews of Ehrlichman and colleagues (Ehrlichman & Weinberger, 1978; Ehrlichman, 1984) or with the review of Hiscock (1986). The most likely explanation for this discrepancy, in our view, is related to the method of review. The narrative reviews generally relied on the *vote-counting* method, in which the ratio of statistically significant studies to nonsignificant studies is the deciding criteria. It is interesting to note that, of the reported significance probability values, most (56.1%) of the hypothesis tests incorporated in the current review were not significant. A traditional review would certainly arrive at a negative conclusion. However, Hedges and Olkin (1985) provide statistical and mathematical arguments that indicate that vote counting frequently fails to detect effects that are small to moderate (Cohen, 1988, d less than 0.5), as in the present study. In fact, according to Hedges and Olkin (1985), the vote-counting method may tend to make the wrong decision more often as the number of studies *increases*.

The meta-analysis has also failed to support a number of contentions in the field. Despite the suggestions that the findings might be clearer for the visual vs. visuospatial construct (Hiscock, 1977; Charlton et al., 1989), we found no evidence for an effect of construct. Although the gender of subjects is often invoked as a potentially major modifier of study outcome, in the aggregate we found no evidence of a difference in studies based on gender. Furthermore, although it is intuitively logical that a stricter criterion (70%) for classification of subjects as left-movers or right-movers might yield stronger effects than a simple majority criterion (51%), this was not supported.

Of course, additional studies may change these conclusions. Although a sample of 29 studies is adequate for metaanalysis review, a larger sample is clearly better. The exclusion of studies that did not conform to the structure of our meta-analysis also limits the strength of our conclusions. In particular, several studies, rather than dividing subjects into left- and right-movers, correlated the percentage of left eye movements with cognitive variables. It would not have been appropriate to include these structurally different studies in the present analysis, so a separate metaanalysis would be required. Also, our results have no relevance regarding the validity of other, noncognitive studies of the individual differences hypothesis. The individual differences hypothesis has been related to hypnotic susceptibility, personality characteristics, emotionality, and biological measures such as electroencephalography (EEG) and regional cerebral blood flow. These areas are open to meta-analytic review.

Although the meta-analysis revealed a small to moderate effect size, study methodology plays a role; weak methodology may obscure a large effect. In closing, we would like to suggest the following methodological changes, which might unveil a larger effect. Subjects could be chosen on the basis of a priori knowledge of their hemisphericity, based, for example, on biological measures such as EEG or rCBF. Only clearly lateralized subjects should be included. Also, as Ehrlichman (1984) and Hiscock (1986) have suggested, more robust eye movement classification, based, not only on the initial eye movement tested in an unnatural setting, but on measures that take into account the full oculomotor pattern in different settings, should be incorporated into the classification algorithm for left-movers and right-movers. In this way, one could test the association between clear and robust individual differences in lateral gaze and biologically validated hemisphericity.

REFERENCES

Alexander, M.P., Benson, D.F., & Stuss, D.T. (1989). Frontal lobes and language. *Brain and Language, 37*, 656–691.

Bakan, P. (1969). Hypnotizability, laterality of eye movements and functional brain asymmetry. *Perceptual and Motor Skills, 28*, 927–932.

Bakan, P., & Shotland, R.L. (1969). Lateral eye movement, reading speed, and visual attention. *Psychonomic Science, 15*(2), 93–94.

Baldinger, A.C. (1980). An investigation of cerebral asymmetry in relation to age and sex using lateral eye movement index. *Dissertation Abstracts International, 41B*, 1131B.

Bangert-Drowns, R.L. (1986). Review of developments in meta-analytic method. *Psychological Bulletin, 99*, 388–399.

Barnat, M. (1972). Some personality correlates of the conjugate lateral eye movement phenomenon. *Dissertation Abstracts International, 33B*, 2337B–2338B.

Becker, B.J. (1987). Applying tests of combined significance in meta-analysis. *Psychological Bulletin, 102*, 164–171.

Berent, S., & Silverman, A.J. (1973). Field dependence and differences between visual and verbal learning tasks. *Perceptual and Motor Skills, 36*, 1327–1330.

Bradshaw, J.L., & Nettleton, N.C. (1983). *Human cerebral asymmetry*. Englewood Cliffs, NJ: Prentice-Hall.

Bradshaw, J.L., & Sherlock, D. (1982). Bugs and faces in the two visual fields: Task order, difficulty, practice and the analytic/holistic dichotomy. *Cortex, 18*, 211–225.

Brown, J.W., & Grober, E. (1983). Age, sex and aphasia type: Evidence for a regional cerebral growth process underlying lateralization. *The Journal of Nervous and Mental Disease, 171*, 431–434.

Bryden, M.P. (1979). Evidence for sex-related differences in cerebral organization. In M.A. Wittig & A.C. Petersen (Eds.), *Sex-related differences in cognitive functioning: Developmental Issues*. New York: Academic Press.

Buffery, A.W.H., & Gray, J.A. (1972). Sex differences in the development of spatial and linguistic skills. In C. Ounsted & D.C. Taylor (Eds.), *Gender differences: Their otogeny and significance*. London: Churchill Livingstone.

Butler, S. (1984). Sex differences in human cerebral function. *Progress in Brain Research, 61*, 443–455.

Carmon, A., Lavy, S., Gordon, H., & Portnoy, Z. (1975). Hemispheric differences in rCBF during verbal and nonverbal tasks. In D.H. Ingvar & N.A. Lassen (Eds.), *Brain work*. Copenhagen: Munksgaard.

Charlton, S., Bakan, P., & Moretti, M. (1989). Conjugate lateral eye movements: A second look. *International Journal of Neuroscience, 48*, 1–18.

Cohen, B.D., Berent, S., & Silverman, A.J. (1973). Field-dependence and lateralization of function in the human brain. *Archives of General Psychiatry, 28*, 165–167.

Cohen, J. (1988). *Statistical power analysis for the behavioral sciences* (2nd ed.). Hillsdale, NJ: Erlbaum.

Combs, A., Hoblick, P., Czarnecki, M., & Kamler, P. (1977). Relationship of lateral eye—movement to cognitive mode, hemispheric interaction, and choice of college major. *Perceptual and Motor Skills, 45*, 983–990.

Crouch, W. (1976). Dominant direction of conjugate lateral eye movements and responsiveness to facial and verbal cues. *Perceptual and Motor Skills, 42*, 167–174.

Crowne, D.P. (1983). The frontal eye field and attention. *Psychological Bulletin, 93*, 232–260.

Day, M.E. (1964). An eye movement phenomenon relating to attention, thought, and anxiety. *Perceptual and Motor Skills, 19*, 443–446.

Domanque, B.B. (1984). Hemisphere dominance, cognitive complexity, and nonverbal sensitivity. *Perceptual and Motor Skills, 58*, 3–20.

Dunn, B., Bartscher, J., & Turaniczo, M. (1989). Relationship between conjugate lateral eye movements, brain organization, and cognitive style. *Brain and Cognition, 10*, 171–188.

Ehrlichman, H. (1984, August). *Methodological issues in lateral eye movement research.* Paper presented at the 1984 meeting of The American Psychological Association, Toronto, Canada.

Ehrlichman, H., & Weinberger, A. (1978). Lateral eye movements and hemispheric asymmetry: A critical review. *Psychological Bulletin, 85*(5), 1080–1101.

Gur, R.E., Gur, R.C., & Marshalek, B. (1975). Classroom seating and functional brain asymmetry. *Journal of Educational Psychology, 67*, 151–153.

Gur, R.C., Gur, R.E., Obrist, W.D., Hungerbuhler, J.P., Younkin, D., Rosen, A.D., Skolnick, B.E., & Reivich, M. (1982). Sex and handedness differences in cerebral blood flow during rest and cognitive activity. *Science, 217*, 659–661.

Gur, R.E., Gur, R.C., Rosen, A.D., Warach, S., Alavi, A., Greenberg, J., & Reivich, M. (1983). A cognitive-motor network demonstrated by positron emission tomography. *Neuropsychologia, 21*, 601–606.

Hantas, M., Katkin, E., & Reed, S. (1984). Cerebral lateralization and heartbeat discrimination. *Psychophysiology, 21*(3), 274–278.

Harnad, S. (1972). Creativity, lateral saccades and the nondominant hemisphere. *Perceptual and Motor Skills, 34*, 653–654.

Hedges, L.V., & Olkin, I. (1985). *Statistical methods for meta-analysis*. Orlando, FL: Academic Press.

Hiscock, M.C. (1975). Some statistical antecedents and dispositional correlates of lateral eye-movement direction. *Dissertation Abstracts International, 36*(1), 942B.

Hiscock, M.C. (1977). Eye-movement asymmetry and hemispheric function: An examination of individual differences. *Journal of Psychology, 97*, 49–52.

Hiscock, M. (1986). Lateral eye movements and dual-task performance. In H.J. Hannay (Ed.), *Experimental techniques in human neuropsychology*. New York: Oxford University Press.

Hoffman, C., & Kagan, S. (1977). Lateral eye movements and field—dependence–independence. *Perceptual and Motor Skills, 45*, 767–778.

Huang, M.S., & Byrne, B. (1978). Cognitive style and lateral eye movements. *British Journal of Psychology, 69*, 85–90.

Hunter, J.E., & Schmidt, F.L. (1990). *Methods of meta-analysis: Correcting error and bias in research findings*. Newbury Park, CA: Sage.

Hynd, G.W., & Semrud-Clikeman, M. (1989). Dyslexia and brain morphology. *Psychological Bulletin, 106*, 447–482.

Jean, P.A. (1982). *Facial processing ability as a function of sex, conjugate lateral eye movements, emotional valence, and familiarity*. Unpublished doctoral dissertation. National Library of Canada.

Johnson, B.T. (1989). *DSTAT: Software for the meta-analytic review of research literature*. Hillsdale, NJ: Erlbaum.

Johnson, B.T., & Eagly, A.H. (1989). Effects of involvement on persuasion: A meta-analysis. *Psychological Bulletin, 106*, 290–314.

Katkin, E.S. (1985). Blood, sweat and tears: individual differences in autonomic self-perception. *Psychphysiology, 22*, 125–137.

Katz, J., & Salt, P. (1981). Differences in task and use of language: A study of lateral eye movement. *Perceptual and Motor Skills, 52*, 995–1002.

Kertesz, A., & Benke, T. (1989). Sex equality in intrahemispheric language organization. *Brain and Language, 37*, 401–408.

Kimura, D. (1969). Spatial localization in left and right visual fields. *Canadian Journal of Psychology, 23*, 445–448.

Kinsbourne, M. (1972). Eye and head turning indicates cerebral lateralization. *Science, 176*, 539–541.

Kite, M.E., & Johnson, B.T. (1988). Attitudes toward older and younger adults: A meta-analysis. *Psychology and Aging, 3*, 233–244.

Lake, D.A., & Bryden, M.P. (1976). Handedness and sex differences in hemispheric asymmetry. *Brain and Language, 3*, 266–282.

Lansdell, H. (1961). The effect of neurosurgery on a test of proverbs. *American Psychologist, 16*, 448.

Lansdell, H. (1962). A sex difference in effect of temporal-lobe neurosurgery on design preference. *Nature, 194*, 852–854.

Levy, J. (1974). Psychobiological implications of bilateral asymmetry. In S.J. Dimond & J.G. Beaumont (Eds.), *Hemisphere function in the human brain*. New York: John Wiley & Sons.

Levy-Agresti, J., & Sperry, R.W. (1968). Differential perceptual capacities in major and minor hemisphere. *Proceedings of the U.S. National Academy of Sciences, 61*, 1151.

Lezak, M.D. (1983). *Neuropsychological assessment*. New York: Oxford University Press.

Light, R.J., & Pillemer, D.B. (1984). *Summing up: The science of reviewing research*. Cambridge, MA: Harvard University Press.

Maccoby, E.E., & Jacklin, C.N. (1974). *The psychology of sex differences*. Palo Alto, CA: Stanford University Press.

Mann, C. (1990). Meta-analysis in the breech. *Science, 249*, 476–480.

McCallum, R. (1979). The utility of conjugate lateral eye movements as an index of information processing style. *Dissertation Abstracts International, 40A*, 2557A.

McGlone, J. (1977). Sex differences in the cerebral organization of verbal functions in patients with unilateral brain lesions. *Brain, 100*, 775–793.

McGlone, J., & Kertesz, A. (1973). Sex differences in cerebral processing of isuospatial tasks. *Cortex, 9*, 313–320.

Milner, B. (1971). Interhemispheric differences in the localization of psychological processes in man. *British Medical Bulletin, 27*, 272–277.

Montgomery, W., & Jones G. (1984). Laterality, emotionality, and heartbeat perception. *Psychophysiology, 21*, 459–465.

Moretti, M.M. (1978). *Conjugate lateral eye movements and performance on the Wechsler Adult Intelligence Scale—Revised*. Unpublished doctoral dissertation. National Library of Canada.

Mullen, B. (1989). *Advanced BASIC meta-analysis*. Hillsdale, NJ: Erlbaum.

Natale, M. (1977). Perception of nonlinguistic auditory rhythms by the speech hemisphere. *Brain and Language, 4*, 32–44.

Nebes, R.D. (1978). Direct examination of cognitive function n, the right and left hemispheres. In M. Kinsbourne (Ed.), *Asymmetrical function of the brain* (pp. 99–137). Cambridge, UK: Cambridge University Press.

Ogle, W. (1971). Lateral eye movements: their relationship to reading speed, cardiac responsivity and ability to process speeded information in the visual and auditory modes. *Dissertation Abstracts International, 33*(3b), 1293B.

Orwin, R.G. (1983). A fail-safe *N* for effect size in meta-analysis. *Journal of Educational Statistics, 8*, 157–159.

Pierro, R., & Goldberger, L. (1982). Lateral eye movements, field dependence and denial. *Perceptual and Motor Skills, 55*, 371–378.

Posner, M.I., Petersen, S.E., Fox, P.T., & Raichle, M.E. (1988). Localization of cognitive operations in the human brain. *Science, 240*, 1627–1630.

Ray, W., Georgiou, S., & Ravizza, R. (1979). Spatial abilities, sex differences, and lateral eye movements. *Developmental Psychology, 15*, 455–457.

Reed, S. (1987). Relationship among hemispheric preference, visceral self perception, autonomic arousal, and emotions. *Dissertation Abstracts International, 47B*, 3991B.

Reivich, M., & Gur, R. (1985). Cerebral metabolic effects of sensory and cognitive stimuli in normal subjects. In M. Reivich & A. Alavi (Eds.), *Positron emission tomography*. New York: Alan R. Liss.

Risberg, J., Halsey, J.H., Wills, E.L., & Wilson, E.M. (1975). Hemispheric specialization in normal man studied by bilateral measurements of the regional cerebral blood flow. *Brain, 98*, 511–524.

Roland, P.E. (1984, November). Metabolic measurements of the working frontal cortex in man. *Trends in Neuroscience*, pp. 430–435.

Rosenthal, R. (1978). Combining results of independent studies. *Psychological Bulletin, 85*, 845–193.

Rosenthal, R. (1979). The "file drawer problem" and tolerance for null results. *Psychological Bulletin, 86*, 638–641.

Rosenthal, R., & Rubin, D.B. (1986). Meta-analytic procedures for combining studies with multiple effect sizes. *Psychological Bulletin, 99*, 400–406.

Russo, M., & Vignolo, L.A. (1967). Visual figure-ground discrimination in patients with unilateral cerebral disease. *Cortex, 3*, 113–127.

Sememza, C., Denes, G., D'Urso, V., Romano, O., & Montorsi, T. (1978). Analytic and global strategies in copying designs by unilaterally brain-damaged patients. *Cortex, 14*, 404–410.

Spanos, N., Pawlak, A., Mah, C., & D'eon, J. (1980). Lateral eye movements, hypnotic susceptibility and imaginal ability in right—handers. *Perceptual and Motor Skills, 50*, 287–294.

Stam, H., & Spanos, N. (1979). Lateral eye movements and indices of non-analytic attending in right handed females. *Perceptual and Motor Skills, 48*, 123–127.

Toombs, N. (1982). Differences in lateral eye movement and hemispheric dominance associated with ability to recall verbal and non-verbal stimuli. *Dissertation Abstracts International, 42A*, 3925A.

Tucker, G., & Suib, M. (1978). Conjugate lateral eye movement (CLEM) direction and it's relationship to performance on verbal and visuospatial tasks. *Neuropsychologia, 16*, 251–254.

Van Kleeck, M.H. (1989). Hemispheric differences in global versus local processing of hierarchical visual stimuli by normal subjects: New data and a meta-analysis of previous studies. *Neuropsychologia, 27*, 1165–1178.

Walker, B.B., & Sandman, C.A. (1979). Human visual evoked responses are related to heart rate. *Journal of Comparative and Physiological Psychology, 93*, 717–729.

Walker, B.B., & Sandman, C.A. (1982). Visual evoked potentials change as heart rate and carotid pressure change. *Psychophysiology, 19*, 520–527.

Walton, A. (1980). Conjugate lateral eye movement, brain dysfunction and asymmetry of hemispheric function. *Dissertation Abstracts International, 40B*.

Weiten, W., & Etaugh, C. (1973). Lateral eye movement as related to verbal and perceptual—motor skills and values. *Perceptual and Motor Skills, 36*, 423–428.

Witkin, H.A., & Asch, S.E. (1948). Studies in space orientation. IV. Further experiments on perception of the upright with displaced visual fields. *Journal of Experimental Psychology, 38*, 762–782.

Zee, D.S. (1986). Oculomotor control. In A.K. Asburg, G.M. McKhann, & W.I. McDonald (Eds.), *Diseases of the nervous system—Clinical Neurobiology* (Vol. 1, pp. 507–519). Philadelphia: Saunders.

Chapter 9

Measuring Individual Differences in Cognition in Schizophrenia and Other Disordered States: Backward Masking Paradigm

Dennis P. Saccuzzo

San Diego State University/University of California,
San Diego Joint Doctoral Program

The study of individual differences in cognition in schizophrenia and other disordered states has been guided primarily by information-processing models. My goal in this chapter is to present an overview for researchers new to the field and for those whose work may benefit from an understanding of theoretical and methodological advances in the field. The primary focus will be on the *visual masking paradigm*, in which a noninformational stimulus (mask) is presented in close temporal succession with an informational target stimulus. I will then discuss a variety of attempts to use the masking paradigm to study individual differences in cognition from a developmental perspective, in mental retardation, and as a function of IQ. Inasmuch as I have had numerous inquiries from investigators on how to effectively use the masking procedure in evaluating individual differences in a variety of groups, I will also discuss major methodological consideration and potential pitfalls.

HISTORICAL PERSPECTIVE

The study of individual differences in cognition in schizophrenia has a long history, as schizophrenia traditionally has been viewed as a cognitive or "thought" disorder. While both major early pioneers in the field, Kraepalin (1896/1919) and Bleuler (1911/1950), agreed that schizophrenia involved a disturbance in attention, Bleuler's emphasis on an associative (i.e., higher brain center) disturbance dominated the field for nearly half a century. For Bleuler the splitting of associations, that is, the isolation of ideas from each other, was the primary disturbance in schizophrenia. Indeed, the term *schizophrenia*, which Bleuler used to describe the disorder, literally means a splitting or fragmenting of mental functions. Splitting of association might cause a patient, for example, to respond to a word in terms of meaning inappropriate to the context in which it is used, resulting in concrete thinking, idiosyncratic concepts, or overinclusion.

Information Processing Models

By the 1960s, frustrated by a failure to make significant inroads to our understanding of schizophrenia and supported by the advent of information processing theory (Averback & Coriell, 1961; Broadbent, 1958; Sperling, 1960; Neisser, 1967; Haber, 1969), a handful of researchers began to argue that the primary disturbance in schizophrenia was not a thought disorder but rather a more fundamental disturbance of the processes that precede and result in thought. According to this early information-processing dysfunction theory, cognitive dysfunction in schizophrenia is the result of a more primary disturbance in the selection and processing of information.

The earliest attempts to view schizophrenia in terms of information processing emphasized attentional processes. Defining *attention* as the process by which we reduce, organize, and interpret the otherwise chaotic flow of information reaching consciousness, McGhie and Chapman (1961) argued that, in schizophrenia, there was a breakdown in the processes by which people normally screen out irrelevant incoming sensory data. Using the verbal reports of schizophrenics to support their position (e.g., "Sometimes when people speak to me my head is overloaded. It's too much to hold at once," p. 105), McGhie and Chapman (1961) hypothesized that the cognitive dysfunction observed in schizophrenic patients was due to a breakdown in the selective inhibitory function of attention.

Venebles (1964) also argued in favor of an attentional dysfunction in schizophrenia. According to Venables there were two major subtypes of schizophrenics: those suffering from a broadening of attention, and those characterized by a restriction of the attentional field. The former, unable to screen out irrelevant information, are bombarded with overwhelming amounts of information; the latter do not take in sufficient information to obtain an accurate view of reality. The cause of the attentional disturbance, Venables believed, was abnormally high or abnormally low arousal levels.

Working independently of Venables, Silverman (1964) reached similar conclusions concerning the primary dysfunction in schizophrenia. Like Venables, Silverman hypothesized that there were two subtypes of schizophrenics: those characterized by a broadening of attention, and those by a restriction or narrowing of attention. For Silverman, the root of the disturbance could be traced to individual differences in *scanning* (sampling environmental stimuli) and *field articulation* (attention to certain segments of a stimulus field and simultaneous inhibition of attention to other segments of the field). According to Silverman, schizophrenics are those individuals who fall on the extremes of individual differences in scanning and field articulation. Thus, for example, schizophrenics with broadening attention scan too much and are flooded with information.

Yates's Slow Processing Theory

Yates (1966) was the first to incorporate a stage model in a theory of schizophrenic cognition. Yates examined four basic stages of information processing: (a) *the perceptual response* (e.g., registration of environmental input by receptors), (b) *speed of information transfer* from receptors to the higher brain centers, (c) *informtion analysis* (e.g., evaluation of input by the higher brain centers, and (d) the *final overt response*. In a review of the literature, Yates (1966) organized empirical studies of schizophrenia in terms of each of the above four stages and concluded that, while stages 1, 3, and 4 were essentially unimpaired, schizophrenics suffered from abnormally slow information processing. Schizophrenics have, Yates argued, a deficiency in handling incoming information and, as a result, experience being flooded by information. Moreover, insufficient information reaches the higher brain centers for analysis to provide an accurate view of reality.

Attempts to provide a direct empirical test of Yates's (1966) slow-processing theory soon followed, using measures of the span of apprehension as the major methodological tool. *Span of apprehension* refers to the amount of information to which a person can simultaneously attend in a single presentation. Theoretical formulations of the span are based on the notion of a brief perceptual memory or "sensory" storage system, which Neisser (1967) called *iconic storage*. Accordingly, environmental input is first registered in the form of a rapidly decaying visual representation or, icon. Information enters iconic storage in parallel and is scanned internally in serial as it is transferred to the higher brain centers for analysis. Theoretically, if the icon dissipates before one of its elements is transferred to the higher brain centers, the information is lost and, therefore, cannot be part of the span of apprehension.

In the typical experiment a visual display is presented briefly and subjects are asked to report all or a portion of what was presented. Investigations of the span of apprehension in the late 1960s and early 1970s demonstrated a reduced span in schizophrenics compared to normal controls (Neale, McIntyre, Fox, & Cromwell, 1969; Spohn, Thetford, & Woodham, 1970; Neale, 1971; Cash, Neale, & Cromwell, 1972).

Studies of the span of apprehension proved to be limited and inconclusive, however. Such studies measure only the amount of information processed, not the speed. Moreover, schizophrenics may process less than normal for a variety of reasons. They may, for example, not select as much information initially. In addition, studies of the span of apprehension provide no control over the duration of the icon. For example, the initial icon or sensory signal may be weaker or more unstable in schizophrenics. Or schizophrenics may process as quickly as normals but still may be unable to report as much information, because the initial sensory signal decayed more rapidly.

THE USE OF VISUAL MASKING METHODOLOGY

In an effort to deal with limitations of the span of apprehension methodology, my colleagues and I introduced visual masking methodology to the study of schizophrenia (Saccuzzo, Hirt, & Spencer, 1974). In a visual masking paradigm two stimuli are presented in close temporal succession: a target or test stimulus containing information, and a noninformational masking stimulus. In a simple case the target can consist of a single letter or number, the mask a pattern of random lines, or a meaningless composite of several letter or numbers. In backward masking, the mask is presented at varying intervals *following* the brief onset or offset of the target.

Assume that a target stimulus has been briefly presented tachistoscopically or on a microcomputer screen monitor for about 20 milliseconds. If the mask is presented quickly enough (i.e., before the target stimulus has been sufficiently processed to permit accurate recognition), overlaps spatially with the target (e.g., both are presented to the same central location), and is of sufficient intensity, the mask will limit the duration that the target is available for processing. As Felsten and Wasserman (1980) state in their review of the literature:

A mask permits the cognitive investigator to do something important that cannot be done by other means, namely, to deliver a pulse of information to the central nervous system with precise control on the duration of that impulse. Without using masking, visual persistence will guarantee that the duration of the information pulse experience by the central nervous system will vary in an exceedingly complex manner. (p. 350)

Studies of visual masking are consistent with anatomical studies that have indicated that input information is analyzed in increasingly refined levels as it is relayed through the nervous system. Consider, for example, the anatomical correlates of visual information processing. Light reflecting from an object in the individual's visual field is resolved by the lens systems and projected onto the back of the retina, where stimulus processing begins with the excitation of photoreceptors (rods and cones). Light energy is transduced into a neural impulse, which is subsequently relayed to the bipolar and then to the gangilion cells, which form the optic nerve. After this retinal level of analysis, in which global features are probably extracted, information is relayed to the optic chiasma, where each optic nerve separates into two distinct paths such that fibers from the right side of each eye (i.e., left visual field) ultimately relay the nerve impulse to the right cerebral hemisphere and those from the left side of each eye (i.e., right visual field) to the left cerebral hemisphere. Central nervous system processing continues as information is relayed along the optic tracts to the lateral geniculate body and finally projected onto visual cortex. Information separated at the optic chiasma may reunite when it reaches or passes through the corpus callosum, which connects the two major hemispheres of the brain.

In a masking experiment the target and mask can be used together in a variety of ways, allowing for a wealth of design possibilities and converging operations. In binocular presentations target and mask are both presented at the center of the visual field, thus involving both retinas and both hemispheres. In monocular presentations the target and mask are presented at the center to a single eye, involving one retina but both hemispheres. In dichoptic presentations the target is presented to one eye and the mask to the other, precluding retinal interaction of the two stimuli. In forward masking, the mask is presented prior to the target stimulus so that all stimulus–mask interactions occur at peripheral (retinal) levels.

MASKING STUDIES IN SCHIZOPHRENIA

Early Studies

The purpose of Saccuzzo et al. (1974) was to evaluate speed of information processing (mental speed) in schizophrenics in order to evaluate Yates's (1966) slow processing speed theory of schizophrenia. To accomplish this purpose, central binocular backward masking methodology was employed. Groups of chronic paranoid and nonparanoid schizophrenics were compared to non-schizophrenic inpatients and normal controls. The task was kept as simple as possible to minimize memory and response requirements. Subjects simply had to determine whether a "T" or "A" was presented in a single letter display and in an eight-letter display containing seven irrelevant letters.

To control for possible differences at the perceptual or iconic stage of processing, Saccuzzo et al. (1974) first determined the minimum stimulus duration necessary for criterion identification of the stimulus when no mask was presented, which was subsequently called the *critical stimulus duration* (CSD). The stimulus was presented at varying durations in a modified staircase method until the subject was able to obtain the criterion of 80 percent correct identifications without a mask.

The CSD was individually determined for each subject and used throughout the masking experiment. Results revealed wide individual differences in the CSD, even within the normal control group. The group means for the CSD, however, differed significantly only between the nonparanoids and other three groups.

In the masking experiment target and mask energy were equated by exposing the mask as well as the target at the previously determined CSD and holding luminance constant. The mask followed the target at one of six randomly presented intervals following off-set of the target: 50-,100-, 150-, 200-, 300-msec, and no mask control. Results indicated slower processing in both schizophrenic groups as reflected in their slower rising masking functions. The reliability of these findings was confirmed by Saccuzzo and Miller (1977) and has since been replicated in several independent laboratories (Balogh & Merritt, 1987a; Schwartz & Winstead, 1982; Green & Walker, 1984).

A potential limitation of these early masking studies is the possibility that the schizophrenics performed less well than normals because of generalized deterioration, rather than due to a specific processing-speed deficit. A number of subsequent studies were conducted to deal with this and other possible limitations.

Ruling Out Generalized Deterioration

Shortly after the publication of Saccuzzo et al. (1974), Birren (1974) reported on a recently completed doctoral dissertation by Kline (1972), which had shown slower rising masking functions in an elderly population compared to younger controls. Birren had taken this masking result as support for slower processing with aging. In fact, according to Birren, the primary underlying factor in cognitive deterioration in aging was a slowing down of information-processing speed.

Birren's report created a problem for me in that, if slow processing was implicated in cognitive deterioration in aging, how could it be the primary deficit in schizophrenia? Obviously, becoming slower processors does not cause older people to become schizophrenic. Intrigued by the apparent similarity between Birren's elderly population and the schizophrenics I had tested, I examined the aging literature. To my surprise, I found that, for just about every deficit found in older adults, a similar one could be found in schizophrenics (see Saccuzzo, 1977). One possible explanation of the similar deficits is that both groups are impaired on a wide variety of tasks due to generalized deterioration. I (Saccuzzo, 1977) suggested that the elderly might make a good comparison group for schizophrenics, since, if both show identical deficits, experimental results would be best interpreted in terms of generalized deterioration rather than ascribed to a more specific or primary deficit underlying either schizophrenia or aging.

Brody, Saccuzzo, and Braff (1980) provided a direct comparison of schizophrenics and the elderly in order to determine if generalized deterioration could account for the masking deficit found in either or both groups. The elderly group was carefully screened for neurological problems, drug and alcohol abuse, and other problems that might impair performance on the masking task. As in Saccuzzo et al. (1974), each subject's CSD was determined in order to equate subjects on initial sensory input and iconic storage variables. Results were striking. The elderly required a significantly higher CSD than both young normal controls and young schizophrenics. Schizophrenics, one the other hand, showed slower rising masking functions than the elderly. These results showed the importance of the CSD control in group masking studies and indicated that the masking deficit in schizophrenics was not due to generalized deterioration.

Further evidence against generalized deterioration has been found in studies of remitted schizophrenics and the schizotypal personality—a disorder that has been genetically linked to schizophrenia but in which full-blown schizophrenic symptoms are absent (Heston, 1966, 1970; Meehl, 1962). Miller, Saccuzzo, and Braff (1979) evaluated remitted schizophrenics who had previously met diagnostic criteria for a schizophrenic disorder but were presently free of symptoms and living in an outpatient setting. Like actively schizophrenic inpatients, the remitted, symptom-free schizophrenics showed slower rising masking functions when compared to normal controls. These results suggested that rather than due to generalized deterioration or a transitory state, slow processing, as evaluated in the masking paradigm, is an enduring trait of individuals with schizophrenia.

Saccuzzo and Braff (1981) subsequently evaluated two subtypes of schizophrenics, those with a good prognosis for recovery and those with a poor prognosis, and matched control groups of depressed inpatients, manic inpatients, and normal controls (hospital staff). The design allowed for testing of the schizophrenic patients throughout acute hospitalization (up to six months) with comparable testing for the controls. Results showed that the impaired masking performance of the poor prognostic group remained constant, whereas an initial masking deficit found in the good prognostics had been ameliorated by the end of their hospital stay. The findings supported the long-held view of at least two major subgroups of schizophrenics: the chronic, poor prognostic schizophrenic, who is characterized by slow information processing as a relatively stable trait; and the good prognostic schizophrenic, who suffers from slow processing only during active schizophrenic episodes.

In support of the above conclusion, Saccuzzo and Schubert (1981) found slower rising masking functions in the genetically linked schizotypal personality. These findings supported the notion of a schizophrenia spectrum in which the genetically linked schizotype, actively psychotic poor prognostic schizophrenic, and remitted poor prognostic schizophrenic can be characterized as suffering from chronically slow information processing speed. Nakano and Saccuzzo (1985) supported these findings by demonstrating a masking deficit in schizotypes who were selected from a college student population using the 2-7-8-MMPI code to identify schizotypes. Masking deficits in the schizotype have also been reported by Braff (1981) and Merritt and Balogh (1984).

In other studies, Braff and Saccuzzo (1982) found that the masking deficit observed in schizophrenics is not due to medication effects. Indeed, medication has a tendency to enhance and normalize schizophrenic masking curves. Braff and Saccuzzo (1985), moreover, demonstrated that the masking deficit in schizophrenia is time linked, being restricted to mid-range interstimulus intervals of 60 to 500 msec. At briefer or longer interstimulus intervals, schizophrenic and control performance is equivalent. This finding of a time linked deficit further argues against generalized deterioration and generalized task difficulty as underlying the masking deficit in schizophrenia.

OTHER APPLICATIONS OF VISUAL MASKING

If the backward masking paradigm has relevance to the measurement of processing speed in schizophrenia, then it should have validity as a measure of processing speed in other groups. Indeed, numerous relevant studies have been conducted. Such studies have indicated developmental difference in masking performance, with rising masking function between ages 5 years and 8 years and between 8 years and 13 years and, as previously indicated, declining masking functions with increased aging. Moreover, the mentally retarded have showed a masking deficit when compared to mental age controls.

Developmental and Mental Age Differences in Masking Functions

The first published group comparison masking study ever published compared children of different ages and found an inverse relationship between age and ability to evade the effects of the mask (Pollack, 1965). Spitz and Thor (1968) subsequently reported a masking deficit in retarded adolescents compared to *chronological age* (CA) but not *mental age* (MA) controls. Two years later, Liss and Haith (1970) provided additional evidence of the relationship between mental age and ability to evade the effects of the mask and introduced a forward versus backward masking paradigm for the first time in a group comparison visual masking study. During the 1970s the superiority (in evading the effects of the mask) of young adults compared to children (Gummerman & Gray, 1972; Miller, 1972; Welsandt, Zupnick, & Meyer, 1973; Blake, 1974) and of mental or chronological age controls compared to persons with mental retardation (Thor, 1970; Galbraith & Gliddon, 1972; Welsandt & Meyer, 1974) was confirmed for binocular presentations under a variety of conditions. The first failure to find a masking deficit in retarded persons was reported by Horstein and Mosley (1979). A few months after this study was published, however, Saccuzzo, Kerr, Marcus, and Brown (1979) did report evidence for such a deficit. As Saccuzzo (1981) subsequently noted, Saccuzzo et al.'s (1979) use of a pattern mask was more discriminating than Hornstein and Mosley's (1979) mask, which consisted only of a flash of light. Furthermore, a year later Mosley (1980) reported a masking deficit in retarded persons.

Lawrence, Kee, and Helliges (1981) failed to find an age-by-masking-interval interaction when they varied the size of the stimulus such that each subject was 75% correct in a no mask condition. The validity of Lawrence et al.'s (1981) procedure, however, can be questioned in view of an earlier study by Farrell (1979) with normal adults. Specifically, Farrell had studied the stimuli used by Lawrence et al. (1981), which consisted of arrows pointing up, down, and to the left or right. Farrell's finding that certain positions are more difficult to identify than others indicates that Lawrence et al. may have confounded task difficulty with masking. In general, it seems safe to conclude that, while more empirical findings would be welcome, performance on the masking task tends to vary directly as a function of mental age.

A decline in speed of processing, as indicated by slower rising masking functions, is also well documented in young–old comparisons (Welsandt et al., 1973; Kline & Birren, 1975; Kline & Szafran, 1975; Walsh, 1976). As previously noted, however, this decline with aging is not so dramatic as the deficits found in schizophrenia when initial levels of input are controlled.

Effects of Other Variables On Masking Functions

As might be expected, alcohol and drugs have an adverse effect on processing speed. Acute alcohol intoxication (Moskowitz & Murray, 1976) and acute marijuana intoxication (Braff, Silverton, Saccuzzo, & Janowsky, 1981) have been shown to impair masking functions, suggesting an impairment in speed of processing with intoxication. Application of masking methodology to a group of patients suffering from dementia has similarly indicated impaired processing speed (Miller, 1977). There is also some evidence of a slight relationship between

processing speed, as evaluated in the masking paradigm, and hypnotic susceptibility (Ingram, Saccuzzo, McNeill, & McDonald, 1979; Saccuzzo, Safran,
Anderson, & McNeill, 1982).

IQ and Masking

In the area of intelligence research, the masking paradigm has a relatively short
but controversial history. Using the masking procedure to arrive at a single index
called *inspection time*, Nettlebeck and Lally (1976) reported an astonishing -.92
correlation between scores on the performance scale of the Wechsler Adult
Intelligence Scales (WAIS) and inspection time. Subsequent investigators
reported a less spectacular, though significant, relationship between inspection
time and intelligence, with a median correlation of about -.45. These positive
findings have been questioned on methodological grounds, however, due to small
sample sizes; the inclusion of mentally retarded persons, which greatly inflates
the correlation due to the extremely disparate range of performance relative to
sample size; and analyses based on extreme scoring subjects (Irwin, 1984;
Nettlebeck, 1982).

In 1986 an entire issue of *Personality and Individual Differences* was devoted
to inspection time (Brenner & Nettlebeck, 1986). The studies supported
previous suggestions (Brand, 1984; Jensen, 1982) that mental speed can account
for between 10 and 20 percent of the variance in adult IQ (Nettlebeck, Edwards,
& Vreugdenhil, 1986; Longstreth, Walsh, Alcorn, Szeszulski, & Manis, 1986).
The existence of contradictory findings (see Lubin & Fernandez, 1986) and
concerns over the validity of inspection time as a measure of processing speed
(Vickers & Smith, 1986), however, indicates that more work is needed before a
relationship between intelligence and processing speed can be firmly
established.

THEORETICAL ISSUES

Although the masking procedure has been used to demonstrate a wide variety of
individual differences, the interpretation of such differences remains open due to
unresolved issues concerning the validity of masking methodological as a
measure of processing speed and numerous methodological issues and pitfalls in
conducting group comparison masking studies. An understanding of these
issues is critical to further advancement our knowledge in this field.

Vastness of the Literature

It is important to recognize the extensiveness of the visual literature. As Allik
and Bachmann (1983) have noted, some 50 to 100 papers are published every

month on visual information processing, iconic memory, visual persistence, and related concepts in an effort to comprehend the functioning of the visual system subserving the transfer and interpretation of information. The application of any specific masking paradigm clearly reflects a highly selective and, by necessity, limited application of specific techniques. As Braff, Saccuzzo, and Gyer (1991) have noted, it is virtually impossible to answer all methodological questions in any one, or even a series of studies. My own rationale in using the masking procedure is based on Felsten and Wasserman's (1980) review and conclusion that the mask allows an investigatior to deliver a pulse of information to the central nervous system with precise control on the duration of that impulse. Nevertheless, researchers who have used the masking procedure have advocated a variety of creative interpretations of their results.

Breitmeyer's Channel Theory

Breitmeyer (1984), for example, has explained masking phenomena in terms of neural channels with differing response characteristics. The Y cells of *transiet* neural channels, he argues, respond to low spatial frequencies and high temporal frequencies with a short latency, rapidly dissipated CNS signal that produces a course pattern of information. The X cells of *sustained* neural channels, by contrast, are responsive to high spatial and low temporal frequencies with a longer latency, more slowly dissipating CNS signal. In short, transient channels deal with fast, rapidly presented information; sustained channels deal with slow to relatively continuous stimulation.

In terms of backward masking, the rapidly occurring and dissipating transient channel actively to the mask occurs during the sustained response to the target stimulus. This transient response is believed to inhibit the stimulus-identifying sustained response to the target. Applying Breitmeyer's theory of masking to schizophrenia, Schwartz and colleagues have argued that schizophrenics might be impaired to abnormally augmented transient responses to the mask or to weak and vulnerable sustained responses to the target (Schwartz, Winstead, & Adinoff, 1983; Schwartz, Whittier, & Schweitzer, 1979).

Knight's Perceptual Organization Theory

Knight (1984), by contrast, has argued in terms of poor perceptual organization as the underlying cause of the poor masking performances found in schizophrenic subjects. Knight, Elliot, and Freedman (1985) compared the effects of a meaningless random noise mask and an informational cognitive mask (a photograph of a real world scene) in good and poor prognosis schizophrenic patients, nonschizophrenic patients, and normal controls. Only the poor prognosis schizophrenics failed to differentiate between the meaningless and cognitive masks. For the other three groups the pattern mask impaired performance only during the first 150 msec, while the cognitive mask impaired performance through the 300-msec delay condition. The poor prognosis schizophrenics, on the other hand, were equally impaired by both types of masks. Knight et al. hypothesized that the poor prognosis schizophrenics suffer from a perceptual organization dysfunction that impairs their ability to determine the meaninglessness of the mask. Consequently, the poor prognosis schizophrenics continue to process a meaningless mask so that its effects are similar to those of a cognitive mask.

Given that the nature of masking effects are far from clear, there appears to be general agreement that a high energy meaningless visual backward mask for central binocular presentations does indeed limit stimulus processing. Under such conditions the masking paradigm may be used to evaluate speed of processing.

METHODOLOGICAL ISSUES

In conducting an actual experiment there are a number of factors that must be considered. These include the nature of the target, stimulus duration, nature of the mask, mask duration, nature of the task, type of response, and a host of other factors.

Target Characteristics

Target stimuli may consist of letters, numbers, geometric symbols, line drawings, words, equations, etc. In working with children, geometric targets are preferable to letters or numbers to reduce the effects of stimulus familiarity as much as possible. In studying the relationships between intelligence and processing, a novel idea would be to vary the informational content or complexity of the target in order to determine if the superiority of high-IQ individuals increases or remains the same as stimulus complexity increases.

Stimulus Duration

Once the physical characteristics of the stimuli have been selected, a researcher must make a number of difficult decisions concerning the stimulus duration. Stimulus duration may be fixed for all subjects or varied for each subject individually in a CSD type procedure. In studying individual differences in intelligence, a fixed stimulus duration, or perhaps two or more levels of stimulus duration, are recommended. The problem with the variable CSD procedure is that one runs the risk of confounding stimulus duration and masking, since the effects of the mask may differ as a function of stimulus duration. In schizophrenia research it was easy to see the value of the CSD procedure to control initial input. In my own research, however, I have also used two or more fixed levels of stimulus duration for all subjects (e.g., Saccuzzo & Schubert, 1981) in order to demonstrate masking deficits when stimulus duration is held constant. In working with normals my colleagues and I have found little evidence of input differences (Saccuzzo & Larson, Rimland, 1986; Saccuzzo & Larson, 1987).

If one or more levels of a fixed stimulus duration is to be used, pilot work will usually be necessary to determine the optimal durations for yielding performance curves between chance and ceiling. Obviously, if the stimulus duration is too long all subjects will be at the ceiling and masking functions will not be observed. Similarly, if the stimulus duration is too short all subjects will be at chance.

In determining the optimal stimulus duration using tachistoscopic procedures, it is important to recognize that the critical variable is actually stimulus intensity, a function of stimulus duration and luminance. In my own work I have tried to hold luminance constant and vary only stimulus duration. It is also important to recognize that the luminance of the prestimulus field (the field into which subjects are looking prior to stimulus presentation) as well as the post exposure luminance both affect processing of the target. To minimize possible confounds, it is usually best to hold constant and equal the luminance in all fields.

Mask Characteristics

There are numerous possibilities for the mask. The mask can simply be a flash of light, or it can be a pattern, or even random noise. Masking experiments with normals (see Kahneman, 1968; Felsten & Wasserman, 1980; Turvey, 1973) have suggested that different types of masks interact with the stimulus at different stages of processing. Moreover, the energy of the mask may be equal to, greater than, or less than that of the target. Finally, the mask may or may not spatially overlay the target.

In my own research the goal has been to use the mask to disrupt stimulus processing and control the duration of the informational pulse delivered to the central nervous system. For this purpose, a pattern mask of equal energy (i.e., equal luminance and stimulus duration) to the target appears to be the most effective choice. In constructing the mask, one can take the various target stimuli and form an unintelligible composite.

Target-Mask Parameters

Having worked out the details of the stimulus and mask, it is now necessary to decide on target-mask parameters. Assuming a target and pattern mask of equal energy, the mask can be presented at varying intervals prior to (forward masking) or following the test stimulus. Theoretically, forward masking is peripheral, due to target-mask interactions at retinal levels, whereas in backward-masking target-mask interactions may occur at central levels. Thus, forward masking can provide a good control over peripheral effects. As more conditions are added, however, testing time increases, which may result in subject fatigue.

It is usually best to include a simultaneous mask (zero stimulus-mask interval). If the mask is effective and the stimulus duration short enough, subjects should be performing at chance levels for a simultaneous mask. Then pilot work is needed to determine about three or four additional stimulus-mask intervals, so that subjects will perform between chance and ceiling. A relatively long stimulus duration to allow subjects to process at ceiling levels is important to have. It is necessary, however, to have intermediate stimulus-mask intervals in order to demonstrate individual differences.

The presentation of stimulus-mask intervals must be randomized or completely counterbalanced. There should be a minimum of 10–20 presentations of the target at each stimulus-mask interval. The more trials the better, but individual sessions greater than 30 to 60 minutes risk confounding the results due to subject fatigue.

The Task

The subject's task may be to identify the target or to discriminate between one of two targets. I prefer the forced-choice discrimination procedure, as it allows the application of signal detection methodology (Green & Swets, 1966). In terms of response, subjects may respond orally or through a push button technique. Either is fine.

CONCLUDING COMMENTS

Despite the large number of studies that have employed the masking procedure to study individual differences in cognition, to date researchers have only scratched the surface in terms of the possibilities. Clearly there is a masking deficit in the schizophrenia spectrum that affects genetically linked schizotypes and appears to be present throughout most of the life of the afflicted individual. There are also developmental differences over the entire life span in response to the mask as well as differences as a function of mental age in retarded populations. Moreover, within the 90–140 IQ range, there may be a direct relationship between IQ and ability to evade the effects of the mask. It is not clear at this point whether fast processing is the primary underlying factor in intelligence, as Jensen, Cohn, and Cohn (1989) have argued, or whether it is simply one of many relatively independent components of intelligence. In the later case, processing speed and intelligence would be related in a curvilinear fashion. An important need is to determine if it is possible to increase the correlation between IQ and masking performance through manipulations of the stimulus-mask characteristics, such as those described herein, and to determine the actual nature of the relationship between IQ and processing speed.

REFERENCES

Allik, J., & Bachmann, T. (1983). How bad is the icon? *Behavior and Brain Science, 6,* 12–13.

Averback, E., & Coriell, A.S. (1961). Short term memory in vision. *Bell Systems Technical Journal, 40,* 309–328.

Balogh, D.W., & Merritt, R.D. (1987). Visual masking and the schizophrenia spectrum: Interfacing clinical and experimental methods. *Schizophrenia Bulletin, 13,* 679–698.

Birren, J.E. (1974). Psychophysiology and speed of response. *American Psychologist, 29,* 816.

Blake, J. (1974). Developmental change in visual information processing under backward masking. *Journal of Experimental Child Psychology, 17,* 133–146.

Bleuler, E. (1950). *Dementia praecox or the group of schizophrenias* (J. Zinkin, Trans.). New York: International Universities Press. (Original work published 1911).

Braff, D.L. (1981). Impaired speed of information processing in nonmedicated schizotypal patients. *Schizophrenia Bulletin, 7,* 499–508.

Braff, D.L., & Saccuzzo, D.P. (1982). The effects of anti-psychotic medication on speed of information processing in schizophrenic patients. *American Journal of Psychiatry, 139,* 1127–1130.

Braff, D.L., & Saccuzzo, D.P. (1985). The time course of information-processing deficits in schizophrenia. *American Journal of Psychiatry, 142,* 170–174.

Braff, D.L., Saccuzzo, D.P., & Gyer, M. (1991). Information processing dysfunction in schizophrenia: Studies of visual backward masking, sensory gating, and habituation. *Handbook of schizophrenia,* New York: Elsever Science Publishers.

Braff, D.L., Silverton, L., Saccuzzo, D.P., & Janowsky, D.S. (1981). Impaired speed of visual information processing in marijuana intoxication. *American Journal of Psychiatry, 138,* 613–617.

Brand, C.R. (1984). Intelligence and inspection time: An ontogenic relationship? In C.J. Turner & H.B. Miles (Eds.)., *Biology of human intelligence.* Nafferton, UK: Nafferton Books.

Brenner, J., & Nettelbeck, T. (1986). Inspection time. *Personality and Individual Differences, 7,* 603–749.

Breitmeyer, B.G. (1984). *Visual masking: An integrative approach.* New York: Oxford University Press.

Broadbent, D.E. (1958). *Perception and communication.* New York: Pergamon.

Brody, D., Saccuzzo, D.P., & Braff, D.L. (1980). Information processing for masked and unmasked stimuli in schizophrenia and old age. *Journal of Abnormal Psychology, 89,* 617–622.

Cash, T.F., Neale, J.M., & Cromwell, R.L. (1972). Span of apprehension in acute schizophrenics: Full-report technique. *Journal of Abnormal Psychology, 69*, 322–326.

Farrell, W.S., Jr. (1979). Coding left and right. *Journal of Experimental Psychology, 5*, 42–51.

Felsten, G., & Wasserman, G.S. (1980). Visual masking: Mechanisms and theories. *Psychological Bulletin, 88*, 324–353.

Galbraith, G.L., & Gliddon, J.B. (1972). Backward visual masking with homeogeneous and pattern stimuli: Comparison of retarded and nonretarded subjects. *Perceptual and Motor Skills, 34*, 903–908.

Green, D.M., & Swets, J.A. (1966). *Signal detection theory and psychophysics.* New York: Wiley.

Green, M., & Walker, E. (1984). Susceptibility to backward masking in schizophrenic patients with positive or negative symptoms. *American Journal of Psychiatry, 141*, 1273–1275.

Gummerman, K., & Gray, L.R. (1972). Age, iconic storage, and visual information processing. *Journal of Experimental Child Psychology, 13*, 165–170.

Haber, R.H. (1969). Perception and thought: An information processing analysis. In J.F. Voss (Ed.), *Approaches to thought* (pp. 1–27). Columbus, OH: Charles E. Merrill Publishing Company.

Heston, L.L. (1966). Psychiatric disorders in foster home reared children of schizophrenic mothers. *British Journal of Psychiatry, 112*, 815–825.

Heston, L.L. (1970). The genetics of schizophrenia and schizoid disease. *Science, 167*, 249–256.

Horstein, H.A., & Mosley, J.L. (1979). Iconic-memory processing of unfamiliar stimuli by retarded and non-retarded individuals. *American Journal of Mental Deficiency, 84*, 40–48.

Ingram, R., Saccuzzo, D.P., McNeill, B., & McDonald, R. (1979). Speed of information processing in high and low susceptible subjects. *International Journal of Clinical Experimental Hypnosis, 27*, 42–47.

Irwin, R.J. (1984). Inspection time and its relation to intelligence. *Intelligence, 8*, 47–65.

Jensen, A.R. (1982). Reaction time and psychometric 'g'. In H.J. Eysenck (Ed.), *A model for intelligence.* New York: Springer-Verlag.

Jensen, A.R., Cohn, S.J., & Cohn, C.M.G. (1989). Speed of information processing in academically gifted youth and their siblings. *Personality and Individual Differences, 10*, 29–34.

Kahneman, D. (1968). Method, findings, and theory in studies of visual masking. *Psychological Bulletin, 70*, 404–424.

Kline, D.W. (1972). *Signal processing time and aging: Age differences in backward dichoptic masking.* Unpublished doctoral dissertation, University of Southern California.

Kline, D.W., & Birren, J.E. (1975). Age differences in backward dichoptic masking. *Experimental Aging Research, 1*, 17–25.

Kline, D.W., & Szafran, J. (1975). Age differences in backward monoptic visual noise masking. *Journal of Gerontology, 30*, 307–311.

Knight, R.A. (1984). Converging models of cognitive deficit in schizophrenia. In W.D. Spaulding & J.K. Cole (Eds.), *Nebraska symposium on motivation, 1983: Theories of schizophrenia and psychosis* (pp. 93–156). Lincoln: University of Nebraska Press.

Kraepalin, E. (1919). *Dementia praecox and paraphrenia* (R.M. Barclay, Trans.). Edinburgh: E & S Livingstone. (Original work published 1896).

Lawrence, V.W., Kee, D.W., & Hellige, J. (1981). Developmental differences in visual backward masking. *Child Development, 51*, 1081–1089.

Liss, P.H., & Haith, M.M. (1970). The speed of visual processing in children and adults: Effects of backward and forward masking. *Perception and Psychophysics, 8*, 396–398.

Longstreth, L.E., Walsh, D.A., Alcorn, M.D., Szeszulski, P.A., & Manis, F.R. (1986). Backward masking, IQ, SAT, and reaction time: Interrelationships and theory. *Personality and Individual Differences, 7*, 643–651.

Lubin, M.P., & Fernanez, J.M. (1986). The relationship between psychometric intelligence and inspection time. *Personality and Individual Differences, 7*, 653–658.

McGhie, A., & Chapman, J. (1961). Disorders of attention and perception in early schizophrenia. *British Journal of Medical Psychology, 34*, 103–116.

Meehl, P.E. (1962). Schizotaxia, schizotypy, schizophrenia. *American Psychologist, 17*, 827–838.

Merritt, R.D., & Balogh, D.W. (1984). The use of a backward masking paradigm to assess information-processing deficits among schizotypics: A re-evaluation of Steronko & Woods. *Journal of Nervous and Mental Disease, 172*, 216–224.

Miller, E. (1977). A note on visual information processing in presenile dementia: A preliminary report. *British Journal of Social and Clinical Psychology, 16*, 99–100.

Miller, L.K. (1972). Visual masking and developmental differences in information processing. *Child Development, 43*, 704–709.

Miller, S., Saccuzzo, D.P., & Braff, D.L. (1979). Information processing deficits in remitted schizophrenics. *Journal of Abnormal Psychology, 88*, 446–449.

Moskowitz, H., & Murray, J.T. (1976). Decrease in iconic memory after alcohol. *Journal of Studies on Alcohol, 37*, 278.

Mosley, J.L. (1980). Selective attention of mildly retarded and nonretarded individuals. *American Journal of Mental Deficiency, 84*, 568–570.

Nakano, K., & Saccuzzo, D.P. (1985). Schizotaxia, visual information processing, and the MMPI 2-7-8 code type. *British Journal of Clinical Psychology, 24*, 217.

Neale, J.M. (1971). Perceptual span in schizophrenia. *Journal of Abnormal Psychology, 77*(2), 196–204.

Neale, J.M., McIntyre, L.W., Fox, R., & Cromwell, R.L. (1969). Span of apprehension in acute schizophrenics. *Journal of Abnormal Psychology, 74*, 593–596.

Neisser, U. (1967). *Cognitive psychology*. New York: Appleton-Century-Crofts.

Nettlebeck, T. (1982). Inspection time: An index for intelligence? *Quarterly Journal of Experimental Psychology, 34*(A), 299–312.

Nettlebeck, T., Edwards, C., & Vreugdenhil, A. (1986). Inspection time and IQ: Evidence for a mental speed-ability association. *Personality and Individual Differences, 7*, 633–641.

Nettlebeck, T., & Lally, M. (1976). Inspection time and measured intelligence. *British Journal of Psychology, 67*, 17.

Pollack, R.H. (1965). Backward figural masking a function of chronological age and intelligence. *Psychonomic Science, 3*, 65–66.

Saccuzzo, D.P. (1977). Bridges between schizophrenia and gerontology: Generalized or special deficits? *Psychological Bulletin, 84,* 595–600.

Saccuzzo, D.P. (1981). Input capability and speed of processing in mental retardation: A reply to Stanovich and Purcell. *Journal of Abnormal Psychology, 90,* 172–174.

Saccuzzo, D.P., & Braff, D.L. (1981). Early information processing deficits in schizophrenia: New findings using schizophrenic subgroups and manic controls. *Archives of General Psychiatry, 38,* 175–179.

Saccuzzo, D.P., Hirt, M., & Spencer, T.J. (1974). Backward masking as a measure of attention in schizophrenia, *Journal of Abnormal Psychology, 83,* 512–522.

Saccuzzo, D.P., Kerr, M., Marcus, A., & Brown, R. (1979). Input capability and speed of processing in mental retardation. *Journal of Abnormal Psychology, 88,* 341–345.

Saccuzzo, D.P., & Larson, G.E. (1987, August). *Variability, effort, and intelligence.* Paper presented at the 95th Annual Convention of the American Psychological Association, New York.

Saccuzzo, D.P., Larson, G.E. & Rimland, B. (1986). Visual auditory and reaction time approaches to the measurement of speed of information processing and individual differences in intelligence. *Personality and Individual Differences, 2,* 659–668.

Saccuzzo, D.P., & Miller, S. (1977). Critical interstimulus interval in delusional schizophrenics and normals. *Journal of Abnormal Psychology, 86,* 261–266.

Saccuzzo, D.P., Safran, D., Anderson, V., & McNeill, B. (1982). Visual information processing in high and low susceptible subjects. *International Journal of Clinical and Experimental Hypnosis, 30,* 32–44.

Saccuzzo, D.P., & Schubert, D.L. (1981). Backward masking as a measure of slow processing in schizophrenic spectrum disorders. *Journal of Abnormal Psychology, 90,* 305–312.

Schwartz, B.D., Winstead, D.K. (1982). Visual processing deficits in acute and chronic schizophrenics. *Biological Psychiatry, 18,* 1311–1320.

Schwartz, B.D., Winstead, D.K., & Adinoff, B. (1983). Temporal integration deficit in visual information processing by chronic schizophrenics. *Biological Psychiatry, 18,* 1311–1320.

Schwartz, B.D., Winstead, D.K., & Adinoff, B. (1983). Visual processing deficits in acute and chronic schizophrenics. *Biological Psychiatry, 17,* 1377–1387.

Schwartz, M., Whittier, O.M., & Schweitzer, P.K. (1979). Evoked responses in retroactively masked stimuli. *Physiological Psycology, 7,* 107–111.

Silverman, T. (1964). The problem of attention in research and theory in schizophrenia. *Psychology Review, 71,* 352–379.

Sperling, G. (1960). The information available in brief visual presentations. *Psychological Monographs, 74* (11, Serial No. 498).

Spitz, H.H., & Thor, D.H. (1968). Visual backward masking in retardates and normals. *Perception and Psychophysics, 4,* 245–246.

Spohn, H.E., Thetford, P.E., & Woodham, F.L. (1970). Span of apprehension and arousal in schizophrenia. *Journal of Abnormal Psychology, 75,* 113–123.

Thor, D.H. (1970). Discrimination of succession in visual masking by retarded and nonretarded normal children. *Journal of Experimental Psychology, 83,* 380–384.

Turvey, M.T. (1973). On peripheral and central processes in vision: Inferences from an information-processing analysis of masking with patterned stimuli. *Psychological Review, 80*, 1–52.

Venables, P.H. (1964). Input dysfunction in schizophrenia. In B.A. Maher (Ed.), *Progress in experimental personality research* (Vol. 1, pp. 1–47). New York: Academic Press.

Vickers, D., & Smith, P.L. (1986). The rationale for the inspection time index. *Personality and Individual Differences, 7*, 609–623.

Walsh, D.A. (1976). Age differences in central perceptual processing: A dichoptic backward masking investigation. *Journal of Gerontology, 31*, 178–185.

Welsandt, R.F., Jr., & Meyer, P.A. (1974). Visual masking, mental age, and retardation. *Journal of Experimental Child Psychology, 18*, 512–519.

Welsandt, R.F., Jr., Zupnick, J.J., & Meyer, P.A. (1973). Age effects in backward visual masking (Crawford Paradigm). *Journal of Experimental Child Psychology, 15*, 454–461.

Yates, A.J. (1966). Psychological deficit. *Annual Review of Psychology, 17*, 111–144.

Section *IV*

Information-Processing Approaches

Chapter 10

Reasoning about Social and Practical Matters

Richard K. Wagner and Ethel L. Parker

Florida State University

The occasion of a recent class reunion provided first-hand support for the common observation that success in school is, at best, a modest predictor of success in later life. I did come across examples of individuals who had distinguished themselves in schooling and in later life (e.g., a smart albeit "geeky" classmate who ranked in the top 25 of our class had become a test pilot and astronaut). But for every example there were counterexamples of individuals with distinguished school records and unremarkable lives thereafter (e.g., the vita of our "most likely to succeed" classmate contained the single entry "housewife") and individuals who blossomed but only after leaving school (e.g., the classmate who would have easily been voted "most likely to fail" had we been permitted to vote on such a category, who has experienced considerable success and wealth in his career as a comic book fiction writer).

Obviously there are many reasons for differential success in and out of school. Career success may be markedly unpredictable. Chance factors such as being in the right career at the right time or knowing the right person appear to play a major role in career success. Motivation for success at one's ultimate career may be very different than one's motivation for success in school. Motivators of career performance (e.g., money, responsibility, power) are different from those of school performance (e.g., grades), and whereas individuals have relatively little say about the tasks they are asked to do in school, individuals sometimes can select careers that require tasks they enjoy.

THE GENERALITY OF COGNITIVE ABILITY

Another potential reason for differential success in and out of school is more directly relevant to intelligence researchers: *Levels of cognitive performance may be much more domain specific than we have assumed—when the domains extend beyond classroom-type tasks.* Classroom-type tasks, the kinds found on many IQ tests as well as in the classroom typically (a) are formulated by others, (b) are well defined, (c) come with all information necessary for solution, (d) are disembedded from an individual's everyday experience, (e) have a single solution, and (f) have a single method for obtaining the correct solution (Neisser, 1976; Wagner & Sternberg, 1985). In contrast, many of the tasks faced in out-of-school contexts including those found in many career pursuits typically (a) have to be formulated or reformulated by oneself, (b) are ill defined, (c) require additional information, (d) are amenable to application of everyday experience, (e) have multiple solutions, and (f) have multiple methods for obtaining solutions.

For classroom-type tasks, the fact of positive manifold (the average correlation in a matrix of correlations among cognitive tasks will be positive) indicates some generality of individual differences in performance. Numerous factor analyses of sets of cognitive variables tell us that this generality is partial rather than complete. Group factors—factors that are less general than *g* but more general than task-specific factors—exist for domains such as mathematical reasoning. Such factors would be unnecessary were there (a) complete generality of individual differences in performance, in which case all of the common variance would be explained by the *g* factor; or (b) no generality of individual differences in performance, in which case there would only be task specific factors. The fact that group factors tend to be correlated (though not perfectly) further supports the partial generality of individual differences in performance.

Whereas there is convincing evidence of the partial generality of individual differences in performance across classroom-type tasks, an implication of research in the area of practical intelligence is that this generality may not extend to beyond classroom-type tasks (Sternberg & Wagner, 1986). Consider several recent examples from the domain of everyday mathematics.

Ceci and Liker (1986) studied 30 experienced horse-race handicappers at an East Coast race track. They were able to model what turned out to be complex cognitive strategies that the handicappers used to predict the probable favorite in a series of races and to predict the top three horses' post time odds. All of the handicappers made better than chance predictions, and some were astonishingly accurate. The interesting point for present purposes was that there was no relation between accuracy of prediction and IQ on the Wechsler Adult Intelligence Test. Lave, Murtaugh, and de la Rocha (1984) studied the ability of adults to make prudent choices at the supermarket among items that could be purchased in different sizes at different prices. The adults varied in their ability and willingness to engage in the kind of proportional reasoning necessary to make prudent choices. The adults were also given a test of formal mathematical reasoning that sampled the same operations required at the supermarket. No relation was found between performance on the test and in the supermarket. Finally, Scribner (1986) studied the practical mathematical reasoning of "unskilled" workers in a milk-processing plant. Experienced plant workers were observed to use a variety of ingenious and effective strategies for counting quantities of milk products that were very different from the kinds of algorithmic procedures taught in school. For example, individuals who assembled batches of products for delivery filled identical orders in different ways, depending on the availability of cases in the vicinity. For example, 10 quarts of milk might be obtained by subtracting 5 quarts from a partial case of 15 quarts, or adding 4 quarts to a partial case of 6 quarts. The method used was the one that required the fewest moves. For a second example, individuals who inventoried milk products rarely used simple counting or multiplication to count items. Rather, they began with the knowledge of how many items a given storage space could hold, and then adjusted the number accordingly. So an inventory taker counting items in a storage area that was nearly filled but had gaps would mentally "fill-in" the gaps to arrive at the number of items the area would hold if it were completely filled, and then adjust the number downward because of the gaps. Alternatively, inventory workers might count items by first visualizing the largest complete rectangle of items in the space, and then adding to that number on the basis of the irregular items about the perimeter.

Evidence that questions the generality of individual differences in levels of cognitive performance to everyday tasks can be found in domains other than practical mathematical reasoning. I have carried out a series of studies in collaboration with Robert Sternberg of career performance in the fields of business management, sales, and academic psychology (Wagner, 1987; Wagner & Sternberg, 1985, 1990). In each of these studies, we constructed measures of tacit knowledge—work-related practical know-how that rarely is taught explicitly—for the domain under study and gave them to individuals of varying levels of experience. An example of work-related tacit knowledge that is helpful to career performance is to "think in tasks accomplished rather than hours spent working." Across the studies performance on measures of tacit knowledge consistently have been better predictors of career performance than IQ typically is, and in none of the studies has the correlation between IQ and tacit knowledge been reliably different from zero. In the most recent study of this series, we gave a tacit knowledge measure to business managers who were participating in the Leadership Development Program at the Center for Creative Leadership (Wagner & Sternberg, 1990). Our measure of managerial performance was rated effectiveness in small-group problem-solving exercises that were simulations of managerial problems faced by two companies. Participants were given a battery of tests, including an IQ test, as a requirement for participation in the program. The best predictor of managerial problem-solving performance was tacit knowledge ($r = -.61$). The negative correlation is due to the fact that the scoring system for the tacit knowledge was based on deviation from an expert prototype, and consequently that low scores were indicative of better performance. IQ was the second best predictor of problem-solving performance ($r = .38$). Of particular interest was that tacit knowledge and IQ contributed independent predictive power, as evidenced by the facts that the correlation between tacit knowledge and IQ ($r = -.14$) was not reliably different from 0, and that, by combining tacit knowledge, IQ, and selected personality variables, nearly all of the reliable variance in the managerial problem-solving variable was accounted for.

Generality of Cognitive Ability to the Social Domain

Classroom tasks and IQ tests differ from many of the tasks we face in our daily lives and careers in that we are asked to perform them in isolation and the content is rarely animate. Yet much of our life is spent working and dealing with others, both at home and at work. To what degree do individual differences in performance on traditional cognitive tasks generalize to social situations?

Mercer, Gomez-Palacio, and Padilla (1986) completed a large cross-cultural study of individual differences in IQ and in social role performance, the results of which question the degree to which individual differences in cognitive ability among children generalize to social problem-solving situations. They studied three samples of children, including random samples of 700 Chicano and 700 Anglo students aged 5 through 11 from the public school population of California, and a sample of 1,100 Mexican students from Mexico City made up of 50 boys and 50 girls at each age level from 6 through 16. The Chicano and Anglo samples were given the WISC-R, and the Mexican sample was given a Spanish version of the WISC-R that was translated and modified slightly by the researchers. The measure of social role performance was the Adaptive Behavior Inventory for Children (ABIC) (Mercer, 1979). The ABIC consists of a set of questions to be answered by a child's primary caretaker about how well the child handles various social problems and responsibilities. Scores are provided for family roles, nonacademic school roles, community roles, peer group roles, earner/consumer roles, and self-maintenance roles.

This is a fascinating study with many interesting results, but for present purposes we shall focus on the limited question of the relation between IQ and social role performance. There were virtually no relations between IQ and any of the ABIC scores for any of the samples. Factor analyses of the matrix of intercorrelations yielded uncorrelated factors for the WISC-R and the ABIC. An interesting aside is that the data refuted Mercer's (1979) assumption in constructing the ABIC that the performance of children across social roles is largely independent. Thus, a given child might be very competent at family roles but not particularly competent at community roles, depending on the child's experiential history and the nature of the demands made by the child's environment. The data, however, were that the ABIC subtest scores were highly intercorrelated. The intercorrelations ranged from .84 to .91, with a median of .89, for the Mexican sample; .68 to .82, with a median of .76, for the Chicano sample; and .63 to .80, with a median of .75, for the Anglo sample. The absolute magnitude of these correlations is inflated by the large age range of the subjects (6 to 16 for the Mexican sample; 6 to 11 for the Chicano and Anglo samples), but the relative magnitude of these correlations compared to those for the WISC-R are informative: The ABIC subtests were more highly intercorrelated than the WISC-R subtests for each of the three samples of children. These results, then, support a fairly general ability for handling social problems and situations that is analogous to, but independent of, psychometric g. This result parallels our factor analyses of subtests on our tacit knowledge measures (Wagner, 1987), which indicated a general ability for practical problems that also was analogous to, but independent of, psychometric g.

Measures of Social Intelligence

In addition to the ABIC and other similar parental interview measures of adaptive behavior, a number of tests have been constructed specifically to measure social intelligence.

The George Washington Social Intelligence Test (Hunt, 1928; Moss, Hunt, Omwake, & Woodward, 1955). This test of social intelligence consists of five subtests that require answering multiple-choice, true-false, or matching questions. Judgment in Social Situations consists of questions about what to do in problem situations involving relations with others. Observation of Human Behavior consists of questions about generalities concerning human behavior. Recognition of the Mental States Behind Words consists of questions about mental states as reflected in target statements. Memory for Names and Faces consists of questions that require matching names to faces that had just been learned. Finally, Sense of Humor consists of question that require picking the best ending of jokes. Unfortunately, scores on the George Washington Social Intelligence Test correlate more highly with IQ test scores than with other criteria more relevant to social functioning, which suggests that the test is largely an IQ test in disguise (Cronbach, 1960).

The Chapin Social Insight Test (Chapin, 1942). This test consists of 25 statements of common social situations. For each statement, the examinee's task is to select the most apt commentary or course of action from among four alternatives. The validity data on the Chapin Social Insight Test have been mixed. On the one hand, and in contrast to the George Washington Test of Social Intelligence, modest correlations between Chapin scores and IQ (e.g., *r*s in the range of .2 to .4) provide some support of discriminant validity (Gough, 1968; Keating, 1978). On the other hand, the fact that Chapin scores do not correlate with other measures of social intelligence questions the convergent validity of the Chapin or the other measures of social intelligence (Sternberg & Smith, 1985).

Six Factor Test of Social Intelligence (O'Sullivan & Guilford, 1966). Perhaps the most recent test of social intelligence to receive widespread interest is one based on Guilford's (1967) Structure of Intellect Model. Using the SOI model, O'Sullivan and Guilford constructed subtests to measure six factors of social intelligence, each of which was measured from three to five proposed tests. The six factors are Cognition of Behavioral Units, Cognition of Behavioral Classes, Cognition of Behavioral Relations, Cognition of Behavioral Systems, Cognition of Behavioral Transformations, and Cognition of Behavioral Implications. Some sample tests include (a) *missing pictures—the examinee chooses from among three photographs the one that best completes the story—a measure of Cognition of Behavioral Systems; (b) expression*—the examinee picks from among four drawings of facial expressions, hand gestures, or body postures, the one that best matches a given expression, gesture, or posture—a measure of Cognition of Behavioral Units; and (c) *social relations*—the examinee picks from among three verbal statements the one that best fits the relationship depicted between a pair of schematic faces—a measure of Cognition of Behavioral Relations. The results of validity studies of the Six Factor Test of social Intelligence have been quite mixed (see, e.g., Matney & McManis, 1977; Osipow & Walsh, 1973; Shanley, Walker & Foley, 1971). In general, studies frequently find that only one of several tests correlates with external criteria in the expected direction, perhaps a reflection of the uneven reliabilities of the tests. In addition, the Six Factor Test scores appear to correlate as highly with IQ as with other more relevant measures.

The Profile of Nonverbal Sensitivity (PONS) (Hall, Rosenthal, Archer, DiMatteo, & Rogers, 1978; Rosenthal, Hall, DiMatteo, Rogers, & Archer, 1979). The PONS consists of 220 audio and video 2-second segments of an individual expressing different affective situations (e.g., expressing motherly love, threatening someone). After each segment, the examinee picks from among two alternatives the phrase that best fits the segment. A number of validity studies of the PONS have been carried out, most by the authors of the test. The divergent validity of the test is supported by only modest correlations with IQ. However, as is the case for several of the other measures of social intelligence, the convergent validity is suspect because there have yet to be convincing demonstrations that PONS scores correlate with appropriate criterion measures of social performance.

A MEASURE OF SOCIAL INDUCTIVE REASONING

Inductive reasoning, which involves inducing rules or concepts from a series of examples, figures prominently in conceptions of intelligence. Thurstone (1938) included inductive reasoning as one of the seven primary mental abilities, and inductive reasoning is at the heart of the Cattell's (1943, 1971) construct of fluid ability (see also Horn, 1968; Snow, 1981).

Induction tasks have been of considerable interest to psychometricians, information-processing psychologists, and learning theorists. Inductive reasoning problems, including analogies (e.g., ELEPHANT is to MOUSE as HIPPO-POTAMUS is to a. RHINOSAURUS, b. MOLE), series completions (e.g., 1, 3, 9 a. 18, b. 27), and classifications (e.g., which goes best with ANT, GRASSHOPPER, and CRICKET? a. MOSQUITO, b. BAT), comprise at least half of the items on many IQ tests (Pellegrino, 1985). These same inductive reasoning problems have figured prominently in information-processing analyses of the processes and knowledge representations that underlie intelligent performance (see, e.g., Pellegrino & Glaser, 1980, 1982; Sternberg, 1977a,b; Whitely & Barnes, 1979). The study of human learning has focused for many years on yet another inductive reasoning task, the concept formation task. In this task, subjects typically are asked to classify a series of stimuli (e.g., shapes of different sizes and colors). Feedback about the correctness of their classification is used by subjects to induce the relevant concept (e.g., large square). It is generally believed that subjects first learn to attend to the appropriate dimensions, and then determine the correct values of the dimensions (Sutherland & Mackintosh, 1971; Trabasso & Bower, 1968; Zeaman & House, 1963).

Inductive reasoning would appear to be essential, not only for doing well on IQ tests and in human learning experiments, but also for intelligent performance in everyday situations. It is almost impossible to imagine how difficult our daily lives would be were we not able to distill our observations about people and events into a manageable set of concepts and rules. However, there may be important differences between the traditional inductive reasoning problems that have served as the basis of the study of human learning and as IQ test items, and the kinds of inductive reasoning tasks that we face in our everyday lives. For example, the categories and concepts that are represented by traditional inductive reasoning problems tend to be well defined, whereas many of the categories and concepts that are useful in everyday situations tend to be ill defined (Rosch & Lloyd, 1978). (Analyses of ill-defined categories have been carried out by Medin & Schaffer, 1978; Smith & Medin, 1981; Posner & Keele, 1968.)

The focus of the study to be reported here was on two additional ways in which the inductive reasoning tasks of everyday life possibly are different from the traditional inductive reasoning problems found on IQ tests and in human learning laboratories. First, the content of a substantial proportion of everyday inductive reasoning problems concerns people and social situations, whereas the content of traditional inductive reasoning problems is almost invariably inanimate.[1] Second, whereas traditional concept formation tasks and many IQ-type inductive reasoning problems attempt to minimize the effects of differences in prior knowledge by focusing on relations among well-defined and common concepts such as color, size, and shape, everyday inductive reasoning tasks would appear to allow, and indeed require, the application of considerable prior knowledge.

We developed the following inductive reasoning task to study inductive reasoning in the social domain. Ten stories were constructed, each consisting of seven episodes in the life of a fictitious main character. The actions of the main character were governed by a defining behavioral characteristic (e.g., adventurous, self-centered, aggressive, shy) that was not revealed to the subject. In each episode, the main character was faced with a choice of two possible responses to a social situation, one of which was consistent with the target behavioral characteristic, the other of which was not. For example, Anne, whose defining behavioral characteristic was adventurous, would be faced with the choice of accepting or rejecting a dare from her peers to do something adventurous. Subjects predicted what the main character would do, and then learned what the main character actually did. This feedback could be used to improve prediction of the main character's behavior in subsequent episodes.

Our goals in this study were to (a) compare children's ability to make correct predictions with their ability to verbalize a reason for their predictions; (b) examine developmental changes in social inductive reasoning; (c) test, albeit indirectly, a specific hypothesis about how children reason about others on our task; and (d) examine relations between individual differences in performance on our measure of social inductive reasoning and IQ. The specific hypothesis about how children reason about others on our task is that children rely on self-knowledge to understand the behavior of another. We tested an implication of this hypothesis, namely, that performance should be higher if there is congruence between one's own behavioral characteristics and those of the character whose behavior is to be predicted.

The social induction task consisted of 10 stories, each of which contained seven episodes.[2] Each story described situations involving a main character

---

[1] There are occasional examples of psychometric induction problems with social content. O'Sullivan and Guilford (1966) used cartoons depicting social situations in their Six Factor Tests of Social Intelligence, and a picture arrangement task using similar cartoons can be found on the Wechsler scales.

[2] The materials are available from the authors.

whose behavior was governed by one of 10 defining behavioral characteristics: extrovert, quitter, sensitive, optimistic, introvert, irresponsible/forgetful, adventurous, aggressive, ambitious, and self-centered. The defining behavioral characteristics were drawn from Rosenberg, Nelson, and Vivekananthan (1968), and they were chosen to represent both positively and negatively valued characteristics. The main characters were given names. Six were female and four were male.

Each episode consisted of a brief description of a situation that concluded with a choice faced by the main character. The following is a sample episode from "aggressive" Jane's story:

> The next day, Jane went to the store to spend some of her allowance. There were a lot of neat things and Jane had a hard time deciding what to buy. She was trying to decide between a Rambo-style squirt gun and a set of paints. Which one do you think she chose, the squirt gun or the paints?

After the first episode, each subsequent episode in a story began with a statement indicating what the main character chose in the previous episode.

IQ estimates were obtained by giving the Block Design and Vocabulary subtests of the Wechsler Intelligence Scale for Children-Revised to the fourth-grade and seventh-grade groups, and the Verbal Reasoning subtest of the Differential Aptitude Tests to the undergraduate group.

We gave our measure to 30 fourth-grade, 28 seventh-grade, and 30 undergraduate students. (An initial try-out at the first-grade level revealed that first-grade children were at chance performance.) The inductive reasoning problems were presented orally. Members of the fourth-grade group responded orally. Members of the seventh-grade and undergraduate groups responded in writing. The inductive reasoning problems were presented first, followed by the ability tests. The ordering of stories, and of episodes within stories, was fixed. All tasks were presented individually to members of the fourth-grade group. The inductive reasoning problems were given in small-group sessions, and the ability measures were individually administered for members of the seventh-grade group. All tasks were presented to the undergraduates in a group session.

For each episode, subjects (a) predicted what the main character would do, (b) provided a reason for their prediction, (c) told what they would choose to do in the situation, and (d) provided a reason for their choice. Members of the undergraduate-student group were not asked to tell what they would choose to do or to provide a reason for their choice because it was deemed to be inappropriate to do so given their age level.

After listening to an episode, and prior to asking subjects to make their predictions, a comprehension check was made to insure that subjects were basing their predictions on accurate information from the episode. Members of the fourth-grade group were asked to repeat the episode. If a mistake was made, it was corrected, the episode was reread, and the subject again was asked to repeat the episode. Members of the seventh-grade and undergraduate groups answered a comprehension question prior to making their prediction. Subjects were instructed to raise their hand if they wanted an episode repeated.

A point was given for each correct prediction, with a maximum possible score of 70 points (7 episodes or trials times 10 stories). We also scored subjects' reasons for their predictions using a three-point scale. A zero was given for a reason unrelated to the defining behavioral characteristic (e.g., for the defining behavioral characteristic of extrovert, "She might be mad"). A *1* was given for an action, feeling, or preference that was congruent with the defining behavioral characteristic (e.g., "She likes to talk"). A *2* was given for mentioning a trait that was congruent with the defining behavioral characteristic ("She's outgoing").

Having a score based on correct predictions and a score based on reasons for predictions allowed us to compare three potential measures of performance on the inductive reasoning problems: a prediction score, a reasons score, and a combined prediction/reasons score. There were no differences in results when analyses were carried out of either of the three performance measures, and there were no obvious differences between the ability to make correct predictions and the ability to provide a reason for the predictions. Because there were no differences among the three performance measures, and because the prediction score avoids the potential problem of bias and subjectivity in scoring reasons for predictions, the results we report are based on the predictions score.

Developmental Differences in Social Inductive Reasoning

Means and standard deviations of prediction scores are presented by group in Table 1. A group-by-trial (episode number) repeated measures analysis of variance with linear and quadratic polynomial contrasts on the repeated-measures factor of trial yielded (a) a reliable effect of group, $F(2, 85) = 63.3, p < .001$; (b) reliable linear, $F(1, 85) = 359.6, p < .001$, and quadratic, $F(1, 85) = 73.5, p < .001$, effects of trial; and (c) reliable group-by-linear trial, $F(2, 85) = 28.6, p < .001$, and group-by-quadratic trial, $F(2, 85) = 13,7, p < .001$, interactions. We will discuss the effects of group, trial and their interaction in turn. It will be helpful to refer to Figure 1, which displays the performance of the groups by trial position, to better visualize the results.

Table 1.   Means and Standard Deviations for Prediction Scores by Group

Group	M	(SD)	Range
4th	42.8	(6.8)	33–57
7th	51.3	(8.5)	37–64
undergraduates	60.9	(2.9)	54–66

Note. The range of scores possible was from 0 to 70.

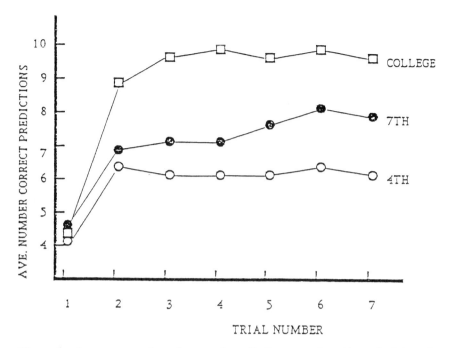

Figure 1.   Average number of correct predictions as a function of trial position and group.

The group means were in the expected order, and each was significantly different from the other two ($p < .05$), which indicates that undergraduates performed better than seventh-grade students, who in turn performed better than fourth-grade students. The linear effect of trial position reflects learning that resulted in improved performance with successive episodes in a story, and the quadratic effect of trial position indicates that this improvement was greater for earlier episodes than for later ones. The group-by-linear trial interaction reflects increasing rates of improvement across grade levels, and the group-by-quadratic interaction suggests that the same was true for the larger increase in performance across early trials. Inspection of the curves in Figure 1 suggests that what differentiated fourth- and seventh-grade students was that the fourth-grade students had reached their maximum level of performance by the second trial, whereas the seventh-grade students continued to improve. The undergraduate students were more like the fourth-grade students than the seventh-grade students in that they did not show much improvement after the second trial either, but unlike the results for fourth-grade students, the leveling off of performance for the undergraduates after the second trial appears to reflect their reaching a ceiling on task performance.

Use of Self-Knowledge in Reasoning About Others

Recall that we hypothesized that subjects might use knowledge about what they would do in trying to understand the behavior of others. We operationalized knowledge about what they would do by asking our fourth- and seventh-grade subjects what they would do if given the choice faced by the main character. Of course, we had no guarantee that our subjects would respond truthfully, but we assumed that their responses would be accurate enough for the purpose of testing our hypothesis, which we did in the following way: We compared performance on trials for which subjects indicated that they would have made the *same* choice the character subsequently made, with performance on trials for which subjects indicated that they would have made a *different* choice from the choice the character subsequently made. We present these results in Figure 2. Note the large disordinal interaction between group and same versus different choice, $F(1, 56)$ = 35.8, $p < .001$. Whereas the predictions of fourth-grade students were more accurate when their self-reports of what they would choose matched what the character chose, the predictions of seventh-grade students were more accurate when their self-reports of what they would choose were the opposite of what the character chose. Our hypothesis, then, was supported for fourth-grade students but refuted for seventh-grade students.

We next examined correlations between our social inductive reasoning scores and estimated IQ based on the Block Design and Vocabulary subtests of the

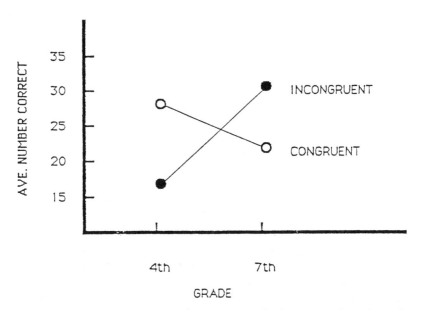

Figure 2. Average number of correct predictions as a function of congruence between subjects' and characters' responses.

WISC-R for the fourth and seventh-grade samples, and the Verbal Reasoning subtest of the Differential Aptitude Tests for the undergraduates. The correlations were not reliably different from zero for either the fourth-grade ($r = -.02$), seventh-grade ($r = -.02$), or undergraduate ($r = -.13$) groups. The correlation for the undergraduate group may have been attenuated by an apparent ceiling effect on the social inductive reasoning task, but that was not the case for the fourth-grade or seventh-grade groups.

We find these preliminary results to be promising. The developmental changes and lack of correlations with IQ support the divergent validation of our task. The interpretable effects of trial position that are similar to those observed in traditional concept formation studies provide indirect support of the validity of our task. The important limitation of our data to date is that we have yet to demonstrate the convergent validity of our task.

CONCLUSIONS

Recent studies of intellectual functioning in practical and social domains underscore the meager generalizability of individual differences in performance on classroom-type tasks to everyday-type tasks. To be sure there remains a statistically significant relation between IQ and performance on everyday tasks, especially correlations are disattenuated for restriction of range and imperfect reliability of measures (see, e.g., Schmidt & Hunter, 1981). But the bottom line is that, in practice, the variance in performance on everyday tasks explained by performance on classroom-type tasks represents little more than a drop in a bucket full of unexplained variance. If, for example, we accept Wigdor and Garner's (1982) figure of .2 as the typical correlation between performance on either IQ or employment tests and job performance, only 4% of variance in job performance is accounted for by test scores. Even the most ardent proponent of using performance on IQ or classroom-type tasks to predict career performance would be happier if the data were more favorable. There is a growing body of evidence—some of which was reviewed and reported in the present chapter— that it is possible to measure intellectual competencies required for success in everyday pursuits, but such measures are in their "psychometric infancy" when compared to IQ tests.

Perhaps the most important implication of recent work in practical and social domains is to reinforce the need for more adequate theories if intelligence. Simply to point out a distinction between the intellectual demands of classroom-type tasks and tasks common to everyday life, as we and others have done, is not a satisfying theoretical state of affairs. Proponents of constructs such as practical or social intelligence bear the ultimate responsibility for proposing a framework (with empirical support) that encompasses classroom- and everyday-type tasks. For a concrete example of kinds of questions that remain to be addressed, consider the basic question of what really differentiates classroom-type and everyday-type tasks. The answer cannot simply be where the task is found. Even a cursory analysis of the classroom environment reveals significant demands on practical and social competencies (Wagner & Kistner, 1990), and academic skills including reading, writing, and mathematical computation are required by many facets of everyday life. One can describe typical characteristics that differentiate classroom-type tasks from everyday-type tasks as we have done earlier, but such a description represents mere armchair speculation.

We are pursuing the study of three factors that we believe to differentiate the kinds of intellectual competence that are required by classroom-type and everyday-type tasks. The first is simply content. Classroom-type tasks and everyday-type tasks differ in problem content. Given individual differences in experience and in facility and motivation for acquiring academic, practical, and social knowledge, differential performance on classroom-type and everyday-type tasks may reflect differences in amount and organization of requisite knowledge. The second factor we are investigating is problem format. The format of classroom-type tasks is often pencil and paper, whereas the "format" of everyday-type tasks tend to be more veridical and less symbolic. The third factor we are investigating is learning history, and more specifically, forgetting history. Much of what we learn soon becomes unaccessible unless it is refreshed through practice or actual use. Differences in what the environment requires on a continuing basis between the environments faced by children in school and adults at work may be a primary cause of ultimate differences in their intellectual competencies and knowledge.

The picture would be so much simpler if there were no differences between the way we reason about academic matters and the way we reason about practical and social ones. Unfortunately, the situation is not simple, and the work ahead is monumental. However, progress in this area is likely to be consequential to a broad understanding of the interactions of knowledge and intellectual processes that underlie complex cognitive performance.

REFERENCES

Cattell, R.B. (1943). The measurement of adult intelligence. *Psychological Bulletin, 40*, 153–193.

Cattell, R.B. (1971). *Abilities: Their structure, growth, and action.* Boston: Houghton-Mifflin.

Ceci, S.J., & Liker, J. (1986). Academic and nonacademic intelligence. In R.J. Sternberg & R.K. Wagner (Eds.), *Practical intelligence: Nature and origins of competence in the everyday world* (pp. 119–142). New York: Cambridge University Press.

Chapin, F.S. (1942). Preliminary standardization of a social insight scale. *American Sociological Review, 7*, 214–225.

Cronbach, L.J. (1960). *Essentials of psychological testing.* New York: Harper & Row.

Gough, H.G. (1968). *Manual for the Chapin Social Insight Test.* Palo Alto, CA: Consulting Psychologists Press.

Guilford, J.P. (1967). *The nature of human intelligence.* New York: McGraw-Hill.

Hall, J.A., Rosenthal, R., Archer, D., DiMatteo, M.R., & Rogers, P.L. (1977). Profile of nonverbal sensitivity. In P. McReynolds (Ed.), *Advances in psychological assessment* (Vol. 4, pp. 179–221). San Francisco: Jossey-Bass.

Horn, J.L. (1968). Organization of abilities and the development of intelligence. *Psychological Review, 75,* 242–259.

Hunt, T. (1928). The measurement of social intelligence. *Journal of Applied Psychology, 12,* 317–334.

Keating, D.P. (1978). A search for social intelligence. *Journal of Educational Psychology, 70,* 218–223.

Lave, J., Murtaugh, M., & de la Rocha, O. (1984). The dialectic of arithmetic in grocery shopping. In B. Rogoff & J. Lave (Eds.), *Everyday cognition: Its development in social context.* Cambridge, MA: Harvard University Press.

Matney, D.C., & McManis, D. (1977). Repression sensitization status and social intelligence characteristics. *Psychological Reports, 41,* 837–838.

Medin, D.L., & Schaffer, M.M. (1978). A context theory of classification learning. *Psychological Review, 85,* 207–238.

Mercer, J.R. (1979). *System of multicultural pluralistic assessment: Technical manual.* New York: The Psychological Corporation.

Mercer, J.R., Gomez-Palacio, M., & Padilla, E. (1986). The development of practical intelligence in cross-cultural perspective. In R.J. Sternberg & R.K. Wagner (Eds.), *Practical intelligence: Nature and origins of competence in the everyday world* (pp. 307–337). New York: Cambridge University Press.

Moss, F.A., Hunt, T., Omwake, K.T., & Woodward, L.G. (1955). *Manual for the George Washington University Series Social Intelligence Test.* Washington, DC: The Center for Psychological Service.

Neisser, U. (1976). General, academic, and artificial intelligence. In L. Restock (Ed.), *The nature of intelligence* (pp. 135–144). Hillsdale, NJ: Erlbaum.

Osipow, S., & Walsh, W.B. (1973). Social intelligence and the selection of counselors. *Journal of Counseling Psychology, 4,* 866–869.

O'Sullivan, M., & Guilford, J.P. (1966). *Six factor test of social intelligence: Manual of instruction and interpretation.* Beverly Hills, CA: Sheridan Psychological Services.

Pellegrino, J.W. (1985). Inductive reasoning ability. In R.J. Sternberg (Ed.), *Human abilities: An information processing approach* (pp. 195–224). New York: W.H. Freeman.

Pellegrino, J.W., & Glaser, R. (1980). Components of inductive reasoning. In R. Snow, P.A. Federico, & W. Montague (Eds.), *Aptitude, learning, and instruction: Cognitive process analyses of aptitude* (Vol. 1). Hillsdale, NJ: Erlbaum.

Pellegrino, J.W., & Glaser, R. (1982). Analyzing aptitudes for learning: Inductive reasoning. In R. Glaser (Ed.), *Advances in instructional psychology* (Vol. 2). Hillsdale, NJ: Erlbaum.

Posner, M.I., & Keele, S.W. (1968). On the genesis of abstract ideas. *Journal of Experimental Psychology, 77,* 353–363.

Rosch, E., & Lloyd, B.B. (Eds.). (1978). *Cognition and categorization.* Hillsdale, NJ: Erlbaum.

Rosenberg, S., Nelson, C., & Vivekananthan, P.S. (1968). A multidimensional approach to the structure of personality impression. *Journal of Personality and Social Psychology, 9,* 283–294.

Rosenthal, R., Hall, J.A., DiMatteo, M.R., Rogers, P.L., & Archer, D. (1979). *Sensitivity to nonverbal communication: The PONS test.* Baltimore: Johns Hopkins University Press.

Schmidt, F.L., & Hunter, J.E. (1981). Employment testing. *American Psychologist, 36,* 1128–1137.

Scribner, S. (1986). Thinking in action: Some characteristics of practical thought. In R.J. Sternberg & R.K. Wagner (Eds.), *Practical intelligence: Nature and origins of competence in the everyday world* (pp. 13–30). New York: Cambridge University Press.

Shanley, L.A., Walker, R.E., & Foley, J. (1971). Social intelligence: A concept in search of data. *Psychological Reports, 29,* 1123–1132.

Smith, E.E., & Medin, D.L. (1981). *Categories and concepts.* Cambridge, MA: Harvard University Press.

Snow, R.E. (1981). Toward a theory of aptitude for learning: Fluid and crystallized abilities and their correlates. In M.P. Friedman, J.P. Das, & N. O'Connor (Eds.), *Intelligence and learning* (pp. 345–362). New York: Plenum.

Sternberg, R.J. (1977a). Component processes in analogical reasoning. *Psychological Review, 84,* 353–378.

Sternberg, R.J. (1977b). *Intelligence, information processing, and analogical reasoning: The componential analysis of human abilities.* Hillsdale, NJ: Erlbaum.

Sternberg, R.J., & Smith, C. (1985). Social intelligence and decoding skills in nonverbal communication. *Social Cognition, 2,* 1168–1192.

Sternberg, R.J., & Wagner, R.K. (Eds.). (1986). *Practical intelligence: Nature and origins of competence in the everyday world.* New York: Cambridge University Press.

Sutherland, N.S., & Mackintosh, N.J. (1971). *Mechanisms of animal discrimination learning.* New York: Academic Press.

Thurstone, L.L. (1938). *Primary mental abilities.* Chicago: University of Chicago Press.

Trabasso, T.R., & Bower, G.H. (1968). *Attention in learning.* New York: Wiley.

Wagner, R.K. (1987). Tacit knowledge in everyday intelligent behavior. *Journal of Personality and Social Psychology, 52,* 1236–1247.

Wagner, R.K., & Kistner, J.A. (1990). Implications of the distinction between academic and practical intelligence for learning-disabled children. In H.L. Swanson & B. Keogh (Eds.), *Learning disabilities: Theoretical and research issues* (pp. 75–92). Hillsdale, NJ: Erlbaum.

Wagner, R.K., & Sternberg, R.J. (1985). Practical intelligence in real-world pursuits: The role of tacit knowledge. *Journal of Personality and Social Psychology, 48,* 436–458.

Wagner, R.K., & Sternberg, R.J. (1990). Street smarts. In K. Clark & M. Clark (Eds.), *Measures of leadership* (pp. 493–504). West Orange, NJ: Leadership Library of America.

Whitely, S.E., & Barnes, G.M. (1979). The implications of processing event sequences for theories of analogical reasoning. *Memory & Cognition, 7,* 323–331.

Wigdor, A.K., & Garner, W.R. (Eds.). (1982). *Ability testing: Uses, consequences, and controversies.* Washington, DC: National Academy Press.
Zeaman, D., & House, B.J. (1963). The role of attention in retardate discrimination learning. In N.R. Ellis (Ed.), *Handbook of mental deficiency* (pp. 159–223). New York: McGraw-Hill.

Chapter 11

Human Intelligence in a Repeated-Measures Setting: Communalities of Intelligence With Performance*

Robert S. Kennedy

Essex Corporation

William P. Dunlap

Tulane University

Janet J. Turnage

University of Central Florida

Robert L. Wilkes

University of Wyoming (Casper)

* Support for this work was under the following: National Aeronautics and Space Administration (Contract NAS9-17326), National Science Foundation (Grant 1S1-8521282), and U.S. Army Medical Research Acquisition Activity (Contract DAMD17-85-C-5095). The authors are indebted to M.G. Smith for data rendering.

INTRODUCTION

We had several motives for conducting and reporting these studies. In developing a battery of tests to measure time-course changes from environmental or psychological stress, we believed the most important characteristic was that the test be stable over many replications (Jones, Kennedy, & Bittner, 1981). Then, because reliability has such a strong, favorable influence on statistical power (Sutcliffe, 1980), especially for "subject own control" studies, we also sought highly reliable tests.

Initially, over 100 traditional and mostly paper-and-pencil-based mental (perceptual, cognitive, information processing) tests were evaluated empirically for these metric properties in a 15-day repeated-measures paradigm (Bittner, Carter, Kennedy, Harbeson, & Krause, 1986). The best three dozen of these were implemented on a microcomputer and then evaluated again. Selection criteria in both cases were that the tests needed to stabilize in less than 10 minutes' practice and test reliability needed to be $r > .707$ for 3-minutes' testing (Kennedy, Wilkes, Dunlap, & Kuntz, 1987). More recently, correlation (Kennedy, Turnage, & Osteen, 1990) and factor analytic studies (Kennedy, Baltzley, Turnage, & Jones, 1989) have helped to define a core battery. These tests have been shown to be sensitive to environmental and toxic agents (Kennedy, Turnage, & Dunlap, 1992; Turnage, Kennedy, Smith, Baltzley, & Lane, 1992), and correlated with simulation of operational tasks (Turnage, Kennedy, Gilson, Bliss, & Nolan, 1988).

Based on the availability of these tests, we believed we could address practical and theoretical cases relevant to intelligence. First, we sought to answer questions about predictive validity of the tests through correlation with holistic measures of intelligence and aptitude. Strong correlations between these tests and intelligence tests were predicted. If this result were obtained, the tests which were predictive could be used to fashion a tool to study time-course changes in intelligence which might be due to various effects, conditions, and treatments (e.g., recovery from head injury, aging, infection). Alternatively, because our retest correlations were very high, and between-task correlations low to moderate, we expected that there would be reliable variance not related to intelligence and aptitude, which logically might suggest "new" factors. The repeated-measures aspect of our work afforded an opportunity to look at some of these relations.

Second, we were interested in clarifying two contrasting theories of intelligence. From the earliest days, the focus in human intelligence testing has been characterized by two main themes that have led to different prediction objectives (Weinberg, 1989). Advocates of the two theories have been referred to as *lumpers* or *splitters* (Mayr, 1982). Binet (Binet & Simon, 1905) (a lumper) focused on intelligence as a "fundamental faculty" and believed that the type of intelligence measured could be assessed using a single index that would be validated by prediction of academic success as opposed to general performance. In contrast, Galton (1983) (a splitter) felt that a variety of human mental capabilities should be assessed in order to predict performance at work. One can see this dichotomy of predictive goals today in the fundamental measurement objectives of the Wechsler Intelligence Scale for Children (WISC-R) (1974) or Wechsler Adult Intelligence Scale (WAIS) (1981) vs. the Armed Services Vocational Aptitude Battery (ASVAB) (1985) or the General Aptitude Test Battery (GATB) (1970). The WISC and WAIS set out to predict abilities thought to be fundamental to the prediction of academic skills, whereas the ASVAB and GATB are more directed toward prediction of skills acquisition and job performance.

The controversy between these two views of intelligence persists today. Amid widespread public debate about the use of standardized tests in schools and in the workplace (e.g., Wigdor & Garner, 1982), proponents of testing consider standardized aptitude tests the best available means of impartial selection on ability. Critics, on the other hand, claim that ability tests measure too little and too narrowly. In recent special issues of the *Journal of Vocational Behavior* (Gottfredson, 1986; Gottfredson & Sharf, 1988), the focus has been on the fairness of using standardized aptitude tests in hiring workers. In fact, lately the debate about fairness in employment testing has been significantly newsworthy since the U.S. Department of Labor has announced that it is discontinuing use of the General Aptitude Test Battery (GATB) for employment selection and referral because of concerns that the test may not adequately serve minority groups ("Science Directorate," 1990). Against this background of sociopolitical issues, there is the fundamental question of how to integrate various psychometric and information processing methodologies in the prediction of discrete performance by standardized intelligence measures. For instance, when Ackerman (1987), using appropriate within-task methodological techniques, reexamined individual differences in skill learning by accounting for crucial task characteristics, he found that intellectual abilities play a substantial part in determining individual differences in skill learning. Central to this question is the issue of the effects of practice on intelligence test scores which in some cases have been shown to increase by nearly a standard score on the average (Mackaman, Bittner, Harbeson, Kennedy, & Stone, 1982). Therefore, we decided to look at changing correlations of these tests with intelligence tests.

Third, we wanted to compare our short test battery with lengthier tests of intellectual functioning. One difficulty in studying intelligence and aptitude with standard predictors of skill acquisition and job performance is that none of the traditionally employed tests is suitable for repeated measures application, because each is too long to function as anything other than a one-time or, at most, several-times measure. A need exists for tests that are short in administration time, that stabilize rapidly with administration and yet are reliable, and that share variance with one-time tests and their predictive goals. For example, if one wishes to index the recovery process of the intellectual function following closed-head injury, then one-time tests are of minimal usefulness. Likewise, if one wishes to study cognitive deficits occasioned by disease, fatigue, stress, or exposure to an environmental hazard (e.g., carbon monoxide exposure, or hypoxia coincident with extreme altitudes), a mental test instrument of a quite different structure is needed. If such instruments are to be used with these predictive goals in mind, their covariance with the one-time measures must be ascertained, and perhaps more importantly, how that shared variance changes with repeated performance on the instruments must be documented.

Generally, two factors limit the covariance with one-time tests: (a) short periods of measurement are equivalent to fewer samples of performance (items)—thus, correlations will suffer because of the Spearman-Brown relation (Anastasi, 1988, p. 121); and (b) to stabilize rapidly with high reliability, the measure will have to differ in some fundamental ways from those items more commonly encountered on one-time intelligence tests. Therefore, we planned to see whether our short tests could be combined to form a strong correlate of intelligence.

Fourth, we were interested in time-course changes in mental functioning. Adaptability is a central theme of modern evolutionary theory and is used as an explanatory principle in behavioral neurosciences. So, too, time-course behavioral change (plasticity, learning, reaction to movements, adaptation) appears in one way or another in most modern theories of intelligence, and was, of course, central to the earlier ones (cf. Ginsburg & Opper, 1969, for a review). In one axis of his triarchic theory, Sternberg (1985) makes distinctions between individual differences in the ability to deal with novel tasks, and differences in postadaptation learning at minimal cost to functional reserve. Yet most single-administration intelligence test batteries do not permit the isolation of these features. Conversely, some individuals may have been exposed to some of a subtests' elements previously, and, because practice often improves scores, this factor can introduce systematic error in such measurement. We suggest that scores on cognitive and information-processing ability tests that can be administered repeatedly might afford some advantage for converging on these methodological problems. A number of studies have focused on the relationship between global measures of intelligence and performance on tasks thought to index specific component abilities and skills (Sternberg, 1977; Detterman, 1984). One purpose of such research is to attempt to establish a firmer understanding of the particular substrates or underlying capabilities necessary for performing well on these global measures of intellectual ability. The usual finding is that moderate correlations are obtained between the global IQ measures and the more specific tasks of cognitive ability. Sternberg (1977) has referred to the ".30 barrier" as the usual upper limit to correlations between IQ and these more basic processes, but, in the correlation of these specific tasks with the tests of intelligence (Ackerman, 1987; Fleishman & Hempel, 1954, 1955), except for occasional studies, generally the time-course changes are not monitored.

Last, we hoped to demonstrate that test development using psychometric criteria first and mental models secondarily could yield a robust tool to measure mental performance. In attempts to decompose the global IQ construct, most mental tests that have been investigated to date have been based on cognitive theory. That is, these tests or tasks have been developed as representations of structural models of intellect, usually thought to take place in stages or steps of information processing (Carroll, 1981). In contrast, we present research from a battery of tests developed specifically from the point of view of psychometric theory (Allen & Yen, 1979), rather than any particular mental model.

In summary, a major part of our purpose in conducting the present studies was to use global IQ measures as criteria or markers against which the performance subtests could be measured, with two major aims. First, we hoped to demonstrate the communalities shared by the performance battery with the more general measures of intellectual functioning; second, we hoped to index the extent to which each subtest had reliable variance not shared with IQ (i.e., the extent to which the battery, as a whole, measured capability beyond what Spearman termed g) (Spearman, 1904). The first aim would be comparable to breaking Sternberg's .30 barrier, while the second would be comparable to demonstrating "new factors" that Hunt and Pellegrino (1986) found can be revealed by microcomputer testing. In addition, an ancillary goal was to determine whether these relationships or communalities change as a function of practice.

EXPERIMENT I

Method

In a preliminary study, 25 college students (8 males and 17 females) were employed in a series of 15 sessions where they received repeated trials of microcomputer-based testing. They were comprised of freshman to juniors and were paid $4.50 per hour for their participation. In this study, we used six microcomputer tests from the Automated Performance Test System (Essex Corporation, 1985) that previously had been shown to be stable and reliable (Bittner, Smith, Kennedy, Staley, & Harbeson, 1985), and three others which were under developmental study. Pertinent information about the tests and their administration may be found in Table 1. They are described more completely elsewhere (Kennedy, Dunlap, Jones, Lane, & Wilkes, 1985). Also, the Wechsler Adult Intelligence Scale (Revised) and eight Wonderlic Personnel tests were administered individually to the subjects within 2 weeks of the microcomputer testing.

NEC PC 8201A. Microcomputer tests were implemented on the NEC PC8201A (NEC Home Electronics, 1983) microprocessor, which is configured around an 80C85 microprocessor with 64K internal ROM. RAM capacity may

Table 1.   Microbased Performance Test Battery Order, Task, and Battery Time

Performance Task Order	Trials/ Battery	Practice Time	Trial Time	Total Task Time in a Battery Less Practice	Total Time on Task for 15 Replications of the Battery Less Practice
Preferred Hand					
Tapping	2	10[1]	10[a]	20	300
Pattern Comparison	1	15	75	75	1125
Two-Hand Tapping	2	10	10	20	300
Grammatical Reason.	1	15	90	90	1350
Nonpreferred Hand					
Tapping	2	10	10	20	300
Manikin	1	10	60	60	900
Sternberg Item					
Recognition	1		60	60	900
Code Substitution	1	10	60	60	900
Landolt C[b]	1	15	60	60	900
Reaction Time	1	15	60	60	900
Vertical Math[b]	1	10	60	60	900
Totals		80	555	585	8775

[a]Times are reported in seconds.
[b]Test did not stabilize.

be expanded to 96K onboard, divided into three separate 32K banks. Visual displays are presented on an 8-line LCD with 40 characters per line. Memory may be transferred to 32K modules with independent power supplies for storage or mailing. The entire package is lightweight (3.8 lbs), compact (110 W × 40 H × 130 D mm), and fully portable with rechargeable nickel cadmium batteries permitting up to 4 hours of continuous operation.

The computerized test battery required about 10 minutes/day and about 2.5 hours overall, slightly less than a single administration of an ASVAB. The correlational findings between the two parts of the WAIS and the stable computerized tests appear in Table 2.

Results

Table 2 shows that the microcomputer tests correlate more strongly with Performance WAIS scores and less strongly with the Verbal scores. The strongest simple correlation between the microcomputer tests and the Full Scale WAIS was for Grammatical Reasoning (a highly cognitive test), although Nonpreferred Hand Tapping (a motor task) was clearly not zero. The r squared values indicate that a substantial proportion of the Performance IQ variance can be predicted from the microcomputer tests ($R^2 = .80$).

INTELLIGENCE AND PERFORMANCE   265

Table 2.   Cross-Correlations Between Microcomputer Performance Tests
and the WAIS

Microcomputer Test	Verbal	Performance	Total Score
Pattern Comparison	05	57**	34
Grammatical Reasoning	41*	63**	66**
Manikin	05	50*	29
Reaction Time	− 13	− 17	− 22
Code Substitution	09	44*	31
Preferred Hand Tap	41*	42*	55**
Nonpreferred Hand Tap	48*	50*	63**
Two Hand Tap	21	37	33
Sternberg Item Recognition	26	23	35
Multiple R	67	89	75
R Squared	45	80	57

* $p<.05$

** $p<.01$

A finer grained analysis of these relationships may be found in Table 3, which details cross-correlations between the individual performance tests and the individual WAIS subtest scores.

In general, it seems apparent that the microcomputer tests have most in common with Block Design and Digit Symbol subtests from the WAIS, and least in common with Information, Vocabulary, and Similarities, the more highly verbal subscales. Some correlations are $r> .30$.

Alternate forms of the Wonderlic were also administered eight times to the 25

Table 3.   Cross-Correlations Between the Microcomputer Performance
Tests and the Various Subtests from the WAIS

WAIS	Stern	PHT	NPHT	NEC Test THT	PC	MK	CS	GR	RT
Info	26	34	28	26	−	−	−	28	−
DSpan	−	36	49*	16	12	−	27	37	−
Vocab	21	21	26	−	−	−	−	33	−
Arith	−	22	35	−	12	−	−	32	−
Compr	−	−	−	13	14	− 18	− 27	−	21
Simil	11	−	−	15	− 16	− 28	− 20	−	− 27
PicCom	−	33	37	30	17	28	22	27	− 29
PicArr	18	14	19	−	29	37	33	40*	− 13
BlkDes	23	49*	50*	71**	59**	48*	16	45*	− 28
ObjAsm	29	34	35	−	27	−	19	41*	− 31
DSym	44*	42*	48*	48*	71**	42*	69**	62**	− 15

* $p<.05$

** $p<.01$

Table 4.   Cross-correlation Between the Microcomputer Tests and the Wonderlic

	Stern	PHT	NPHT	THT	PR	Man	CS	GR	RT
Wonderlic	16	41	40	39	20	03	04	26	-45

subjects, and, although performance improved over sessions, the intercorrelations from form to form were not high perhaps because of the homogeneity of the population. The correlations appeared to be stable after the second administration and the average score of the last three Wonderlic test administrations was selected for additional analyses. Table 4 shows that the correlations between the microcomputer tests and the Wonderlic were of only modest size, and it is clear that only the motor tests showed appreciable commonality. The multiple regression coefficient predicting Wonderlic from the collective microcomputer tests was $r = 0.62$.

Discussion

In this preliminary study, the correlation between the microcomputer battery tests and the WAIS IQ showed that a substantial portion of the performance subskill variance could be accounted for by this self-contained, self-administered short battery of computerized tests. At this stage of test battery development, we believed that addition of arithmetic and verbally-based tests might improve correlation.

It was of more than passing interest that there were strong relations between motor tasks and IQ and some of the correlations exceeded the .3 boundary described by Sternberg (1977). This was surprising, because the population in the present study was reasonably homogeneous being from a single, small community college in Casper, Wyoming, average ages between 18 and 25, and two-thirds of the population female. Furthermore, for a task as simple as hand tapping, to show the highest correlation with verbal subskill and the second highest intercorrelation with a full scale IQ was provocative. Jensen and Monro (1979) hypothesized that complex reaction times should be better predictors of general intelligence (g) and simple reaction times. Certainly this procedure is borne out by the present data in that the Sternberg, a complex motor response task, has a higher correlation than simple reaction time with the WAIS IQ. Furthermore, Jensen and Monro (1979) found that motor speed showed a strong relation as complex reaction time to g, an unexpected finding but one that might relate to the strong relation to tapping and IQ of the present results.

Part of the reason for the weak relationship to Wonderlic, we thought, was that the test is a short IQ measure (12 minutes) and, while it stabilized with reasonable rapidity, the retest reliability of only .58 obtained in this sample limits the extent to which it may be intercorrelated with external indices.

Therefore, it is not surprising to find that it had low correlations with the computerized test battery. Corrected-for-attenuation (Allen & Yen, 1979, p. 68) values showed considerably higher relationships between the microcomputer tests and the Wonderlic, implying that, with a more heterogeneous sample and larger Wonderlic reliabilities, larger correlations may be obtained with the computerized tests.

EXPERIMENT II

Method

Subjects. The research subjects were again obtained from undergraduate psychology classes at Casper College in Wyoming. The sample consisted of 26 subjects (18 women and 8 men) who ranged in age from 18 to 38 and were in good physical and mental health. They were comprised of freshmen to juniors and were paid $4.50 per hour for their participation. Motivation appeared to remain high over the 13 hours (approximate) of study obligations.

Criterion mental tests. Four different global aptitude/ability paper-and-pencil measures were employed in the study.

(1) The American College Testing Program (ACT) (1973) provides ability subscale scores in English, Math, Social Science, and Science as well as an overall composite score (Aiken, 1985). The ACT is used by institutions of higher learning for prediction, advising, and placement purposes. While the Composite Score is regarded as a good indicator of general intelligence, the test also indexes high school and college achievement.

(2) The Wechsler Adult Intelligence Scale-Revised (Wechsler, 1981) provides both Verbal and Performance subscale scores and is one of the most widely used indicators of general intelligence. In clinical settings the test is also used as a diagnostic aid for disorders associated with brain damage and learning disabilities.

(3) Four forms of the Wonderlic Personnel Test (Wonderlic, 1983) were administered to each subject. The forms (I, II, IV & B) are parallel and each is administered in 12 minutes of testing. The Wonderlic is used in business and industry for personnel selection and placement and has normative data available for various occupations and educational levels. The Wonderlic purports to measure "ability to learn" and is regarded as a short-form measure of general intelligence; however, it does not provide subscale measures of verbal and quantitative abilities.

(4) The Armed Services Vocational Aptitude Battery (ASVAB) was obtained from a book of facsimile tests (Steinberg, 1986) widely available in bookstores throughout the continental United States and used to practice for the ASVAB. As in the original ASVAB, this battery is composed of 10 subtests: General Science, Arithmetic Reasoning, Word Knowledge, Paragraph Comprehension,

Numerical Operations, Coding Speed, Auto and Shop Information, Mathematics Knowledge, Mechanical Comprehension, and Electronic Information. Like the true ASVAB, the test may be administered in 144 minutes; however, instructions and procedures significantly increase the total testing time. One combination of ASVAB subtest scores serves as the Armed Forces Qualification Test (AFQT) which determines acceptance into a particular branch of the U.S. Armed Services. Other scores are also derived from the ASVAB and serve to identify aptitude and training placement. The true ASVAB test is regarded as a measure of general intelligence with both verbal and quantitative components. There are no known normative psychometric data for the facsimile test.

Microcomputer-based Assessment. The performance battery used was the Automated Performance Test System (APTS) with subtests selected based on previously exhibited stability and reliability. The test evaluation and development of the battery is more fully described by Kennedy et al. (1987), Turnage et al. (1992).

Six of the eight tests selected for the core performance battery were from the APTS battery of an original set of 30 performance measures found to be most statistically suitable for repeated-measures applications and were employed in Experiment I. These were Pattern Comparison; Nonpreferred Hand Tapping; Code Substitution; Simple Reaction Time; Grammatical Reasoning; and Manikin. Two additional subtests were selected from the Unified Tri-Service Cognitive Performance Assessment Battery (UTC-PAB) (Englund, Reeves, Shingledecker, Thorne, Wilson, & Hegge, 1987), which is another battery composed of a variety of subtests that measure varying degrees of cognitive and visual-motor processing abilities. These subtests were Associative Memory and Matrix Rotation. Correlational analyses (Kennedy et al., 1990) suggested that these tests add elements not tapped by the other tests of the APTS battery. A brief description of each subtask is provided below:

(1) Nonpreferred Hand Tapping (NTAP). The participant is required to alternately press the indicated keys as fast as he or she can with two fingers of the nonpreferred hand. Performance is based on the number of alternate key presses made in the allotted time. Kennedy, Wilkes, Lane, and Homick (1985) described tapping as a psychomotor skill assessing factors related to skilled fine motor performances. This test is similar to the other tests in the Tapping series using Preferred and Two-Hands, but has generally higher retest reliability.

(2) Pattern Comparison (PC). The Pattern Comparison task (Klein & Armitage, 1979) is accomplished by examining two patterns of asterisks that are displayed on the screen simultaneously. The participant is required to determine if the patterns are the same or different and respond with the corresponding "S" or "D" key. Patterns are randomly generated with similar and different pairs presented in random order. According to Bittner, Carter, Kennedy, Harbeson, and Krause (1986), Pattern Comparison "assesses an integrative spatial function

neuropsychologically associated with the right hemisphere" (p. 699). Recent field testing with a microcomputer adaptation of the task (Kennedy, Dunlap, et al., 1985; Kennedy, Wilkes, et al., 1985; Wilkes, Kennedy, Dunlap, & Lane, 1986) resulted in strong recommendations for inclusion of Pattern Comparison in repeated-measures microcomputer test batteries.

(3) Grammatical Reasoning (GR). The Grammatical Reasoning Test (Baddeley, 1968) requires the participant to read and comprehend a simple statement about the order of two letters, *A* and *B*. Five grammatical transformations of statements about the relationship between the letters or symbols are made. The five transformations are: (a) active versus passive construction, (b) true versus false statements, (c) affirmative versus negative phrasing, (d) use of the verb *precedes* versus the verb *follows,* and (e) *A* versus *B*, mentioned first. There are 32 possible items arranged in random order. The subject's task is to respond "true" or "false," depending on the verity of each statement. Performance is scored according to the number of transformations correctly identified. Grammatical Reasoning is described as measuring "higher mental processes" with reasoning, logic, and verbal ability, important factors in test performance (Carter, Kennedy, & Bittner, 1981). According to Bittner et al. (1986), Grammatical Reasoning "assesses an analytic cognitive neuropsychological function associated with the left hemisphere" (p. 699). Previous studies with Grammatical Reasoning, identified in Bittner et al. (1986), have indicated that the task is acceptable for use in repeated-measures research. Recent field testing with a microcomputer version of the task (Kennedy, Wilkes, et al., 1985; Kennedy, Dunlap, et al., 1985; Wilkes et al., 1986) have resulted in strong recommendations for inclusion of Grammatical Reasoning in repeated-measures microcomputer test batteries.

(4) Reaction Time-1 Choice (RT1). The Visual Reaction Time Test (Donders, 1968) involves the presentation of a visual stimulus and measurement of a response latency to the stimulus. The subject's task is to respond as quickly as possible with a key press to a simple visual stimulus presented on a flat panel liquid crystal display (LCD). Latency of LCD response and of key press are both less than 7 msec each. A short tone precedes at a random interval to signal that a "change" in the status of the stimulus is about to occur. The participant observes the stimulus for the change and then presses the response key as quickly as possible. Simple reaction time has been described as a perceptual task responsive to environmental effects (Krause & Bittner, 1982) and has been recommended for repeated-measures research (Bittner, et al., 1986; Kennedy, Dunlap, et al., 1985).

(5) Associative Memory (AM). This is a memory test (Underwood, Boruch, & Malmi, 1977) that requires the participant to view five sets of three-letter trigrams that are paired with the numbers 1 to 5, and to memorize this list. After an interval, successive trigrams are displayed, and the participant is required to press the key of the number corresponding to that letter set. In previous research

(Krause & Kennedy, 1980) this associative memory task, using percent correct score, was recommended for inclusion in a performance test battery for environmental research.

(6) Manikin (MK). This performance test (Benson & Gedye, 1963) involves the presentation of a simulated human figure in either a full-front or full-back facing position. The figure has two easily differentiated hand-held patterns. One of the two patterns is matched to a pattern appearing below the figure. The subject's task is to determine which hand of the figure holds the matching pattern and respond by pressing the appropriate microprocessor key. Pattern type, hand associated with the matching pattern and front-to-back figure orientation are randomly determined for each trial. The Manikin Test is a perceptual measure of spatial transformation of mental images and involves spatial ability (Carter & Woldstad, 1985). Bittner et al. (1986) recommended the use of the Manikin Test latency scores, and Carter and Woldstad (1985) identified the Manikin Test for inclusion in microcomputer repeated-measures batteries.

(7) Matrix Rotation (MR)—PAB. This test (Phillips, 1974) assesses spatial orientation and short-term memory. A series of 5×5 cell matrices that contain five illuminated cells per matrix are presented (singly). The participant compares successive displays to determine if they are the same (*S*) or different (*D*). Matrices are considered alike if the same matrix is rotated either 90 degrees to the left or 90 degrees to the right from the previously displayed matrix. Two successive matrices are never presented in exactly the same orientation. The stimulus remains on the screen until the subject makes a response.

(8) Code Substitution Test (CS). There is an adaptation of the version of the test contained in the Wechsler Adult Intelligence Scale (Wechsler, 1958). This test is designed to measure associative learning ability and perceptual speed. A string of nine letters and nine digits (numbers) are displayed across the screen in an arrangement so that the digit string is immediately below the letter string. Letters and digits are randomly paired for each test and their order is randomly assigned in the coding string. A test letter is presented at the bottom of the screen below the coding strings. The participant is to indicate which digit corresponds to that test letter in the display strings. The letter and digit associates change at 10-second intervals.

Practice times and trial durations for each of the performance battery subtests are provided in Table 5. As can be seen, the actual time required for these particular subtests to be administered as a battery was a little less than 20 min, which in contrast to the global IQ measures is shorter. The same apparatus, a NEC PC8201A, was used.

Procedure. Subjects were first tested with the global paper-and-pencil measures of mental ability. The ASVAB testing (3-hour administration time) and four replications of the Wonderlic (1-hour administration time) were conducted under group testing conditions. The ASVAB scores were obtained first, followed

Table 5. Microcomputer Subtests, Subtest Order, Time, Practice and Feedback Information, and Total Battery Administration Time

Order of Tests	Practice Time	Feedback	Trial Time	Trials/ Battery	Total Battery Task Time Less Practice	Total Battery Task Time For 7 Replications
1. PC	30	yes	180[a]	1	180	1260
2. GR	30	yes	180	1	180	1260
3. MK	30	yes	180	1	180	1260
4. RT1	none	no	180	1	180	1260
5. AM	none	no	90	1	90	630
6. CS	30	yes	180	1	180	1260
7. MR	30	yes	180	1	180	1260
8. NTAP	10	yes	10	2	20	140
Total	160		1180	9	1190	8330

[a]All time data reported in seconds.
PC—Pattern Comparison
GR—Grammatical Reasoning
MK—Manikin
AM—Associative Memory
RT1—Reaction Time
CS—Code Substitution
MR—Matrix Rotation
NTAP—Nonpreferred Tapping

on a separate occasion by the Wonderlic testing. Scores for the standardized American College Testing (ACT) test (Aiken, 1985) were obtained, with subjects' permission, through existing college files.

Prior to testing with the microcomputer-based battery, subjects were given a thorough introduction to the use of the self-administered testing system within a monitored classroom. They were encouraged to ask questions and to resolve difficulties. Testing procedures were reviewed, personal testing schedules were established, and handouts concerning procedure and scheduling were provided to each subject. Subjects were required to complete seven replications of the APTS battery within a 3-week period with multiple battery replications on a single test day not permitted. All self-testing was conducted within controlled laboratory rooms reserved for data collection associated with this study. Subjects were encouraged to self-test on an every-other-day basis (personal schedule permitting). If more than 7 days elapsed between replications of the battery, an abbreviated "warm-up" practice battery was required, but this occurred on only 4% of the sessions. Subtest order, practice, feedback, testing time, and instructions were held constant. Previous field testing with this portable testing system, the NEC PC 8210A, had been carried out successfully (Kennedy, Wilkes, et al., 1985; Wilkes et al., 1986).

Subject study obligations were concluded with the administration of a WAIS-R. The WAIS-R testing (approximately 1.25 hours of administration time) was

Table 6. Descriptive Statistics for the Global Measures of Intelligence Criterion Mental Tests

Tests[a]	N	Mean	SD	Skew	Kurtosis
ASVAB	27	322.1	29.7	-1.21	5.59
ACT	23	80.4	23.5	-0.44	0.06
WONLK	27	104.2	21.4	-0.43	1.19
WVER	26	106.1	12.8	0.52	-0.14
WPER	26	107.9	12.7	0.27	-0.37
WAIS	26	107.8	13.2	0.54	-0.11

[a]Criterion Mental Test Codes
ASVAB—Armed Services Vocational Aptitude Battery (summed composite-all tests)
ACT—American College Testing Program (composite score)
WONLK—Wonderlic Personnel Test (summed composite of four administrations)
WVER—Wechsler Adult Intelligence Scale—Revised (verbal score)
WPER—Wechsler Adult Intelligence Scale—Revised (performance score)
WAIS—Wechsler Adult Intelligence Scale—Revised (composite score)

conducted under laboratory conditions by a qualified psychometrist. The WAIS-R testing signaled the completion of all research obligations and qualified a subject for final payment.

Results

Descriptive statistics for the global measures of intelligence are provided in Table 6. WAIS-R scores were at approximately the 70th percentile for persons of equivalent age and approximately average for a college group. The ACT scores were also about average for a college population. Wonderlic mean scores appeared consistent with this relation, that is, a mean score slightly better than average for men and women in general. There were no comparable data for the ASVAB and raw scores were used for all analyses.

Correlations among the global measures of intelligence may be found in Table 7. Most of these tests are highly correlated with each other and all correlations are significant ($p < .01$). Since the literature implies that total scores for the

Table 7. Correlations[a] Among Measures of Intelligence

	ASVAB	ACT	WONLK	WVER	WPER	WAIS
ASVAB						
ACT	0.745[b]					
WONLK	0.818	0.821				
WVER	0.611	0.781	0.761			
WPER	0.564	0.633	0.639	0.648		
WAIS	0.631	0.777	0.769	0.944	0.860	

[a]Correlations are based on $N = 27$ subjects, with ACT $N = 23$ the exception
[b]All correlations are significant at $p < 0.01$

Table 8.   Means and Standard Deviations (N = 27) of Performance Tests

Subtests	1	2	3	Trials 4	5	6	7
PC (NC)[a]	109	119	125	128	129	130	132
	(21)[b]	(19)	(19)	(21)	(22)	(22)	(20)
GR (NC)	39	37	44	44	47	48	48
	(910)	(15)	(11)	(14)	(17)	(16)	(14)
MK (NC)	72	83	95	101	103	107	109
	(28)	(32)	(32)	(29)	(33)	(34)	(32)
RT1(RL)	453	366	311	311	323	330	329
	(242)	(151)	(62)	(69)	(84)	(97)	(88)
NC (NC)	19	57	60	65	64	63	66
	(19)	(19)	(18)	(11)	(11)	(12)	(14)
CS (NC)	61	63	66	66	66	67	67
	(9)	(6)	(6)	(5)	(5)	(6)	(6)
MR (NC)	65	76	80	81	81	84	86
	(23)	(22)	(24)	(24)	(24)	(25)	(25)
NTAP (N)	31	33	34	34	35	35	35
	(10)	(10)	(10)	(9)	(8)	(9)	(9)

[a]Codes: (N) = Number of Hits, (NC) = Number Correct, (RL) = Response Latency
[b]Standard deviations in parentheses.

tests of Table 7 may be expected to possess retest reliabilities (not shown) of $r >$ 0.80 or 0.90 for each of the tests, one would expect these tests to share a minimum of 15% and a maximum of 95% common variance when corrected for attenuation.

The means and standard deviations for the APTS performance subtests (see Table 8) indicated that both means and standard deviations stabilized within the testing period, with most tests stabilizing by Trial 3. Number correct (NC) was the response measure used for all tests except Tapping and Reaction Time for which number of hits (N) and response latency (RL) are the most appropriate measures, respectively (Kennedy et al., 1990).

Table 9 shows the stabilized retest reliability in the diagonal (in parentheses) for the eight microcomputer tests and cross-task correlations among the performance test trials. Stabilized retest reliability is defined as the average intertrial correlation within the matrix of trial-to-trial correlations for each test including and after the trial of stability. Trial of stability was determined by agreement between two independent analysts regarding the trial at which means, standard deviations, and intertrial correlations appear to plateau (i.e., reach stability). A correlation matrix of the stabilized between-task correlations for the APTS appears above the diagonal in Table 9. Below the diagonal we have calculated corrected-for-attenuation values, as an index of overlap with other tests. It may be seen that the reliabilities of these tests are high (average $r = .91$) and even when corrected for attenuation (regardless of sign) the correlations among the eight tests within the battery are only moderate (average $r = .31$),

Table 9. Cross-task Correlations (Above Diagonal) Reliabilities (In Parentheses[a]) and Corrected-for-Attenuation Values (Below Diagonal) Among Stabilized Performance Test Trials

	PC	GR	MK	RT1	AM	CS	MR	NTAP
PC	(0.92)	0.46 *	0.55 *	−0.69**	−0.11	0.62**	0.41	0.32
GR	0.49	(0.94)	0.36	0.48 *	0.20	0.39	0.12	0.25
MK	0.58	0.38	(0.97)	−0.27	−0.05	0.50 *	0.32	0.43
RT1	−0.77	−0.53	−0.30	(0.86)	0.14	−0.62**	−0.05	−0.34
AM	−0.12	−0.22	−0.05	0.16	(0.88)	0.02	0.09	0.09
CS	0.70	0.44	0.55	−0.72	0.02	(0.85)	0.25	0.53 *
MR	0.45	0.13	0.34	−0.06	0.10	0.29	(0.90)	0.10
NTAP	0.34	0.26	0.44	−0.37	0.10	0.58	0.11	(0.97)

[a]Reliabilities (in parentheses) calculated on the average of last three trials

* $p < 0.05$

**$p < 0.01$

which implies a multifactor battery and is consistent with factor analysis studies with these tests (Kennedy, Baltzley, Turnage, & Jones, 1989).

Cross-correlations between intelligence test score measures and the eight microcomputer-based subtests are shown in Table 10. Virtually all of these are positive (Reaction Time, Response Latency, the exception) ranging from $r = 0.03$ to $r = 0.81$. The average cross-correlation for the microcomputer-based battery range from $r = 0.10$ to $r = 0.66$. Generally, the highest relationships are seen with the ACT and Wonderlic and the lowest with tests from the WAIS-R performance subtests.

Table 10. Cross-Correlations[a] Between Intelligence Measures and Microbased Subtests

	ACT	WONLK	ASVAB	WVER	WPER	WAIS	AVG r
PC	0.65**	0.68**	0.81**	0.63**	0.56**	0.64**	0.66
GR	0.52**	0.52**	0.53**	0.28	0.25	0.28	0.40
MK	0.50**	0.66**	0.62**	0.42*	0.39*	0.44*	0.51
RT1[b]	−-.50**	−0.65**	−0.66**	−0.40*	−0.40*	−42*	−0.57
AM	0.14	0.03	−0.10	0.22	0.10	0.21	0.10
CS	0.42*	0.59**	0.65**	0.30	0.50**	0.40*	0.47
MR	0.02	0.24	−0.25	0.43*	0.23	0.39*	0.18
NTAP	0.39	0.35	0.34	0.18	0.15	0.17	0.26
Average r	0.52	0.46	0.50	0.36	0.32	0.37	

[a]Correlations are based on N = 27, with ACT N = 23 the exception

[b]Negative correlations for RT1 are due to scoring method (response latency); sign ignored in adding columns.

*$p < 0.05$ (one tail)

**$p < 0.01$

Table 11.   Multiple Correlations of Each IQ Measure Predicted by the
Microbased Battery Subtests

TESTS	R	R-Squared	Adjusted R	F	df	P
ASVAB	0.87	0.75	0.80	6.82	8/18	.000
ACT	0.85	0.72	0.75	4.53	8.14	.007
WONLK	0.84	0.71	0.76	5.59	8/18	.001
WVER	0.74	0.54	0.57	2.52	8/17	.052
WPER	0.63	0.40	0.34	1.40	8/17	.266
WAIS	0.72	0.52	0.55	2.34	8/17	.067

As can be seen in Table 11, the multiple correlations between the performance battery and the various IQ or "g" measures are uniformly high. Furthermore, even after correction for shrinkage, the correlations are still substantial, except in the case of the WAIS based measures, where although positive, the relations are at best moderate. It is important to note that the strongest relationships are with the ACT and ASVAB which are both general intelligence tests whose basic purposes are for selection.

A final analysis of these data involved assessing the relationship of the battery of performance subtests to general IQ or g measures at various stages of practice on the cognitive-performance tests. For purposes of this analysis, Replications 2 and 3 of the APTS were considered to be early trials, Replications 4 and 5 to be middle trials, and Replications 6 and 7 to be trials late in practice. Multiple correlations of the "core" battery and the general IQ measures as a function of practice are shown in Table 12. As can be seen, the strength of the relationship between the core battery and both the WAIS and the Wonderlic decreased as practice proceeded. On the other hand, the correlations with the ASVAB and ACT scores did not appear to change dramatically as a function of practice. All multiple correlations were reasonably high even when corrected for shrinkage.

Table 12.   Multiple Correlations Between the Core Performance Battery
and Reference Tests of Intellectual Ability as Functions of Practice

	Early R	Mid R	Late R	Early ^aR_c	Mid R_c	Late R_c
ASVAB	0.86	0.88	0.83	0.79	0.84	0.75
ACT	0.85	0.80	0.84	0.56	0.44	0.55
Wonderlic	0.89	0.86	0.81	0.84	0.79	0.71
WVER	0.79	0.74	0.71	0.67	0.58	0.53
WPER	0.72	0.67	0.59	0.55	0.43	0.20
WAIS-R	0.78	0.75	0.70	0.65	0.59	0.50

^aR_c = Corrected for shrinkage

Discussion

In two studies, a series of mental acuity tests, implemented on a portable microcomputer, were related to established holistic measures of intelligence. The findings of Experiment I were largely supported in Experiment II, but with some exceptions. The scores for the microcomputer-based performance tests generally stabilized quickly and demonstrated adequate reliabilities. Correlations among the microcomputer-based tests were generally moderate to low (range of $r = .02$ to .69), and given the high retest reliabilities of all the tests, strongly suggest a multifactor structure of the performance test battery.

Four different global measures of intelligence were intercorrelated and revealed considerable overlap. When the holistic measures of intelligence were compared to the microcomputer-based subtests, the correlations varied from essentially zero ($r = .02$ for Matrix Rotation and ACT) to $r = .81$ for Pattern Comparison with the ASVAB. This finding is consistent with that of Hunt and Pellegrino (1986) and Detterman (1984) and implies that microcomputer-based tests are tapping factors available from more traditional paper-and-pencil and individually administered tests. However, the retest reliabilities of the microcomputer tests are so large (i.e., $r > .707$) that it is evident there is considerable additional predictive power in the microcomputer tests. It is also clear that all of these highly practiced performance subtests but one (Associative Memory) exceeded Sternberg's (1977) barrier of .30. Thus, these tests fall somewhere between what Sternberg termed "basic processes" and global intellect, but probably closer to the latter.

The results of this study reveal that stable measures of performance implemented on a microcomputer test battery bear a strong relationship to global measures of intelligence, such as the synthetic ASVAB, ACT, Wonderlic, and to a lesser extent, performance subtests of the Wechsler Adult Intelligence Scale. Multiple correlational analyses of these microcomputer tests regressed against criterion scores on global measures of intelligence revealed 64% common variance (*after adjustment*) for the synthetic ASVAB, 56% for the ACT, and 58% for the Wonderlic, and about 30% of the full scale Wechsler Adult Intelligence Scale. This experiment shows that in a short period of time (the microcomputer battery of selected tests only takes 20 minutes for each administration) it is possible to account for a substantial portion of variance in global measures of intelligence. Thus, over half of the variance of the much longer ASVAB (over 2.4 hours) and ACT (3.5 hours) can likely be predicted by this shorter microcomputer battery. Because predictive validity could be expected to increase as retest reliabilities increase, following the Spearman prophecy formula (Anastasi, 1988), we theorize that, if a battery like the APTS were two to three times as long, it could add 10%–20% additional variance, particularly if, in the selection of subtests, one were to capitalize on the reliability and predictive validity of the test and adjust their length in battery accordingly.

The best performance tests for predicting all holistic intelligence measures are Pattern Comparison and Simple Reaction Time, with Manikin a close third. Note that these tests do not have any obvious verbal content and so may be likely to be collectively "culture-free." Recently, and curiously, these same three tests were shown to be related to performance of a landing task in a flight simulator (Turnage et al., 1988). At some future time, too, it may be instructive to determine the extent to which these performance measures reflect possible motivational components.

The findings summarized in Table 12 regarding changes in correlation between the performance battery and various IQ or g measure as functions of practice on the cognitive-performance battery are both interesting and important. The general tests for which the multiple correlation coefficients clearly fall as a function of practice were the WAIS and Wonderlic which are tests thought to be relatively pure measures of IQ. The global tests that were more stable relative to stage of practice were the ASVAB and ACT, both of which are tests that are more slanted toward performance and achievement. Fleishman and Hempel (1954, 1955), among others, have studied the change in factorial structure of performance tests as a function of stage of practice, and refer to the process underlying later trial skilled performance as the emergence of "automaticity." Fleishman and Rich (1963) found parallel findings of correlations that drop with practice between reference tests of intellectual ability with what they termed skill development tasks. A recent summary of the history, data, and theory of the relationship of skilled performance to global measures of intellectual ability can be found in Ackerman (1987). In agreement with Ackerman (1989), and in contrast to the contentions of Henry and Hulin (1987), whether validity for the prediction of performance falls off with practice is clearly related to the type of performance and to the type of predictor considered. The ASVAB and ACT scores continue to have good predictive power after considerable practice on the performance battery. To the extent that APTS test may be considered a surrogate for real-world tasks (e.g., Turnage et al., 1988), one might also argue that ASVAB and ACT may also be serving this same function at the present time (Zeidner, 1987).

A major finding of the current work is that the correlations between the core microbased performance battery and the ASVAB and ACT (tests used primarily for selection purposes) are both substantial and relatively stable. Since ASVAB has been shown to be related to military grades and job performance (Zeidner, 1987), there are also implied relevances of the APTS tests for military applications, such as how to measure fitness for duty by performance impairment tests, or online monitoring of performance impacts of stressors.

CONCLUSIONS

In summary, we believe that at least one predictive goal of cognitive performance testing can be achieved on a repeated measures basis, if one is willing to identify more with the goals of Galton (the splitter) than with those if Binet (the lumper). The multifactorial subtests of the APTS battery correlated about as well with the ASVAB and the ACT at the end of performance as at the beginning. Less encouraging were the correlations with the WAIS and the Wonderlic, which suggest that performance early in the trial sequence is better correlated with these more academic IQ measures than in later performance. Perhaps these latter correlations could be strengthened by the inclusion of more verbally and mathematically oriented tasks in the battery. What is presently (and perhaps will remain) unclear is how the relations between the one-time tests and the repeated measures battery might change if the former were given repeatedly.

REFERENCES

Ackerman, P.L. (1987). Individual differences in skill learning: An integration of psychometric and information processing perspectives. *Psychological Bulletin, 102*(1), 3–27.

Ackerman, P.L. (1989). Within-task intercorrelations of skilled performance: Implications for predicting individual differences? (A comment on Henry & Hulin, 1987). *Journal of Applied Psychology, 74,* 360–364.

Aiken, L.R. (1985). Review of ACT Assessment Program. *Ninth Mental Measurements Yearbook, 1,* 29–31.

Allen, M.J., & Yen, W.M. (1979). *Introduction to measurement theory.* Monterey, CA: Brooks/Cole.

American College Testing Program, Research and Development Division. (1973). *Assessing students on the way to college: Technical report for the ACT assessment program.* Iowa City, IA: ACT Publications.

Anastasi, A. (1988). *Psychological testing* (6th ed.). New York: MacMillan.

Armed Services Vocational Aptitude Battery (ASVAB). (1985). Washington, DC: U.S. Government Printing Office.

Baddeley, A.D. (1968). A three-minute reasoning test based on grammatical transformation. *Psychonomic Science, 10,* 341–342.

Benson, A.J., & Gedye, J.L. (1963). *Logical processes in the resolution of orientation conflict* (Report No. 259). Farnborough, UK: Royal Air Force, Institute of Aviation Medicine.

Binet, A., & Simon, T. (1905). Methodes nouvelles pour le diagnostic du niveau intellectuel des anormaux. *Annee Psychologique, 11,* 191–244.

Bittner, A.C., Jr., Carter, R.C., Kennedy, R.S., Harbeson, M.M., & Krause, M. (1986). Performance evaluation tests for environmental research (PETER): Evaluation of 114 measures. *Perceptual and Motor Skills, 63,* 683–708.

Bittner, A.C., Jr., Smith, M.G., Kennedy, R.S., Staley, C.F., & Harbeson, M.M. (1985).

Automated portable test system (APTS): Overview and prospects. *Behavior Research Methods, Instruments and Computers, 17,* 217–221.

Carroll, J.B. (1981). Ability and task difficulty in cognitive psychology. *Educational Researcher, 10,* 11–21.

Carter, R.C., Kennedy, R.S., & Bittner, A.C., Jr. (1981). Grammatical reasoning: A stable performance yardstick. *Human Factors, 23,* 587–591.

Carter, R.C., & Wolstad, J.C. (1985). Repeated measurements of spatial ability with the Manikin test. *Human Factors, 27*(2), 209–219.

Detterman, D.K. (1984, August). *Computer-assisted assessment of cognitive abilities.* Paper presented at the 92nd Annual Meeting of the American Psychological Association, Toronto, Canada.

Donders, F.C. (1969). On the speed of mental processes (W.G. Koster, Trans.). *Acta Psychologica, 30,* 412–431.

Englund, C.E., Reeves, D.L., Shingledecker, C.A., Thorne, D.R., Wilson, K.P., & Hegge, F.W. (1987). *Unified Tri-service Cognitive Performance Assessment Battery (UTC-PAB): I. Design and specification of the battery* (Rep. No. 87–10). San Diego, CA: Naval Health Research Center.

Essex Corporation. (1985). *Automated portable test system.* Orlando, FL: Brochure.

Fleisham, E.E., & Hempel, W.E., Jr. (1954). Changes in factor structure of a complex psychomotor test as a function of practice. *Psychometrika, 19,* 239–252.

Fleishman, E.A., & Hempel, W.E., Jr. (1955). The relation between abilities and improvement with practice in a visual discrimination reaction task. *Journal of Experimental Psychology, 49,* 301–316.

Fleisham, E.A., & Rich, S. (1963). Role of kinesthetic and spatial-visual abilities in perceptual-motor learning. *Journal of Experimental Psychology, 66,* 6–11.

Galton, F. (1883). *Inquiries into human faculty and its development.* London: Macmillan.

General Aptitude Test Battery. (1970). Washington, DC: U.S. Government Printing Office.

Ginsburg, H., & Opper, S. (1969). *Piaget's theory of intellectual development: An introduction.* Englewood Cliffs, NJ: Prentice-Hall.

Gottfredson, L.S. (Ed.). (1986). The "g" factor in employment (Special issue). *Journal of Vocational Behavior, 33*(3).

Henry, R.A., & Hulin, C.L. (1987). Stability of skilled performance across time: Some generalizations and limitations on utilities. *Journal of Applied Psychology, 72,* 457–462.

Hunt, E.B., & Pellegrino, J. (1986). Testing and measures of performance. *Proceedings of the 27th Annual Meeting of the Psychonomic Society* (p. 385). New Orleans, LA.

Jensen, A.R. & Munro (1979). Reaction time, movement time, and intelligence. *Intelligence, 3,* 121–126.

Jones, M.B., Kennedy, R.S., & Bittner, A.C., Jr. (1981). A video game for performance testing. *American Journal of Psychology, 94,* 143–152.

Kennedy, R.S., Baltzley, D.R., Dunlap, W.P., Wilkes, R.L., & Kuntz, L.A. (1989). *Microcomputer-based tests for repeated-measures: Metric properties and predictive validities* (EOTR 89-02). Orlando, FL: Essex Corporation.

Kennedy, R.S., Baltzley, D.R., Turnage, J.J., & Jones, M.B. (1989). Factor analysis and predictive validity of microcomputer-based tests. *Perceptual and Motor Skills, 69,* 1059–1074.

Kennedy, R.S., Dunlap, W.P., Jones, M.B., Lane, N.E., & Wilkes, R.L. (1985). *Portable human assessment battery: stability, reliability, factor structure, and correlation with tests of intelligence* (Final Rep.). Washington, DC: National Science Foundation. (NTIS Order # PB88-116645/AO3)

Kennedy, R.S., Turnage, J.J., & Dunlap, W.P. (in press). A portable, computerized, self-administered test battery capable of evaluating drug action over repeated testings. In P.D. Garzone, J. Fleishaker, & M. Eldon (Eds.), *Pharmocokinetics pharmacodynamics, Vol. 4: Cognitive function measures: Application in patient studies.* Cincinnati: Harvey Whitney.

Kennedy, R.S., Turnage, J.J., & Osteen, M.K. (1990, March). *Performance of performance tests: Comparison of psychometric properties of 24 tests from two microcomputer-based batteries* (USAARL Rep. No. CR-90-1). Fort Rucker, AL: U.S. Army Aeromedical Research Laboratory.

Kennedy, R.S., Wilkes, R.L., Dunlap, W.P., & Kuntz, L.A. (1987). Development of an automated performance test system for environmental and behavioral toxicology studies. *Perceptual and Motor Skills, 65,* 947–962.

Kennedy, R.S., Wilkes, R.L., Lane, N.E., & Homick, J.L. (1985). *Preliminary evaluation of a microbased repeated-measures testing system* (Tech. Rep. No. EOTR-85-1). Orlando, FL: Essex Corporation.

Klein, R., & Armitage, R. (1979). Rhythms in human performance: $1^{1}/_{2}$-hour oscillations in cognitive style. *Science, 204,* 1326–1328.

Krause, M., & Bittner, A.C., Jr. (1982). *Repeated measures on a choice reaction time task* (Rep. No. NBDL-82R006). New Orleans: Naval Biodynamics Laboratory. (NTIS No. AD A121904)

Krause, M., & Kennedy, R.S. (1980). Performance Evaluation Tests for Environmental Research (PETER): Interference susceptibility test. *Proceedings of the 7th Psychology in the DoD Symposium* (pp. 459–464). Colorado Springs, CO: USAF Academy.

Mackaman, S.M., Bittner, A.C., Jr., Harbeson, M.M., Kennedy, R.S., & Stone, D.A. (1982). Performance Evaluation Tests for Environmental Research (PETER): Wonderlic Personnel Test. *Psychological Reports, 51,* 635–644.

Mayr, E. (1982). *The growth of biological thought.* Cambridge, MA: Belknap Press.

NEC Home Electronics (USA), Inc. (1983). *NEC PC-8201A user's guide.* Tokyo: Nippon Electric Co. Ltd.

Phillips, W.A. (1974). On the distinction between sensory storage and short-term visual memory. *Perception and Psychophysics, 6,* 283–290.

Science Directorate Opposes Department of Labor's Suspension of GATB. (1990, August/September). *APA Science Agenda,* p. 5.

Spearman, C. (1904). The proof and measurement of association between two things. *American Journal of Psychology, 15,* 72–101.

Steinberg, E.P. (1986). *Practice for the armed services test.* New York: Acco Publishing Co.

Sternberg, R.J. (1977). *Intelligence, information processing, and analogical reasoning: The componential analysis of human abilities.* Hillsdale, NJ: Erlbaum.

Sternberg, R.J. (1985). *Beyond IQ: A triarchic theory of human intelligence.* Cambridge, UK: Cambridge University Press.

Sutcliffe, J.P. (1980). On the relationship of reliability to statistical power. *Psychological Bulletin, 88*(2), 500–515.

The Psychological Corporation. (1981). *Wechsler adult intelligence scale-revised.* New York: Harcourt Brace, & Jovanovich.

Turnage, J.J., Kennedy, R.S., Gilson, R.D., Bliss, J.P., & Nolan, M.D. (1988, December). *The use of surrogate measurement for the prediction of flight training performances* (Final Rep., IST Faculty Grant Award). Orlando, FL: Institute for Simulation and Training, University of Central Florida.

Turnage, J.J., Kennedy, R.S., Smith, M.S., Baltzley, D.R., & Lane, N.E. (1992). Development of microcomputer-based mental acuity tests. *Ergonomics, 35*(10), 1271–1295.

Underwood, B.J., Boruch, R.F., & Malmi, R.A. (1977, May). *The composition of episodic memory* (ONR Contract No. N00014-76-C-0270). Evanston, IL: Northwestern University. (NTIS No. Ad A040696).

Wechsler, D. (1958). *Measurement and appraisal of adult intelligence* (4th ed.). Baltimore: Williams and Wilkins.

Wechsler, D. (1974). *Wechsler intelligence scale for children-revised.* Baltimore: Williams and Wilkins.

Wechsler, D. (1981). *WAIS-R manual: Wechsler adult intelligence scale-revised.* New York: The Psychological Corporation.

Weinberg, R.A. (1989). Intelligence and IQ. *American Psychologist, 44*(2), 98–104.

Wigdor, A.K., & Garner, W.R. (1982). *Ability testing: Uses, consequences, and controversies.* Washington, DC: National Academy Press.

Wilkes, R.L., Kennedy, R.S., Dunlap, W.P., & Lane, N.E. (1986). *Stability, reliability, and cross-mode correlation of tests in a recommended 8-minute performance assessment battery* (Tech. Rep. No. EOTR-86-4). Orlando, FL: Essex Corporation.

Wonderlic, C.F. (1983). *Wonderlic personnel test.* Northfield, IL: E.F. Wonderlic.

Zeidner, J. (1987). *The validity of selection and classification procedures for predicting job performance* (IDA Paper P-1977). Alexandria, VA: Institute for Defense Analysis.

Chapter 12

Stimulus Organization and Stimulus Detection: Intelligence-Related Differences

S.A. Soraci, Jr., A.A. Baumeister, and M.T. Carlin

Department of Psychology and Human Development
John F. Kennedy Center
Vanderbilt University

Herb Simon (1981) has emphasized that a critical characteristic of an intelligent system is the ability to extract "from the problem environment new information about regularities in its structure." The present authors agree with this statement, and the research we have conducted over the past several years has

This research was supported by the National Institute of Child Health and Human Development Research Program Project Grants # HD15051, # HD23682, # HD27336, & 1K04 HD00921–01 awarded to the John F. Kennedy Center for Research on Education and Human Development at Vanderbilt University. Special thanks to Theodore P. Hoehn for helpful comments on an earlier draft of this manuscript.

Reprint requests should be sent to Dr. Salvatore A. Soraci, Jr., Box 45, George Peabody College, Vanderbilt University, Nashville, TN 37203.

been directed at variables involving stimulus organization, in the context of a theoretically motivated approach toward relational learning. Because basic properties of stimuli such as similarity–dissimilarity and novelty–familiarity are intrinsically relational, the ability to detect such relational information is essential to adaptive functioning. There is substantial evidence that individuals of varying levels of intellectual functioning exhibit differential performances on tasks that demand relational responding (Greenfield, 1985; Soraci, Deckner, Baumeister, & Carlin, 1990a). Converging evidence from various studies conducted by the present investigators and others suggests that a critical factor in the performance discrepancies between retarded and nonretarded individuals is a differential sensitivity to relational information (Soraci et al., 1990a). The present chapter provides some background on theoretical precursors that initially inspired the development of the paradigms to be discussed, and an overview of the research conducted by the present investigators directly relevant to an understanding of relational information processing.

The approach we have taken, i.e., an examination of the influence of stimulus organization variables in the learning of interstimulus relations, has relevance both for cognitive/developmental approaches and behavior–analytic perspectives (see Figure 1). Cognitive/developmental research has tended to focus on sophisticated conceptual and rule-based skills requisite for effective problem solving. The approach has typically posited mediational mechanisms and attempted to chart the course of their development (Baumeister, 1984; Bransford, Sherwood, Vye, Rieser, 1986; cf. Gibson, 1979). Behavior-analytic approaches, on the other hand, have emphasized the importance of stimulus control in the learning of interstimulus relations (cf. Mackay & Sidman, 1984). This latter approach, however, has underemphasized the complexity of environmental structure (Soraci, Carlin, Deckner, & Baumeister, 1990b).

In several of the studies we will be discussing in this chapter, an attempt is made to enhance effective problem solving via structural manipulations of the stimulus array that render the formats conducive to the selection of relevant stimulus relationships. Such structural manipulations can involve relatively sophisticated rule utilization, such as oddity (Soraci et al., 1987), or encoding processes in the context of rapid information presentations (Caruso & Detterman, 1983; Soraci et al., 1990b). There is thus a focus on the critical role of the information presentation format in effective stimulus detection. One commonality between recent approaches toward situated cognition (Brown, Collins, & Duguid, 1989) and our orientation is a strong emphasis on the importance of exploring and examining how a particular learning situation structures cognitions. As Brown et al. state, "activity and perception are importantly and epistemologically prior—at a nonconceptual level—to conceptualization in that it is on them that more attention needs to be focused" (p. 41). As a brief advance organizer it should be noted here that the chapter is divided into two sections. The first section discusses *global* stimulus organization, and the second section

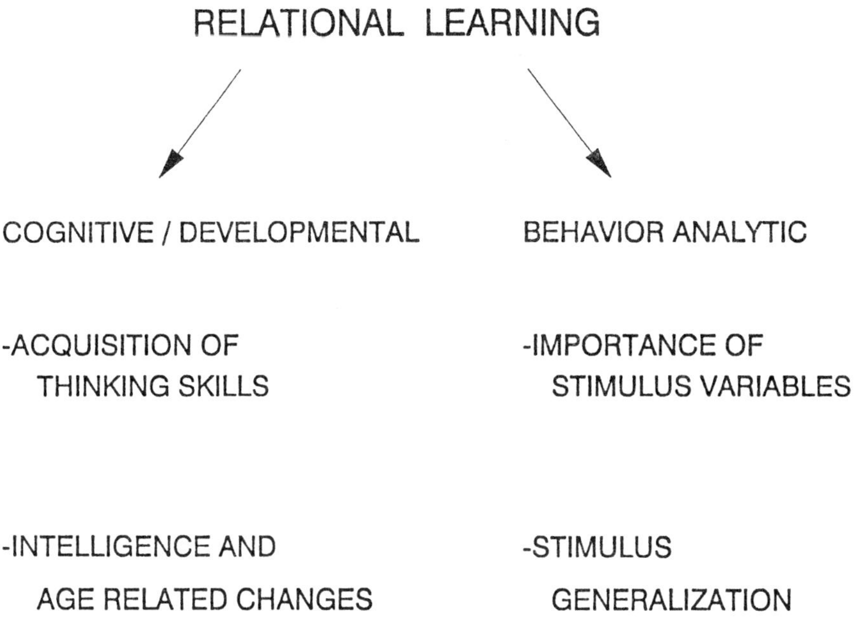

RELATIONAL LEARNING

COGNITIVE / DEVELOPMENTAL   BEHAVIOR ANALYTIC

-ACQUISITION OF   -IMPORTANCE OF
   THINKING SKILLS   STIMULUS VARIABLES

-INTELLIGENCE AND   -STIMULUS
   AGE RELATED CHANGES   GENERALIZATION

Figure 1.   Implications for the study of relational learning.

emphasizes research on *stimulus-specific* organization. By global organization, we are referring to organizational parameters involving multiple stimuli in an extant visual array. Such stimuli can be arranged and rearranged in the context of a particular visual and/or auditory array. By stimulus-specific organization, we are referring to organizational manipulations of a single target stimulus, presented at rapid presentation rates.

Historical Precursors

In his book *The Perception of Stimulus Relations*, Reese (1968) emphasized the long history in psychology of research focusing on the subject's detection and discrimination of interstimulus relations. Early investigators (Kohler, 1929; Kuenne, 1946; Lawson, 1960) analyzed tasks such as transposition in attempts to delineate the *effective stimulus* (Hilgard, 1956), i.e., the stimulus critical for a particular discrimination. Transposition, for example, would be demonstrated when a subject who has learned to select the larger of two triangles selects the larger of the new pair of triangles even though the currently smaller member is the same size as the larger member of the original pair. This emphasis on the *relative* rather than absolute qualities of the stimulus was clearly evidenced in Kohler's work also. Kohler demonstrated that a chick would select the brighter of two gray squares across a wide range of brightness comparisons. In referring to Kohler's approach toward discrimination learning, Gibson (1960) stated that "the simplest explanation would be that the effective stimulus in the experiment was the direction of the difference in brightness in the field of view" (p. 697). Gibson is emphasizing an obvious but essential point: that procedures that induce comparing and contrasting of a plurality of stimuli are the *sine qua non* of relational learning. One of the present authors argued more than 20 years ago (Baumeister, Beedle, & Hawkins, 1964) that relational tasks such as transposition should be emphasized in understanding the locus of intelligence–related differences. We pursue this line of reasoning both with respect to global and stimulus–specific organization.

The Focus on Relational Information

Most discriminations, whether they involve novelty–familiarity judgments (as in studies of language acquisition using the exclusion paradigm), same—different judgments (as in the oddity paradigm), or relative judgments (as in choosing the larger of two triangles), require the utilization of relational information. Depending on their structural organization, multistimulus visual and auditory arrays can provide greater or lesser amounts of information specifying relations among stimulus elements (Soraci, Barlean, Haenlein, & Baumeister, 1986; Uttal, 1983). It has been well established that individuals who vary with respect to intellectual functioning also exhibit performance differences on relational tasks such as oddity and match-to-sample. In these tasks, an individual stimulus presented in a particular experimental context does not have discrete informational value independent of its relation to other stimuli (Sugimura, 1981). Rather, the informational value of the stimulus is determined by the context in which the stimulus appears (Gibson, 1979; Sekuler & Blake, 1985). We thus find relevant to the present proposal the work on stimulus organization (Caruso & Detterman, 1983), "contrastive learning" principles (Gibson, 1979), and the important behavior–analytic thinking concerned with the role of observing (Dinsmoor, 1985) in establishing equivalence relations (Mackay & Sidman, 1984; McIlvane et al., 1987; Sidman & Tailby, 1982).

Mediational interpretations of developmental changes in areas such as discrimination learning are prevalent now and have been prominent historically (Kail & Hagen, 1977). The present investigators' approach to inducing effective discriminative responding, including performances based on relational learning, does not require the subject to utilize sophisticated cognitive and/or metacognitive mediational strategies; nor does this approach require the provision of semantically rich contexts (cf. Campione & Brown, 1984). Our approach emphasizes perceptual/attentional variables rather than cognitive mediation (Soraci et al., 1990a). Whereas cognitive theories have invoked mediational processes such as rule application and decision making, a concept emphasized in our work is the *structure* of the visual and auditory arrays presented in the task. Gibson (1979) suggested that the visual array possesses a structure that specifies certain invariant stimulus relationships. According to this model, stimulus information is directly perceived; i.e., the organism detects information specifying relevant relationships in the visual array. Attention thus becomes the orienting or "attuning" of the perceptual system to stimulus information. *Perceptual learning* here refers to the progressive differentiation by the organism of stimulus information, rather than the cognitive elaboration of stimulus information alleged to be impoverished.

Several investigators have assumed that the ability to detect similarities (Mervis & Rosch, 1981) and/or novelty (Fagan, 1985) involves relatively higher order cognitive processes such as categorization. Our approach, however, examines structural manipulations of stimulus organization at the perceptual or "front end" in an attempt to *induce* cognitive skills such as categorization or rule application. In this sense, our view is quite consonant with recent perspectives on "distributed intelligence" (Pea & Kurland, 1984) that emphasize the importance of the interface between the individual's knowledge and environmental structure.

Nettlebeck (1985) hypothesized that the impaired performance of mentally retarded persons may be attributable to a centrally mediated attentional limitation. As previously stated, the present investigators assume that an important limitation of people of lower intellectual functioning is a decreased sensitivity to relational information. This sensitivity affects early phases of the information–processing sequence. All subsequent functions such as retention, valuative judgment, and response selection are necessarily impaired by such attentional deficits (Guilford, 1967).

GLOBAL ORGANIZATION: THE ODDITY PARADIGM

Oddity learning is a form of relational discrimination learning that requires the subject on each trial to choose one distinct stimulus from a display that also contains a set of stimuli that do not differ from one another. In the context of the oddity task, such learning has been posited to involve attentional (House, Brown & Scott, 1974; Scott & House, 1978; Zeaman & House, 1979), perceptual (Soraci et al., in 1991; Zentall, Hogan, Edwards, & Hearst, 1980), and conceptual (Gollin & Schadler, 1972) factors. In order to respond correctly, the subject must attend to and compare a minimum of three stimuli presented simultaneously (see Figure 2). Such a task requires primary attention to the relations among stimuli (Stella & Etzel, 1986). In an important respect, therefore, the oddity task demands the antithesis of what has been called *overselective attention* (Lovaas, Koegel, & Schreibman, 1979).

A particularly stringent test of oddity acquisition is the reversal assessment, in which the previously correct odd stimulus becomes the multiple nonodd

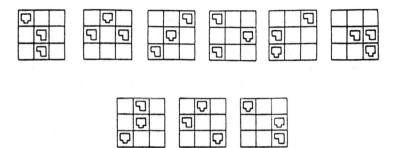

Figure 2.   Example of stimulus trials (top row) and the associated reversal trials (bottom row) used in the initial phase to assess oddity performance with three-element arrays (From Soraci et al., 1987).

stimulus element, while the previously nonodd element becomes the single odd stimulus that is the new correct choice. Reliable selection of this stimulus on the first trials of such tests indicates that the subject is responding on the basis of the relational aspects of the visual array. Children with low MAs—both developmentally delayed children and young, normal children—typically are unsuccessful on reversal assessments, particularly those involving only three element displays (Greenfield, 1985; Soraci et al., 1987, 1990a), which provide the minimal amount of relational information necessary for oddity responding. One method of facilitating oddity performance is to increase the number of identical, nonodd stimuli in each array (see Figure 3). When an odd stimulus is embedded in a two-dimensional array of many nonodd homogeneous distractors, its uniqueness is more readily perceived than when presented with few such distractors. This procedure has proven effective in several studies (Gollin, Saravo, & Salten, 1967; Gollin & Schadler, 1972; Sidman & Stoddard, 1968; Zentall et al., 1980). From the perspective of Gollin et al. and that of the present investigators, as the number of nonodd elements increases, the perceptual

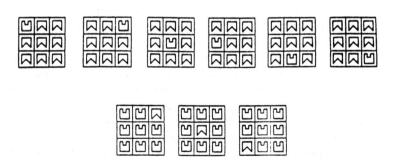

Figure 3.   Example of stimulus trials (top) and reversal trials (bottom) for the intervention phase utilizing nine-element arrays. (From Soraci et al., 1987).

salience of the odd stimulus increases and learning is facilitated. Interestingly, this view also is consonant with the operant perspective of Dinsmoor (1985), that the greater the degree of disparity between a stimulus and the context in which it is embedded, the greater the salience of the stimulus. Increases in stimulus salience evoke increases in observing behavior; and greater observing of and attending to relevant stimuli increases the probability of correct responding.

In the studies by Gollin et al. (1967), Gollin and Schadler (1972), and Zentall et al. (1980), subjects did not consistently transfer from arrays with many nonodd distractors to arrays with few nonodd distractors. A factor that may have accounted for these failures to transfer was the structure of the experimental task. Specifically, the structure of the visual arrays provided to the subjects may have provided only minimal or impoverished relational information. For example, Gollin and Schadler's (1972) use of stimuli positioned in a row may have induced visual scanning of individual elements rather than attention to the "perceptual field," which would make interstimulus relationships more salient. Because the three-element horizontal row is used frequently in oddity studies, this factor may have confounded results and reduced comparability with studies using other forms of stimulus presentation. As another example, Ellis and Sloan (1959) found poor oddity performance in young retarded children. In their study, however, three-dimensional forms were used, which may have evoked scanning of discrete characteristics of the stimuli. Such scanning may have interfered with the detection of the critical holistic oddity perception.

In the several oddity studies we have conducted, we have utilized a matrix that the subject could view holistically—that is, all the stimuli, both odd and nonodd, could be viewed simultaneously. This allows for manipulation of interstimulus relations globally—that is, across the particular visual array presented on each trial. As an example, in some studies the number of nonodd stimuli was increased from three during baseline to eight in an intervention phase (Soraci et al., 1983, 1987). The assumption underlying this intervention was that the perceptual salience of the odd stimulus, specifically its relationship to the nonodd stimuli, would be enhanced. Using young, developmentally delayed children as subjects, we have consistently found that accurate oddity responding is rapidly acquired with the change from baseline to intervention. Following exposure to the nine-element arrays during intervention, the children also demonstrated successful transfer when re-presented with the three-element arrays throughout large numbers of training trails during baseline. It is noteworthy that this transfer, as assessed by the stringent reversal assessment of oddity acquisition, was achieved in subjects at a developmental stage wherein such oddity responding has been regarded as atypical (i.e., MAs of less than 5 years). In addition, these subjects all had developmental delays of at least six months.

The children's successful performance on reversal trials is regarded as having required the utilization of relational information because the similarity and dissimilarity dimensions tested in the oddity task, like novelty-familiarity dimensions, are inherently relational (Greenfield, 1985; Hayek, 1952). That is, a stimulus is "similar" or "dissimilar" only with respect to its relationship to other stimuli. We suggested, therefore, that it was the relationship among the stimuli that was made more discriminable by the intervention.

Further, we have demonstrated that once children acquire the oddity performance with arrays containing eight nonodd stimuli, they then become able to respond correctly to arrays that contain only two nonodd stimuli. Soraci et al. (1987) also demonstrated transfer of oddity responding across stimulus types and, in a 6-week follow up, maintenance of oddity responding over time.

Stimulus Contiguity and Stimulus Adjacency: Unresolved Issues

The enhanced performances with respect to oddity acquisition demonstrated in several studies by the present investigators have been accomplished by utilizing 3 x 3 matrices with all cells filled as the maximally effective intervention (Bryant, Deckner, Soraci, Baumeister, & Blanton, 1988; Soraci, Alpher, Deckner, & Blanton, 1983; Soraci et al., 1987). While at one level this manipulation simply involves an increase in the number of nonodd elements provided in a visual array, several other factors could be operative in the enhanced detection. For example, with all cells filled, stimulus contiguity is necessarily enhanced. Stimulus contiguity, an analog to "clustering" in the visual domain, not only provides enhanced critical features, but the provision of such stimulus adjacencies provides for a more homogenous distractor field. Such contiguity/adjacency effects are clearly related to enhanced detection performances (Caruso & Detterman, 1983; Soraci et al., 1990b; Uttal, 1983). Secondarily, a filled nine-cell matrix contains no blank cells. Though the potential informational relevance of a blank cell is arguable, it is clearly the case that matrices containing blank cells render three potential stimulus values per cell (i.e., odd stimulus, nonodd stimulus, or blank), into simply two possibilities, odd or nonodd.

In a recently completed study, Bryant, Soraci and Carlin (1992), in order to delineate the organizational parameters responsible for effective oddity performance with nine-element arrays, examined oddity performance by manipulating both number of elements and stimulus contiguity in the context of the oddity paradigm. A brief perusal of the matrices presented in this task (Figure 4) indicates that the level of spatial contiguity is manipulated in both a four- and a nine-element stimulus array, allowing for the possibility of delineating interaction effects. Results indicated that, as predicted, both spatial contiguity and number of elements influenced oddity detection. However, the interaction obtained demonstrated that contiguity effects were more powerful, and in fact had a greater effect in the four-element array. In fact, four-element contiguous stimulus arrays resulted in performance relatively equivalent to the nine-element low-contiguity arrays. Although the subjects utilized in this experiment were nonretarded children with MAs of less than five, an extension of this study is

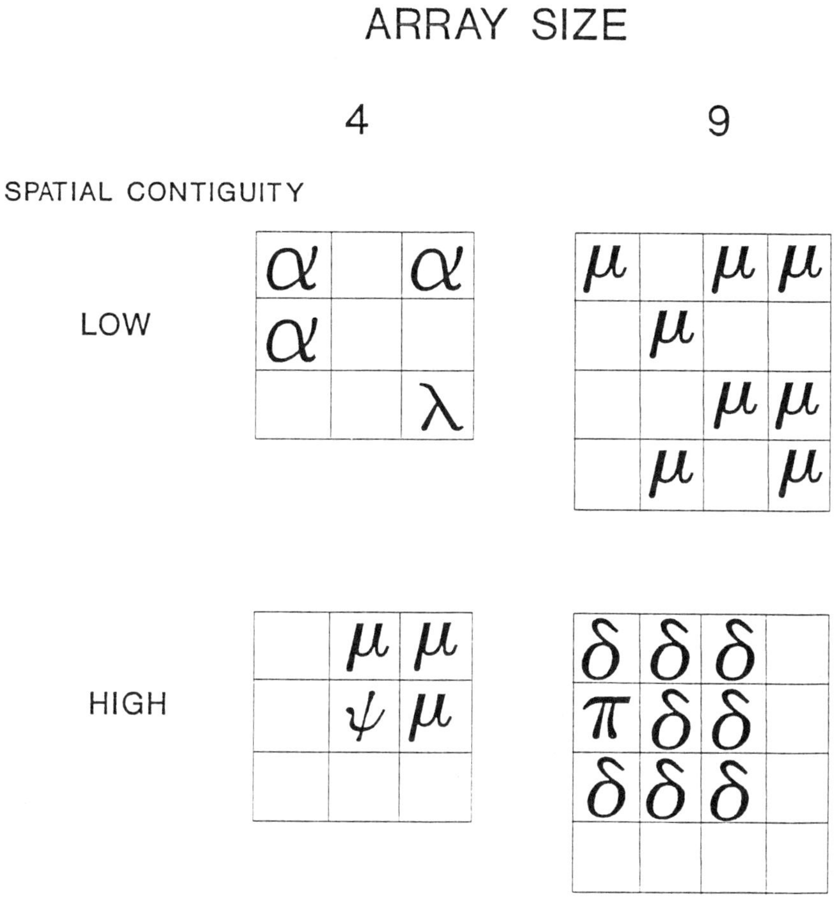

ARRAY SIZE

Figure 4. Experimental design and sample arrays for each of the four experimental groups (From Bryant et al., 1990).

planned with mildly mentally retarded children in order to examine the relationship between the manipulated organizational parameters and intellectual functioning. In this cross-group comparison, interactions of interest would involve high and low levels of spatial contiguity for retarded and nonretarded children. One possible outcome is that retarded children will require, in addition to an increase in the number of elements in the array, spatially contiguous stimuli in order to detect the odd stimulus effectively.

We have suggested that mentally retarded children do not have an immutable information-processing deficit as such; instead, they may have a lower sensitivity to relational information, and this reduced sensitivity may be amenable to interventions that make the relationships among stimuli more salient. The initial evidence, however, suggested a lower sensitivity to relational information in the mentally retarded only in the visual domain. The question remained as to whether this deficit was domain specific or reflected a more general phenomenon (cf. Gibson, 1979; Spelke, 1976). Thus, it was important to evaluate the ability of mentally retarded individuals to detect changes in relational information among auditory stimuli. This was our next step.

The Auditory Domain

Detection of alterations in the pattern and/or relationship among individual auditory stimuli has been shown to be correlated with changes in cardiac beats per minute (Graham & Clifton, 1966). Specifically, in nonretarded infants, cardiac response to alterations in the pattern of six auditory tones was characterized by a curvilinear function (Kinney & Kagan, 1976). Cardiac deceleration was greatest at moderate levels of discrepancy and less at both minimal and high levels of discrepancy. However, Kinney and Kagan's dishabituation patterns consisted either of a reordering of the component tones of the habituation sequence, which altered the relationship among tonal elements, or replacement of one or more of the original tones with novel tones.

Chang and Trehub (1977), on the other hand, directly evaluated relational sensitivity by using an additional set of manipulations. They reordered the component tones, much as Kinney and Kagan (1976) had done, and they also transposed the entire tonal pattern up or down three semitones, thereby preserving the pattern while changing individual tonal elements. Differential response to the transposed and discrepancy conditions would indicate a differential sensitivity to relational aspects of the auditory array. They found that infants demonstrated cardiac deceleration in response to moderate levels of discrepancy between the habituation and dishabituation patterns when reordered, but not when the specific tones of the pattern were transposed. In a variation of the Chang and Trehub study, we compared, via changes in cardiac response, the sensitivity of retarded and nonretarded adults to alterations in the relationship among individual auditory tones (Soraci et al., 1986). Retarded individuals demonstrated a lower sensitivity than nonretarded individuals to alterations of the relational information provided by the auditory tones.

The results of the Soraci et al. (1986) study thus extended to retarded individuals the findings that cardiac deceleration is curvilinearly related to the magnitude of discrepancy between tonal patterns. More importantly, this curvilinear function was less pronounced in retarded as compared to nonretarded groups, and this suggests a lower sensitivity in retarded individuals to alterations in relational information. This interpretation is supported by the observations in our visual oddity studies that retarded individuals' performances improved following manipulations designed to enhance the salience of relational information (Soraci et al., 1987). Furthermore, the findings in the auditory domain suggest that the hypothesized lower sensitivity of retarded individuals to relational information is crossmodal and thus may constitute a general phenomenon. Although Gibson (1979) did not address mental retardation, the foregoing is consistent with a Gibsonian perspective inasmuch as the detection of invariance, as distinguished from detection of specific stimulus characteristics, is independent of modality.

Relational Learning and Respondent Conditioning

An additional point should be made about the study in which the dependent variable was cardiac activity. The other studies we have discussed examined changes in behavior mediated by higher levels of the central nervous system, referred to as the performances produced by operant conditioning or instrumental learning, and viewed as voluntarily emitted. In contrast, the cardiac dependent variable was an example of a response mediated by the autonomic nervous system, referred to as the response produced in respondent or Pavlovian conditioning, and characterized as involuntarily elicited. Recently, Rescorla (1988) quotes passages from a number of general psychology texts illustrating that Pavlovian conditioning continues to be regarded by psychologists as a matter of a previously neutral stimulus acquiring the ability to elicit the response originally elicited by an unconditioned stimulus. In reviewing a large number of studies, Rescorla demonstrated that this traditional description is wholly inaccurate. He indicated that contemporary investigators describe such conditioning as "the learning of relations among events so as to allow an organism to represent its environment." Thus, these investigators no longer see Pavlovian conditioning as a kind of low-level mechanical process in which the control over a response is passed from one stimulus to another. Instead, modern conceptions (a) view the learning that results from exposure to relations among events as the primary means by which an organism represents the structure of its world, (b) assume that Pavlovian conditioning must have considerable richness both in the relations it represents and in the ways its representations influence behavior, and (c) emphasize the information that one stimulus gives about another.

Rescorla (1988) describes recent research demonstrating that perceptual relations that naturally occur among events, such as similarity and the partwhole relation, influence the formation of Pavlovian associations. The partwhole relation is a particularly interesting perceptual relation, because in the natural environment partial information about an object or event frequently serves as a signal of the entire object or event. Similarly, in the natural environment a stimulus that is similar to another is frequently predictive of he appearance of the other. Consequently, it is important in the adaptation of an organism to its environment that Pavlovian conditioning be especially sensitive to such naturally occurring perceptual relations. The cardiac studies just described indicate the generality of the observation first made in an operant or instrumental learning modality by providing analogous evidence in an entirely different but equally important modality, responses in the domain of Pavlovian conditioning.

Crossmodal Relational Information

Whereas our aforementioned cardiac study (Soraci et al., 1986) demonstrated differential responding to relational characteristics of auditory patterns in retarded and nonretarded adults, this was with respect to only one modality. Up to this point, we had not utilized a bimodal intervention. In a recently completed study we had the opportunity to conduct in collaboration with several researchers at the Shriver Center, we examined a method designed to facilitate learning of the apparently difficult, three-stimulus oddity task directly (Soraci et al., 1991). The hypothesis was that the salience of an odd visual stimulus could be enhanced through synchronized presentation of auditory stimuli. One tone sounded simultaneously when each of two nonodd visual stimuli was displayed and a clearly different tone sounded when the odd visual stimulus appeared. For the reasons noted above, oddity learning has been of interest to a large number of investigators, and numerous approaches to establishing oddity performance have been explored. However, we know of no bimodal interventions that have been investigated. Consonant with a Gibsonian (1979) perspective, which assumes that stimulus invariance may be detected in different modalities or sensory channels simultaneously, we predicted facilitation of oddity performance when relational information was provided in two modalities concurrently.

In order to assess oddity acquisition comprehensively, both reversal assessments and assessments with novel sets of stimuli were employed. As suggested, a number of investigators have described reversal probes as a particularly stringent assessment of oddity acquisition. However, such a test does not assess generalization of the performance to other stimuli. The novel set assessments were included to assess the generalization of oddity performance to novel stimuli directly. Six of the seven subjects in this study demonstrated the acquisition of oddity responding in both a reversal and a novel set format. Additionally, these six subjects demonstrated generalization to a visual-only condition upon a return to baseline.

As noted, Dinsmoor (1985) has claimed that, in the early stages of discrimination learning, more functional observing occurs when the disparity between the $S+$ and $S-$ is large than when it is small. Soraci et al. (1987) noted the relevance of such a view to their study of the facilitatory effects of increasing the number of nonodd stimuli in a visual oddity task. The auditory intervention can be viewed similarly as a method of increasing the disparateness (and hence the observing of differences) of the odd and nonodd stimuli, by indicating the uniqueness or oddity of the $S+$ in two modalities concurrently.

One might also consider the possibility that the facilitation by the tones resulted because preexperimental experience had taught the children that changes in the auditory environment are often accompanied by simultaneous and characteristic visual changes. Having detected an auditory stimulus difference, were the children then more likely to look for an accompanying visual stimulus difference? Such a hypothesis seems reasonable and perhaps even likely. Perception of differences among successively presented tones probably requires less advanced prerequisite behavior than does careful scanning and comparison of letterlike forms.

A similar argument can be made for facilitation of reversal performance. One can view the tones on each original problem as a stimulus pattern unique to that problem. Although the actual order of tone presentations varied unsystematically across trials, all trials within a problem were alike in presenting one odd tone (e.g., a higher one) and two nonodd tones (e.g., two lower ones). On a reversal, the oddity relationship was preserved, but the tone pattern was different (e.g., now two higher tones and one lower). This changed pattern could conceivably serve the function suggested above for individual tones—directing the child's detection to the visual counterpart of the new acoustic pattern.

Resolution of an Anomaly: Oddity Learners versus Nonlearners

The results discussed thus far with respect to the oddity paradigm provide resolution of an unanswered question from Stoddard's (1968) research. Stoddard demonstrated that children tested on an oddity task with tilted lines as stimuli could be characterized as being oddity learners or nonlearners. Subjects who were oddity *learners* did not demonstrate, on a match-to-sample posttest, learning of the specific direction of tilt of individual stimuli. Surprisingly, however, oddity *nonlearners* did demonstrate learning of a specific direction of tilt of individual stimuli. In the Soraci et al. (1987) study discussed previously, relational information per se was enhanced; the learning demonstrated was relational in that it was not linked to a specific stimulus configuration. The rule—that is, of choosing the odd or "different" stimulus—did not require attending to features of an individual stimulus in isolation. As Stella and Etzel (1986) have recently shown, holding the S + (in the oddity study, the "different" stimulus) constant and varying the S − stimuli (i.e., nonodd distractors) results in greater visual orienting to the S − stimuli. This greater attention to the nontarget stimuli, particularly on an oddity task, should lead to better performance, since the "oddity" of a stimulus is determined by its *surround*. This perspective implies that overattending to specific stimuli in isolation, as was perhaps the case with Stoddard's oddity nonlearners, impairs learning of the critical oddity rule, which should apply regardless of the specific stimulus configuration presented on each trial. Malott (1984) has recently suggested that an examination of the acquisition of rule-governed behavior is important, because rule-governed behavior is another repertoire lower functioning children need in order to approximate normal performance.

STIMULUS-SPECIFIC ORGANIZATION:
THE DETECTION PARADIGM

Caruso and Detterman (1983) demonstrated that retarded subjects were slower and committed more errors on a stimulus encoding task than nonretarded subjects, but that varying degrees of stimulus organization were processed in a similar manner by both groups. Stimuli used in the Caruso and Detterman task were nonverbal checkerboard-like patterns. The advantage of using such stimuli is that they are quantifiable on each of three stimulus structure variables: symmetry, number of adjacencies, and number of cells filled. Although Caruso and Detterman found no intelligence-related differences on such tasks, sample duration in their task was subject determined, and correlations between decision times and stimulus structure variables were examined across a continuum of either highly organized or random sets. Intermediate levels of stimulus organization did not comprise a discrete factor in their study.

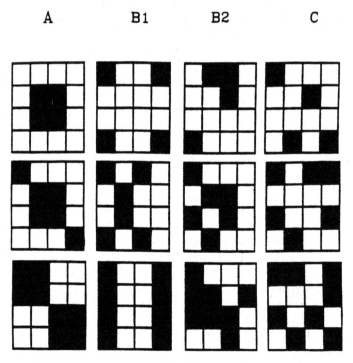

Figure 5.   Stimuli used in the study: (A) High Structure, high symmetry-high adjacency, (B1) Moderate Structure, high symmetry-low adjacency, (B2) Moderate Structure, low symmetry-high adjacency, (C) Low Structure, low symmetry-low adjacency (From Soraci et al., 1990b).

A recent study completed in our laboratory (Soraci et al., 1990b) utilized stimulus configurations similar to those designed by Caruso and Detterman (see Figure 5), but we presented these stimuli at 150-msec durations, which allowed for only central scanning (Estes, 1965). In addition to varying stimulus organization parameters, the *disparity* between target and distractor was also manipulated, across high, low, *and* moderate levels of stimulus organization. The target-distractor disparity manipulation, essentially a stimulus contrast variable, has been addressed previously in our discussion of Dinsmoor (1985) and Gibson's (1979) work. Utilizing 150-msec stimulus durations, we essentially replicated Caruso and Detterman's results at high and low levels of stimulus organization. That is, both high- and low-functioning subjects benefited from high levels of stimulus organization relative to lower, more randomlike patterns. However, Caruso and Detterman had not included a discrete level of moderate stimulus organization. The interaction we found in our study indicated that, whereas there were no differences at either high or low levels of stimulus organization between nonretarded and retarded individuals, there were significant differences at moderate levels of stimulus organization (see Figures 6 and 7). Lower functioning subjects were found to ineffectively encode stimuli at both *moderate* and *low* levels of stimulus organization. Such poor performance was only found for nonretarded subjects at low levels of stimulus organization. More importantly, in examining the ability of subjects to utilize relational information-that is, to capitalize on target-distractor disparity, nonretarded subjects benefited from high and moderate levels of disparity whereas retarded subjects were only able to utilize extremely disparate target-distractor differences-that is, when the target was of high organization and the distractor was low, or vice versa.

The importance of this finding is that, even though differences in intelligence appear to be related to encoding differences involving central scanning processes, the differences only appear to be salient at *moderate* levels of stimulus organization. Taking into consideration the fact that most stimuli, whether in the real world or laboratory situations, tend to have moderate (i.e., mixed) degrees of organizational parameters such as symmetry and adjacency, such encoding differences as obtained in this study could have implications for intelligence-related differences across a wide range of tasks. Additionally, lower functioning individuals appear less able to utilize target-distractor disparities than higher functioning individuals, although lower functioning individuals do benefit from extreme target-distractor disparity. This appears to be another case where intelligence-related performance differences interact with target/surround relational characteristics.

In the second phase of the study, the investigators assessed the relationship between stimulus organization and stimulus discriminability. That is, deficits in performance may have resulted from differential detection rates for stimuli within and across different groupings. To assess the inter- and intraclass

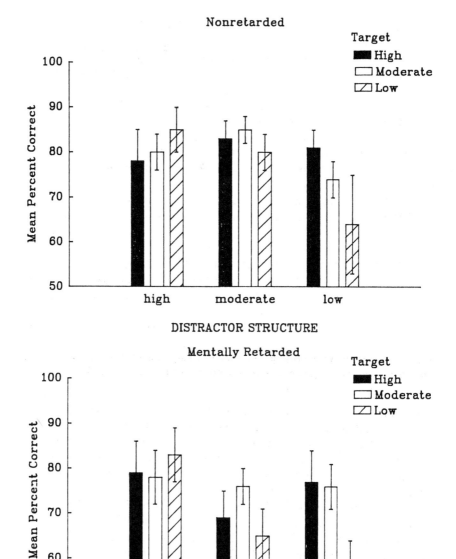

Figure 6.   Depiction of detection accuracies for retarded and nonretarded subjects as a function of target and Distractor structure. (From Soraci et al., 1990b).

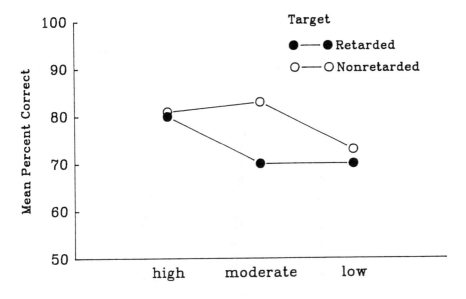

Figure 7.   Detection accuracy for retarded and nonretarded subjects as a function of Distractor stimulus structure (From Soraci et al., 1990b).

comparabilities of the stimuli employed, a sorting task was performed by a group of nonretarded subjects to determine whether stimuli were consistently grouped into the appropriate structural organization categories, either high, moderate, or low, as determined a priori. Results indicated that subjects did sort the stimuli into the structural organization categories with high accuracy. These results suggest that the stimulus variables (e.g., symmetry and number of adjacencies) comprising the checkerboard patterns were directly related to the discriminability of the stimuli on the rapid presentation match-to-sample task.

A follow-up study (Carlin & Soraci, in press) was conducted to determine whether similar intelligence-related differences would be obtained with stimuli varying solely with respect to axis of symmetry. In addition, both checkerboard patterns *and* formlike polygon stimuli (i.e., Palmer & Hemenway, 1978) were studied. Symmetry was manipulated in four ways: double symmetry, vertical symmetry, horizontal symmetry, and asymmetry. Results from the two-choice match-to-sample task indicated that performance was enhanced (a) when target stimuli were vertically symmetrical, and (b) with the presence of increased target-distractor disparity (i.e., vertically symmetrical target-asymmetrical distracter). Interestingly, the detection rates for checkerboard patterns and the more "ecologically valid" formlike polygon stimuli were equivalent.

It should be noted that the intelligence-related differences identified by Soraci et al. (1990b) were found using stimuli which varied with respect to symmetry *and* number of adjacencies. The lack of group differences in the Soraci et al. (1989) study may have resulted from the fact that the perception and identification of symmetries are basic processing tasks unmediated by higher order cognitive processes (i.e., strategies), which frequently differentiate groups varying in level of intelligence. In addition, the disparity between two stimuli differing with respect to axis of symmetry may have been too great to differentiate groups varying in intelligence level. House (1966) proposed that the greater facilitative effect of symmetrical stimuli than equally redundant asymmetrical stimuli was due to other factors inherent in the figures, such as number of adjacencies (i.e., visual clusters). The grouping of individual elements into a single feature or cluster requires higher order cognitive processing. The inability of mentally retarded subjects to process (i.e., perceptually organize) this type of information as efficiently as nonretarded individuals may account for the intelligence-related differences indicated in the Soraci et al. (1990b) study and the absence of such findings in the Soraci et al. (1989) study, in which number of adjacencies was not included as an independent factor.

To assess the role of perceptual organization in the detection of checkerboard stimuli varying with respect to symmetry *and* adjacencies, a rapid presentation signal-detection task was employed. The lack of significant group *by* stimulus type (high, moderate, or low organization) differences indicated that the retarded and nonretarded individuals processed the stimuli in a similar manner. However, significant group differences for d' and recognition accuracy demonstrated that the two groups were not equally sensitive to the information provided at such brief exposures. Specifically, the mentally retarded subjects required significantly more time for inspection of the target stimulus to obtain an equal amount of stimulus information from the target. These results further support the notion that the locus of intelligence-related differences on detection tasks is a lower sensitivity to interstimulus relations, as assessed in the two-choice match-to-sample task, and not necessarily a general difference in perceptual encoding.

RELATIONAL LEARNING, PERCEPTUAL ENHANCEMENT, AND THE NEW VIDEODISC TECHNOLOGY

Virtually all of the aforementioned research the present investigators have been involved with has entailed the use of computer-based training and assessment formats. The attempt has been to facilitate relatively sophisticated rule-based skills such as oddity and match-to-sample via appropriate perceptual modifications of visual arrays. Bransford et al. (1986) have recently emphasized the importance of perceptual learning in any kind of teaching format, since the individual's successful access to his or her knowledge base is typically dependent upon a *prior* detection of relevant stimulus relationships.

We see our approach as very consonant with modern videodisc technology, since such technology enables an efficacious utilization of visual presentations and rapid presentation of successive visual formats (Rock, Bransford, Maisto, & Moray, 1987). Rock et al., in discussing the application of such videodisc technology to training of successful clinicians, point out that such technology enables *contrast-based* training—i.e., precisely the approach toward relational learning that we have been discussing in this chapter. Such rapid-access video technology also enables one to select small, precise components of visual arrays, which can be compared and contrasted an unlimited number of times.

In short, we envision the potential interface of modern videodisc technology with a battery of relational tasks. With the development of an appropriate taxonomy of relational tasks, one might imagine a series of training programs that focus on a range of cognitive skills, from lower level match-to-sample-like performance which is requisite for successful receptive vocabulary learning (McIlvane et al., 1987) to more sophisticated *conceptually based* skills, which are necessary for reading comprehension (Anderson, 1985). We believe this marriage of a relational taxonomy, in terms of experimental tasks in conjunction with effective videodisc technology that enables precise visual and/or auditory presentations, holds great promise for the future of teaching learning and thinking.

RELEVANCE FOR CONNECTIONIST MODELS

We have already discussed Rescorla's (1988) emphasis on the importance of perceptual relations in conditioning. Rescorla is essentially attempting to demonstrate the utility of classical associationistic perspectives in more complex learning problems. We wish to emphasize that relational perspectives such as Rescorla's and the one we are presenting in the present chapter are quite consonant with contemporary connectionist models that have emerged in cognitive psychology.

Traditionally, computer metaphors have invoked the utilization of rules, inferences, and hypotheses as integral parts of symbolic, computational models. Modern connectionist or *parallel* models, however, do not require the existence of an internal symbolic medium (McClelland & Rummelhart, 1986; Rummelhart & McClelland, 1986). In such connectionist views, computations are performed via the interaction of an extensive network of nodes or *units*. The sophisticated output obtained from such programs, which, for example, can simulate rudimentary speech perception or category learning, are solely dependent upon the interaction of the nodes in the network. Hatfield (1986) has recently referred to such an approach as a "noncognitive functional analysis." The functional algorithms, as Hatfield claims, are nonsymbolic and involve lawful relationships between stimulus input and perceptual response. Such algorithms are instantiated by the neural net. The notion of *information* in such a view is "defined in terms of the relation between real world events" (1986, p. 10). Hatfield (1986) is here referring to relations involving patterns of light at the retina, geometric properties of the array, etc.

The important point about the relevance of such connectionist models for learning, as Rescorla has claimed, is that such models can result in the production of relatively complex outputs—yet such output is contingent upon the interaction of multiple associations only. Note the approach of the present investigators concerning "rule-based" or inferential processes alleged to be requisite for oddity learning (House et al., 1974). We have designed modifications of the stimulus arrays so as to make salient the critical dimensions of difference. Such an approach "bypasses" a mediational or symbolic conceptually based rule induction, and strives to induce such rule utilization via perceptually based manipulations. Thus, the notion of complex outputs being dependent upon relatively simplistic multiple interactions is of direct relevance, both for connectionist models and the present perspective. It is perhaps instructive for the reader to not two quotations, one by Rescorla, an ardent behaviorist:

> Connectionist theories of this sort bear an obvious resemblance to theories of Pavlovian conditioning. Both view the organism as using multiple associations to build an overall representation, and both view the organism as adjusting its representation to bring it into line with the world, striving to reduce any discrepancies. (Rescorla, 1988, p. 159)

And the other by the Gibsons in an earlier work:

> in this theory, perception gets richer in differential responses, not in images. It is progressively in *greater* correspondence with stimulation, not in less. Instead of becoming more imaginary it becomes more discriminating...learning is...a matter of improvement—of getting in closer touch with the environment. (Gibson & Gibson, 1955, p. 34)

The aforementioned quotations, although enunciated by scientists of quite different theoretical persuasions, clearly emphasize the importance of focusing on environmental structure, and the relationship of such structure to perception. The present authors thus find an interesting parallel between connectionism, respondent conditioning, and a Gibsonian emphasis on stimulus structure, in their sharing of a theoretical parsimony that harks back to classical associationism.

CONCLUSION

We believe that our approach toward the examination of global and stimulus-specific stimulus organization and its influence on stimulus detection in the context of intelligence-related differences is consonant with Norman's (1981) suggested criteria for future cognitive science research. These include "goal-directed, conceptually based research planning" and "the decomposition of difficult problems into smaller, nearly independent issues." We believe that the examination of rule-based acquisition in the context of the oddity paradigm and of organizational influences on stimulus detection in rapid information-processing tasks has promise for contributing to the understanding of basic processes and their relationship to general intelligence (Sternberg, 1987).

REFERENCES

Anderson, R.C. (1985). Role of the reader's schema in comprehension, learning, and memory. In R.C. Anderson, J. Osborn, & R.J. Tierney (Eds.), *Learning to read in American schools: Basal readers and content texts*. Hillsdale, NJ: Erlbaum.

Baumeister, A.A. (1984). Some methodological and conceptual issues in the study of cognitive processes with retarded people. In P.H. Brooks, R. Sperber, & C. McCauley (Eds.), *Learning and cognition in the mentally retarded* (pp. 1–38). Hillsdale, NJ: Erlbaum.

Baumeister, A.A., Beedle, R., & Hawkins, W.F. (1964). Transposition in normals and retardates under varying conditions of training and test. *American Journal of Mental Deficiency, 69*, 114–120.

Bransford, J., Sherwood, R., Vye, N., & Rieser, J. (1986). Teaching thinking and problem solving: Research foundations. *American Psychologist, 41*(10), 1078–1089.

Brown, J.S., Collings, A., & Duguid, P. (1989). Situated cognition and the culture of learning. *Educational Researcher, 18*(1), 32–42.

Bryant, J.T., Deckner, C.W., Soraci, S.A., Jr., Baumeister, A.A., & Blanton, R.L. (1988). Oddity learning in developmentally delayed children: Facilitation by means of familiar stimuli. *American Journal on Mental Retardation, 93* (2), 138–143.

Bryant, J.T., Soraci, S.A., Jr., & Carlin, M.T. (1992). *Oddity facilitation as a function of array size and spatial contiguity*. Manuscript in preparation.

Campione, J.C., & Brown, A.L. (1984). Learning ability and transfer as sources of individual differences in intelligence. In P. H. Brooks, R. Sperber, & C. McCauley (Eds.), *Learning and cognition in the mentally retarded* (pp. 265–293). Hillsdale, NJ: Erlbaum.

Carlin, M.T., & Soraci, S.A., Jr. (in press). Similarities in the detection of stimulus symmetry by persons with and without mental retardation. *American Journal on Mental Retardation*.

Caruso, D.R., & Detterman, D.K. (1983). Stimulus encoding by mentally retarded and nonretarded adults. *American Journal of Mental Deficiency, 87*(6), 649–655.

Chang, H.W., & Trehub, S.E. (1977). Auditory processing of relational information by young infants. *Journal of Experimental Child Psychology, 24*, 324–331.

Dinsmoor, J.A. (1985). The role of observing and attention in establishing stimulus control. *Journal of the Experimental Analysis of Behavior, 43*, 365–381.

Ellis, N.R., & Sloan, W. (1959). Oddity learning as a function of mental age. *Journal of Comparative and Physiological Psychology, 52*, 228–230.

Estes, W.K. (1965). A technique for assessing variability of perceptual span. *Proceedings of the National Academy of Sciences*, *54*, 403–407.

Fagan, J.F. (1985). A new look at infant intelligence. In D.K. Detterman (Ed.), *Current topics in human intelligence: Research methodology* (Vol. 1, pp. 223–246). Norwood, NJ: Ablex Publishing Corp.

Gibson, J.J. (1960). The concept of the stimulus in psychology. *American Psychologist*, *15*, 694–703.

Gibson, J.J. (1979). *The ecological approach to visual perception*. Boston: Houghton-Mifflin.

Gibson, J.J., & Gibson, E.J. (1955). Perceptual learning: Differentiation or enrichment? *Psychological Review*, *62*(1), 32–41.

Gollin, E.S., Saravo, A., & Salten, C. (1967). Perceptual distinctiveness and oddity-problem solving in children. *Journal of Experimental Child Psychology*, *5*, 586–596.

Gollin, E.S., & Schadler, M. (1972). Relational learning and transfer in young children. *Journal of Experimental Child Psychology*, *14*, 219–232.

Graham, F.K., & Clifton, R.K. (1966). Heart-rate change as a component of the orienting response. *Psychological Bulletin*, *65*, 305–320.

Greenfield, D.B. (1985). Facilitating mentally retarded children's relational learning through novelty-familiarity training. *American Journal of Mental Deficiency*, *90*, 343–348.

Guilford, J.P. (1967). *The nature of human intelligence*. New York: McGraw-Hill.

Hatfield, G. (1986). *Representation and content in some (actual) theories of perception*. Baltimore: The Johns Hopkins University, Cognitive Neuropsychology Laboratory.

Hayek, F.A. (1952). *The sensory order: An inquiry into the foundations of theoretical psychology*. Chicago: University of Chicago.

Hilgard, E.R. (1956). *Theories of learning* (2nd ed.). New York: Appleton-Century Crofts.

House, B.J. (1966). Discrimination of symmetrical and asymmetrical dot patterns by retardates. *Journal of Experimental Child Psychology*, *3*, 377–389.

House, B.J., Brown A.L., & Scott, M.S. (1974). Children's discrimination learning based on identify or difference. In H.W. Reese (Ed.), *Advances in child development and behavior* (Vol. 9). New York: Academic Press.

Kail, R.V., Jr., & Hagen, J.W. (Eds.). (1977). *Perspectives on the development of memory and cognition*. Hillsdale, NJ: Erlbaum.

Kinney, D.K., & Kagen, J. (1976). Infant attention to auditory discrepancy. *Child Development*, *47*, 155–164.

Kohler, W. (1929). *Gestalt psychology*. New York: Liveright.

Kuenne, M.R. (1946). Experimental investigation of the relation of language to transposition behavior in young children. *Journal of Experimental Psychology*, *36*, 471–490.

Lawson, R. (1960). *Learning and behavior*. New York: The MacMillan Company.

Lovaas, O.I., Koegel, R.L., & Schreibman, L. (1979). Stimulus over-selectivity in autism: A review of research. *Psychological Bulletin*, *86*, 1236–1254.

Mackay, H.A., & Sidman, M. (1984). Teaching new behavior via equivalence relations. In P.H. Brooks, R. Sperber, & C. McCauley (Eds.), *Learning and cognition in the mentally retarded* (pp. 493–513). Hillsdale, NJ: Erlbaum.

Malott, R.W. (1984). Rule-governed behavior, self-management, and the developmentally disabled: A theoretical analysis. *Analysis and Intervention in Developmental Disabilities*, *4*, 199–209.

McClelland, J.L., & Rumelhart, D.E. (1986). *Parallel distributed processing* (Vol. 2). Cambridge, MA: MIT Press.

McIlvane, W.J., Kledaras, J.B., Munson, L.C., King, A.J., DeRose, J.C., & Stoddard, L.T. (1987). Controlling relations in conditional discrimination and matching by exclusion. *Journal of the Experimental Analysis of Behavior*, *48*(2), 197–208.

Mervis, C.B., & Rosch, E. (1981). Categorization of natural objects. *Annual Review of Psychology*, *32*, 89–115.

Nettlebeck, T. (1985). Inspection time and mild mental retardation. In N. R. Ellis (Ed.), *International review of research in mental retardation* (Vol. 13, pp. 109–141). New York: Academic Press.

Norman, D.A. (1981). Twelve issues for cognitive science. In D.A. Norman (Ed.), *Perspectives on cognitive science* (pp. 265–295). Hillsdale, NJ: Erlbaum.

Palmer, S.E., & Hemenway, K. (1978). Orientation and symmetry: Effects of multiple, rotational, and near symmetries. *Journal of Experimental Psychology*, *4*, 691–702.

Pea, R.D., & Kurland, D.M. (1984). On the cognitive effect of learning computer programming. *New Ideas in Psychology*, *2*(2), 137–168.

Reese, H.W. (1968). *The perception of stimulus relations*. New York: Academic Press.

Rescorla, R.A. (1988). Pavlovian conditioning: Its not what you think it is. *American Psychologist*, *43* (3), 151–160.

Rock, D.L., Bransford, J.D., Maisto, S.A., & Moray, L.C. (1987). The study of clinical judgment: An ecological approach. *Clinical Psychology Review*, *7*, 645–661.

Rumelhart, D.E., & McClelland, J.L. (1986). *Parallel distributed processing* (Vol. 1). Cambridge, MA: MIT Press.

Scott, M.S., & House, B.J. (1978). Repetition of cues in children's oddity learning and transfer. *Journal of Experimental Child Psychology*, *25*, 58–70.

Sekuler, R., & Blake, R. (1985). *Perception*. New York: Alfred A. Knopf.

Sidman, M., & Stoddard, L.T. (1967). The effectiveness of fading in programming in a simultaneous form discrimination for retarded children. *Journal of the Experimental Analysis of Behavior*, *10*, 3–15.

Sidman, M., & Tailby, W. (1982). Conditional discrimination vs. matching to sample: An expansion of the testing paradigm. *Journal of the Experimental Analysis of Behavior*, *37*, 5–22.

Simon, H.A. (1981). Cognitive science: The newest science of the artificial. In D.A. Norman (Ed.), *Perspectives on cognitive science* (pp. 13–26). Hillsdale, NJ: Erlbaum.

Soraci, S.A., Jr., Alpher, V.S., Deckner, C.W., & Blanton, R.L. (1983). Oddity performance and the perception of relational information. *Psychologia*, *26*, 175–184.

Soraci, S.A., Jr., Barlean, J.L., Haenlein, M., & Baumeister, A.A. (1986). Lower sensitivity to alternations of auditory relational information in mentally retarded than in nonretarded adults. *Physiological Psychology*, *14*(3 & 4), 146–149.

Soraci, S.A., Jr., Deckner, C.W., Baumeister, A.A., & Carlin, M.T. (1990a). Attentional functioning and relational learning. *American Journal on Mental Retardation*, *95*(3), 304–315.

Soraci, S.A., Jr., Carlin, M.T., Deckner, C.W., & Baumeister, A.A. (1990b). Detection of stimulus organization: Evidence of intelligence-related differences. *Intelligence*, *4*(2), 435–447.

Soraci, S.A., Jr., Deckner, C.W., Haenlein, M., Baumeister, A.A., Murata-Soraci, K., & Blanton, R. (1987). Oddity performance in preschool children at risk for mental retardation: Transfer and maintenance. *Research in Developmental Disabilities*, *8*, 137–151.

Soraci, S.A., Jr., Deckner, C.W., Baumeister, A.A., Bryant, J.T., Mackay, H.A., Stoddard, L.T., & McIlvane, W.J. (1991). Generalized oddity performance in preschool children: A bimodal training procedure. *Journal of Experimental Child Psychology*, *51*, 280–295.

Spelke, E. (1976). Infants' intermodal perception of events. *Cognitive Psychology*, *8*, 53–60.

Stella, M.E., & Etzel, B.C. (1986). Stimulus control of eye orientations: Shaping S+ only versus shaping S− only. *Analysis and Intervention in Developmental Disabilities*, *6*, 137–153.

Sternberg, R.J. (1987). A unified theory of intellectual exceptionality. In J.D. Day & J.G. Borkowski (Eds.), *Intelligence and exceptionality: New Directions for theory, assessment, and instructional practices*. Norwood, NJ: Ablex Publishing Corp.

Stoddard, L.T. (1968). An observation on stimulus control in a tilt discrimination by children. *Journal of the Experimental Analysis of Behavior*, *11* 321–324.

Sugimura, T. (1981). Children's oddity learning as a function of interaction and task. *Psychologia*, *24*, 193–201.

Uttal, W.R. (1983). *Visual form detection in 3-dimensional space*. Hillsdale, NJ: Erlbaum.

Zeaman, D., & House, B.J. (1979). A review of attention theory. In N.R. Ellis (Ed.), *Handbook of mental deficiency, psychological theory and research* (2nd ed.). Hillsdale, NJ: Erlbaum.

Zentall, T.R., Hogan, D.E., Edwards, C.A., & Hearst, E. (1980). Oddity learning in the pigeon as a function of the number of incorrect alternatives. *Journal of Experimental Pyschology: Animal Behavior Processes*, *6*, 278–299.

Author Index

A

Abelson, R.P., 141, *152*
Ackerman, P.L., 261, 262, 277, *278*
Adinoff, B., 229, *236*
Aiken, L.R., 267, 271, *278*
Alavi, A., 175, *183,* 193, *214*
Albert, M.S., 58, *76*
Alcorn, M.D., 228, *235*
Alexander, J., 109, *117*
Alexander, M.P., 190, *213*
Allen, L., 14, *27,* 32, *51*
Allen, M.J., 263, 266, *278*
Allik, J., 228, *233*
Allport, A., 56, 60, 69, *76*
Alpher, V.S., 289, 290, *305*
Amatruda, C., 32, *51*
Amin, D., 167, 168, *169*
Amsterdam, J.B., 59, *78*
Anastasi, A., 262, 276, *278*
Anderson, J.R., 97, *112*
Anderson, R.C., 301, *303*
Anderson, V., 228, *236*
Apicella, A., 160, *170,* 175, 179, *185*
Appelbaum, M.I., 4, 10, 14, 15, 16, 17, 19, 20, 21, *25, 27,* 148, *150*
Archer, D., 246, *255, 256*
Arlin, P.K., 112, *112*
Armitage, R., 268, *280*
Asch, S.E., 192, *217*
Ashman, A.F., 97, *118*
Atkinson, R.C., 97, 98, 99, *112, 114,* 126, *149*
Atwood, M.E., 91, *116*
Averback, E., 220, *233*

B

Babcock, R.L., 58, *80*
Bachelder, B.L., 97, *112, 113*
Bachmann, T., 228, *233*
Backman, L., 58, *76*
Baddeley, A.D., 101, *113,* 269, *278*
Bakan, P., 190, 192, 193, 195, 197, 198, 206, 211, *213, 214*
Baker, C.T., 14, *28*
Baker, L.A., 179, 182, *183, 184*
Baldinger, A.C., 201, 206, *213*
Balogh, D.W., 224, 226, *233, 235*
Ball, K., 57, 58, *79*
Baltes, P.B., 55, 59, *76*
Baltzley, D.R., 260, 268, 274, *279, 281*
Bangert-Drowns, R.L., 193, 197, *213*
Banich, M., 109, *117*
Bannatyne, A., 122, 123, *149*
Barenbaum, E.M., 144, *152*
Barker, W.W., 160, *170,* 175, *185*
Barlean, J.L., 286, 292, 294, *305*
Barnat, M., 199, 206, *213*
Barnes, G.M., 247, *256*
Barrett, P.T., 173, 176, 178, 179, 181, *183, 184*
Barron, J.L., 173, *185*
Bartscher, J., 203, 206, *214*
Baumeister, A.A., 284, 286, 288, 289, 290, 292, 294, 295, 296, 297, 298, 299, 300, *303, 305, 306*
Baumrind, D., 22, *26*
Bayley, N., 14, *26,* 32, *46*
Beach, D.R., 127, 128, *151*
Beck, E.C., 172, *185*

307

Wilson, K.P., 268, *279*
Wilson, M., 144, *154*
Wilson, R.S., 20, *29*
Winstead, D.K., 224, 229, *236*
Witkin, H.A., 192, *217*
Wohlwill, J.F., 4, 9, 13, 25, *29*
Wolf, A., 175, 176, *183*
Wolfe, J.M., 69, 71, 72, 73, *76, 81*
Wolfson, J., 44, *53*
Wolstad, J.C., 270, *279*
Wonderlic, C.F., 267, *281*
Wong, B.Y.L., 127, 128, 129, 132, 144, *153*
Wong, R., 127, *154*
Wong, T.M., 109, *115*
Woodham, F.L., 22, *236*
Woodward, L.G., 245, *255*
Worden, P.E., 141, *154*
Worthen, D., 142, *152*
Wright, F., 123, *151*
Wu, J., 160, 161, *169, 170*, 174, 175, 179, *184*

Y
Yalow, E., 95, *119*
Yamamoto, Y.L., *170*

Yanikoglu, B.A., 69, *80*
Yantis, S., 98, 99, 99n, *116*
Yarrow, L.J., 41, 43, *54*
Yates, A.J., 221, 223, *237*
Yen, W.M., 263, 266, *278*
Yonekura, Y., 175, *183*
Yoshii, F., 160, *170*, 175, 179, *185*
Young, A.B., 160, 161, *169*
Young, C.W., 176, *186*
Younkin, D., 195, *214*
Yu, J., 157, 158, 159, 161, 162, 163, 165, 166, 167, 168, *170*

Z
Zajonc, R.B., 23, *29*
Zeaman, D., 247, *257*, 287, *306*
Zee, D.S., 192, *217*
Zeef, E.J., 58, *77*
Zeidner, J., 277, *281*
Zentall, T.R., 287, 288, 289, *306*
Zhang, Y., 182, *187*
Zonderman, A.B., 87, *113*
Zupnick, J.J., 227, *237*

Subject Index

A

Alzheimer's disease, 175
Auditory stimuli, 292–293
Automated Performance Test System (APTS), 268–271
Averaged evoked potential (AEP) research, 172–174

B

Backward masking, *see* Visual masking paradigm
Bayley Scales of Infant Development, 32
Binet, Alfred, 32–33
Breitmeyer's channel theory, 229

C

California First Year Mental Scale, 32
Cattell Infant Scale, 32
Cerebral glucose metabolism research, 174–176
Cognitive ability, generality of, 242–245
Cognitive aging, 56–59; *see also* Visual-cognitive aging
Cognitive architecture, 56
Cognitive components approach, 89–95
  and problem representation, 91–93
  and strategy and metacognitive components, 93–95
Cognitive correlates approach, 95–107
  in extremely talented, 100–102
  literature on, 97–99
    weakness in, 100
  new data, 102–106
Communication in LD children, 144–147

D

Confluence Model, 23–24
Connectionist models, 301–302
Critical stimulus duration (CSD), 224–225, 230–231
Cross-modal transfer, 36–37, 40–41

D

Detection paradigm, 296–300
Developmental functions, 5–6
  environmental contributions to, 21–23
  hereditary contributions to, 20–21
Developmental profile; *see also* Developmental functions
  potential causes of changes in, 19–25
Domain-specific knowledge, 91, 242–243
Down Syndrome, 38

E

Employment testing, 261
Engram RNA, 173
Epstein's phrenoblysis hypothesis of brain and mental periodization, 10–13

F

Fels Longitudinal Study, 11, 14–15
Fluctuation variance, 45

G

Gaze shift, *see* Lateral eye movements
General mental performance, 3
  individual differences in the developmental functions for, 13–25
  species-general developmental functions for, 8–13

321